Outsourcing Global Services

TECHNOLOGY, WORK AND GLOBALIZATION

The Technology, Work and Globalization series was developed to provide policymakers, workers, managers, academics, and students with a deeper understanding of the complex interlinks and influences between technological developments, including information and communication technologies, work organizations, and patterns of globalization. The mission of the series is to disseminate rich knowledge based on deep research about relevant issues surrounding the globalization of work that is spawned by technology.

Also in this series:

GLOBAL SOURCING OF BUSINESS AND IT SERVICES
Leslie P. Willcocks and Mary C. Lacity

ICT AND INNOVATION IN THE PUBLIC SECTOR
Francesco Contini and Giovan Francesco Lanzara

EXPLORING VIRTUALITY WITHIN AND BEYOND ORGANIZATIONS
Niki Panteli and Mike Chiasson

OFFSHORE OUTSOURCING OF IT WORK
Mary C. Lacity and Joseph W. Rottman

KNOWLEDGE PROCESSES IN GLOBALLY DISTRIBUTED CONTEXTS
Julia Kotlarsky, Ilan Oshri and Paul C. van Fenema

GLOBAL CHALLENGES FOR IDENTITY POLICIES
Edgar Whitley and Ian Hosein

E-GOVERNANCE FOR DEVELOPMENT
Shirin Madon

Outsourcing Global Services

Knowledge, Innovation and Social Capital

Ilan Oshri, Julia Kotlarsky
and
Leslie P. Willcocks

First published 2008 by
PALGRAVE MACMILLAN

Palgrave Macmillan in the UK is an imprint of Macmillan Publishers Limited,
registered in England, company number 785998, of Houndmills, Basingstoke,
Hampshire RG21 6XS.

Palgrave Macmillan in the US is a division of St Martin's Press LLC,
175 Fifth Avenue, New York, NY 10010.

Palgrave Macmillan is the global academic imprint of the above companies
and has companies and representatives throughout the world.

Palgrave® and Macmillan® are registered trademarks in the United States,
the United Kingdom, Europe and other countries.

ISBN-13: 978–0–230–20667–0
ISBN-10: 0–230–20667–0

This book is printed on paper suitable for recycling and made from fully
managed and sustained forest sources. Logging, pulping and manufacturing
processes are expected to conform to the environmental regulations of the
country of origin.

A catalogue record for this book is available from the British Library.

A catalog record for this book is available from the Library of Congress.

10 9 8 7 6 5 4 3 2 1
17 16 15 14 13 12 11 10 09 08

Printed and bound in Great Britain by
Cromwell Press Ltd, Trowbridge, Wiltshire

CONTENTS

LIST OF TABLES

List of Figures

ACKNOWLEDGMENTS

Julia and Ilan would like to thank Leslie for his support, intellectual stimulus, and friendship. We would never be where we are without you.

We would also like to thank our little daughter, Hadar, first, for patiently waiting a couple of weeks after the workshop to be born, so that we could wrap it up properly. And second, for allowing us to review these articles and provide feedback to the authors in between night-time feeds.

Ilan would also like to thank Warwick Business School for accommodating him: Warwick University has always been a good place to get work done. Ilan would also like to thank the following friends and colleagues: Leslie Willcocks, Katy Mason, Paul van Fenema, Sue Newell, Shan-Ling Pan, and Tom Mom. I have learned a lot from each one of you. Ilan would like to thank his parents, Jacob and Hannah, his brother Uri and his family, and sisters, Yael, Shosh, and her family for their love and support.

Julia thanks her colleagues at Warwick Business School for promoting the Workshop at various academic conventions. Special thanks goes to her friends Karin Oppelland and Viara Popova who came to visit (and looked after) her two weeks before the due date, which allowed Ilan to travel to Val d'Isere for the Workshop. We spent a fun week while Ilan and Leslie were running the Workshop and enjoying their skiing (!). Julia would also like to thank her parents, Irina and Michael, and her brother Pavel for their support, advice, and constant interest in her academic achievements.

Leslie would like to thank Julia and Ilan for making the annual Global Sourcing Workshops truly happen – sine qua non – and Joe and Antonio for their support in this. He would like to thank his wonderful colleagues at London School of Economics Information Systems and Innovation Group for providing a place for ideas, work, and fun. Also, all the participants of the workshops for their considerable contributions, and sense of adventure (!). And of course Stephen Rutt and all at Palgrave Macmillan for their unremitting support for the Technology, Work and Globalization series, in which this book is placed.

SERIES PREFACE

Technology is all too often positioned as the welcome driver of globalization. The popular press neatly packages technology's influence on globalization with snappy sound bites, such as "any work that can be digitized, will be globally sourced." Cover stories report Indians doing U.S. tax returns, Moroccans developing software for the French, Filipinos answering U.K. customer service calls, and the Chinese doing everything for everybody. Most glossy cover stories assume that all globalization is progressive, seamless, intractable, and leads to unmitigated good. But what we are experiencing in the twenty-first century in terms of the interrelationships between technology, work, and globalization is both profound and highly complex.

We launched this series to provide policy makers, workers, managers, academics, and students with a deeper understanding of the complex interlinks and influences between technological developments, including information and communication technologies, work organizations, and patterns of globalization. The mission of this series is to disseminate rich knowledge based on deep research about relevant issues surrounding the globalization of work that is spawned by technology. To us, substantial research on globalization considers multiple perspectives and levels of analyses. We seek to publish research based on in-depth study of developments in technology, work, and globalization and their impacts on and relationships with individuals, organizations, industries, and countries. We welcome perspectives from business, economics, sociology, public policy, cultural studies, law, and other disciplines that contemplate both larger trends and micro-developments from Asian, African, Australian, and Latin American, as well as North American and European viewpoints.

The first book in the series, *Global Sourcing of Business and IT Services* by Leslie Willcocks and Mary Lacity is based on over 1000 interviews with clients, suppliers, and advisors and 15 years of study. The specific focus is on developments in outsourcing, offshoring, and mixed sourcing practices from client and supplier perspectives in a globalizing world. We found many organizations struggling. We also found other practitioners adeptly creating global sourcing networks that are agile, effective, and cost efficient. Nevertheless, they did so only after a tremendous amount of trial-and-error and close attention to details. All our participant organizations acted in a context of fast-moving technology, rapid development of supply side offerings, and ever-changing economic conditions.

Knowledge Processes in Globally Distributed Contexts by Julia Kotlarsky, Ilan Oshri, and Paul van Fenema, examines the management of knowledge processes of global knowledge workers. Based on substantial case studies and interviews, the authors – along with their network of coauthors – provide frameworks, practices, and tools that consider how to develop, coordinate, and manage knowledge processes to create synergetic value in globally distributed contexts. Chapters address knowledge sharing, social ties, transactive memory, imperative learning, work division, and many other social and organizational practices to ensure successful collaboration in globally distributed teams.

Offshore Outsourcing of IT Work by Mary Lacity and Joseph Rottman examines the practices for successfully outsourcing IT work from Western clients to offshore suppliers. Based on over 200 interviews with 26 Western clients and their offshore suppliers in India, China, and Canada, the book details client-side roles of chief information officers, program management officers, and project managers and identifies project characteristics that differentiated successful from unsuccessful projects. The authors examine ten engagement models for moving IT work offshore and describe proven practices to ensure that offshore outsourcing is successful for both client and supplier organizations.

Exploring Virtuality within and beyond Organizations by Niki Panteli and Mike Chiasson argues that there has been a limited conceptualization of virtuality and its implications on the management of organizations. Based on illustrative cases, empirical studies, and theorizing on virtuality, this book goes beyond the simple comparison between the virtual and the traditional to explore the different types, dimensions, and perspectives of virtuality. Almost all organizations are virtual, but they differ theoretically and substantively in their virtuality. By exploring and understanding these differences, researchers, and practitioners gain a deeper understanding of the past, present, and future possibilities of virtuality. The collection is designed to be indicative of current thinking and approaches, and provides a rich basis for further research and reflection in this important area of management and information systems research and practice.

ICT and Innovation in the Public Sector by Francesco Contini and Giovan Franceso Lanzara examines the theoretical and practical issues of implementing innovative ICT solutions in the public sector. The book is based on a major research project sponsored and funded by the Italian government (Ministry of University and Research) and coordinated by Italy's National Research Council and the University of Bologna during the years 2002–2006. The authors, along with a number of coauthors, explore the complex interplay between technology and institutions, drawing on multiple theoretical traditions such as institutional analysis, actor network theory, social systems theory, organization theory, and transaction costs economics. Detailed case studies offer realistic and rich lessons. These case studies include e-justice in Italy and Finland, e-bureaucracy in Austria, and Money Claim On-Line in England and Wales.

In addition to these first five books, several other manuscripts are under development. These forthcoming books cover topics of ICT in developing countries, global ICT standards, and identity protection. Each book uniquely meets the mission of the series.

We encourage other researchers to submit proposals to the series, as we envision a protracted need for scholars to deeply and richly analyze and conceptualize the complex relationships among technology, work, and globalization.

LESLIE P. WILLCOCKS
MARY C. LACITY
November 2007

NOTES ON CONTRIBUTORS

Niels Bjørn-Andersen is Professor at Centre for Applied ICT at Copenhagen Business School. He is the research director of a number of large research projects, for example the (1) "Third Generation ERP-systems" with Microsoft (2) ITAIDE on the introduction of new e-customs systems for facilitation of international trade with among others IBM and SAP as well as (3) e-Media project with four other research institutions and nine companies on the future of the media sector. He has published more than 50 journal articles in journals like *Journal of MIS; Information and Management; Journal of IT, IEEE Transactions* and the like, and he has more than 150 other publications.

Esther Ruiz Ben is Assistant Professor at the Institute of Sociology of the Technical University of Berlin. Her main areas of interest include Sociology of Professions, Theories of Gender and Intersectionality, Economic Sociology, Sociology of Technology. Esther's most recent research focuses on the impact of Internationalization dynamics on tasks and knowledge transformation in the German IT industry.

Donald Chand is a Professor of information and process management at Bentley College in Waltham, MA. His current research interests are in the areas of global collaboration and process measurements. He has published in the *Communications of the ACM, Journal of ACM, IEEE Software*, and the *Journal of Management Systems.*

Dr. Gary C. David is an Associate Professor of Sociology at Bentley College. Dr. David's research examines the role of intergroup relations and intercultural communication in the formation of social relationships among distributed teams through a workplace studies perspective. Current projects include a study of the medical transcription industry, cross-boundary information sharing between government agencies, and the development of virtual workplace communities in distributed organizations. Dr. David has developed training programs on the use of "everyday ethnography" as a device to decreasing social distance and increasing rapport in the pursuit of collaborative work. He has published numerous articles and chapters internationally across a range of disciplines.

Paul C. van Fenema (Ph.D. Erasmus University) is an Associate Professor at Netherlands Defence Academy, The Netherlands, and a part-time Assistant Professor at Tilburg University. He held positions at RSM Erasmus University and Florida International University. His research focuses on coordination and knowledge management in global IS projects and High Reliability Organizations. His work has been published or is forthcoming in among others *MIS Quarterly, Journal of International Business, Information Systems Journal, European Journal of Information Systems,* and *Decision Support Systems* (www.paulcvanfenema.com).

Sirkka L. Jarvenpaa is the James Bayless/Rauscher Pierce Refsnes Chair in Business Administration at the University of Texas at Austin. She is the director of the center for Business, Technology, and Law. Her interests include virtual teams and organizations. Her work appeared in *Organization Science* and many other leading IS journals.

Séamas Kelly is Director of the Centre for Innovation, Technology and Organization (CITO) at UCD School of Business, University College Dublin. He holds a Ph.D. in Management Studies/Information Systems from the University of Cambridge, and his primary research interests concern the relationship between knowledge, ICT, and forms of organizing.

Helmut Krcmar holds the Chair for Information Systems at Technische Universität München. He worked at the IBM Los Angeles Scientific Center, the Leonard Stern School of Business, NYU, and Baruch College, CUNY as well as Hohenheim University, Stuttgart. His research interests include Information and Knowledge Management, Service Management, CSCW as well Information Systems in Health Care and eGovernment. He has published numerous works on these topics, among others "Information Management," 2004, 4th edition, Springer.

Dr. Julia Kotlarsky is an Assistant Professor of Information Systems, Warwick Business School, UK. She holds a Ph.D. degree in IS and Management from Rotterdam School of Management Erasmus (The Netherlands). Her main research interests revolve around social and technical aspects involved in the management of globally distributed IS teams and IT outsourcing. Julia published her work in journals such as *Communications of the ACM, European Journal of Information Systems, Information Systems Journal, Journal of Information Technology,* and others.

Stefanie Leimeister is a full-time researcher and Ph.D. student at the Chair for Information Systems at Technische Universität München. She received a Master's degree in Communication Science from Hohenheim University, Stuttgart. Her research focus is on IS outsourcing, especially IS outsourcing governance and relationship management. She has published her work in several national and international conferences, books, and journals.

Volker Mahnke is a professor of Strategic Management of IS at Copenhagen Business School. His research focuses on the intersection of information technology, economics, and strategy. Dr. Mahnke's research has appeared in some 60 papers. Outlets included journals such as *IEEE Transactions on Professional Communication*, *Journal of Management Studies*, *Management International Review*, *International Journal of Technology Management*, *Journal of Management*; *Academy of Management Best Paper Proceedings*. His current research interest is focused on the interface between advances in ICT, IT enabled business development, outsourcing of knowledge intensive work, and innovation models.

Ji-Ye Mao is a Professor and Associate Dean in the School of Business, Renmin University of China. Prior to his current appointment, he has taught at the University of Waterloo in Canada (1995–2001) and the City University of Hong Kong. In addition, he was a Visiting Scientist at the IBM Toronto Lab (User-Centered Design Lab, 2000–2001). He holds a Ph.D. in MIS from the University of British Columbia (1995), MBA from McGill University, and B.Eng. from Renmin University of China (1985). His areas of research include user participation in the design and implementation of information systems, human-computer interaction (HCI), IT outsourcing management. His research has appeared in *Communications of the ACM*, *Journal of MIS*, and major *HCI* journals. He is on the editorial board of the *Journal of Database Management, Journal of AIS* (Association for Information Systems), and *Information and Management*.

Sue Newell is the Cammarata Professor of Management at Bentley College, US and Professor of Information Management at Warwick University, UK. Sue was a founding members of IKON (Innovation, Knowledge, and Organizational Networking Research Centre), reflecting her research focus on exploring innovation processes using knowledge and organizational networking perspectives.

Camilla Noonan is a lecturer in International Business at UCD School of Business, University College Dublin. She holds a Ph.D. in Economics from the University of Reading and her primary research interest lies in the area of Corporate Technological Change and International Business.

Dr. Ilan Oshri is an Assistant Professor of Strategic Management, Rotterdam School of Management Erasmus, The Netherlands. Ilan holds a

Ph.D. degree in technological innovation from Warwick Business School (UK). His main research interest lies in the area of learning and innovation in global teams. Ilan has published widely his work in journals and books which include *IEEE Transactions on Engineering Management, Communications of the ACM, European Journal of Information Systems, Journal of Strategic Information Systems, Journal of Information Technology, Information Systems Journal,* and others.

Albert G. Plugge is a research associate at the department of Information and Communication Technology at Delft University of Technology and holds a degree in Telecommunications. He lectures in Information Technology and Information Management. His research interests include the organizational and economic aspects of information management in general and the outsourcing and offshoring of information systems in particular.

Joseph W.z Rottman is an Assistant Professor of Information Systems at the University of Missouri-St. Louis. His primary research interests are centered on global sourcing and innovation diffusion. His publications have appeared in the *Sloan Management Review, IEEE Computer, MIS Quarterly Executive, Journal of Information Technology, and Information Systems Frontiers.* He is on the Editorial Board for *MIS Quarterly Executive* and Senior Editor (USA/Americas) for the *Journal of Information Technology.*

João Resende-Santos is Associate Professor of International Studies at Bentley College. His field of specialization is international relations, with a focus on international security and theory, and also US–Latin American relations. His areas of research include Brazilian foreign relations, with publications on Brazilian foreign relations, dependency theory, and regional security. His recent book is "Neorealism, States, and the Modern Mass Army" (Cambridge University Press).

Vinay Tiwari is a Ph.D. candidate at RSM Erasmus University. He received his B.Tech. from IIT Kanpur, India, and his M.Phil. in Business Research (cum laude) from RSM Erasmus University, The Netherlands. He has previously worked in the Indian IT industry. His work is forthcoming in *MIS Quarterly.* His research interests include issues of coordination, communication, and understanding during outsourcing.

Paul W.L. Vlaar obtained his Ph.D. at RSM Erasmus University. He currently works at VU University Amsterdam, The Netherlands. His research has been published in *MIS Quarterly, Organization Studies* and

Group & Organization Management. In 2008, his book entitled "Contracts and Trust in Alliances: Creating, Appropriating and Discovering Value" will be published by Edward Elgar.

René W. Wagenaar was a full professor of ICT at Delft University of Technology. René worked with great enthusiasm at building a dynamic ICT section, e-government, and services program and high quality education and research programs at the crossroads of ICT, policy, and management. He passed away unexpectedly during a short vacation in Switzerland.

Jonathan Wareham is an Associate Professor of Information Systems at ESADE. His research focuses on the intersection of information technology, economics, and strategy. Dr. Wareham's research has been published or forthcoming in such journals and proceedings as *MIS Quarterly* and *IEEE Transactions*. He currently serves as Associate Editor for *Information Systems Research*.

Michaela Wieandt is a doctoral candidate and junior researcher at the Institute of Sociology of the Technical University of Berlin. Her main areas of interest include Sociology of Organizations, Economic Sociology, theories of consulting, knowledge management and learning, theories of power and internationalization processes. Michaela's most recent research focuses on power relations in IT consulting projects.

Gerard M. Wijers received his Ph.D. degree (cum laude) in Computer Science at Delft University of Technology. In 2002, he had joined the international management consultancy firm Morgan Chambers as principal consultant on sourcing, contracting and, business architectures. In 2007, he became director of the business line Sourcing Management. Morgan Chambers is nowadays part of EquaTerra. He combines his position with a Senior Research Fellowship at Delft University on Sourcing and IT management. He is program director of the Executive Master of IT management program of Delft University.

Prof. Leslie Willcocks is Head of the Information Systems and Innovation Group and Professor of Technology Work and Globalization at the London School of Economics and Political Science. He holds a Ph.D. from the University of Cambridge and is visiting professor at Erasmus and Melbourne Universities. He is also coeditor of the *Journal of Information Technology*. Leslie has coauthored 26 books and over 180 refereed papers on information systems management, IT and business process outsourcing, IT-enabled change, IT evaluation, and social theory and philosophy for information systems.

On the soft side of global IT outsourcing: innovating in relationships, social capital, and knowledge

Ilan Oshri, Julia Kotlarsky, and Leslie Willcocks

By 2009, revenues from offshore outsourcing of information technologies (IT) will exceed $US30 billion, and over the next five years the compound annual growth rate in this industry is expected to be about 20 percent (Willcocks and Lacity 2007). By 2006, over 200 firms from the Forbes 2000 companies had offshored IT and business process outsourcing activities totaling about $9 billion. The phenomenon of offshore outsourcing is certainly expanding, and indeed at a faster rate than more domestic forms of IT and business process outsourcing. It has become increasingly important to understand the phenomenon, not least as a basis for suggesting what directions it will take, its impacts, how it has been conducted, and how its management can be better facilitated. These issues lie at the heart of the present book.

These points are particularly pertinent because recent evidence suggests that a number of offshore outsourcing relationships have failed to live up to some of their promises (e.g., Aron and Singh 2005; Lacity and Rottman 2008). The reasons for this are many, ranging from poor quality delivered by vendors to rising management costs that result in frustration and disappointment. Collaboration between remote sites and the ability to share and transfer knowledge between dispersed teams have been mentioned by past research (e.g., Kotlarsky and Oshri 2005; Oshri et al. 2008) as imperative to successful IT offshore outsourcing projects. In addition, our own research highlights certain capabilities that vendors and clients should develop, the governing structures they need to put in place, and the bonding activities they need to promote and make time for (Kotlarsky et al. 2007; Oshri et al. 2007a, b; Willcocks and Lacity 2007).

Drafts of the present chapters were first presented at the First Global Sourcing Workshop, held in Val d'Isere, France, in March 2007. This annual gathering of academics and practitioners offers a stage to discuss and develop cutting edge ideas and research concerning IT and business process outsourcing and offshoring. In 2007, the Workshop focused on services, knowledge, and innovation in IT outsourcing and offshoring. Some 21 papers were presented and, on the basis of the Workshop, and after paper revision and improvement, the present 11 chapters emerged as strong, insightful, and innovative contributions to both academic and practitioner understandings of the emergent field. The Workshop offered us much-needed information and perceptive commentary on how global sourcing trends were developing, what practices were working, and what was not going so well. The majority of the papers also provided rich detailed case studies enabling the processes and management of offshoring to be tracked at the micro-level over time. But looking across the contributions, one major insight stood out above all others: the critical importance of what we call here the "soft side" of global IT outsourcing; in other words, of the social, organizational, processual, knowledge, relationship, and expertise aspects and their impact on offshoring and outsourcing effectiveness.

The chapters of this book give wide and in-depth coverage to the global IT sourcing phenomenon. The research has been carried out in client organizations and suppliers. Most major economic sectors are represented, and the geographical spread and diversity of types of sourcing is considerable. Thus, Chapter 1 looks at German client experiences of outsourcing, Chapter 2 at Scandinavian experiences of using Indian suppliers, while Chapter 3 studies five Dutch clients and Chapter 4 researches Chinese supplier experiences in Japan, Europe, and the U.S.A. Chapter 5 looks at a U.S. company's attempts to coordinate wholly owned sites in Ireland, India, and the U.S.A., while Chapters 6, 7, and 8 look at U.S.A.–India, Ireland–India and Netherlands–India outsourcing relationships respectively. Chapters 9 and 10 have their primary focus on Germany and nearshoring to Poland, but also to Romania and Slovakia as well as offshoring to India. Our final chapter looks at a major Indian supplier delivering services to a Dutch global bank from centers in Mumbai, the Netherlands, Sao Paulo, Budapest, and Luxembourg.

All the chapters make innovative contributions, and advance our understanding of how offshoring, nearshoring, and outsourcing is being, and can be, conducted. Each chapter goes beyond any rhetoric of prematurely declared success, to carefully reveal the ongoing complexity and sheer hard work inherent in getting human beings of different cultures, in different time zones, often with different levels and types of expertise, and with different incentives to collaborate to achieve IT work. In looking at the 11 chapters we found it relatively easy to organize them into three areas, with each chapter making a primary innovation in at least one of these. The three areas are relationship management, social capital, and knowledge. Let us look at these innovative contributions in more detail.

Innovations in relationship management

The first chapter *Exploring relationships in information systems outsourcing: a typology of IS outsourcing relationships* is by Stefanie Leimeister and Helmut Krcmar. The authors point out several key gaps not considered in the extant research: (1) research on relationship management in interorganizational contexts has enumerated a great number of relationship factors, but has failed to integrate these factors into an overall outsourcing context; (2) Social Exchange and Expectation Confirmation Theory can help to foster a comprehensive view on outsourcing relationships, including an exchange perspective between individual actors, as well as involving market interactions and context; (3) classifications from other business-to-business relationship management approaches are not that applicable to IS outsourcing relationships due to the specific nature of information systems in an organization; and (4) classifications of relationships in information systems outsourcing are often one-sided and do not provide an exhaustive set of dimensions for describing an outsourcing relationship type. The authors use social exchange and expectation confirmation theory to develop an innovative, research-based, fivefold classification of effective relationship types dependent on context.

The second chapter *offshore middlemen: transnational intermediation in technology sourcing* is by Volker Mahnke, Jonathan Wareham, and Niels Bjorn-Andersen. It explores the highly interesting, potentially valuable, and under-researched role of the "middleman" in offshore outsourcing. The researchers show that in recent years we have seen the emergence of this new breed of entity, operating as an offshore intermediary. Such entities specialize in bridging cultural, expertise, and communication gaps between a vendor and a client. The chapter examines the experiences of I-Technolgies, a Scandinavian company specializing in assisting Scandinavian clients to find and work with offshore suppliers. The chapter pinpoints the boundary-spanning capabilities needed, and explores the cultural, distance, pre and postcontractual management aspects involved in operating as an intermediary transnational offshoring relationships.

The third chapter by A.G. Plugge, G.M. Wijers, and R.W. Wagenaar is entitled *IT outsourcing from a client perspective: exploring client developments and their impact on supplier capabilities*. Their research on five client organizations demonstrates that the Social Interaction approach's main focus on environmental, atmosphere, and exchange developments in a relationship do in fact impact meaningfully on a client's experiences of outsourcing. These developments also impact on supplier capabilities. The 12 supplier capabilities identified in Willcocks and Lacity (2007) do have to be strengthened to meet present and future client demands. The authors find that the newly identified capability "business market knowledge" needs to be added to the capability set of suppliers.

The fourth chapter is *Operational capabilities development in mediated offshore software services models* by Sirkka L. Jarvenpaa and Ji-Ye Mao. It examines the capabilities developed by Chinese vendors operating according to the mediated offshoring business model. The chapter focuses on understanding the capabilities needed by such vendors to deliver services successfully. In particular, they examine the development of operational capabilities, which are those involved in the provision of a service or a product. These consist of three types: client-specific capabilities, process capabilities, and human resources capabilities. Jarvenpaa and Mao conclude the chapter, based on data collected in four Chinese firms, by suggesting that human resources capabilities are the most important in this specific context.

The role of social capital

The section focusing on social capital begins with *Integrated collaboration across distributed sites: the perils of process and the promise of practice* by Gary C. David, Donald Chand, Sue Newell, and João Resende-Santos. The authors deal with the issue of collaboration between offshore and on-site teams. By applying World-Systems Theory, the researchers are able to examine collaboration across their case study organization as the relationships between all remote sites, instead of using the traditional approach in which the research focus has been on a single site or a group of sites. As a result, this chapter innovates by highlighting the role that the socio-political organizational context plays in creating relationships and generating tensions between sites. The chapter concludes that tensions and breakdowns are also the result of how members of a globally distributed team perceive themselves: as core or periphery. Consequently, the key issue is power, and not just culture or the information and communication technologies deployed, thus explicitly introducing political issues into applications of the concept of social capital in offshoring contexts.

There follows a chapter by Joseph W. Rottman entitled *Successful knowledge transfer within offshore supplier networks: a case study exploring social capital in strategic alliances.* The chapter considers social capital as the vehicle through which value is created in offshore outsourcing relationships. Rottman argues that it is important who the supplier knows in the client organization and vice versa. Through these social relationships, knowledge can flow and value can be created for both client and vendor. A case from a Fortune 100 manufacturing firm illustrates the importance of social capital and its impact on knowledge transfer and on the management of global IT suppliers.

The social capital theme is continued in the next chapter, *Risk, anxiety, and the production of comfort/trust in the context of globalized modes of working: the case of an Ireland-India IS offshoring relationship.* Here, Séamas Kelly and Camilla Noonan focus on the "relationship work" required to produce and sustain a sense of emotional comfort on the part of a client in the context of, or what was perceived as, an extremely unfamiliar and risky venture. In so doing, they innovate by synthesizing a novel theoretical perspective for illuminating key aspects of the phenomenon in question, by drawing mainly on Anthony Giddens' ideas on risk, trust, and globalization, supplemented by important contributions from other authors. A striking feature of their analysis is the amount of effort, care, and attentiveness that was required to establish productive social relations, notwithstanding the apparent value congruity of the two firms involved. These efforts, however, contributed to the creation of important social capital that gave the project a new robustness which sustained it during difficult periods.

Our final chapter focusing primarily on social capital issues is *Requirements analysis in offshore IS development: remote bridging of differences in understandings.* Here, Paul C. van Fenema, Vinay Tiwari, and Paul W.L. Vlaar use a financial services offshore development project to illustrate how organizations need insight into strategies for dealing with coordinating various domains and varying levels of understandings, and the situations in which they should be deployed. The innovative strategies found in this study – translation, specialization, and generalization – represent alternatives for cooperating across sites, and for investing in capabilities.

Translation aims for a transactive interaction pattern, aimed at the correct execution of comprehensively defined requirements by offshore team members. This strategy would match situations of high time pressure, high precision, or high levels of turnover. Specialization is likely to fit best with projects calling for great depth of expertise. Second, specialization calls for offshore organizations to invest resources in developing technical expertise among on-site team members, who are encouraged to remain involved in a project for a prolonged period of time. Third, generalization further extends the need for offshore personnel to actively participate in the global team. When such a strategy is deployed, customers are expected to pay a premium, which enables on-site and offshore team members to enhance value creation by jointly exploring new opportunities. The authors' findings allow practitioners in offshore settings to better assess the options they have for developing sufficiently similar understandings among members of on-site and offshore vendor teams – an extremely critical aspect in offshore ISD.

Knowledge and outsourcing

In Chapter 9 *Global expertise and quality standards in ICT offshore projects,* Esther Ruiz Ben focuses on two German-based case studies of nearshoring and offshoring to Poland, India, Rumania, and Slovakia. Her innovative work shows how the knowledge and expertise needed in offshore IT projects are related to quality management systems and time. The research suggests that temporal norms and regulations are related not only to working practices but also to project deadlines as essential links to customers in software development. In practice, temporal norms constitute important dimensions of expertise definition. Moreover, her analysis emphasizes the important role that quality standards have in structuring expertise. Quality standards also play a very important role as internal controlling and timing instruments of knowledge, working, and communication processes, as well as an external mechanism beyond the ICT network to gain market advantages. The research suggests that establishing domains of practice from a long-term perspective in the client organization supports the expertise transfer in offshore projects and the engagement of experts in the improvement of quality management systems.

Michaela Wieandt's chapter is also concerned with knowledge and expertise transfer. In *Step by Step: the development of knowledge transfer and collaboration in a nearshore software development project,* she shows how employees of onshore and nearshore sites of a medium-sized German software development company established a transactive-memory-oriented knowledge base in an incremental manner. Important factors enabling collaboration included the arrangement of the division of labor, a high social and organizational integration of the nearshore workers, as well as equal control mechanisms for all sites. The author concludes that it is more useful when a company's management communicates the near-shore concept to all its employees. Incentives for the on-site employees are important for raising their dedication to putting the concept successfully into practice. In particular, project managers play a key role and should be adequately supported. Project managers' ability to structure work, to lead, and motivate employees are basic factors for the success of a near-shore project. Furthermore, the establishment of a Transactive Memory System appears to be very important because it eases knowledge transfer and communication. Similarly, team-building processes in dispersed working situations are key. This is effectively supported by an integration of, and equal treatment of, the nearshore employees through a comprehensive socialization into the organizational context, work procedures, and routines encompassing on-site on-the-job-training, joint company training programs, and team rotation.

The knowledge, expertise, and collaboration themes of this section are examined again in the final chapter, in which Ilan Oshri, Julia Kotlarsky, and Leslie Willcocks describe their study of a major outsourcing arrangement between ABN AMRO Bank and Tata Consultancy Services. In *Managing dispersed expertise in IT offshore outsourcing: lessons from Tata Consultancy Services,* the authors show how a large Indian supplier organized its knowledge and expertise to service its global client from bases in the Netherlands, Sao Paulo, Budapest, Mumbai, and Luxembourg. The study concludes that all global suppliers are going to need to develop similar knowledge systems and processes if they are to continue to compete effectively in the near future. The authors also point to four challenges for clients. They must understand the benefits they will receive from a provider's expertise management strategy. Clients must understand their own costs implicit in a provider's expertise management strategy. Clients must safeguard their intellectual property. And finally, clients need to leverage the relationship advantage. If TCS and other major IT outsourcing providers do go down the expertise management route, as described in this chapter, then clients could reap one significant, but unanticipated, benefit: they could learn how to better manage their own expertise and knowledge.

Conclusion

The book brings many innovative, key insights together into the relationship, social capital, and knowledge themes that are only just emerging as critical for effective use of offshoring, nearshoring, and outsourcing.

The chapters show that global IT sourcing should be treated as a context-dependent scenario. What is critical for the American middleman might not be imperative for the Chinese mediating firm. Second, the chapters bring together vendor/client capabilities, along with the broader picture of the supply network, and also the micro-processes involved in managing knowledge transfer and globally distributed collaboration. These are indeed the building blocks of any global sourcing relationship. But, beyond this, the chapters illustrate in rich detail that the essentially human, "soft" side of outsourcing is critical to researcher insights and understanding, and also to practitioner management effectiveness. In putting together this book our intention is to make valuable contributions to these communities, and their objectives.

References

Aron, R. and Singh, J. (2005) Getting Offshoring Right. *Harvard Business Review*, 8(12): 135–143.

Kotlarsky, J. and Oshri, I. (2005) Social Ties, Knowledge Sharing and Successful Collaboration in Globally Distributed System Development Projects. *European Journal of Information Systems*, 14(1): 37–48.

Kotlarsky, J., Oshri, I., Kumar, K., and van Hillegersberg, J. (2007) Globally Distributed Component-Based Software Development: An Exploratory Study of Knowledge Management and Work Division. *Journal of Information Technology*, 22(2): 161–173.

Lacity, M. and Rottman, J. (2008) *Offshoring IT Work,* Palgrave Macmillan: London.

Oshri, I. Kotlarsky, J., and Willcocks, L.P. (2007a) Managing Dispersed Expertise in IT Offshore Outsourcing: Lessons from Tata Consultancy Services. *MISQ Executive*, 6(2): 53–65.

Oshri, I., Kotlarsky, J., and Willcocks, L.P. (2007b) Missing Links: Building Critical Social Ties for Global Collaborative Teamwork. *Communications of the ACM,* 50(12): 63–67.

Oshri, I., van Fenema, P., and Kotlarsky, J. (2008) Knowledge Transfer in Globally Distributed Teams: The Role of Transactive Memory. *Information Systems Journal.* (DOI 10.1111/j.1365-2575. 2007.00243.x).

Willcocks, L. and Lacity, M. (2007) *Global Sourcing of Business and IT Services*, Palgrave Macmillan: London.

CHAPTER 1

Exploring relationships in information systems outsourcing: a typology of IS outsourcing relationships

Stefanie Leimeister and Helmut Krcmar

Introduction

Information systems (IS) outsourcing continues to be an important issue on the agenda of corporate IT executives (Luftman et al. 2006). However, the IS outsourcing market is changing and diversified approaches to outsourcing practices have been emerging over the past three decades (Dibbern et al. 2004; Lee et al. 2003). Starting with long-term outsourcing projects in the 1980s, organizations today face a turbulent and dynamic business environment and thus tend to seek increasingly selective, short-term, and often multi-vendor outsourcing arrangements (Cohen and Young 2006). Outsourcing has evolved beyond providers merely taking over a function and performing higher quality work at lower cost. Outsourcing arrangements have become more sophisticated not only with regard to the service itself but also with regard to the seemingly boundless global delivery of IT components (Rottman and Lacity 2004). Besides forms of short-term selective outsourcing, strategic partnerships and alliances, often referred to as transformational outsourcing (Linder 2004), have become an emerging trend. In this context, risk-sharing models and collaborative service development of innovative IT services have begun to shape customers' expectations toward the IT service provider (Leimeister et al. 2006b).

Despite these various approaches to outsourcing, however, many arrangements fail to live up to expectations and have to be interrupted, renegotiated, or even prematurely terminated (Kern et al. 2002; Lacity and Willcocks 2003).

The extensive variety of outsourcing approaches has contributed to increased complexity and a Babylonian confusion of sourcing practices, rather than to successful outsourcing arrangements with satisfied clients and vendors. Key reasons for such outsourcing failures include an underestimation of the complexity of an outsourcing venture, divergent and incongruous expectations of both parties toward the venture, and a lack of understanding of the imperative need for a continuous governance of the outsourcing relationship (Cohen and Young 2006). It has become obvious that a detailed and appropriately structured contractual agreement is a necessary, but often not a sufficient, governance mechanism for outsourcing success (Goles and Chin 2005; Klepper 1995, 1997). Governing beyond traditional contractual clauses toward a closer relationship-focused management that operates "within the spirit of the contract" then becomes necessary (Kern and Willcocks 2000). Moreover, relationship management in IS outsourcing is fundamentally different from other interorganizational relationships due to the business-critical, pervasive, and complex nature of IS in an organization (Dibbern et al. 2004).

Because of the contradictory outsourcing experiences and the peculiarities of IS outsourcing relationships outlined above, researchers have increasingly turned their attention to the management of the relationship between client and vendor in IS outsourcing (McFarlan and Nolan 1995; Klepper and Jones 1998; Lee and Kim 1999; Kern and Willcocks 2000; Lee et al. 2000; Kern et al. 2002; Kim and Chung 2003; Lee et al. 2003; Goles and Chin 2005; Sargent 2006).

Although several studies emphasize the importance of this relationship for the success of an outsourcing arrangement (Kern 1997; Lee and Kim 1999), little research has been directed toward a thorough examination and analysis of outsourcing relationships compared to other IS outsourcing research streams (Goles and Chin 2005). Most studies that have evaluated the relationship dimension in IS outsourcing (Lee and Kim 1999; cf. Goles 2001; Goles and Chin 2005) have focused on elaborating general relationship factors. However, the role and relevance of certain relationship factors varies between different outsourcing settings and according to the varying expectations of clients and vendors toward an outsourcing venture. Extant research distinguishes different *outsourcing forms and objects* (e.g., datacenter/infrastructure outsourcing, application hosting), but it does not consider the appropriate *types of outsourcing relationships* that result from expectations toward these outsourcing arrangements.

This chapter addresses these issues by developing a typology of different IS outsourcing relationships. The typology is regarded as a prerequisite to be able to suggest a specialized governance concept for a successful management of the identified types.

This chapter is structured as follows. The first section looks at social exchange and expectation confirmation theory as the underlying theoretical constructs that will guide us through the research context and also serve as the basis for the relationship type framework. Then, the extant literature is systematically reviewed and key factors of outsourcing relationships are derived. From the literature review and consideration of theoretical approaches, we develop key categories through which the relationship types can be structured and described in a framework. In the empirical evidence section, we discuss the key findings from preliminary exploratory expert interviews from which constitutive relationship types can be drawn and described through the framework categories. The concluding section discusses consequences and application areas of the identified relationship types and offers an outlook on future research.

Theoretical background

Theoretical foundation

Theoretical considerations of IS outsourcing research have focused overwhelmingly on economic theories such as transaction cost economics (TCE; Williamson 1979). In many ways, TCE seems to be the ideal theoretical foundation for IS outsourcing because it specifically addresses make-or-buy decisions based on the generic attributes of assets and describes appropriate ways to govern customer–supplier relationships from an economic point of view (Lacity and Willcocks 2003). However, while an outsourcing arrangement depends very much on the governance of the contractual relation element – which is the core proposition of TCE – an exclusively economic view falls far short of a comprehensive understanding of an outsourcing relationship because it views the actor as not interacting with another actor but rather directly with the market and thus does not include the perspective of exchanges between individual actors (Kern and Willcocks 2000). As this chapter focuses on the overall relationship aspect of an outsourcing venture, social theories are used as appropriate theoretical approaches to understand the phenomenon of outsourcing relationships.

Social exchange theory and related theories

Social or relational exchange theory reflects the exchange aspect and is one of the most appropriate theories to explain interorganizational behavior. Evolving from the junction of economics, sociology, and psychology, social exchange theory was developed and advanced by Blau (1964), Cook (1977), Emerson (1962), and Homans (1958) to understand the social behavior of humans in an economic context. It focuses on dyadic exchange relations involving the transfer of resources for mutual benefit of the actors. Over time, it has been enriched by different facets, varying from a technical economic analysis (Blau 1964) to the psychology of instrumental behavior (Homans 1958). In the context of IS outsourcing research, social exchange theory has served as an underlying theoretical model for explaining outsourcing relationships (e.g., Lee and Kim 1999; Kern and Willcocks 2000). A quite similar approach is followed in relational exchange theory. This is based on the notion that exchanging parties are in mutual agreement that the resulting outcomes of the exchange are greater than those that could be attained through other forms of exchange (Goles and Chin 2002). For this reason the exchange partners consider the exchange relationship valuable enough to devote resources toward its maintenance and development (Anderson and Narus 1984; Dwyer et al. 1987).

In addition to social and relational exchange theory, two related theoretical approaches need to be mentioned in the context of reciprocal exchanges between actors: (1) social contract theory proposes revamping classical contract theory so that it caters for the prior and future actions of individuals participating in exchange relations (Macneil 1980). Macneil argues that the traditional view of contract law does not adequately address the empirical realities of relational norms. (2) Similarly, psychological contract theory focuses on mutual obligations. A psychological contract refers to people's mental beliefs and expectations in relation to their mutual obligations in a contractual relation (Rousseau 1995).

Expectation confirmation theory

The underlying principle of reciprocal interaction between the involved actors entails mutual expectations toward the exchange relation. The expectations of both parties toward the relationship thus strongly determine the relationship and the perceived satisfaction of both parties. Expectation Confirmation Theory originated from the marketing and consumer behavior area. It states that expectations together with the following perceived performance lead to post-purchase satisfaction (Oliver 1977, 1980). Disconfirmation – either positive or negative – stems from the interaction of expectations with performance. Outperforming expectations cause positive disconfirmation, while lower performing expectations lead to negative disconfirmation.

Expectations are the anticipated or estimated behavior and precede the perceived outcome or performance of a relationship. In contrast to individual consumer behavior situations, in outsourcing exchange relationships the expectations of both parties have to be considered. Because perceived performance and overall success or satisfaction are highly dependent on the individual expectations of each participant, these expectations have to be congruent to achieve mutual benefits and perceived success of an outsourcing relationship.

Expectation Confirmation Theory has also been applied in the context of outsourcing IS applications (Application Service Provision (ASP)). Susarla et al. (2003) found that expectations in relation to ASP services have a significant influence on the performance evaluation of ASPs.

Prior research on IS outsourcing relationships: state of the art and literature review

The relationship perspective in IS outsourcing

Outsourcing can be termed a contractual-based exchange relation (Kern and Willcocks 2000) and a form of strategic information partnership which offers both parties mutual access to information, resources, and customers (Konsynski and McFarlan 1990). Interorganizational relationships have been researched from various perspectives and in several academic disciplines: among them are general management (Oliver 1990; Ring and Van de Ven 1994), marketing (Dwyer et al. 1987; Anderson and Narus 1990), psychology (Smith 1998), and IS (Henderson 1990; Konsynski and McFarlan 1990; Lasher et al. 1991).

Integrating the definitions of IS outsourcing and interorganizational relationships leads to a specific definition of an outsourcing relationship adopted from Goles and Chin (2005, 49) that will also be followed in this research:

> an ongoing ... linkage between an outsourcing vendor and customer arising from a contractual agreement to provide one or more comprehensive IT activities, processes, or services with the understanding that the benefits attained by each firm are at least in part dependent on the other.

Despite a shared understanding of interorganizational relationships between various disciplines, relationship management in IS outsourcing is fundamentally different from other interorganizational or outsourcing relationships. This difference arises from the nature and inherent characteristics of IS and information technology. General relationship management approaches as developed, for example, in marketing business-to-business relationships, strategic management, or other contractual literature are not necessarily applicable to IS outsourcing for several reasons. Although not necessarily strategic or a differentiating asset from competitors, information technology is business-critical and pervasive throughout the organization (Lacity and Willcocks 2001; Dibbern et al. 2004). It is not a homogenous function, but rather is interrelated with practically all organizational activities (Willcocks et al. 1996). Moreover, IS is complex in nature and also a permanent focus of change due to a company's IS needs, technology leaps, and the inherent difficulty of specifying IS in every detail upfront for a long period of time (Lacity and Willcocks 2003; Dibbern et al. 2004). Hence, relationship management approaches or typologies from other academic disciplines (e.g., TCE) may not be applicable to the context of relationships in IS outsourcing. New approaches have to be developed that consider the specific features inherent to IS.

IS outsourcing relationships are a multifaceted and complex phenomenon. The literature thus provides various relationship factors that determine an outsourcing relationship (Kern 1997; Kern and Willcocks 2000; Goles 2001; Alborz et al. 2004; Goles and Chin 2005). To gain a systematic overview of this vast variety of elements several authors have grouped such relationship factors into two distinct categories: inherent, sustainable characteristics that underlie a relationship, and ongoing, operational factors that affect the daily routines of the relationship (Henderson 1990; Lambe et al. 2000; Goles and Chin 2005). Goles and Chin (2005) suggest a detailed and systematic conceptualization of these factors, distinguishing between the *attributes* of an outsourcing relationship and its *processes*.

While a detailed discussion of such relationship factors is beyond the scope of this chapter, an overview of the factors extracted from a variety of papers related to relationships in various disciplines (mainly marketing, behavioral science, psychology, sociology, economics, administrative science, and IS) is given in Table 1.1. Despite the exorbitant number of relationship factors, research has failed to integrate these factors into an overall outsourcing context and the expectations of both parties.

Table 1.1 Relationship factors in various disciplines

References	Age of relationship	Commitment	Communication	Conflict/conflict resolution	Consensus	Cooperation	Coordination	Cultural similarity/cultural fit	Flexibility/adaptation	Influence	Information sharing	Interdependence	Joint action	Joint expectations	Norm development	Personal and social bonds/networks	Power	Reputation	Service quality	Top management support	Trust
(Aalders 2002)	X					X					X	X	X							X	
(Anderson et al. 1984)	X	X	X	X		X	X	X		X		X	X			X	X	X		X	X
(Bensaou and Venkatraman 1995)		X										X									
(Cook 1977)		X																			
(Dahl 1957)												X					X				
(de Loof 1998)			X	X		X		X	X			X					X				X
(DeSanctis and Jackson 1994)							X														
(Dwyer 1980, 1987)		X	X	X								X		X	X		X				X
(Emerson 1962)												X					X				
(Fitzgerald and Willcocks 1994)		X						X	X												
(Fontenot and Wilson 1997)		X																			
(Goles 2001; 2005)		X	X	X	X	X	X	X	X			X					X				X
(Grover et al. 1996)	X		X		X				X					X					X		X
(Gupta and Iyer 2003)		X						X													
(Heide and John 1990)		X	X						X			X			X						
(Henderson 1990)		X	X					X				X					X	X		X	X
(Kanter 1994)		X	X	X	X	X						X					X				X

Continued

Table 1.1   Continued

References	Age of relationship	Commitment	Communication	Conflict/conflict resolution	Consensus	Cooperation	Coordination	Cultural similarity/cultural fit	Flexibility/adaptation	Influence	Information sharing	Interdependence	Joint action	Joint expectations	Norm development	Personal and social bonds/networks	Power	Reputation	Service quality	Top management support	Trust
(Kern 1997, 2000)	X	X	X		X		X									X					X
(Klepper 1994; 1995; 1997)		X	X		X					X			X	X		X					X
(Konsynski et al. 1990)						X					X								X		
(Korsgaard et al. 1995)		X		X																	X
(Lacity and Hirschheim 1993; Lacity 1998)											X	X									
(Lasher et al. 1991)								X											X		
(Lee et al. 1999)	X	X	X			X	X				X	X	X							X	X
(Malone and Crowston 1990, 1994)						X															
(Mejias et al. 1996)				X																	
(Mohr and Spekman 1994)		X	X	X		X					X	X									X
(Monczka et al. 1998)		X	X	X		X					X	X									X
(Moorman et al. 1993)																					X
(Morgan and Hunt 1994)		X		X		X	X			X											X

Continued

Table 1.1   Continued

References	Relationship factor																				
	Age of relationship	Commitment	Communication	Conflict/conflict resolution	Consensus	Cooperation	Coordination	Cultural similarity/cultural fit	Flexibility/adaptation	Influence	Information sharing	Interdependence	Joint action	Joint expectations	Norm development	Personal and social bonds/networks	Power	Reputation	Service quality	Top management support	Trust
(Narus and Anderson 1987)						X															
(Pfeffer and Salancik 1978)								X				X									
(Pruitt 1981)	X																	X			
(Rai et al. 1996)				X															X		
(Griffin and Baldwin 1994)		X		X	X				X								X	X			X
(Rosenberg and Stern 1971)																X					
(Rousseau 1995)																					X
(Sargent 2006)														X					X		
(Scanzoni 1983)	X		X	X																	
(Sethuraman et al. 1988)												X							X		X
(Simpson and Mayo 1997)		X																			X
(Spekman et al. 1997)					X							X									
(Stern et al. 1973)													X		X						
(Willcocks and Choi 1995)				X				X													X
(Wooldridge and Floyd 1989)		X		X																X	
(Zaheer et al. 1998)																					X

Approaches to the classification of IS outsourcing relationships

The literature shows that the first approaches to a systematization of IS outsourcing relationships do exist (Nam et al. 1996; Kern et al. 2002; Kishore et al. 2003). Nam et al. (1996) propose a two-dimensional framework for describing four outsourcing relationships and expand this framework by proposing an evolution of these relationships across the identified types (Kishore et al. 2003). Kern et al. (2002) also classify four main types of IS outsourcing relationships along two other dimensions.

Although contributing to a more systematic understanding of outsourcing relationship arrangements, these approaches are too one-sided as they include only two selected dimensions, rather than an exhaustive set of dimensions, for describing an outsourcing relationship type.

Research gap

The analysis of the state of the art in the literature reveals several gaps that have not been considered in the extant research:

1. Research on relationship management in interorganizational relationships has enumerated a great number of relationship factors but has failed to integrate these factors into an overall outsourcing context.
2. Social Exchange and Expectation Confirmation Theory can help to foster a comprehensive view on outsourcing relationships, including an exchange perspective between individual actors instead of interaction with the market and the context perspective.
3. Classifications from other business-to-business relationship management approaches are hardly applicable to IS outsourcing relationships due to the specific nature of IS in an organization.
4. Classifications of relationships in IS outsourcing are often one-sided and do not provide an exhaustive set of dimensions for describing an outsourcing relationship type.

Constitutive factors of outsourcing relationships

As shown before, a vast variety of relationship factors can be identified in the literature. To gain an overall perception of an IS outsourcing relationship, these factors have to be expanded with the inclusion of general factors that need to be considered in an outsourcing arrangement (e.g., motivation for outsourcing, outsourcing object).

For the purpose of this chapter and to develop a framework within which relationship types of outsourcing arrangements can be allocated and described, we grouped the most important relationship factors and general outsourcing factors into four categories, building upon and expanding the relationship properties of Kern and Willcocks (2000). The categories and their subsequent factors were the basis for the development of the framework for describing and differentiating outsourcing relationships.

Strategic intent and expectations

Strategic intent focuses on what Kern and Willcocks (2000) call the contextual dimension of an outsourcing relationship. It encapsulates the objectives and expectations of the client toward the outsourcing engagement and also defines the role of the vendor. Derived from Expectation Confirmation Theory, expectations comprise economic and technical, as well as social or political, aspects of the relationship. Such expectations and objectives in turn are determined by the internal and external environment and challenges of both client and vendor (Lacity and Hirschheim 1994). In rather simple commodity outsourcing arrangements, the strategic impact is low and focuses on IT efficiency or access to a technical resource pool rather than on business transformation or technical leadership. Also, the involvement of the service provider in proactive planning and developing of new IS in the client firm plays a minor role compared, for example, to strategic alliance arrangements (Kishore et al. 2003).

Relationship architecture

The relationship architecture comprises the structure and conditions of an outsourcing arrangement. The network architecture, mutual dependency, or relationship duration are factors that determine the arrangement, and experience a wide variety in different outsourcing settings. Concerning relational architectures, Sambamurthy and Zmud (2000) distinguish between (1) strategic architectures that reflect relatively stable relationships with a limited number of partners (2) extended networks that arise for providing external commodity IT, and (3) virtual networks, which are loose arrangements with a large number of potential partners as needed.

Depending on the focus of the outsourcing relationship, various architectures might be appropriate to fulfill the expectations. Value-based IT innovations can be achieved best through strategic network architectures. IT efficiency might be accomplished in extended networks, and virtual networks are the appropriate means for temporarily limited consultation or implementation projects where specific know-how is required for a special task (Sambamurthy and Zmud 2000).

Another important issue mentioned in the context of social exchange theory has to be considered in the architecture of an outsourcing arrangement, that is, the power relation between client and vendor. Asymmetries in the power relations result from mutual dependencies (Easton 1992). They become critical if the impact of one party is dominant and leads, for example, to the danger of opportunistic behavior. In long term, stable outsourcing relationships, where large parts of the information technology have been outsourced to a vendor, the vendor most often dominates the outsourcing relationship due to lock-in effects. In selective outsourcing arrangements a client can distribute the risk to various vendors and thus minimize the overall risk (Kern 1997). Lacity and Willcocks (2003) emphasize that well-balanced power structures play a major role when common goals and expectations are pursued.

Governance and monitoring mechanisms

Contracts as formal mutual agreements engaged in by both parties have traditionally been an essential part of every outsourcing arrangement and the primary vehicle of governing outsourcing relationships. "Contracts, however, are not panaceas" (Clark et al. 1995).

Despite the importance and value of a written formal contract, outsourcing research has acknowledged that reliance on a legal contract alone is insufficient, given the complexities of real-life outsourcing arrangements and the rapid changes in technology and organizational environments (Koh et al. 2004; Leimeister et al. 2006a). Specifying long-term exchange relations such as outsourcing arrangements is complex, as they have to cover various unspecified obligations and thus are inherently incomplete. Incomplete contract theory suggests that not all possible events during an outsourcing venture can be predicted and included upfront in contract clauses (Richmond et al. 1992; Gietzmann 1996; Beulen and Ribbers 2002, 2003). Rendering contracts is expensive, often inflexible, and adaptation is costly.

In addition to formal, outcome-based governance styles, behavior-based governance mechanisms or informal relational norms are often set in place as interorganizational management structures that go beyond legal structures (Behrens 2006). Structural liaison devices or informal relational norms evolve over time through continuous collaboration and cooperation. They embrace implicit rules that define values such as trust, commitment, fairness, or flexibility among the participants. Informal governance is an adequate means in strategic alliance or joint service development structures, as these arrangements depend highly on structures beyond contractual clauses.

Interactions

Derived from social exchange theory, interaction-related factors emphasize behavioral mechanisms and interactions between the parties. They can be characterized by such dimensions as transfer of skills, information sharing, risk/benefit sharing, trust, and the role of cultural similarity between client and vendor (Kern and Willcocks 2000). Many authors claim that focusing on mutual and shared goals is crucial for a successful outsourcing relationship. Such a view, however, does not consider that there is an inherent adversarial nature in the contracts, "in that a dollar out of the customer's pocket is a dollar in the supplier's pocket" (Lacity and Willcocks 2003). Lacity and Willcocks (2003) thus emphasize the need to embrace the dynamics and development potential as the primary success factor of an outsourcing relationship. They suggest three interaction forms for outsourcing relationships: tentative, cooperative, and collaborative. The important message here is that each side must have equal power so that they can achieve fair outcomes.

Another aspect to be considered is the experience of the client with an outsourcing venture. In many cases, experience solely focuses the vendor's experience and capabilities with outsourced IT services (Kishore et al. 2003). For establishing and managing a long-term interaction the experience of the customer – the experience of the organization as a whole and the IT manager or CIO likewise – is a vital success factor.

Research context and framework for relationship types

Research context

The introduced relationship categories show fundamental areas that are important in different outsourcing arrangements. For an effective and

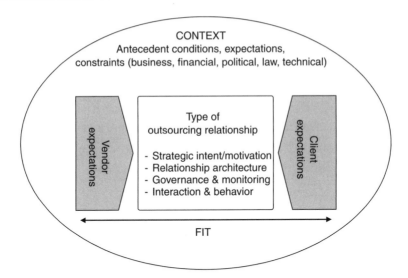

Figure 1.1   Research context

successful management of an outsourcing venture two aspects have to be considered: first, the context (i.e., expectations, antecedent conditions, and constraints) of both client and vendor in relation to the outsourcing venture and, second, the fit of the relationship type resulting from the expectations of each side. It is argued that this fit will determine each side's satisfaction with the relationship. Figure 1.1 depicts this interplay and the research context that underlies the typology to be developed in this chapter. It shows that client's expectations as well as vendor's expectations result in a certain type of outsourcing relationship. Only if both types of the outsourcing relationship match can an overall perceived satisfaction lead to a successful outsourcing venture.

A framework for types in IS outsourcing relationships

The literature has revealed that the first approaches to a systematization of IS outsourcing relationships (Nam et al. 1996; Kern et al. 2002; Kishore et al. 2003) are in general too one-sided, as they are not collectively exhaustive dimensions for describing an outsourcing relationship type. As the field of IS outsourcing has become more complex and diversified over the years, it becomes necessary to include various factors into the analysis of relationship types.

Relationship dimension \ Type	Type A	Type B	Type C	...
Strategic intent & expectations				
Relationship architecture				
Governance and monitoring				
Interaction				

Figure 1.2   Framework for types in IS outsourcing relationships

Therefore, we suggest a comprehensive framework for describing outsourcing relationships along a variety of relationship dimensions, as depicted in Figure 1.2.

Empirical evidence on expectations toward IS outsourcing relationships

Data collection

Based on the literature-based findings on relationship factors and the developed framework for classifying the relationship types, first, empirical evidence of different outsourcing types was gathered through 18 explorative, semi-structured expert interviews with Chief Information Officers (CIO) of outsourcing clients as well as sales and account managers of IT service providers. Although not accounting for a large sample size, these interviews serve as initial exploratory empirical evidence to support the conceptual idea of differentiating various outsourcing relationship types. The interviews covered antecedent conditions of the outsourcing decision, expectations toward the outsourcing relationship, and parameters of the current setting. Across the interviews the expectations in relation to the capabilities and conditions of an outsourcing arrangement and also the characteristics and importance of the relationship factors differed significantly. Table 1.2 gives an overview of the expert interviews which were conducted.

Results

Throughout the interviews, all interview partners stressed the importance of relational aspects in the outsourcing arrangement. The expectations in

Table 1.2 Overview of expert interviews

Interview partner (position)	Industry	Contract duration	Experience of expert with IS outsourcing	Areas of outsourced IT/ outsourcing portfolio	Expectations toward outsourcing partner/success factors of relationship	Identified or assigned type of relationship
Customer A Chief Information Officer (CIO)	Telecommunication	Current contract: since 2004, before that different vendor from 1998, contract duration: 5 years	>15 years experience both as client and vendor	Infrastructure (Desktop, Laptop, WAN, LAN, Messaging, Telephone, Server&Storage)	• Expert know-how/best of breed for technology and processes • Cost reduction: scale effects, synergies • Customized solution • Proactive suggestions for improvement • IT support for new products	Technology Excellence (Partner for Excellence)
Customer B Chief Information Officer (CIO)	Media/television	Current contract: since 2005, contract duration 4 years, before that: 3–year contract from 1996	>4 years	Infrastructure (Network, WAN, SAP, data bases), Call center Application Hosting	• Flexible adaptation toward changed customer demand/ adaptability/quick availability (business critical for live TV) • Specified competencies, responsibilities • Peak demand orientation because of dynamic end consumer demands • Industry know-how of provider	Mixed motives, rather commodity supplier (supportive role)

Customer C Head of IT	Banking/finance	Since 2001, then backsourced IT; current contract since 2004, contract duration 3 years	>5 years	Current: SAP, Desktop-services, On-site-support, Help desk before also: Networks, data center	• Cost reduction • Professional expertise: expert know-how, State-of-the-Art know-how of technology and processes • Fit of delivery model of client and vendor • Flexible adaptation of customer's business development: internationalization, M&A	Commodity supplier (supportive role)
Customer D Head IT-Management	Manufacturing/chemistry	Since 1996, contract duration 7 years, current contract since 2003, duration 5 years	>4 years	Network, SAP, special applications	• Industry know-how of provider • Transparent, specified contract with special service level agreements (SLA) • Fit of delivery model of client and vendor	Commodity supplier (supportive role)
Customer E Chief Information Officer (CIO)	Aerospace	Since 1999, contract duration 3 years (twice), current contract duration 5 years	>4 years	Networks (WAN, LAN), data center, applications, desktop	• Proactive suggestions for efficiency and improvement • Not bureaucratic, but rather slim processes • Quick response and flexible adaptation to customer needs	Mixed motives: reliance partner (Long-term stability partner), Technology excellence

Continued

Table 1.2 Continued

Interview partner (position)	Industry	Contract duration	Experience of expert with IS outsourcing	Areas of outsourced IT/ outsourcing portfolio	Expectations towards outsourcing partner/ success factors of relationship	Identified or assigned type of relationship
Customer F Associate partner Strategic IT management	Consulting	Since 2000, contract duration revolving (rollover, extendable)	>5 years	Total outsourcing to single vendor: infrastructure (server, desktops), Application Outsourcing, BPO (help desk, call center)	• Focus on core competencies • Technological innovation explicitly not expected • Stability with long-term partnership ,ongoing, stable delivery of operations • Cost reduction	Reliance partner (Long-term stability Partner)
Customer G Project leader cost management	Banking	n/a, short-term period (on project-basis)	n/a	Selective outsourcing, only application development	• Cost reduction • Buy-in of external know-how, no important drivers: benefit-risk share, knowledge transfer, innovation potential	Commodity supplier (supportive role)
Customer H Head of IT operations	Insurance	Since 2002, contract duration revolving (rollover, extendable)	>4 years	Infrastructure, help desk, printing services	• Cost reduction • "learning," knowledge transfer	Commodity supplier (supportive role)
Customer I CIO	Insurance	n/a, contract duration revolving (rollover, extendable)	>7 years	Infrastructure (network, WAN, SAP, data center), applications	• Cost efficiency, transparency • Flexibility due to volatile business, technical innovation explicitly expected	Mixed motives: Technology excellence (Partner for excellence), Commodity supplier

Role	Industry / Service	Duration		Scope	Drivers	Relationship type
Customer J Head of IT/Project Management, CIO	Transport/logistics	Since 2001 (mother company since 1998)	n/a	Infrastructure (hosts, SAP, desktop services), applications	• Focus on core competencies • Innovation (understood as cost reduction) • No important drivers; knowledge transfer	Commodity supplier (supportive role)
Vendor A Account manager	IT services (full service provider) Current customer in Banking/Finance	Current contract: since 2004, contract duration 10 years	n/a	IT systems, special banking applications	• Transfer of risks to vendor (dynamic end consumer demands in transaction business of banks) • Flexibility of monetary model: pay-on-production • Innovative delivery and market model	Mixed motives: Joint service development partner/strategic alliance partner
Vendor B Account manager	IT services (full service provider) Current customer in health care/medicine	Current contract duration between 1 and 3 years	n/a	Infrastructure, applications (ASP)	• Industry know-how of provider • Transfer of risks to vendor: risk/benefit sharing • Collaborative service development of innovative service in ASP medical area	Joint service development partner
Vendor C EMEA Program manager and competency leader, relationship alignment solutions	IT services (full service provider)	Contract duration approx. 5 years (customer tendency shorter)	>6 years	Full service provision: infrastructure, applications, business processes	• Exchange of values • Information sharing, open communication • Explicit consideration of mutual interests • Adaptation of cultures and processes of the partner	Strategic alliance partner

27

Continued

Table 1.2 Continued

Interview partner (position)	Industry	Contract duration	Experience of expert with IS outsourcing	Areas of outsourced IT/ outsourcing portfolio	Expectations toward outsourcing partner/ success factors of relationship	Identified or assigned type of relationship
Vendor D Managing consultant Strategy and change	IT services (full service provider) Same company as Vendor C	Contract duration approx. 5 years (customer tendency shorter)	n/a	Full service provision: infrastructure, applications, business processes	• Relevance and type of relationship management depends on desired relationship form • Success factors: SLA compliance, customer satisfaction • Quality of service delivery • Day-to-day working relationship	Mixed motives, no dominant type identified
Vendor E Leader resource management and reporting, service manager	IT services (full service provider)	Contract duration approx. 3–5 years	n/a	Full service provision: infrastructure, applications, business processes	• Vendor must be proactive, demonstrate up-to-date technology capabilities • Reputation of service provider, industry knowledge • Fit of delivery model of client and vendor • Information and knowledge exchange and transfer • Financial issues: cost reduction	Mixed motives, no dominant type identified

Vendor F Sales manager	IT services (full service provider) Same company as Vendor E. Current customers in aeronautic&defense, industrial manufact.	Contract duration application hosting and man.: approx. 3 years Full outsourcing: 5 years	n/a	Full service provision: infrastructure, applications, business processes Current customer focus: enterprise services	• High security policy required (due to industry requirements) • Cost reduction not expected: on the contrary: customer expects higher costs due to special security compliance • Trust extremely important, social and personal bonds	Strategic alliance partner
Vendor G Sales director out-tasking and outsourcing solutions	IT services (full service provider)	Contract duration approx. 3–5 years (4 years ago: 4–7 years)	n/a	Full service provision: infrastructure, applications, business processes	• Fit of delivery model: vendor looks for large-scale enterprise customers • Demonstration of vendor capabilities: vendor must show experience • Customer expectation: cost reduction • Customer expectation: native language of call center agents	Commodity supplier (supportive role)
Vendor H Client manager	IT Services (full service provider) Current customers in the public sector	Contract duration approx. 4–7 years	n/a	Full service provision: infrastructure, applications, business processes	• Fit of delivery model • Continuous benchmarking • Stable partnership required for long-term business value → stability, not necessarily strategic advantages expected	Reliance partner (long-term stability partner)

relation to the outsourcing partner and the overall outsourcing venture, however, varied significantly in the interviews. The perceived differences become most obvious in the varying characteristics and relevance of the relationship categories.

Strategic intent, expectations, and context

Regarding current business challenges, all interviewees emphasized the dynamics of the business environment and the resulting need for flexibility and efficient business processes. From this situation, the interview partners derived different motivations and expectations in relation to their outsourcing partner. Three of the interview partners focused on cost reduction and IT efficiency as their overall goal for the outsourcing relationship. Two other interview partners in turn highlighted the desire for proactive suggestions for improvement of processes, costs, and the development of competitive advantages.

> *For me, it is especially important that the vendor does not approach me in an "acquisition mode", but rather in an "improvement mode". The vendor is too reactive and not proactive. Making things better means a hassle for the vendor, but my vendor is only successful if I am successful. I am successful if my processes are efficient and ahead of the competition. So I expect improvement potential of my vendor.* (CIO, customer A)

One customer even strives for more expectations: Vendor G mentions that his customer explicitly expects a shared development of innovative ASP services in the medical sector for his end consumer, coupled with a shared benefit-risk model.

Relationship architecture

As a consequence of the evolution of various forms and models of outsourcing arrangements, the interviews reflect the trend toward a multi-sourcing strategy. Almost all of the interview partners engaged more than one IT service provider. Regarding the contract duration, a drift toward short outsourcing ventures can be stated. This, however, seems to be connected with the experience of the clients. The greater the experience with outsourcing in general and with the specific vendor becomes, the more customers dare to engage in long-term arrangements. One major issue in this context is also the industry knowledge of the vendor, as client B states: "A working distribution of responsibilities and a shared understanding of my business problems is crucial to the relationship. The vendor has to understand the challenges and constraints of my business and my industry" (CIO, customer B).

Governance and monitoring

In parallel with the literature, the distinction between formal, outcome-based and informal, behavior-based governance mechanisms could be found in practice. While all interview partners emphasized the importance of a formal contractual agreement as fundamental for the outsourcing relationship, two interview partners explicitly govern their relationship through informal, behavior-based mechanisms. In their view, a contract exclusively is not sufficient for a successful relationship, but rather a cooperative management beyond contractual clauses. These two interview partners regard their IT service provider not as a commodity supplier, but rather as a strategic partner: "The contract is essential. However, once I have to get out the contract and make reference to the specific clauses, it is too late. The relationship is damaged" (CIO, customer E).

Interaction

Regarding the reciprocal interaction between the parties, the interview partners stressed two aspects: first, the power dependency relation between client and vendor, and second the delivery model of the vendor. In both aspects, the balance and fit between the expectations of both parties play a major role. Negotiating at eye level was mentioned as a vital success factor:

> We were no match for the delivery model of the vendor. The vendor was the "big boss" and imposed his processes and resources on us. We are a small business and the methods and instruments of the vendor were in not relation to our needs and monetary power. In the end, the deal was not profitable for our vendor and he let us feel it. (Head of IT, customer C)

Types of IS outsourcing relationships

To develop a typology of different outsourcing relationship types, we allocated the expectations and experiences gathered in the expert interviews to the framework. We conducted a thorough content analysis (Krippendorff 1980) by searching for structures and patterned regularities in the different expert interviews. While we found mixed and sometimes incongruent motives and characteristics in some expert interviews, in general, we could derive five different, alternative, and exclusive relationship types that followed a certain underlying motive and represent constitutive patterns of expectations: Commodity Supplier, Technology Excellence, Reliance Partner, Joint Service Development Partner, and Strategic Alliance Partner (see Figure 1.3).

The most common type – also found to be dominant in the selection of expert interviews that were conducted – is the *Commodity Supply Relationship*. Here the objective is to achieve IT efficiencies by hiring external resources. In such relationships, the focus is on cost reduction or rendering IT as a variable cost. The vendor is regarded as a utility provider offering services from a resource pool on a short-term, often as-needed, basis. Ties of the relationship in terms of trust, commitment, and informal exchange are quite loose. An appropriate governance mechanism is the formal, outcome-based control via contracts. Strategic elements and long-term competitive advantages cannot be expected in this type.

Another relationship is *Technology Excellence*, where the vendor is chosen for "best-in-class" capability, "future-proofing" on the technological front, and proactive innovation in technological applications (Kern et al. 2002). This relationship is often established for a project-based short-term duration, where the vendor is regarded as a partner for excellence. This relationship also mostly requires outcome-based governance mechanisms.

A third type is the *Reliance Partner*. This relationship requires more commitment, trust, and informal exchange, since significant portions of the client's IT operations are transferred to the external vendor for a long period. Also, the coordination costs and barriers for changing the partner are higher compared to the first two relationship types. It is important to note that long-term and large-scale outsourcing arrangements are not necessarily strategic alliances (Kishore et al. 2003). A long-term, stable vendor can provide noncore, commodity IT capabilities without a strategic or transformational component.

Joint Service Development is a highly innovative relationship type, just beginning to evolve in practice. This relationship is neither a short-term commodity outsourcing type nor a fully strategic type. The focus is on collaborative service engineering, where both partners engage in working together and developing selected outsourcing services together on a risk-reward-basis for a medium period of time. Governance in this relationship type is best achieved through behavior-based forms. The extent of mutual dependency is high, and this type also involves strategic elements such as gaining competitive advantage through joint knowledge from both partners. The specification for outsourced services is difficult to define completely *a priori*, as the outcomes are ambiguous and dynamic. This type is the answer to clients' requests for innovation in IS outsourcing. While not being a long-term reliance partner or a long-term strategic alliance partner, a joint service development partnership focuses on the question of how an outsourcer can contribute to innovation and deliver value to the client. An example of this type was found in practice: a client in the medical sector explicitly requested the development of a new business model/product of an innovative medical ASP service of his IT service provider that the client could in turn offer to his clients, that is, hospitals. The development of such services was intended to be a mutual and joint project where both parties dedicated their resources and took the risk and rewards alike.

Finally, *Strategic Alliance Partnership* – often labeled as transformational outsourcing – involves working together and sharing the risks and rewards. Coordination is – similar to joint service development – much more complex, and monitoring is best achieved through behavioral-based mechanisms and relational norms. This type involves a long-term engagement with high commitment of both partners, and experience of outsourcing is required for a successful undertaking.

Based on the review of relationship factors in the literature and our exploratory empirical results, we can now propose types more comprehensively. Moreover, we extend the existing literature not only by being able to describe the types in more detail but also by identifying a new type of outsourcing relationship, that is, joint service development.

Figure 1.3 depicts the types in more detail and characterizes them along the proposed categories.

Conclusion and outlook on further research

The contribution of this chapter is an advancement of knowledge regarding the characteristics of the relationship in different IS outsourcing arrangements. Key relationship factors were derived from the extant literature and grouped into constitutive relationship categories that are relevant in an IS outsourcing arrangement. As elaborated above, classifications from other relationship management approaches are hardly applicable to IS outsourcing relationships due to the specific nature and role of IS in an organization. In explorative expert interviews, first, the supporting evidence for different characteristics of the relationship factors was elaborated, which led to a

Type / Dimension	Commodity supplier (supportive role)	Technology excellence (partner for excellence)	Reliance partner (long-term stability partner)	Joint service development partner	Strategic alliance partner	Supporting references for dimension (examples)
Strategic intent/expectations/context						
Strategic intent and motivation for outsourcing	IT efficiency, cost reduction	IT efficiency, cost reduction, access to world-class technological expertise	Business value, performance, stability, focus on core competencies	Business value, innovation, collaborative Service engineering/know-how fusion	Business transformation, strategic alliance partner	(Kern et al. 2002) (Kishore et al. 2003) (Alborz et al. 2004)
Strategic impact on client's IS components	⟳	⟳	⟳	⟳	⟳	(Nam et al. 1996), (Kishore et al. 2003)
Expectation/role of service provider	Utility provider, access to commodities	Solution provider "best in class"	Stable solution provider	Joint service development partner		McFarlan et al. 1995
Motivation of technical capability	Gain access to technical resources from a resource pool	Gain leading-edge technology, "future-proofing"	Gain access to technical resources from a resource pool	Distinctive technical leadership	Distinctive technical leadership	(Kern et al. 2002)
Involvement of service provider in proactive planning&development of new IS in the client firm	Hardly	extremely important	important	extremely important/crucial	extremely important	(Kishore et al. 2003)
Extent of competitive advantage, business value leveraged and positioning through outsourcing	⟳	⟳/⟳	⟳/⟳	⟳	⟳	(Kishore et al. 2003)
Extent of future development of interorganizational relationship (evolution)	⟳	⟳/⟳	⟳	⟳	⟳	(Kishore et al. 2003)
Influence on long-term strategy	⟳	⟳	⟳	⟳	⟳	(Kishore et al. 2003)
Relational Architecture						
Barriers/switching costs to change/mutual dependency	⟳	⟳/⟳	⟳	⟳	⟳	(Nam et al. 1996), (Lee et al. 1999), (Goles et al. 2005), (McFarlan et al. 1995)
Shared goals	⟳	⟳	⟳/⟳	⟳	⟳	(Easton 1992), (Lacity et al. 2003)
Duration of relationship/contract period	short-term	short-term	long-term	mid-term	long-term	(McFarlan et al. 1995), (Fitzgerald et al. 1994), (Lee et al. 1999)
Time horizon of relationship	Project-based, (ongoing)	Project-based	ongoing	Ongoing/ (project-based)	ongoing	(Kishore et al. 2003)
Relational architecture (strategic, extended, virtual)	virtual/ extended	virtual/ extended	extended/ (strategic)	extended/ (strategic)	strategic	(Sambamurthy et al. 2000)

Figure 1.3 A typology of different IS outsourcing relationships

Dimension / Type	Commodity supplier (supportive role)	Technology excellence (partner for excellence)	Reliance partner (long-term stability partner)	Joint service development partner	Strategic alliance partner	Supporting references for dimension (examples)
Object focus of relationship	specific to project/service	specific to service/technology	specific to service	joint service development	strategic alliance	(Kishore et al. 2003)
Outcomes of IS relationship	well defined	well defined	well defined, but dynamic	ambiguous/dynamic	ambiguous/dynamic	(Kishore et al. 2003)
Specification of outsourced information services	well defined	well defined	well defined	difficult to specify a priori	difficult to specify a priori	(Kishore et al. 2003)
Extent of substitution by vendors (amount of outsourced services)	◐	◐	◐	◔	◔	(Nam et al. 1996)
Role of experience with outsourcing	◐	◔ / ◐	◔	◔	◔	(Lee et al. 1999)
Governance mechanisms						
Governance or control mechanism (formal/informal, outcome-based, behavior-based, relational norms)	formal, outcome based	formal, outcome-based	formal, outcome-based	formal, behavior-based, also informal based on rel. norms	formal, behavior-based, also informal based on rel. norms	(Behrens 2006; Kishore et al. 2003)
Role/level of contractual control	◐	◔ / ◐	◐	◔	◔	(Kishore et al. 2003) (Klepper et al. 1998)
Extent of outcome fixed in contractual agreement	◐	◐	◔/◐	◔ /dynamic	◔ /dynamic	(Behrens 2006)
Interactions						
Importance of informal information channels	◐	◔	◔	◐	◐	(Kishore et al. 2003)
Transfer and sharing of information	◐	◐	◔	◐	◐	(Lee et al. 1999)
Need for profit/risk sharing incentives	◐	◐	◔/◐	◐	◐	(Kishore et al. 2003), (Lee et al. 1999)
Need for Profit/risk sharing incentives	◐	◐	◔/◐	◐	◐	(Kishore et al. 2003) (Lee et al. 1999)
Transfer of skills	◐	◐	◔	◐	◐	(Kishore et al. 2003)
Extent of vendor's managerial control & decision-making authority	◐	◔	◐	◐	◐	(Kishore et al. 2003)
Coordination costs and intensity	◐	◔	◐	◐	◐	(Kishore et al. 2003)
Commitment of client and vendor	◐	◐	◔	◐	◐	(Lee et al. 1999), (Goles et al. 2005)
Role of trust between parties	◐	◐	◔	◐	◐	(Henderson 1990; Kern 1997; Lee et al. 1999), (Goles et al. 2005)
Need for cultural similarity	◐	◔	◐	◐	◐	(McFarlan et al. 1995), (Klepper et al. 1998), (Lee et al. 1999)

Legend: ◔ = high, ◑ = medium, ◐ = low

distinction of five different relationship types. We found the typology useful in elucidating important relationship management areas, highlighting not only the outsourcing relationship's contractual, social, and economic characteristics but also many additional elements found to have relevance in practice. The typology is only an initial step toward a more comprehensive understanding of different expectations of both client and vendor regarding the outsourcing relationship. It provides a foundation for future positivist research where the different types have to be validated on a broader empirical basis to advance this exploratory approach. Subsequent research should thus take into account the preliminary nature of this study.

Several managerial implications emerge from this chapter. First, clarifying the different expectations of both parties and the corresponding relationship type that matches one to the other is a crucial precondition for establishing effective relationship mechanisms of a successful partnership for both partners. Indeed, quite a few organizations contract and manage tightly for cost efficiency in a commodity supplier arrangement, but then also expect the sort of risk sharing and business transformation that can only be obtained from a strategic alliance partnership – a clear mismatch of mutual expectations (Kern et al. 2002) caused by mixed and incongruent motives. The framework can help both parties think through their outsourcing expectations and what the implications of this analysis might be for relationship arrangements, governance, and resource focus. It might also be of greater interest to examine appropriate governance mechanisms, not only for a certain relationship type but also in case there is a misfit of expectations.

Last, it will be interesting to conduct thorough and longitudinal research on the evolution of relationship types. As found in this study, the most common and still predominant type is the commodity supplier relationship. However, it remains to be seen whether outsourcing relationships will tend to evolve toward the extreme edges of the typology (i.e., the commodity type and the strategic type) or if the innovation type of joint service development will be an attractive future model for delivering IT services.

References

Aalders, R. (2002) The IT Outsourcing Guide, Chichester, NY: John Wiley & Sons.

Alborz, S., Seddon, P.B., and Scheepers, R. (2004) Impact of Configuration on IT Outsourcing Relationships, *Proceedings of the Tenth Americas Conference on Information Systems*, New York, 3551–3560.

Anderson, J.C. and Narus, J.A. (1984) A Model of the Distributor's Perspective of Distributor-Manufacturer Working Relationships. *Journal of Marketing*, 48(4): 62–74.

Anderson, J.C. and Narus, J.A. (1990) A Model of Distributor Firm and Manufacturer Firm Working Partnerships. *Journal of Marketing*, 54(1): 42–58.

Behrens, S. (2006) Governance and Information Systems Outsourcing Success: A Contingency Perspective, *Proceedings of the Multikonferenz Wirtschaftsinformatik*, Passau, 101–116.

Bensaou, M. and Venkatraman, N. (1995) Configurations of Interorganizational Relationships: A Comparison between U.S. and Japanese Automakers. *Management Science*, 41(9): 1471–1492.

Beulen, E. and Ribbers, P. (2002) Managing Complex IT Outsourcing-Partnerships, *Proceedings of the 35th Hawaii International Conference on System Sciences – 2002*, Hawaii, USA, 1–10.

Beulen, E. and Ribbers, P. (2003) IT Outsourcing Contracts: Practical Implications of the Incomplete Contract Theory, *Proceedings of the 36th Hawaii International Conference on System Sciences*, Hawaii, USA, 2003.

Blau, P. (1964) *Exchange and Power in Social Life*, New York: John Wiley & Sons.

Clark, T.D., Zmud, R.W., and McCray, G.E. (1995) The Outsourcing of Information Services: Transforming the Nature of Business in the Information Industry. *Journal of Information Technology*, 10(4): 221–237.

Cohen, L. and Young, A. (2006) *Multisourcing: Moving beyond Outsourcing to Achieve Growth and Agility*, Boston, MA, USA: Harvard Business School Press.

Cook, K.S. (1977) Exchange and Power in Networks of Interorganizational Relations. *The Sociological Quarterly*, 18(Winter): 62–82.

Dahl, R.A. (1957) The Concept of Power. *Behavioral Science*, 2(3): 201–215.

de Loof, L.A. (1998) Information Systems Outsourcing: Theories, Case Evidence and a Decision Framework, in L.P. Willcocks and M.C. Lacity (eds) *Strategic Sourcing of Information Systems*, Chichester, NY: John Wiley & Sons, 249–282.

DeSanctis, G. and Jackson, B. (1994) Coordination of Information Technology Management: Team-Based Structures and Computer-Based Communication Systems. *Journal of Management Information Systems*, 10(4): 85–110.

Dibbern, J., Goles, T., Hirschheim, R., and Jayatilaka, B. (2004) Information Systems Outsourcing: A Survey and Analysis of the Literature. *The DATA BASE for Advances in Information Systems*, 35(4): 6–102.

Dwyer, F.R. (1980) Channel-Member Satisfaction: Laboratory Insights. *Journal of Retailing*, 56(2) Summer: 45–65.

Dwyer, F.R., Schurr, P.H., and Oh, S. (1987) Developing Buyer-Seller Relationships. *The Journal of Marketing*, 51(2): 11–27.

Easton, G. (1992) Industrial Networks: A Review, in B. Axelson and G. Easton (eds) *Industrial Networks: A New View of Reality*, London, Routledge, 1–34.

Emerson, R.M. (1962) Power-Dependence Relations. *American Sociological Review*, 27(1): 31–41.

Fitzgerald, G. and Willcocks, L.P. (1994) Contracts and Partnerships in the Outsourcing of IT, *Proceedings of the Fifteenth International Conference on Information Systems*, Vancouver, Canada, 91–98.

Fontenot, R. and Wilson, E. (1997) Relational Exchange: A Review of Selected Models for a Prediction Matrix of Relationship Activities. *Journal of Business Research*, 39(1): 5–12.

Gietzmann, M.B. (1996) Incomplete Contracts and the Make or Buy Decision: Governance Design and Attainable Flexibility. *Accounting, Organizations and Society*, 21(6): 611–626.

Goles, T. (2001) The Impact of the Client-Vendor Relationship on Information Systems Outsourcing Success, in *Unpublished Dissertation*. *Bauer College of Business*, University of Houston, Houston.

Goles, T. and Chin, W.W. (2002) Relational Exchange Theory and IS Outsourcing: Developing a Scale to Measure Relationship Factors, in R. Hirschheim, A. Heinzl, and J. Dibbern (eds) *Information Systems Outsourcing: Enduring Themes, Emergent Patterns and Future Directions*, Berlin, Heidelberg: Springer, 221–250.

Goles, T. and Chin, W.W. (2005) Information Systems Outsourcing Relationship Factors: Detailed Conceptualization and Initial Evidence. *SIGMIS Database*, 36(4): 47–67.

Griffin, R.K. and Baldwin, D. (1994) Self-Management Information System for the Service Industry: a Conceptual Model. *Journal of Management Information Systems*, 10(4) Spring: 111.

Grover, V., Cheon, M.J., and Teng, J.T.C. (1996) The Effect of Service Quality and Partnership on the Outsourcing of Information Systems Functions. *Journal of Management Information Systems*, 12(4): 89–116.

Gupta, B. and Iyer, L.S. (2003) A Theoretical Framework for Measuring the Success of Customer Relationship Management Outsourcing, in Hershey, PA. (ed.) *Business Strategies for Information Technology Management*, London and Melbourne: IRM Press; distributed by Independent Publishers Group, Chicago, 149–159.

Heide, J.B., and John, G. (1990) Alliances in Industrial Purchasing: The Determinants of Joint Action in Buyer-Supplier Relationships, *Journal of Marketing Research (JMR)*, 27 (1): 24–36.

Henderson, J.C. (1990) Plugging into Strategic Partnerships: The Critical IS Connection. *Sloan Management Review*, 31(3): 7–18.

Homans, G.C. (1958) Social Behavior as Exchange. *American Journal of Sociology*, 63(6): 597–606.

Kanter, R.M. (1994) Collaborative Advantage: The Art of Alliances. *Harvard Business Review*, 72(4): 96–108.

Kern, T. (1997) The *gestalt* of an Information Technology Outsourcing Relationship: an Exploratory Analysis, *Proceedings of the Eighteenth International Conference on Information Systems*, Atlanta, GA, 37–58.

Kern, T. and Willcocks, L. (2000) Exploring Information Technology Outsourcing Relationships: Theory and Practice. *The Journal of Strategic Information Systems*, 9(4) December: 321–350.

Kern, T., Willcocks, L.P., and van Heck, E. (2002) The Winner's Curse in IT Outsourcing: Strategies for Avoiding Relational Trauma. *California Management Review*, 44(2): 47–69.

Kim, S. and Chung, Y.-S. (2003) Critical Success Factors for IS Outsourcing Implementation from an Organizational Relationship Perspective. *Journal of Computer Information Systems*, 43(4): 81–90.

Kishore, R., Rao, H., Nam, K., Rajagopalan, S., and Chaudhury, A. (2003) A Relationship Perspective on IT Outsourcing. *Communications of the ACM*, 46(12): 87–92.

Klepper, R. (1994) Outsourcing Relationships, in M. Khosrowpour (ed.) *Managing Information Technology Investment with Outsourcing*, Harrisburg: IDEA Group Publishing, 218–243.

Klepper, R. (1995) The Management of Partnering Development in I/S Outsourcing. *Journal of Information Technology*, 10(4): 249–258.

Klepper, R. (1997) The Management of Partnering Development in IS Outsourcing, in L.P. Willcocks and M.C. Lacity (eds) *Strategic Sourcing of Information Systems: Perspectives and Practices*, Chichester, NY: John Wiley & Sons, 305–326.

Klepper, R. and Jones, W. (1998) *Outsourcing Information Technology, Systems and Services*, Upper Saddle River, NJ: Prentice Hall.

Koh, C., Ang, S., and Straub, D.W. (2004) IT Outsourcing Success: A Psychological Contract Perspective. *Information Systems Research*, 15(4): 356–373.

Konsynski, B.R. and McFarlan, E.W. (1990) Information Partnerships – Shared Data, Shared Scale. *Harvard Business Review*, 68(5): 115–120.

Korsgaard, M.A., Schweiger, D.M., and Sapienza, H.J. (1995) Building Commitment, Attachment, and Trust in Strategic Decision-Making Teams: The Role of Procedural Justice. *The Academy of Management Journal*, 38(1): 60–84.

Krippendorff, K. (1980) Content Analysis: An Introduction to Its Methodology, Beverly Hills, CA. USA: Sage.

Lacity, M.C. and Hirschheim, R.A. (1993) *Information Systems Outsourcing – Myths, Metaphors and Realities*, Chichester, NY: John Wiley & Sons.

Lacity, M.C. and Hirschheim, R.A. (1994) Realizing Outsourcing Expectations: Incredible Expectations, Credible Outcomes. *Information Systems Management*, 11(4): 7–18.

Lacity, M.C. and Willcocks, L. (2001) *Global Information Technology Outsourcing*, Chichester, NY: John Wiley & Sons.

Lacity, M.C. and Willcocks, L. (2003) IT Sourcing Reflections: Lessons for Customers and Suppliers. *Wirtschaftsinformatik*, 45: 115–125.

Lambe, C.J., Spekman, R.E., and Hunt, S.D. (2000) Interimistic Relational Exchange: Conceptualization and Propositional Development. *Journal of the Academy of Marketing Science*, 28(2): 212–225.

Lasher, D., Ives, B., and Jarvenpaa, S. (1991) USA-IBM Partnerships in Information Technology: Managing the Image Project. *MIS Quarterly*, 15(4): 551–566.

Lee, J.-N., Huynh, M.Q., Chi-wai, K.R., and Pi, S.-M. (2000) The Evolution of Outsourcing Research: What is the Next Issue? IEEE Computer Society, *Proceedings of the 33rd Hawaii International Conference on System Sciences-Volume 7.*Lee, J.-N., Huynh, M.Q., Kwok, R.C.-W., and Pi, S.-M. (2003) IT Outsourcing Evolution–Past, Present, and Future. *Communications of the ACM*, 46(5): 84–89.

Lee, J.-N. and Kim, Y.-G. (1999) Effect of Partnership Quality on IS Outsourcing Success: Conceptual Framework and Empirical Validation. *Journal of Management Information Systems*, 15(4): 29–61.

Leimeister, S., Böhmann, T., and Krcmar, H. (2006a) Anticipating and Considering Customers' Flexibility Demands in IS Outsourcing Relationships, *Proceedings of the 14th European Conference on Information Systems*, Göteborg, Sweden.

Leimeister, S., Böhmann, T., and Krcmar, H. (2006b) Relationship Archetypes in Information Systems Outsourcing Arrangements: An Exploratory Analysis, *Proceedings of the Twelfth Americas Conference on Information Systems*, Acapulco, Mexico, 2133–3237.

Linder, J.C. (2004) Transformational Outsourcing. *MIT Sloan Management Review*, 45(2): 52–58.

Luftman, J., Kempaiah, R., and Nash, E. (2006) Key Issues for IT Executives 2005. *MIS Quarterly Executive*, 5(2): 27–45.

Macneil, I.R. (1980) The New Social Contract: An Inquiry into Modern Contractual Relations, New Haven, CT: Yale University Press.

Malone, T.W. and Crowston, K. (1990) What Is Coordination Theory and How Can It Help Design Cooperative Work Systems? in *Proceedings of the 1990 ACM Conference on Computer-Supported Cooperative Work*, Los Angeles, CA, United States: ACM Press.

Malone, T.W. and Crowston, K. (1994) The Interdisciplinary Study of Coordination. *ACM Computing Surveys (CSUR)*, 26(1): 87–119.

McFarlan, F.W. and Nolan, R.L. (1995) How to Manage an IT Outsourcing Alliance. *Sloan Management Review*, Winter: 9–23.

Mejias, R., Shepard, M., Vogel, D., and Lazaneo, L. (1996) Consensus and Perceived Satisfaction Levels: A Cross-cultural Comparison of GSS and non-GSS Outcomes within and between the United States and Mexico. *Journal of Management Information Systems*, 13(3): 137–161.

Mohr, J. and Spekman, R. (1994) Characteristics of Partnership Success: Partnership Attributes, Communication Behavior, and Conflict Resolution Techniques. *Strategic Management Journal*, 15(2): 135–152.

Monczka, R.M., Petersen, K.J., Handfield, R.B., and Ragatz, G.L. (1998) Success Factors in Strategic Supplier Alliances: The Buying Company Perspective. *Decision Sciences*, 29(3) Summer: 553–577.

Moorman, C., Deshpandé, R., and Zaltman, G. (1993) Factors Affecting Trust in Market Research Relationships. *Journal of Marketing*, 57(1): 81–101.

Morgan, R.M. and Hunt, S.D. (1994) The Commitment-Trust Theory of Relationship Marketing. *Journal of Marketing*, 59(3): 20–38.

Nam, K., Rajagopalan, S., Rao, H.R., and Chaudhury, A. (1996) A Two-Level Investigation of Information Systems Outsourcing. *Communications of the ACM*, 39(7): 36–44.

Narus, J. and Anderson, J. (1987) Distribution Contributions to Partnerships with Manufacturers. *Business Horizons*, 30(5): 34–42.

Oliver, C. (1990) Determinants of Interorganizational Relationships: Integration and Future Directions. *Academy of Management Review*, 15(2): 241–265.

Oliver, R.L. (1977) Effect of Expectation and Disconfirmation on Postexposure Product Evaluations – an Alternative Interpretation. *Journal of Applied Psychology*, 62(4): 480.

Oliver, R.L. (1980) A Cognitive Model of the Antecedents and Consequences of Satisfaction Decisions. *Journal of Marketing Research*, 17(4): 460–469.

Pfeffer, J. and Salancik, G.R. (1978) *The External Control of Organizations*, New York: Harper and Row.

Pruitt, D.G. (1981) *Negotiation Behavior*, New York: Academic Press.

Rai, A., Borah, S., and Ramaprasad, A. (1996) Critical Success Factors for Strategic Alliances in the Information Technology Industry: An Empirical Study. *Decision Sciences*, 27(1): 141–155.

Richmond, W.B., Seidmann, A., and Whinston, A.B. (1992) Incomplete Contracting Issues in Information Systems Development Outsourcing. *Decision Support Systems*, 8(5): 459–477.

Ring, P.S. and Van de Ven, A. (1994) Developmental Processes of Cooperative Interorganizational Relationships. *Academy of Management Review*, 19(1): 90–118.

Rosenberg, L.J. and Stern, L.W. (1971) Conflict Measurement in the Distribution Channel. *Journal of Marketing Research (JMR)*, 8(4): 437–442.

Rottman, J.W. and Lacity, M.C. (2004) Twenty Practices for Offshore Sourcing. *MIS Quarterly Executive*, 3(3): 117–130.

Rousseau, D. (1995) *Psychological Contracts in Organizations: Understanding Written and Unwritten Agreements*, Thousand Oaks, CA: Sage Publications Inc.

Sambamurthy, V. and Zmud, R.W. (2000) Research Commentary: The Organizing Logic for an Enterprise's IT Activities in the Digital Era–A Prognosis of Practice and a Call for Research. *Information Systems Research*, 11(2): 105–114.

Sargent, A. (2006) Outsourcing Relationship Literature: an Examination and Implications for Future Research, *Proceedings of the 2006 ACM SIGMIS CPR conference*, Claremont, CA: ACM Press.

Scanzoni, J. (1983) Social Exchange and Behavioral Interdependence, in R. Burgess and T. Huston (eds) *Social Exchange in Developing Relationships*, New York: Academic Press, 61–98.

Sethuraman, R., Anderson, J.C., and Narus, J.A. (1988) Partnership Advantage and Its Determinants in Distributor and Manufacturer Working Relationships. *Journal of Business Research*, 17(4): 327–347.

Simpson, J. and Mayo, D. (1997) Relationship Management: A Call for Fewer Influence Attempts. *Journal of Business Research*, 39(3): 209–218.

Smith, J.B. (1998) Buyer-Seller Relationships: Similarity, Relationship Management, and Quality. *Psychology and Marketing*, 15(1): 3–21.

Spekman, R.E., Salmond, D.J., and Lambe, C.J. (1997) Consensus and Collaboration: Norm-regulated Behaviour in Industrial Marketing Relationships. *European Journal of Marketing*, 31(11/12): 835–856.

Stern, L.W., Sternthal, B., and Craig, C.S. (1973) Managing Conflict in Distribution Channels: A Laboratory Study. *Journal of Marketing Research (JMR)*, 10(2): 169–179.

Susarla, A., Barua, A., and Whinston, A.B. (2003) Understanding the Service Component of Application Service Provision: An Empirical Analysis of Satisfaction with ASP Services. *MIS Quarterly*, 27(1): 91–123.

Willcocks, L. and Choi, C.J. (1995) Co-Operative Partnership and "Total" It Outsourcing: From Contractual Obligation to Strategic Alliance? *European Management Journal*, 13(1): 67–78.

Willcocks, L., Fitzgerald, G., and Lacity, M. (1996) To Outsource IT Or Not? Recent Research on Economics and Evaluation Practice. *European Journal of Information Systems*, 5(3): 143–160.

Willcocks, L. and Lacity, M. (1998) *Strategic Sourcing of Information Systems: Perspectives and Practices*, Chichester, NY: Wiley & Sons.

Williamson, O.E. (1979) Transaction-Cost Economics: The Governance of Contractual Relations. *Journal of Law and Economics*, 22(2): 233–261.

Wooldridge, B. and Floyd, S.W. (1989) Strategic Process Effects on Consensus. *Strategic Management Journal*, 10(3): 295–302.

Zaheer, A., McEvily, B., and Perrone, V. (1998) Does Trust Matter? Exploring the Effects of Interorganizational and Interpersonal Trust on Performance. *Organization Science*, 9(2): 141–159.

CHAPTER 2

Offshore middlemen: transnational intermediation in technology sourcing

Volker Mahnke, Jonathan Wareham, and Niels Bjørn-Andersen

Introduction

The migration of IT outsourcing relationships to lower cost regions such as India and China continues with few indications of abatement (King 2005). The primary motivation for this trend continues to be labor cost arbitrage. However, a secondary incentive, higher levels of skill and specialization, is also cited more frequently in managerial discourse (Dedene and DeVreese 1995; Pfannenstein and Tsai 2004). Most of the offshoring literature studies the outsourcing firm (Mahnke et al. 2005), but there is also a growing and important body of literature focusing on the outsourcing vendor (Levina and Ross 2003). This paper focuses on the intermediation capabilities necessary to span boundaries between a client and an offshoring partner's value creation systems.

Although firms are increasingly aware of offshoring possibilities, their ability to exploit them is far more limited. Frequently, the anticipated benefits in offshore outsourcing partnerships are not realized, complicated by lack of international experience, competency gaps (Cusumano 2006), poor relational capabilities (Lane and Lubatkin 1998), and cultural distance (Gopal et al. 2002; Sahay et al. 2003). As a consequence, organizations may reach out to an external provider of boundary spanning capabilities to traverse such gaps: that is, someone who can facilitate the exchange of expertise across two groups who hold different goals, values, and technical languages (Allen and Cohen 1969; Aldrich and Herker 1977; Tushman and Scanlan 1981). Thus, we examine one possible method of how companies may successfully span such boundaries and thereby reduce many of the complexities of offshore relationships.

A firm may require offshore intermediation capabilities that facilitate the advantages of offshore outsourcing while mitigating its most severe challenges; that is dealing with the cultural, professional, and operational complexities of managing relationships across borders. Whenever such capabilities cannot be internally developed by a vendor or client, a third-party intermediary may be required. Accordingly, this paper examines the function of the offshore intermediary, a new breed of offshore "broker" or "middleman" providing offshore intermediation capabilities. Specifically, we offer novel, empirical, and theoretical insight into a largely unexplored area of offshore outsourcing by illuminating the question of *what* offshore intermediaries do, and *when* in the offshoring process they add value to the relationship. While several authors mention the increasing importance of the phenomenon (Field 2002; Rottman and Lacity 2004; Rottman 2006), there is a lack of theory development to systematically describe how offshore intermediation capabilities add value, in the context of software development specifically, or offshore service provision in general.

Despite the prominent value-adding role of intermediaries in all sectors of the economy, the subject has commanded most attention in the financial literature (Rousseau and Wachtel 1998) where intermediaries are effectively "middlemen," brokering transactions between buyer and seller (Rubinstein and Wolinsky 1987). Intermediaries have been heralded for their ability to aggregate supply and demand, provide market transparency and liquidity, mitigate moral hazard and adverse selection by clearing transactions and providing trade financing, hold inventories to absorb variations in supply and demand, and re-bundle portfolios of goods and services across multiple suppliers (Rubinstein and Wolinsky 1987; Spulber 1999).

While many of the traditional functions of intermediation remain important for the facilitation of offshore systems development (e.g., coordinating multiple vendors), there are also important extensions that we attempt to define and explore in this article. In the realm of offshore systems development, a new breed of intermediary has emerged to moderate differences in culture, communication style, technical capabilities, and overall offshoring maturity. The task is one of intellectual, rather than financial arbitrage. Unlike trade in financial assets, intermediated services cannot rely on standard interfaces with structured technological syntax to the same degree (Lee and Kim 1999; Mahnke 2001; Mahnke et al. 2006). As such, offshore intermediaries offer a set of capabilities that are idiosyncratic to sourcing knowledge-intensive services across international regions through a unique set of competencies. A crucial requirement is to establish "structured technological dialogue" that allows clients to specify requirements, and permits vendors to trace interdependencies and impacts on overall system performance (Monteverde and Teece 1995). Thus, one key task of the offshore intermediary is to develop inter-firm social and intellectual capital (Nahapiet and Goshal 1998; Miranda and Kavan 2005) to create interfaces allowing for inter-firm knowledge identification, knowledge-sharing, and knowledge-combination across company and cultural boundaries.

Consistent with traditional intermediation theory (Rubinstein and Wolinsky 1987; Spulber 1999), our argument acknowledges that in any form of exchange, parties have the option to transact directly with the other partner or transact through an intermediary. A middleman will want some form of economic compensation for their services, so the value that the intermediary provides should exceed the cost of using these. But exactly where this tradeoff occurs is poorly understood. For example, Field (2002) argued that large companies like JP Morgan or General Electric have the scale and experience to directly transact with tier-one vendors in India (e.g., see discussion of The Bank of New York in Field (2002)). However, smaller companies are relegated to tier -2 and tier -3 providers, where quality decreases, and clients thereby incur substantially greater risks in managing an offshore partnership. As a result, it may be in these situations that the intermediary justifies its costs. In fact, one optimistic estimate suggests that over half of all offshoring partnerships will be brokered or intermediated in the future, as intermediaries make the offshore market more accessible to small and medium sized companies (Field 2002).

An important point of clarification is that the functions provided by offshore intermediaries are boundary spanning capabilities that can be offered by a variety of organizational forms, be they internal, external, or a combination thereof. The external market for offshore intermediaries seems to be converging around two main types. Law firms tend to be legal experts who specialize in contract formulation, enforcement, termination and dispute resolution, as well as the overall negotiation of terms and conditions prior to the contract formulation. In contrast, consultancies such as IBM Global Services or PriceWaterhouseCoopers bring domain expertise and process capabilities to the overall ongoing management of the offshore contract. Hence, where there is a tendency to group offshore intermediaries as either legal or operational, this distinction is not entirely valid. Both consultants and law firms operate at many stages of the intermediation process, although there are natural specializations by individual firms.

As a first step toward a deeper understanding of offshore intermediation capabilities, this paper offers insights into how transnational intermediaries offer offshore intermediation services; how they learn from markets, institutions, suppliers, and clients in different locations; and how they use such learning to develop intermediated systems development across changing global market conditions. Specifically, we present preliminary evidence and theoretical arguments for four major intermediary capabilities: (i) intermediating cultural distance, (ii) intermediating cognitive distance, (iii) pre-contractual preparation and negotiation, and (iv) post-contractual operational management.

Accordingly, the remainder of the paper is structured as follows. Section 2 outlines the most pressing boundary spanning challenges that both client and vendor have to address when considering offshore development. Section 3 employs a grounded theory-based analysis (Strauss and Corbin 1990) of a case intermediary and its interaction with three clients, to offer initial evidence of the functions of the transnational intermediary. Section 4 continues the theory building using evidence from the case study, and formulates propositions concerning the contingencies of offshore intermediation. We conclude the paper in section 5 with a discussion of limitations, future research and managerial implications.

Offshore systems development: key challenges

The literature on outsourcing IT partnerships is extensive and often highlights the unexpected complexities of managing outsourcing relationships (Earl 1996; Mahnke et al. 2005). Frequently, the anticipated cost reductions promised in outsourcing partnerships are not realized due to unforeseen complications. Specifically, the costs of vendor search and contracting, quality assurance, conflict resolution, coordination of interdependencies, as well as overall relationship management and nurturance, are often cited as unanticipated challenges for those organizations recently initiated to the practice of outsourcing (Barthelemy 2001; Lee et al. 2004).

Agerfalk and Fitzgerald (2006) develop a framework that places these relative costs and benefits across different categories. Specifically, they suggest that global software development offers challenges and rewards in (a) communication, (b) coordination and (c) control of systems development, because of (i) temporal distance, (ii) geographical distance and (iii) cultural distance. They specify the commonly perceived benefits of offshore system development as reduced cycle time from follow-the-sun development, access to a better skilled labor pool as well as best practice, and of course, reduced development costs. However, these benefits also have costs such as asynchronous communication, lack of face-to-face communication, reduced task awareness and shared vision, as well as cultural differences that lead to conflicts in communication styles, work practices, cooperation, values and incongruent understandings.

Other authors echo the thesis that the recognized complexities of managing IT outsourcing partnerships can assume greater severity when it is conducted across international boundaries (Gopal et al. 2002; Sahay et al. 2003). In fact, a great deal of evidence suggests that spatial, temporal and cultural disparities between vendor and client are frequent sources of complication and dissatisfaction that further exacerbate the innate challenges in a purely domestic outsourcing relationship (Gopal et al. 2002; Murthy 2004).

For example, Cusumano (2006) argues that, despite the fact that 80 of the world's 117 SEI CMMI (SEI 2005) Level-5 companies are based in India, there are many hidden costs of offshoring systems development to India that erode the expected financial savings. These include travel back and forth to customer sites, competency disparities when formulating specifications, redoing work because of communications difficulties, or the constant re-work resulting from iterative development across geography and culture (Cusumano 2006).

As an illustration, consider that many of the standard tools of systems development and design are premised on a shared understanding and shared context (Sese et al. 2006). But formal methods (Zave and Jackson 1997) that prescribe the use of mathematical logic as an avenue to formally specify and communicate user requirements may be insensitive to cultural disparities. And even though the language of mathematics is universal across cultures, its use in requirements specification varies substantially. However, more pragmatic and commercially applied approaches to systems development such as UML or agile development are clearly more sensitive to cultural disparities. For example, object-oriented design using UML (Booch et al. 1999) is premised on the idea that concepts have a clear and well-delimited meaning. This is evidenced by Rumbaugh et al. (1991, 21): "We define an object as a concept, an abstraction, or a thing with crisp boundaries and meaning for the problem at hand." However, when asked to explain how universal classes are defined, Gabriel, a designer of an OO language, contends, "That it is a fundamental question for which there is no easy answer. I try things" (Booch 1994, 145). As such, common forms of commercial systems development assume the ontological existence of universal concepts, yet they are more pragmatic concerning the epistemology of identifying and delimiting classes. This ad hoc process of class definition is particularly sensitive to differences in culture, as pragmatic solutions emerge out of the local context. If the analyst and programmer do not share some basic interpretation and understanding of terms, classes or concepts, then misfits between an organization's requirements and the offshore solution are likely.

The classic body of theoretical discourse most relevant to this challenge is the literature on boundary spanners (Allen and Cohen 1969; Aldrich and Herker 1977; Tushman and Scanlan 1981). The idea of boundary spanning has been applied generally in knowledge management (e.g., Carlile 2004; Cross and Parker 2004) and, in particular, in the implementation and use of information systems (Levina and Vaast 2005), and may contribute to our understanding of what capabilities offshore intermediaries provide. Cross and Parker (2004), for example, define boundary spanners as "vital individuals," facilitating the sharing of expertise across two groups who hold different goals, values, and languages. Such individuals can assume different roles ranging from information processing, through interpreting and translating knowledge, to negotiating meaning and transforming knowledge (Carlile 2004). When engaging separate groups in dialogue, boundary spanners may use "boundary objects" (e.g., Star 1989; Boland and Tenkasi 1995; Carlile 2002; Bechky 2003), which provide a common reference point to coordinate distributed work among heterogeneous actors (Star 1989). For example, Boland and Tenkasi (1995) suggest that boundary objects may be narratives developed in work practices to facilitate a shared frame of reference among individuals. However, role conflict will emerge, for example, when boundary spanners apply an information processing approach where a knowledge transformation approach would be warranted (Carlile 2004; Wareham et al. 2007).

While the boundary spanning literature is clearly relevant in providing a higher level conceptualization of negotiating relationship across cognitive or cultural gaps, it has largely focused on how individual agents become, and function as, boundary spanners (Levina and Vaast 2005). Our purpose is to extend the general concepts of boundary spanning and to apply them in a very specific type of organization, the offshore intermediary. Our main research questions follow:

1. What value adding capabilities do offshore intermediaries provide?
2. Under what circumstances are clients more likely to engage in intermediated offshore relationships versus direct ones?

As mentioned, the literature concerning boundary spanning is relatively mature. However, the theoretical and empirical literature addressing offshore intermediation is limited. Accordingly we proceed by presenting a case study of an offshore intermediary in a grounded theory-building exercise that will help address our research questions.

Case exemplar: offshore intermediation

The following section presents initial evidence to substantiate a framework for offshore intermediation emerging from our study. The case follows, with a discussion and formulation of propositions.

About this research

The data were collected by two researchers throughout the year 2006 from interviews with the case company as well as three of its major clients. Eight informants from the case company included the CEO, CIO, two project lead managers and a number of line employees. We intentionally spoke to informants at different levels of the organization to assure data representativeness, and sampling data from stratified sources which appropriately represented the organization or the phenomenon studied. Toward this goal, we also interviewed three major clients from different sectors including security, financial services and health care. In addition to personal interviews, other sources of primary data included telephone interviews and email correspondence. Finally, archival data, such as company internal documents and websites, were also employed by the third researcher to corroborate the findings of the first two researchers across the case study and provide internal control for researcher bias.

Case evidence: I-Technologies

I-Technologies, founded in 1999, is an IT consultancy specializing in matching Scandinavian clients with offshore service providers. A central emphasis is facilitating cultural and professional connections to new markets and software development opportunities, and providing project management and contract management services.

A variety of unsuccessful off-shoring ventures has led I-Technologies to the conclusion that most clients are totally unprepared for any type of offshore relationship. As such, the company has focused its efforts on three main functions: (a) project scope definition and requirements specification,

(b) development of project management and communication skills, and (c) formulation of contracts, quality criteria, and conflict resolution.

One of the first intermediation clients who approached I-Technologies in 2001 was a leading Danish security firm, DANSECURE. DANSECURE is now well under way with the first offshore outsourcing efforts. Before turning to I-Technologies, the IT manager of DANSECURE explained: "We had already asked our present supplier if they could outsource some of the tasks to countries with low costs. Everybody had been very positive toward the idea and, if everything turned out fine, I imagined that half of our outsourcing would soon be taken over by sub-contractors in low cost countries."

However, after unsuccessful attempts with direct offshore solutions with Indian vendors during 1999–2002, the same manager commented, "We have chosen to outsource the outsourcing. Of course, the extra link via I-Technologies makes the assignment more expensive. It would probably be possible to save something by arranging it all by ourselves, but we do not have the critical mass or the desire to move into an area where we do not have any experience" [DANSECURE IT Manager]. Today, the security firm estimates that it saves 33% on the solutions completed in India. The Indian employees spend more time on solving a task, but the price per hour is much lower. Consequently, total costs are lower while the system development quality matches or exceeds local levels. On the other hand, "there are extra costs that we have to include, for example, system specifications, translation of documents, and the extra coordination time" [DANSECURE Financial Controller].

By contrast, not engaging I-Technologies services means that "clients would incur substantial vendor selection costs, system transition costs, costs associated with cultural and professional training of employees, as well as contract management costs and significant travel and re-location expenses" [I-Technologies Project Manager]. Of course, "over time, clients learn to do things we provide, and they may seek to cut us out of business as they learn how to deal with the Indians; but this is an inevitable part of the life as an intermediary like us" [I-Technologies Founder].

The goal of I-Technologies is to help the outsourcing company partially recover these costs. As the I-Technologies manager responsible for the DANSECURE cooperation explains, "Our experience has shown that we need some kind of cultural interface when managing offshore contracts. Scandinavians communicate directly and have little social hierarchy. Indians, on the other hand, have a hierarchical culture. Furthermore, Indians prefer not to say no to anyone and will often say yes – meaning 'yes I understand you,' not 'yes, I agree -we will have this done on time'."

I-Technologies solution to this is to hire Indians and bring them on site in Scandinavia. At the same time, I-Technologies provide Scandinavian clients with a Scandinavian interface manager situated in India. In this manner, staff from both regions work side by side and develop common ground, and "…their common experience allows them to foresee and avoid problems that might result from miscommunication," as an Analyst of I-Technology comments.

Another customer of I-Technologies, the major financial service provider SCANCARD, experienced a distinct problem with disparities in working styles. "A CMMI level 0 or 1 organization like us will be less formal in documenting the development process, changes, etc. This means that there is much more ad hoc problem solving which can result in sloppy, but functional code" [SCANCARD IT Manager]. As a response, I-Technologies also hire developers that have experience working for or with CMMI level 5 developers. CMMI was developed to create consistent quality levels across a large set of military contractors writing very complicated code, but "…most programmers from us would find working with CMMI level 5 development houses cumbersome and overly formalized. For most businesses, this is pure overkill" [SCANCARD IT Manager].

The role of the intermediary with CMMI level 5 development vendors is not to program: rather, they help in the requirements specification and change requests phase to translate the requirements of the client into the language of the code developers. In iterative development, they help liaison between client and vender. "Our clients frequently do not understand the necessity of all the demands made by our developers. They see them as excessively thorough. Our job is to bridge this gap, communicate to both sides in their own terms, as well as to ensure consistent expectations, understanding, and translation to reach overall compatibility in the relation" [I-Technologies Project Manager].

The first main function encompasses many of the tasks normally addressed in common systems development methodologies. Here, I-Technologies complete a thorough analysis of the motivations (labor arbitrage, access to expertise, etc.) defining project scope, interdependencies, and detailed specifications. As one of the lead mangers stated, "We often encounter clients who simply have not understood their own motivations for the offshore move. This is doomed to fail by definition, because nobody in the organization has determined what might constitute success." Accordingly, I-Technologies sees one of its key value-adding functions in overcoming the difficulties of delimiting the project scope. "Most clients think off-shoring is just a matter of picking up the phone and ordering. They have become quite surprised at the amount of time it actually takes us to ask the right questions, and define a project that is constrained but feasible. As technology consultants, we have experienced this time and time again, and our clients are always taken back by what a lengthy process requirements specification actually is" [I-Technologies Project Manager].

The second main function relates to fact that new systems require some kind of change in organizational processes, where it is important to develop the management's internal project management and communication skills. "With big projects requiring new processes, there is a huge risk that we manage the offshore development that produces great software, but then it all falls to the ground once we deliver it. Unfortunately, we have had to learn this the hard way" [I-Technologies Project Manager]. Accordingly, I-Technologies will often invest considerable resources in educating the client's management with the appropriate change management tools. Here, classical reengineering methods (e.g., Hammer 1995) are applied to ensure that the processes are aligned with the software, and that visible project leaders are given adequate communication skills to manage the organizational transformation. "We can coordinate the development of software that is both inexpensive and sophisticated, but if we deliver it to a client who does not know what to do with it, it makes little difference" [I-Technologies Project Manager].

The third and perhaps least appreciated function of I-Technologies is in vendor management, where cultural intermediation is required in the translation between the two parties, e.g. offshore contract formulation, especially because the definition of verifiable quality criteria tenable to international law enforcement often remains elusive. Given the frequently substantial cognitive and cultural distance, the likelihood of unfulfilled expectations concerning function and quality is high. Contract enforcement is complicated in lieu of some objective quality criteria that can be understood and verified by both client and vendor. The case informants emphasized that the processes for conflict resolution are paramount to the success of the relationship, and are often neglected in offshoring contracts. "It is not a question of *if*, but *when* the conflict is going to happen and how we are going to handle it. This can make the difference between a small bump in the road and a full-blown legal fight. Experience has told us that well functioning conflict resolution procedures are probably the most critical tool in any offshore development project," as the CIO of PROHEALTH, a major client in the insurance sector, comments.

As an intermediary, I-Technologies is often not in a position to negotiate conflict resolutions between client and vendor. The risk is too large that clients view them as agents of the vendor, and many vendors view them as agents of the client. In these cases, important intermediation services include the establishment of governance structures and communication channels so that conflicts are detected quickly and arbitration is effective. In the case of PROHEALTH, where multiple offshore vendors are employed, I-Technology assumes coordination of vendors and sub-contractors via a local delivery centre in India. Such localized handling of several Indian sub-contractors includes a phase of identification and negotiation with a set of potential vendors and sub-contractors in the local market. In instances where multiple sub-contractors are employed I-Technology adds value by managing interdependencies and any conflicts to guarantee a "seamless" and coherent process for PROHEALTH across many suppliers.

Table 2.1 highlights examples of challenges and responses offered by the offshore intermediary from a temporal perspective that is both pre-and post contractual.

We follow with a similar breakdown of the boundary spanning forms that mitigate cultural and cognitive distance (see Table 2.2). We present these separately because they are in many ways orthogonal; that is, equally relevant to both pre- and post- contractual phases.

Not all clients of I-Technology exhibit an exclusively positive experience with the offshore-intermediation services provided by I-Technology.

Table 2.1 Transnational intermediation: pre & postcontractual phases

Phase	Description	Problems addressed	Responses	Value adding activities
Pre-contractual: Prepare clients for offshoring relationship.	Formalized process under which intermediary works intensively with client to prepare for interaction with offshore vendor.	Inability to identify appropriate vendors. Inability to define and delimit projects. Lack of skills to codify requirements. Lack of experience in negotiating contract terms.	Project definition and pilot; mapping the detailed requirements; product documentation; vendor search; contract formulation and negotiation. Systems development tools such as gap analysis, UML, requirements specification, as well as possible organization/ process reengineering. In addition, intermediary knows to "ask right questions."	Experience augmentation. Managing expectations. Creating relational awareness.

Continued

Table 2.1   Continued

Phase	Description	Problems addressed	Responses	Value adding activities
Post-contractual: manage offshore operations.	Brings operational experience and best practice in managing offshore development. Tools of project and client management are marshaled to monitor quality and service, provide mechanisms of conflict resolution, project scope management, and project termination.	Lack of project management skills. Lack of quality control skills. Integration of off-site code into legacy systems. Need to monitor quality standards.	Assist project management for client; identify a champion from client who will take command of the project; identify the actual project management; assistance in vendor management; establish clear communication channels and policies; evaluate and modify work collaborative processes; contract formulation with definition of outcomes, measures, and quality control; define processes of conflict resolution.	Avoiding experience traps. Neutralizing collaborative failure sources. Maintaining relational awareness.

Table 2.2   Boundary spanning forms: cultural and cognitive

Function	Description	Problems addressed	Response	Value adding activities
Intermediate cultural distance	Intermediates differences in culture that are manifested in communication styles (high and low context communication), individualism vs. collectivism, and temporal sense (linear vs. poly-synchronous time perceptions), and other cultural differences that would significantly impact the likelihood of a successful off-shoring relationship.	Lack of cultural understanding. Inability to communicate effectively. Inability to interpret cultural symbols.	Intermediary maintains staff with nationalities from both regions. These staff are experienced in foreseeing common disparities in communication, work, and thought styles of the two (or more) regions.	Mapping cultural differences. Cultural training and specialized translations. Determining associated knowledge transfer costs.

Continued

Table 2.2 Continued

Function	Description	Problems addressed	Response	Value adding activities
Intermediate cognitive distance	Intermediates differences in relative skill levels that might prohibit successful communication and common understanding between client and vendor. Well-known example is CMMI levels. CMMI level 5 providers work in highly systematic and structured way that may clash with clients' less formalized work style.	Lack of awareness of system requirements. Inability to outline budgets and timeframes. Misunderstanding with regard to documentation requirements.	Intermediary has experience with CMMI systems and actively employs staff who have worked in CMMI level 5 organizations. These professionals are technical specialists functioning as liaison between the highly systematic CMMI 5 vendor and less specialized clients who would have difficulties speaking a similar "technical language."	Specialized translations between client's perceived needs and vendor's requirements. Codifying interfaces so that specifications can be crafted. Creating common ground to facilitate understanding.

A Swedish fashion retailer, for example, after a short time using the intermediary, cancelled the contract: "Our reason for hiring I-Technologies was to have a scout into alien territory; our goal was, over time, to learn the territory ourselves...Despite having been open about this, we found I-Technology was trying to prevent us from learning and adapting to the Indian partner." Another former client, NORDBANK, voices similar concerns: "Our goal is to become able to scale up our offshore operations rapidly, but I-Technology seems to slow us down in this effort: we wonder whether higher investments upfront would have enabled us to learn faster later on, but now it is hard to say." One director at I-Technology, commenting on these cases, argues: "Admittedly, we had a rapid growth and at times our client's demands outpaced our ability to serve their needs...and it is also a growing reality that clients require direct contacts to clients, thus, increasingly we are acting as an enzyme like business model. We facilitate complex offshore relations on an ongoing basis. Accordingly, we seek to migrate with our client needs toward shorter term and simultaneously more complex projects."

Theory building

The theoretical analysis and the empirical insights obtained from the grounded approach used in analyzing the case study will be presented in three sections: (a) theoretical framework, (b) propositions regarding the value of transnational intermediaries, and (c) interdependencies.

Theoretical Framework

Our analysis led us to summarize: the disparities needing intermediation capabilities first of all could usefully be grouped into cultural and cognitive factors. Secondly, we found that it was useful to distinguish between contract negotiation and the operational period where the work is completed. The grounded work in I-Technologies corroborated the view that these two dimensions were indeed relevant in making sense of the case. Accordingly, we propose the following theoretical framework, as shown in Table 2.3. This is a 2x2 matrix with cultural/cognitive on the one dimension and pre-contractual/post-contractual on the other. To prepare for the discussion following, we furthermore indicate that we will propose four sets of propositions, to be discussed in the next section, followed by a discussion and a fifth set of propositions concerning interdependencies.

Table 2.3   Framework of intermediary functions

		Propositions III	**Propositions IV**
		Precontractual	**Postcontractual**
Propositions I	**Cultural distance**	• *Vendor search to ensure cultural compatibility.* • *Establish communication channel and cultural liaisons.*	• *Co-located cultural liaisons mitigate misunderstanding.* • *Clearly defined processes for communication and coordination.*
Propositions II	**Cognitive distance**	• *Project scope definition.* • *Common expectations.*	• *Project management and reengineering skills.* • *Quality monitoring.* • *Change management.* • *Conflict resolution.*

Propositions regarding the value of transnational intermediation

Cultural disparities. The first major function that we have identified for transnational intermediaries is the mitigation of cultural disparities. Our case demonstrated that cross-cultural tensions are a frequent source of turbulence in offshoring partnerships. As such, the intermediary responded by hiring staff that represent all concerned national regions, thereby bridging any dissonance caused by communication style differences.

The cultural gaps between Northern Europe and India are generally well documented (Trompenaars and Hampden-Turner 1997). For example, highly individual cultures, such as Anglo-American or North European ones, tend to use low-context communication where the information (message) is very explicit. Individuals will typically shape their thinking and communication as if it was addressed toward themselves. By contrast, collectivist cultures, such as Asian ones, tend to use high-context communication with more implicit information. Collective thinking and communication emphasizes the needs of the group more than the individual, and this significance is seen in the information exchanged (Hofstede 1980; Trompenaars and Hampden-Turner 1997). Accordingly, it is well documented that divergent cultural patterns (cultural distance) can lead to inefficient communication (Te'eni 2001; Markus and Kitayama 1991).

However, the manner in which these patterns produce friction in a transnational client-vendor work relationship is more subtle (Markus and Kitayama 1991). Unless the outsourcing firm understands and manage these differences in the initial search, in the contract negotiation phase, and later in the on-going business relationships, substantial conflicts are likely to arise and erode the potential benefits. While it is easy to acknowledge differences in social hierarchy or temporal perception intellectually, normative solutions to the disparities are more elusive. Specific cultural knowledge is costly to transfer, as it is location-specific or "sticky" to the geographic, organizational or institutional context in which it was created (von Hippel 1988; Wareham and Gerrits 1999). Accordingly, transnational intermediation must be responsive to the type of knowledge and its implicit transfer costs (Kogut and Zander 1992; Armbrüster & Kipping 2003). As such, the intermediary with experienced staff and culturally-aware managers from both regions can more easily foresee and transgress well-known differences in work and communication patterns caused by disparities in communication styles and values.

By mapping and creating awareness of the consequences of cultural differences in the process of cross border system development, the relevant drivers of knowledge transfer costs can be understood and influenced. In addition, especially in the case of de-novo entry in offshore location, the intermediary can mitigate cultural entry barriers. For instance, the intermediary can influence how long it takes for the offshore business model to become operative from the initiative to a working project organization. Moreover, the intermediary can assist in defining how much a client has to invest initially to establish an offshore relationship. Transnational intermediation capabilities may also create value through compressing cycle times by minimizing cross-cultural entry barriers. Accordingly, we suggest the following propositions:

> **P 1a**: *Transnational offshore intermediation capabilities add value through reducing the costs of cultural disparities.*
>
> **P 1b**: *Clients whose staff are less experienced in dealing with cross-cultural issues will benefit more from the use of a third-party intermediary than clients whose staff are more experienced in dealing with cross-cultural issues.*

Cognitive distance. The second function of transnational intermediaries is the mitigation of cognitive distance. Te'eni defines cognitive distance as the initial gap between the sender and receiver's interpretations before transmitting the messages (Te'eni 2001, 282). This can result from differences in current information or from different ways of thinking and communicating. In an offshoring context, cognitive distance often arises when relatively lesser-skilled clients attempt to access a high level of expertise at comparatively lower costs (Mahnke et al. 2005). This is precisely where an offshore intermediary can add value.

Task coordination in offshore outsourcing benefits from a large and consistent "shared knowledge set" about problems and possible solutions (Mahnke and Overby 2007). However, great expertise differentials between outsourcer and vendor can often hinder collective knowledge sharing, introduce cognitive distance and, consequently, complicate cross-border knowledge sharing (Argote 1999). Specifically, with most of the CMMI level-5 development houses being located in India (Cusumano 2006), the differences between working styles here and in western companies can be large. Through time, CMMI has grown to be considered exclusively virtuous, the higher evaluation the better. However, the very high level of structure and formalization comes at a price, and it is often excessive for most business needs, where a possibility for modification after testing and flexible response is advantageous. The transnational intermediary helps transgress and translate the working requirements and styles of both parties.

Whereas codified knowledge often results from abstracting and establishing cause-effect relations expressed in written form, un-codified knowledge often results from local experience, is context-dependent, and remains embodied in the firm's employees (von Hipple 1988). As such, one can expect that the larger the proportion of un-codified knowledge, the more costly is interface identification and inter-firm system integration. Thus, intermediaries create value by articulating and codifying interface knowledge to decrease the client's costs of knowledge transfer. The off-shore intermediary adds value by offering specialized translations between perceived client needs and vendor requirements, codifying interfaces so that contracts can be crafted and systems can be connected, as well as by creating sufficient common ground to facilitate understanding and avoid conflict (Monteverde and Teece 1995; Mahnke et al. 2006). Mitigating differences in systems development methods or styles, our case company accomplished this by hiring analysts and developers with substantial experience with CMMI vendors. Accordingly, we suggest the following propositions:

P 2a: *Transnational offshore intermediation capabilities add value through reducing the costs of cognitive distance.*

P 2b: *Clients who have significant differences in their approach to software development compared to their offshore vendors will benefit more from the use of the intermediary than clients who do not have these differences.*

Pre-contractual. The third major function of transnational intermediaries is a comprehensive preparation of the client for an off-shoring relationship. Many of the fiascos in off-shoring can be traced to the fact the client was not appropriately prepared for the off-shoring outsourcing relationship due to a lack of prior experience (Willcocks and Lacity 1998). Some of the outsourcing relations that Lacity et al. (1995) examined experienced disastrous results because they lacked the expertise to select vendors, evaluate a vendor's past performance, and to negotiate sound contracts. As they suggest, a company cannot control what it does not understand, and the client's preparedness cannot be assumed, neither on an organizational nor application level.

The activities through which transnational intermediaries help prepare clients for offshore system development include creating awareness of the off-shoring objectives, developing analytical understanding of organizational and programmatic interdependencies, and a joint and explicit evaluation of the relevance of the client's and vendor's prior experience for the current joint off-shoring project. In addition, opening parochial and ethnocentric mindsets will create awareness of the possibilities and limitations of experienced and planned offshore software development activities. Transnational offshore intermediation adds value by establishing common expectations, defining project scope and contractual mechanisms. Table 2.1 highlights a number of the specific actions used by our case intermediary, which include: project definition and detailed requirements specification, vendor search, contract formulation and negotiation. Accordingly, we suggest the following propositions:

> **P 3a**: *Transnational offshore intermediation capabilities add value by preparing the client for offshoring partnerships (pre-contractual intermediation).*
> **P 3b**: *Clients who have little experience in offshore vendor identification, screening, selection, requirements specification and contract negotiations will benefit more from a third-party intermediary than clients who do have this experience.*

Post-Contractual. The fourth major function of the transnational intermediary is to act as a process facilitator in the going concern between the offshore-vendor and its clients. An offshore relation is not a static affair, but an ongoing learning process of mutual adaptation. In the offshore development process, unforeseen disagreements occur, which can trigger a process of hidden conflict impeding smooth interaction. This opens the door to post-contractual haggling and misunderstanding (Williamson 1996), and simultaneously stresses the importance of psychological contracts in governing offshore outsourcing relations (Miranda and Kavan 2005). Hence, not only is contract formulation critical, but defining objective deliverables and measurable performance/quality criteria requires considerable prior shared knowledge – be it in the form of intellectual or social capital (Nahapiet and Goshal 1998).

Whenever guaranteeing measurable project outcomes is impossible between parties, the transnational intermediary creates value by formulating a process that can detect misunderstanding and resolve pending conflicts efficiently (Barzel 1982). Hence, the transnational intermediary can be instrumental in defining the process of conflict resolution (Dyer and Singh 1998) such that parties can quickly resolve differences and avoid costly litigation across multiple legal systems and consequent project delays.

In this case, the intermediary mediates the conflict by identifying and bringing to the surface the cultural and cognitive disparities (e.g., explicit versus implicit communication styles, formal versus informal work styles). The intermediary then creates relational awareness by explicating assumptions and defining a common vocabulary from which joint future action can proceed (Carlile 2002, 2004). Previous experience, especially when tacitly accumulated in diverse contexts and projects, may also lead to "superstitious" learning and erroneous inference between past failures/successes and future courses of action. As such, by explicating implicit assumptions, the intermediary helps reduce the negative effects of experience traps.

Finally, depending upon the scope of the project, the client may not be equipped with the necessary internal project management skills within his/her own organization to spearhead an externally developed project. Here, the intermediary may work with the client to ensure that the appropriate communication channels, implementation skills, and structures are present in-house, so that inter-firm governance structures can be tailored to relational requirements (Dyer and Singh 1998). Through the continuous nurturing of cooperative skills, sources of collaborative failure are neutralized and relational awareness can be developed. Thus, offshore intermediation capabilities mitigate the process conflict and misunderstanding caused by spatial differences and knowledge partitioning (co-location etc.). Accordingly we propose the following propositions:

> **P 4a**: *Transnational offshore intermediation capabilities add value by managing on-going offshore partnerships and operations (post-contractual intermediation).*
> **P 4b**: *Clients will benefit more from third-party intermediation the lower their experience in complex project management, formalized conflict resolution, quality evaluation and systems integration skills.*

Interdependencies

In considering the framework and the propositions, it is important to stress that pre- and post- contractual value creation by transnational intermediaries are richly interrelated, as are the processes of mitigating cultural and cognitive distance. For example, insufficient preparation, erroneous expectations, and a lack of self-awareness can result in an increased likelihood of post-contractual haggling and conflict. Likewise, greater cultural misunderstandings normally exacerbate technical miscommunication. As such, we transpose the pre- and post-contractual intermediation categories against the cultural and cognitive in an effort to trace the interdependencies (see Figure 2.1). While this representation

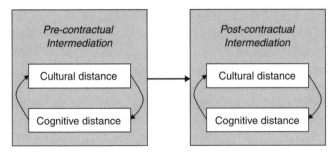

Figure 2.1   Interdependencies of offshore intermediation (Propositions 5)

only superficially highlights how the functions interrelate and reinforce each other, it does indicate how the emphasis on one stage can render benefits in the other.

Pre-contractual intermediation can help mitigate the problems of cultural distance through optimal vendor search, where cultural compatibility is emphasized. The experience of the intermediary in common cultural conflicts will facilitate affective focus on the technical aspects that plague all outsourcing arrangements. Moreover, co-located cultural liaisons facilitate contract formulation and language choice that is suitable to both client and vendor and their relative legal systems. In a similar fashion, pre-contractual intermediation will emphasize the technical disparities that are likely to be contentious between client and vendor. The intermediary's experience will guide pre-contractual negotiations to form the project scope and expectations that are feasible, service levels and operational metrics that are objective and measurable, as well as project management procedures to avoid project scope creep and divergent expectations. These carefully executed phases of client preparation are clearly correlated with a higher probability of fulfilled expectations. Accordingly, we propose the following propositions:

> **P 5a**: *Clients who engage a third-party intermediary at an early stage (pre-contractual) will experience a reduced likelihood of problems in the operational (post-contractual) stage of the offshore partnership.*
>
> **P 5b**: *Clients who engage a third-party intermediary to mitigate the problems of cultural distance will experience a reduced likelihood of problems of cognitive distance.*
>
> **P 5c**: *Clients who engage a third-party intermediary to mitigate the problems of cognitive distance will experience a reduced likelihood of problems of cultural distance.*

Discussion and conclusion

Unlike financial intermediation, the intermediation of offshore systems development work cannot be understood as the simple exchange of well-defined products or instruments. It is a task of intellectual, rather than financial arbitrage, and is often riddled by complications of cultural and professional distance, as well as the disparate international experience of the parties involved. Accordingly, we argue that there is a need for boundary spanning capabilities in offshore systems development partnerships -a need that can be fulfilled by offshore intermediaries. We have provided theoretical arguments and preliminary evidence for four major intermediary functions: (i) intermediating cultural distance, (ii) intermediating cognitive distance, (iii) preparing client for offshoring relationship (pre-contractual intermediation), and (iv) managing offshoring relationship (post-contractual intermediation).

We contribute to the IS outsourcing literature by identifying a new role in offshore system development efforts. Rather than taking the perspective of the offshore vendor or client, as in previous research, we provide a novel view of the offshore middleman. As mentioned, some estimates suggest that more than 50% of all offshoring partnerships will be brokered by intermediaries in the future (Field 2002). While the phenomenon has been mentioned in the previous offshoring literature, (Field 2002; Rottman and Lacity 2004; Rottman 2006), it has, to our knowledge, yet to receive in-depth empirical or theoretical attention.

Empirical justification for our findings is presented as a case exemplar, which serves to substantiate our theory development efforts regarding transnational offshore-intermediation. Focusing on a middleman such as I-Technologies allows us to zoom in on the role of an intermediary function in pure form,[*] and to develop theory on what, how, and where software development tasks are performed. While we believe that we make an important contribution to the literature on required intermediation capabilities in offshore software development, we leave open the questions of by whom, and in which legal form, an intermediation functions shall be best performed. As Field (2002) observes, the man-in-the-middle may, but does not have to, be placed in separate legal entity as was the case with I-Technologies. At times, firms choose to internalize the middleman function to deal directly with offshore vendors. At other times, a global software vendor might assume the function by providing a local interface to clients, while internalizing project management functions for the vendor.

The market for offshore intermediaries is presently clustering toward two types, legal and operational. Both legal and operational intermediaries participate in pre- and post- contractual phases, although there is a clear tendency for the consultancies to focus on operations, where legal firms focus on vendor search, contract specifications, monitoring and termination. However, this is not an exclusive pattern.

Limitations

Our study has a number of limitations that deserve attention. First, our evidence is fairly limited and originates from a single organization, supplemented by market research. Moreover, our empirical understanding of this phenomenon is nascent at best. While several of the functions we identified are well understood, (e.g. managing multiple vendors), offshore sourcing of knowledge-intensive software development services creates a series of new challenges and remedies. An interesting empirical question for future research is to what extent transnational intermediation capabilities are similar to the capabilities of traditional consultancies. Important similarities include the fact that both businesses include knowledge management challenges (e.g., Armbrüster & Kipping 2003). However, there are also important differences. For example, while consultancies conventionally mediate between clients and the professional labor market, the transnational intermediary we studied mediates between clients and vendors in offshore locations.

Another significant limitation in our study is a lack of attention awarded to the relative costs of using an intermediary. It is well known that intermediaries realize financial compensation or economic rents when providing their services. This represents an accounting-based cost and can likely be partitioned in a comparative financial analysis of intermediated versus direct exchanges. However, it is also well known that introducing a third-party to a transaction introduces additional coordination and communication costs, which could have detrimental effects on the partnership. Given the nascent stage of the discourse on offshore intermediation, our analysis attempted to delineate the ostensible benefits. However, similar attention to the relative costs of intermediated exchanges can help balance our understanding as it matures.

Future research

Future research will benefit from larger sample sizes that allow empirical corroboration and increased theoretical advances that would help to focus and refine research efforts in this area. Moreover, as our empirical evidence is based on offshore systems development, we have focused our arguments on this task. However, this is only one business function with its associated processes. There is already a strongly growing market for Business Process Outsourcing in other areas, from relatively routine functions (e.g., call centers, accounting, technical support) to knowledge intensive and innovation-centric research (e.g., financial services, medical services, management consulting, and R&D) where the phenomenon of business process off-shoring could prove very beneficial. In such research, the definition and verification of orthogonal properties, such as a) transaction antecedents, b) generalizable properties of common processes, and c) sector-specific variables, will be a useful guide for future research into transnational intermediation.

In addition, as mentioned previously, future research can benefit from an understanding of the differences between intermediaries and traditional consultancies, as well as a greater emphasis on the financial and non-financial based costs of intermediated exchanges.

Finally, the boundary spanning literature highlights the dynamic, evolutionary nature of boundary spanning capabilities (Levina and Vaast 2005). Specifically, boundary spanning capabilities can reside with a third-party initially, but through time, may be transferred and acquired by the client and vendor. As such, a static view of offshore intermediation will ignore the knowledge transfer and learning effects that would surface in a lifecycle analysis. Future research could focus on the evolutionary nature of the relationship and study how these boundary spanning capabilities emerge or migrate at various loci within the relationship. Undoubtedly, the discourse on offshore intermediation is nascent. We hope that our framework and research propositions will prove useful for future research in assessing the managerial implications of this trend.

Note

* By pure form we mean that this company does nothing other than offshore intermediation. Other companies do bundle functions such as own software development and consulting with their offshore intermediating capabilities.

References

Agerfalk, P. and Fitzgerald, B. (2006) Flexible and Distributed Software Processes: Old Petunias in New Bowls? *Communications of the ACM*, Oct.: 27–34.

Aldrich, H. and Herker, D. (1977). Boundary Spanning Roles and Organization Structure, *Academy of Management Review*, 2: 217 231.

Allen, T.J. and Cohen, S.I. (1969). Information Flow in Research and Development Laboratories, *Administrative Science Quarterly*, 4: 12–19.

Armbrüster, T. and Kipping, M. (2003) Strategy Consulting at the Crossroads. Technical Change and Shifting Market Conditions for Top-Level Advice, *International Studies of Management and Organization*, 4: 19–42.

Argote, L. (1999) *Organizational learning: Creating, retaining and transferring knowledge.* Norwell, MA: Kluwer.

Barthelemy, J. (2001) The Hidden Costs of IT Outsourcing, *Sloan Management Review* 42(3): 60–69.

Barzel, J. (1982) Measurement Costs and the Organization of Markets. *Journal of Law and Economics* 25(1): 27–48.

Bechky, B.A. (2003) Sharing Meaning Across Occupational Communities: The Transformation of Understanding on a Product Floor. *Organization Science* 14(3): 312–330.

Boland, R. J. and Tenkasi, R.V. (1995) Perspective Making and Perspective Taking in Communities of Knowing. *Organization Science*, 6(4): 350–372.

Booch, G. (1994) *Object-Oriented Analysis and Design.* Addison-Wesley.

Booch, G., Rumbaugh, J.E. and Jacobson, I. (1999) *The Unified Modeling Language User Guide.* Addison-Wesley, 2000.

Carlile, P. R. (2002) A Pragmatic View of Knowledge and Boundaries: Boundary Objects in New Product Development. *Organization Science* 13(4): 442–455.

Carlile, P. R. (2004) Transferring, Translating, and Transforming: An Integrative Framework for Managing Knowledge Across Boundaries. *Organization Science*, 15(5): 555–568.

Cross, R.L. and Parker, A. (2004) *The Hidden Power of Social Networks: Understanding How Work Really Gets Done in Organizations,* Harvard Business School Press: Boston.

Cusumano, M. (2006) Envisioning the Future of India's Software Services Business. *Communications of the ACM*, 49(10): 15–17.

Dedene, G. and DeVreese, J.P. (1995) Realities of Off-Shore Reengineering. *IEEE Software*, 12(1): 35.

Dyer, J. and Singh, H. (1998) The Relational View: Cooperative Strategy and Sources of Interorganizational Competitive Advantage. *Academy of Management Review*, 23(4): 660–679.

Earl, M. (1996) The Risks of Outsourcing IT. *Sloan Management Review*, 37(3): 26–32.

Field, T. (2002) The Man in the Middle. CIO Magazine, April 1, 2002, accessed on Feb. 10th, 2007. http://www.cio.com/archive/040102/middle.html

Gopal A., Mukhopadhyay, T. and Krishnan, M. (2002) The Role of Software Processes and Communication in Offshore Software Development. *Communications of the ACM*, 45(4): 193–200.

Hammer, M. (1995) *The Reengineering Revolution*, HarperCollins New York, NY.

Hofstede, G. (1980) *Culture's Consequences: International Differences in Work Related Values*, Newbury Park, CA: Sage.

Keil, M. and Mann, J. (2000) Why Software Projects Escalate: An Empirical Analysis and Test of Four Empirical Models. *MIS Quarterly*, 24(4): 631–664.

King, W.R. (2005) Outsourcing Becomes More Complex. *Information Systems Management*, 22(2): 89.

Kogut, B. and Zander, U. (1992) Knowledge of the Firm, Combinative Capabilities, and the Replication of Technology. *Organization Science*, 3(3): 383–397.

Lacity, M., Willcocks, L. and Feeny, D. (1995) Information Technology Outsourcing: Maximizing Flexibility and Control. *Harvard Business Review*, May–June: 84–93.

Lane, P. and Lubatkin, M. (1998) Relative Absorptive Capacity and Interorganizational Learning. *Strategic Management Journal*, 19(5): 461–477.

Lee, J. N. and Kim, Y.G. (1999) The Impact of Knowledge Sharing, Organizational Capability and Partnership Quality on IS Outsourcing Success. *Journal of Management Information Systems* 15(4): 29–61.

Lee, J.N., Miranda, S.M. and Kim, Y.M. (2004) IT Outsourcing Strategies: Universalistic, Contingency, and Configurational Explanations of Success. *Information Systems Research*, 15(2): 110–131.

Levina, N. and Ross, J.W. (2003) From the vendor's Perspective: Exploring the Value Proposition in IT Outsourcing. *MIS Quarterly*, 27(3): 331–364.

Levina, N. and Vaast, E. (2005) The Emergence of Boundary Spanning Competence in Practice: Implications for Implementation of and use of Information Systems. *MIS Quarterly*, 29(2): 335–363.

Mahnke, V. (2001) The Process of Vertical Dis-Integration: An Evolutionary Perspective on Outsourcing. *Journal of Management and Governance*, 5(3–4): 353–379.

Mahnke, V., Overby, M. and Oscan, S. (2006) Make and/or Buy of IT-enabled Service Innovation. *Industry and Innovation*, 13(2): 189–207.

Mahnke, V. and Overby, M.L. (2007) Coping with Failure Sources in R&D Consortia. *International Journal of Technology Management*, 14(1): 13–35.

Mahnke, V., Overby, M.L. and Vang, J. (2005) Strategic Outsourcing of IT Services: Theoretical Stocktaking and Empirical Challenges. *Industry and Innovation*, 12(2):205–253.

Markus, H. and Kitayama, S. (1991) Culture and the Self: Implications for Cognition, Emotion, and Motivation. *Psychological Review*, 98(2): 224–253.

Miranda, S. and Kavan, B. (2005) Moments of Governance in IS outsourcing. Conceptualization Effects of Contracts on Value Capture and Creation. *Journal of Information Technology*, 20(3): 152–169.

Monteverde, K. and Teece, D. (1995) Technological Dialog as Incentive for Vertical Integration in the Semi-Conductor Industry. *Management Science*, 41(10): 1624–1638.

Murthy, S. (2004) The Impact of Global Outsourcing on IT Providers. *Communications of the AIS*, 14(article 25): 1.

Nahapiet, J. and Ghoshal, S. (1998) Social Capital, Intellectual Capital and the Organizational Advantage. *Academy of Management Review*, 38(2): 242–266.

Pfannenstein, L.L. and Tsai, R.J. (2004) Offshore Outsourcing: Current and Future Effects on American IT Industry. *Information Systems Management*, 21(4): 72–80

Rottman, J. W. (2006) Successfully Outsourcing Embedded Software Development. *IEEE Computer*, 39(1): 55–61.

Rottman, J. and Lacity, M. (2004) Twenty Practices for Offshore Sourcing. *MIS Quarterly Executive*, 3(3): 117–130.

Rousseau, P.L. and Wachtel, P. (1998) Financial Intermediation and Economic Performance: Historical Evidence from Five Industrialized Countries. *Journal of Money, Credit and Banking*, 30(4): 657–678.

Rubinstein, A. and Wolinsky, A. (1987) Middlemen. *Quarterly Journal of Economics*, 102(3): 581–594.

Rumbaugh, J.E., Blaha, M.R., Premerlani, W.J, Eddy, F. and Lorensen, W. (1991) *Object-Oriented Modeling and Design*. Prentice-Hall: Englewood Cliffs, NJ.

Sahay S., Nicholson, B. and Krishna, S. (2003) *Global IT Outsourcing: Software Development Across Boarders*, Cambridge University Press: Cambridge, UK.

SEI (2005) *Software Engineering Institute,* **http://www.sei.cmu.edu/cmmi/** accessed on January 12, 2007.

Sese, F., Wareham, J. and Bonet, E. (2006) Words and Objects in Information Systems Development: Six Paradigms of Information as Representation, *Proceedings of the 14th European Conference on Information Systems.* Gothenburg, Sweden, 2006.

Spulber, D.F. (1999) *Market Microstructure: Intermediaries and the Theory of the Firm.* Cambridge: UK: Cambridge University Press.

Star, S.L. (1989) The Structure of Ill-structured Solutions: Heterogeneous Problem-solving, Boundary Objects and Distributed Artificial Intelligence, in M. Hans and L. Gasser (eds), Distributed Artificial Intelligence (Vol. 2). Menlo Park, CA: Morgan Kauffman, 37–54.

Strauss, A.L. and Corbin, J. (1990) *Basics of Qualitative Research: Grounded Theory Procedures and Techniques*, Newbury Park, CA: Sage.

Te'eni, D. (2001) A Cognitive-Affective Model of Organizational Communication for Designing IT. *MIS Quarterly*, 25(2): 251–312.

Trompenaars, F. and Hampden-Turner, C. (1997) *Riding the Waves of Culture: Understanding Diversity in Global Business,* 2nd edition, McGraw-Hill: New York.

Tushman, M.L. and Scanlan, T.J. (1981) BoundarySpanning Individuals: Their Role in Information Transfer and their Antecedents. *Academy of Management Journal*, 24(1): 286–305.

von Hippel, E. (1988) *The Sources of Innovation*, New York: Oxford University Press.

Wareham, J. and Gerrits, H. (1999) De-contextualizing Competence: Can Business Best Practice be Bundled and Sold? *European Management Journal*, 17(1): 39–49.

Wareham, J., Mahnke, V., Bjørn-Andersen, N. and Peters, S. (2007) Communication Metaphors-in-Use: Technical Communication and Offshore Systems Development. *IEEE Transactions on Professional Communication*, 50(2) June: 93–108.

Willcocks, L. and Lacity, M. (1998) *Strategic Sourcing of Information Systems: Perspectives and Practices*, John Wiley & Sons Ltd: New York.

Williamson, O.E. (1996) *The Mechanisms of Governance*, New York: Oxford University Press.

Zave, P. and Jackson, M. (1997) Four Dark Corners of Requirements Engineering. *ACM Transactions on Software Engineering and Methodology* 6(1): 1–30.

CHAPTER 3

IT outsourcing from a client perspective: exploring client developments and their impact on supplier capabilities

Albert G. Plugge, Gerard M. Wijers, and René W. Wagenaar

Introduction

IT outsourcing is an area that is developing rapidly, requiring a solid relationship between customers and suppliers. Kern and Willcocks (2001) have argued that relationships in IT outsourcing have received little attention in conceptual and empirical research. Yet all researchers emphasize the importance of the relationship between client and supplier as being critical. A relationship is defined as "a long-term commitment, a sense of mutual cooperation, shared risk and benefits, and other qualities consistent with concepts and theories of participatory decision making" (Henderson 1990, 8). While IT outsourcing relationships have been addressed in the literature (Klepper 1994, 1995; McFarlan and Nolan 1995; Willcocks and Kern 2001), only a few researchers have researched the relationship between client and supplier and most of them have been inconclusive (Kern and Willcocks 2002, 4). Empirical research by Lacity and Willcocks (2000a) has shown that a number of client organizations encountered severe problems. These problems can be observed in six areas: strategy, cost, management, operations, contracts, and technology. In four of these areas, strategy, management, operations, and technology, suppliers are causing problems due to insufficient skills in business and IT. Many problems and challenges in outsourcing arrangements are related to the IT supplier capabilities. The IS outsourcing literature often cites "access to the capabilities and experience" of the provider as one of the main reasons why firms outsource (Gurbaxani 1996; Poppo and Zenger 1998; Quinn 1999), and that IT service provider capabilities are probably the most critical factor for success (Clark et al. 1995; McFarlan and Nolan 1995; DiRomualdo and Gurbaxani, V. 1998). While previous studies have discussed interorganizational relationships (Alborz et al. 2003; Kern and Willcocks 2000, 2002) with regard to outsourcing, they have failed to recognize relevant client developments and their impact on IT supplier capabilities. As a result, we only have partial understanding of these elements in IT outsourcing arrangements.

The objective of this chapter is to research key client developments and, subsequently, the impact of these developments on supplier capabilities. As argued by Kern and Willcocks (2002), more exploratory research is necessary to understand the relationship between client and supplier related to these developments. Therefore, this chapter makes the following contributions. First, we have constructed an exploratory study with an orientation on the client side, exploring relevant developments. Second, we have categorized this set of client developments and empirically validated this categorization. Finally, we have studied the impact of the client development and related this to IT supplier capabilities.

Conceptual framework

Interaction approach

Although IT outsourcing relationships have received some attention in the literature (Klepper 1994; McFarlan and Nolan 1995; Kern and Willcocks 2000, 2001; Alborz et al. 2003), all of the studied relationships showed a limited scope, as the context of the relationship was neglected. The relationship between clients and suppliers can be studied from several theoretical perspectives. Aspects like the context and behavior are important to fathom this relationship. Therefore, this study is based on an interorganizational relationship (IOR) theory. As an approach (the) IOR theory proves to be highly useful. In addition to behavioral and structural dimensions, it examines the conditions of a dyadic interfirm relationship (Kern and Willcocks 2001). The IOR is particularly valuable in analyzing interorganizational coordination and cooperation (Cunningham and Tynan, 1993; Bensaou and Venkatraman 1996). Moreover, IOR theory focuses on interactions between parties that are geared toward the joint accomplishment of objectives of the individual parties. However, when studying relationships we can recognize multiple dimensions that are not all covered by IOR theory. Following a literature review of IT outsourcing relationships, Hakansson (1982) developed an "interaction approach" that was derived from IOR theory. Applying this interaction approach, we are able to substantiate its different dimensions. The interaction approach has received empirical validation in the literature on both Marketing (Hakansson 1982) and IT (Cunningham and Tynan 1993; Leek et al. 2000).

Therefore, we conducted an exploratory research into client–supplier relationships, investigating relevant client developments that occur during an IT outsourcing arrangement. Applying an exploratory-descriptive study is useful to be extended later (Denzin, 1978). In addition to the Hakansson interaction approach, Kern and Willcocks (2002) argue that most of the literature has focused either on behavior or management aspects, but none has focused on the interaction, the structure, or the context of these. Building on the work of Kern and Willcocks, the interaction approach to relationships is used during this empirical research as a basis for exploring client developments due to its more comprehensive and holistic view of the client environment.

Figure 3.1 illustrates the basic interaction model based on dyadic client-supplier arrangements.

The model can be divided into three categories of variables that influence the interaction between both parties: their mutual environment, the atmosphere, and the exchange process. As to the first category, the environment of both client and supplier organization is influenced by market

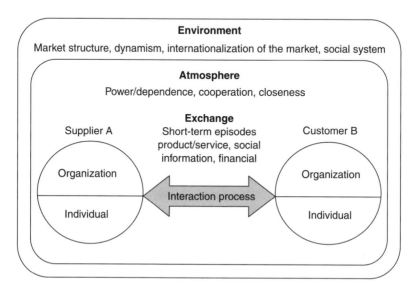

Figure 3.1   Interaction approach, adopted from Hakansson (1982)

developments, the extent of market dynamics, and the social system, among other factors. The second category, the atmosphere, characterizes the relationship more directly and can be expressed in terms of power/dependency, the level of cooperation and the overall social distance between client and supplier. These dimensions are more behavioral and define the relational atmosphere. Finally, the third category, the exchange process, concerns the interaction: product/service exchange, information exchange, financial exchange, and social exchange. Using the Hakansson interaction approach, the model shown in Figure 3.1, will provide a comprehensive view of IT outsourcing relationships.

As the model is applied from an organizational point of view, the individual client and supplier representatives are not within the scope of this research.

IT supplier capabilities

After we have identified the key client developments, we will discuss the impact of these developments on IT supplier capabilities. As a consequence of their decision to outsource, clients invest in their core capabilities to establish a solid outsourcing relationship with their IT supplier (Kern and Willcocks 2001). Also, the IT suppliers need to invest in their core capabilities (Feeny et al. 2005). After all, excellent capabilities are a decisive factor for the client in selecting an IT supplier. In defining the topic "capability," the following generic description will be used: "The IT capability will refer to an assembly of skills, techniques, and know-how developed over time that enable an organization to acquire, deploy and leverage IT investments in pursuit of business strategies" (Lacity and Willcocks 2001). Previous studies related to capabilities refer to an organization (Ethiraj 2005) and the influence of dynamism (Teece et al. 1997; Eisenhardt and Martin 2000). Although supplier capabilities are important, there is insufficient insight from empirical research into this subject. Feeny et al. (2005) have researched IT supplier capabilities, initially focusing on IT outsourcing. Later they extended their scope to business process outsourcing. This research resulted in a widely adopted model for identifying IT supplier capabilities: see Figure 3.2. Since several capabilities are strongly related to each other, Feeny et al. (2005) have developed a model that consists of three organizational competences: Delivery, Transformation, and Relationship. An organizational competence can be defined as a group of interrelated capabilities.

The delivery competence determines the extent to which a supplier is able to react to the client's day-to-day needs in delivering operational services. This competence includes capabilities such as business

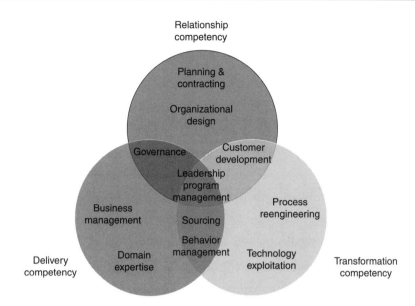

Figure 3.2 IT supplier capability model (Feeny 2005)

management, domain expertise, behavior management, and sourcing. The second competence is related to the area of transformation. Most clients expect that the supplier will improve the quality of the service and reduce the cost. The transformation competence is a bundle of capabilities: technology exploitation, process reengineering, program management, and customer development. The third and perhaps most important competence focuses on the relationship between supplier and client, with capabilities such as planning and contracting, organizational design, governance and leadership. Our research builds on the work of Feeny et al. (2005), in that the identified key client developments are related to IT supplier capabilities.

Conceptual framework

In this section, the conceptual framework for our empirical research is explained.

We constructed a conceptual framework, as illustrated in Figure 3.3, that is based on Hakansson's (1982) interaction approach in combination with the supplier capability model developed by Feeny et al. (2005).

Our conceptual framework consists of three interrelated constructs: environment, atmosphere, and exchange.

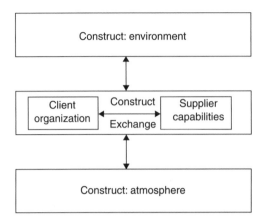

Figure 3.3   Research model for identifying client developments

The construct environment affects the client organization through aspects such as market developments, market dynamism, and the social system. These environmental developments will provide more insight into the context related to market and business. From a client perspective it is important to identify the impact on the client organization and thus on the existing outsourcing relationship. The second construct, which has received more research from a behavioral point of view, concerns developments that arise in the atmosphere between client and supplier. Examples include trust, the effect of power and dependency, and the level of cooperation. The third construct, addressing exchange, relates to the elements of client organization and supplier capabilities. By investigating this construct we are able to identify the type of developments that possibly affect supplier capabilities. Our empirical study encompasses all three constructs to identify key developments.

Research approach

The goal of this study is to address the paucity of empirical research (Yin, 1994) into the client–supplier relationship. We address the key developments that occur during an outsourcing arrangement from a client perspective. Subsequently, we discuss the impact of these developments on supplier capabilities. In this way, we provide a better understanding of the client side of an outsourcing arrangement. We assume that key developments within a client organization will influence the supplier side and therefore have an impact. This chapter sets out to answer two broadly defined research questions: *What are the key developments that arise in the organization and environment of the client?* Second, we will investigate the following question: *What is the impact of client developments on supplier capabilities?* It is the intention to use the insights derived from the answers as a basis for further inquiry into IT supplier organizations.

About this research

This research is derived from the study of five client organizations in five different sectors in the Dutch business community (see Table 3.1).

Table 3.1   Case studies

Case studies	Industry	Sourcing strategy	Start of the deal	Length of the deal	Total size of the deal (million)	Number FTE trans-ferred	CIO	Vendor man.	IT man.
Company A	Banking	Selective	2002	5 years	Euro 1.800	2000	1	1	2
Company B	Retail	Selective	2002	5 years	Euro 467	800	1	2	1
Company C	Chemicals	Selective	1999	5 years	Euro 100	80		2	2
Company D	Telecomm-unications	Selective	2001	5 years	Euro 1.400	950	1	2	2
Company E	Manufac-turing	Selective	2001	5 years	Dollar 1.000	500	1	1	2

Although there are differences between these five client organizations, they were selected due to the similarities in their IT outsourcing arrangements. All of the selected client organizations are market leaders in their specific market sector and operate in an intense and dynamic environment. Each client organization has at least four years of experience in managing the relationship with their suppliers. Their geographical scope varies from European to global. From an IT perspective, outsourced IT activities include: office automation, business applications, software development, and IT infrastructure. Due to the broad approach several similarities and differences can be analyzed. During our interviews with the respondents we observed that all the client organizations applied a selective outsourcing strategy. The choice of selective outsourcing mitigates the risks for the client, while at the same time encouraging competition between the suppliers. While it is not yet possible to draw definitive conclusions from the investigated client organizations, the variations in the categories across the different industry sectors will yield some interesting observations. The results that are discussed in this chapter are indicative of the challenges and developments that both clients and suppliers have to go through.

Findings

As the selected client organizations are acting in a competitive climate within their industry, the different constructs give a rich overview of important developments. During this research we found different motivations for the client organizations to outsource their IT activities. On the one hand, some of them (e.g., banking, manufacturing) have started to define which activities are core and which are not from a business perspective. The strategic choice for outsourcing was therefore considered well. On the other hand, due to their precarious financial situation at the start of this millennium client organizations in the retail and telecommunication markets had purely financial motives for outsourcing their IT environment. Because these companies were forced into outsourcing, the preparation time for a rigorous sourcing process was restricted, which brought about unnecessary risks. These different strategic starting points affect the evaluation of developments and client expectations toward suppliers.

Environmental developments

Studying the environmental developments, we have found some well-known similarities. In general, all of the analyzed companies believe that the IT outsourcing market has become mature in the past ten years. Client organizations have become more experienced in managing the relationship and more capable of controlling risks. Analyzing the preparation for outsourcing of client organizations by mitigating the risks and looking for business advantage, Lacity and Willcocks (2001) came to a similar conclusion.

Studying the environmental developments resulted in three important distinctions. The first distinction is related to the company's experience in the field of IT outsourcing. Companies in the process of their first generation outsourcing arrangement have a distinct cost focus and adhere strictly to the contractual agreements. Their most important concern is to achieve their financial goals and to build a relationship with an IT supplier. However, companies in the process of a second generation outsourcing arrangement approach outsourcing from a holistic viewpoint, applying the lessons learned during their first experience. Topics such as the value added of the IT supplier, catering to market dynamics, and creating agility become more important. The second distinction is the significance of a partnership between client and supplier. Looking at financially driven outsourcing arrangements, we found that the importance of a partnership with external suppliers is restricted to a role as preferred supplier only. However, companies that consider outsourced IT activities to be strategic appreciate the holistic value of suppliers and regard them as partners. A third distinction can be made with respect to the discussion of environmental developments. Clients in the banking and manufacturing industries proactively exchange this information with their suppliers on a regular basis. The objective of these regular meetings is to share company developments and challenges, so that suppliers can anticipate changes in the provision of their services or even adapt to a new situation. We found that the chemicals firm had irregular meetings with suppliers. At the retail and telecommunication firms we even saw that meetings with suppliers were entirely lacking. From the perspective of the interaction approach, the identified key client developments based on the environment are highlighted below.

Globalization

The first key development is the effect of *globalization* on the client organization. As a result of fierce competition, the rise of new entrants in the playing field and an expanding business strategy, globally operating client organizations focus more and more on their core business activities. The influence of globalization underpins the research of Holway (1998). Globalization is one of the major forces that have been driving changes in the software and computer services industry. IT activities like application development and maintenance are offshored to low-wage countries like India and China. Improvements in Internet reliability and functionality have led to a rapid decrease in communication costs. Bangalore is now as near as a "local" branch office. Another consequence of globalization is that companies are expanding their business to new countries.

The investigated chemicals company, for instance, observed a market shift toward Asia while at the same time new players entered the market. To serve their customers and to sustain their businesses they were forced to open sales offices and even a production plant near their customers. Suppliers will be challenged into following the client organization to new countries. It may be assumed that this will certainly affect supplier capabilities. From the perspective of the client, questions that arise are, first, "Is the supplier capable of following our company to new countries all over the world?" and from a global viewpoint, "Can a supplier run a project in 80 countries simultaneously?" The answers to these questions are important for clients, to establish if a supplier acquires new businesses:

> *We run a global business, while the market is shifting toward Asia and new entrants are arising. Due to the process of globalization, we were forced to carve out our pharmaceutical division and open a production plant and sales offices in Asia. Customers become more critical buying our products because of fierce competition. Actually, the customer drives our direction of tomorrow.* (Director global sourcing Company C)

Market dynamics

The second identified key development is the influence of *market dynamics*. Acting in a competitive climate means that it is important to respond to the changing business needs of clients. The dynamics of the market with new entrants, fierce competition, and regulation, will continuously affect companies in all respects. The client organizations have to reduce their time to market to meet customer demands. In turn, the IT supplier must be able to respond quickly. This requires a business mindset to anticipate new business needs:

> *To anticipate new market developments, the IT department of the company and external suppliers needs to have a business mindset to understand the required needs. New business services are less labour-intensive and at the same time another marketing and sales approach is needed. Suppliers have to be involved in this process by deploying their knowledge and insights.* (Business manager Company D)

As a result, the supplier needs to be more flexible as an organization and to increase the agility of its company, which is also argued by Oosterhout et al. (2006). In some market segments, the developments are so intense that end users (e.g., consumers) force companies into a complete transformation with regard to both processes and services. An example is the telecommunications market, where traditional processes were based on lead times and where present and future processes will be available "on demand." As the introduction of triple play packages (voice, Internet, and television) contains a high IT component, and the IT environment that enables these services has been outsourced to external suppliers, we argue that the impact on supplier capacities is also extensive.

Legislation

The third key development concerns *legislation*. In addition to general legislation, firms that are market leaders also have to comply with specific legislation. From a market perspective, legislation applies to, for instance, the determined markets, the dimension of the market share, and regulated client services. From a financial perspective, legislation such as Sarbaines-Oxley affects companies substantially. In addition, Basel II is affecting companies in the banking market. New legislation may also relate to human resource management with regard to illness, taxation, or hiring temporary staff. Especially when a company is present on a global scale, different legislation is applied in different countries, which increases the complexity. Client and supplier have to describe these processes in detail to be compliant. As companies have to report on legislation, this influences the facilitating IT systems, which, in turn, are outsourced to suppliers. Although both parties are partly responsible for the adaptation to the legislation, the client organization retains the responsibility for compliance:

> *Legislation becomes more and more important, due to our expanding businesses to new countries. Since we outsourced together with the IT environment also our IT auditors to a third party, internally we experience a lack of relevant knowledge according to this topic.* (Vendor manager Company A)

The impression of the researched client organizations is that suppliers are struggling with increasing legislation, due to the level of details in the processes. Clients assume that insufficient supplier capabilities are most often the cause of this struggle.

Atmosphere developments

The developments in the atmosphere also show similarities and differences. Similarities could be found in three areas: the mutual relationship, the culture, and the contract. First, with regard to the relationship all the interviewed respondents indicated the importance and value of a good relationship with their supplier. More important than the formal agreements, the key factor in the relationship is the supplier's employees. Enthusiastic and dedicated supplier staff will overcome challenges. This underpins previous research of Kern and Willcocks (2000, 2001, 2002) and Levina and Ross (2003). However, when a supplier omits to invest in the client relationship, the overall performance declines. Second, we also found similarities with regard to the culture. All of the client organizations underline the value of a cultural fit between client and supplier, and several client organizations (e.g., banking, retail, and telecommunications) confirmed that cultural aspects were a part of the selection criteria:

> *The cultural differences within the global supplier organization are enormous. The US handles a directive policy, while Europe seeks the way of consensus. In our negotiation with the global supplier we have determined that cultural differences within their organization can be "dealbreaking."* (Head of IT services Company B)

The third similarity concerns the contractual agreement with suppliers. The performance with regard to the contract strongly influences the relationship (Currie and Seltsikas 2001). With one of the companies, for example, an elaborate 800-page contract was produced. When a new supplier team was assigned during the transition phase, the new supplier team was insufficiently aware of the contract details. This caused much delay, which had a negative effect on the relationship. Following the interaction approach, the identified key client developments with respect to the atmosphere are discussed below.

Innovation

A key development that will seriously affect the supplier capabilities is the increasing interest of client organizations in *innovation*. In general, we found a growing need for sharing new innovative products and services. In particular, companies that are involved in the second generation outsourcing arrangements are looking at adding more value to the relationship and discuss innovation. They have seen that cost reduction alone cannot meet new business requirements. Innovations concern the improvement of business processes, procedures, and technology. Companies in the banking and manufacturing markets have even included innovation in the contract. In the interview with the investigated banking company, an IT executive stated that the contract specifically encouraged suppliers to take the initiative in suggesting innovative solutions. During a previous sourcing contract the company had learned that innovation had to form a part of a mutual agreement to prevent suppliers relying on existing services only. However, an IT executive of the retail company indicated that innovation was an *ad hoc* affair which is not laid down in a contract. The interviews indicate that innovation does not start automatically; it has to be organized. However, practice shows that suppliers are reserved and reactive in discussing and implementing new innovations. So, the expectations of client organizations and the practice of suppliers diverge.

Sourcing strategy

Another key development is the client's *sourcing strategy.* In situations in which the client has decided to implement a selective sourcing strategy, and therefore to apply a best-of-breed strategy, a competition model in relation to the supplier is introduced. This competition model is based on the principle of a continuous challenging of the suppliers to get the best price/performance ratio when contracts are renewed or new contracts are tendered. This competition model results in a proactive role of the suppliers. After all, during a contract period they are never sure if they will win additional contracts when the client is tendering. The supplier cannot afford to lose their focus on the client organization, which is one of the objectives of the customer. Since research (Lacity and Willcocks 2000a, 2000b; Kern and Willcocks 2001) has revealed that selective outsourcing is the more common practices, the market expectation is that the supplier competition model will be deployed more often. This is a key development that will also impact the supplier's capabilities:

> *Our company decided to implement a selective sourcing strategy, so we could select the best suppliers in their market segment. To improve the quality of the services and acquire the best price/performance ratio, we introduced a mult- sourcing strategy competition. This means that all suppliers are able to bid on additional contracts. A single supplier who is responsible for an IT service is not certain of extra business when the contract is extended.* (Business manager Company A)

Exchange developments

Exploring developments with regard to the exchange of services, several similarities and differences were found during the interviews. We address two identified similarities. First, all clients divide the exchange of services into three categories: the design and delivery of IT services, monitoring and reporting, and financial transactions. According to the exchange of services, most clients appreciate regular contact with their supplier, preferably on a day-to-day basis. Their motivation is that frequent mutual contact promotes the cooperation between both parties so that results will be achieved quickly. A second similarity is that the interviewed respondents evaluate the delivery of IT services as generic and not as specifically developed for their organization. Only in situations in which new temporary projects are set up, do processes manifest an *ad hoc* character. Addressing developments according to the exchange of services, two differences between the interviewed respondents could be found. First, the outsourcing contract will often lead to several management issues. In general, the interpretation of the contract is a subject for debate with the supplier. Remarkably, client organizations who have outsourced their IT environment for financial reasons, like the companies in the retail and telecommunications markets, discuss the contract from a financial point of view. The second difference we recognized is related to the characteristics of exchange processes, in particular to the question of whether they are generic or specific. The vehement dynamism in the telecommunications market, for instance, leads to a dramatic transformation of the telecommunication company in a very short time frame. As a result, the company has outsourced the development and implementation of a state-of-the-art all IP multimedia network, which is so brand-new that even the supplier has to develop specific tailor-made processes. As the outsourcing is based on financial reasons, the discussions with the supplier will typically concern additional payments for developing these specific processes. Applying the interaction approach, key client developments with respect to the exchange category are discussed below.

Architecture

Interestingly, clients ascribe value to the role of designing the *IT architecture* which can be identified as a key development. Owing to the division of the IT environment into separate entities and as a result of applying a selective sourcing strategy, the role of the IT architecture becomes more and more important. Hence, entities, processes, and interfaces have to be described in a detailed way to record the agreed responsibilities so that risks are mitigated and continuity is guaranteed. After all, well-designed IT services can produce significant improvements in the organizational performance. All client organizations are of the opinion that they need to work closely together with the architects on the supplier side, as in designing the IT landscape both client and supplier have to be involved. When the client decides to offshore application development, cultural aspects play a major role in jointly designing IT entities. During the interviews it appeared that IT architecture alignment is becoming more important when more parties – client, overall supplier integrator, and sub-contractors – are involved in defining the IT landscape. Therefore, architecture as a key development will not only affect the client organizations but also the supplier. This means that the supplier needs to have the right architecture capabilities in-house to tune the IT services to the client architecture.

Flexibility

A second key development that was found concerns the clients' requirements for *flexibility* of the supplier. As indicated earlier, acting in a dynamic market requires a growing need for flexibility which will require a proactive attitude of suppliers. A fast response to changing business needs demands a flexible mindset from the supplier. Addressing flexibility, we have to distinguish between the expectations of a client and the performance of a supplier. The client expects a highly flexible organization on all levels, with proactive employees catering for all their needs. In practice, however, suppliers are struggling with flexibility for various reasons. Although flexibility may not have been seen as a value added in the acquisition phase of the outsourcing arrangement, the suppliers will still need to take this into account when designing the supply organization. An inadequate mindset with regard to flexibility will affect the mutual relationship negatively:

> *The flexibility requirements toward suppliers are very high as they arise from a strong business need. By introducing new financial services, suppliers sometimes globally have to bring into action additional personnel with the right skills. This will result in a contrast of interest. We demand a high flexibility, while the supplier wants to equally distribute their personnel.* (Business manager Company A)

Offering flexibility from the point of view of the supplier is more than a behavioral aspect.

Synthesis

Analyzing the three different constructs, we observed that they all interact with each other due to dynamic changes. We found developments that occur in the context of the client organization and define how companies have to deal with market dynamics and the competitive climate in the industry. When client organizations respond to market developments by introducing new business services, we argue that even the context of the client organization is affected. Identifying key developments answers our first research question: *What are the key developments that arise in the organization and environment of a client?*

The investigated client organizations are of the opinion that key developments within their organization and their environment cause a major impact on supplier capabilities.

Our research demonstrates that clients discuss new developments with suppliers on a regular basis. Also the researched client organizations underline the impact of client developments on supplier capabilities. Strikingly, we found that during the exchange of information, both clients and suppliers ignore discussion of this impact altogether. They fail to address the importance of capabilities as an important and critical factor for success. We establish that neglecting developments and capabilities is in contrast to the statement of clients that both aspects are essential in adapting to changing circumstances.

Impact on IT supplier capabilities

As described in the research approach, the second phase of this research consists of relating the client developments to IT supplier capabilities to define their impact. Based on the previous research of Feeny et al. (2005), and contributing to the development of a supplier capability model, the discussion will provide answers to the second research question: *What is the impact of client developments on supplier capabilities?* After coding the interviews, we identified the relationship between the different constructs, the relevant client developments, and the relation to supplier capabilities (illustrated in Table 3.2). Studying the supplier capability model of Feeny et al. (2005), we were able to analyze all the capabilities in depth. Subsequently, we identified the relations between client developments and the affected supplier capabilities.

Globalization

The addressed key development "globalization" concerns a set of two supplier capabilities. First, the organizational design capability is needed to design a delivery model to provide the agreed services. If the client is followed globally, a smart and flexible global delivery model is required. The second capability that is involved is leadership.

Table 3.2 Operationalization of constructs

Construct	Key developments	Supplier capabilities
Environment	Globalization	Organizational design
	Market dynamics	Domain expertise
	Legislation	Process reengineering
Atmosphere	Innovation	Process reengineering
		Technology exploitation
	Sourcing strategy	Leadership
Exchange	Architecture	Domain expertise
		Process reengineering
		Governance
	Flexibility	Business management
		Sourcing
		Program management

Translating market dynamics, business, and internal client developments into a strategy with concrete planning and action calls for a professional supplier capability. And this is what leadership is all about. As the number of companies outsourcing their activities on a global scale is increasing, these supplier capabilities become more important. So the impact of globalization on the discussed capabilities is high. Suppliers must adapt the capability model to stay in business. Various clients feel that only a limited number of suppliers is supporting their customers on a global scale.

Market dynamics

The second key development refers to the dynamics in the market. By taking market dynamics into account the supplier shows that he is aware of the actual market circumstances and, consequently, has developed leadership capabilities. The supplier capability model developed by Feeny et al. (2005) states the importance of the leadership capability. However, in describing this capability Feeny et al. (2005) focus on identification of client needs and delivering the balance of activities that are required to achieve present and future success. When we analyze the supplier capability model, we observe a lack of knowledge and experience of market developments on the IT supplier side. This implies that the supplier capability model has to be extended with an additional capability to address market knowledge and entrepreneurship. This conclusion is underlined by various clients such as the banking and retail companies.

Legislation

Legislation is another key development that relates to important supplier capabilities. Legislation is increasing in various areas, including the market, international law, and IT standardization. Suppliers have to adapt their systems and processes to these circumstances which challenge the process reengineering capability. The experience of client organizations like the banking, manufacturing, and retail companies illustrates that suppliers are struggling in this area. They assign only a few employees. Our research illustrates that this capability must be strengthened to meet present and future client needs.

Innovation

An important key development that is mentioned by clients is the increasing interest in innovation. Client organizations divide innovation into two entities: process and technology. Process improvements are necessary to improve, for instance, the delivery chain of activities. Suppliers may propose innovative solutions to meet the increasing client demands. This indicates that the supplier process reengineering capability is affected. The second entity regards the technical aspect of innovation which is related to the supplier technology exploitation capability. Although they dispose of innovative ideas and solutions, the overall impression of clients is that suppliers do not have the right skills or an entrepreneurial mindset. Suppliers adopt a reactive attitude and as a result they will miss opportunities. In the developed supplier capability model of Feeny et al. (2005), this entrepreneurial capability is missing. We argue that suppliers have to develop this entrepreneurial capability in view of the increasing client demands for innovation.

Sourcing strategy

Another key development is choice of a sourcing strategy, which affects the leadership capability of suppliers.

Particularly, clients who are involved in second generation outsourcing arrangements prefer a supplier competition model. The supplier leadership capability is necessary to retain existing business and to win new business. This requires a proactive mindset and a good relationship with the client organization. Clients who are involved in second generation outsourcing arrangements also pay more attention to the IT supplier's value added with regard to innovation. Our research establishes that a stronger capability is required.

Architecture

Architecture is a key development that is related to three supplier capabilities. First, the supplier needs a profound domain expertise in the area of architecture. IT architecture is the starting point from which all the IT entities are derived. Aiming at standardization, clients rationalize applications and platforms to create a more simple and efficient IT landscape. Therefore, a sound "target-architecture" is a guarantee for establishing a coherent IT environment. Second, the process reengineering capability is required to align the IT service processes, in particular when several suppliers are involved in delivering an end-to-end service. Finally, the capabilities described above include the governance capability of the supplier. Interviews with respondents from the industries of banking, retail, and telecommunications illustrate that clients experience insufficient knowledge.

Considering the importance of IT architecture, which is even greater in the case of a selective sourcing strategy, these capabilities deserve the supplier's full attention.

Flexibility

The last key development is the increasing client need for flexibility. First of all, from a supplier perspective flexibility is associated with the business management capability by consistently delivering services in line with both the client service level agreements and their own business plans. With clients emphasizing this key development, suppliers are very challenged in achieving this objective. Second, the sourcing capability of the supplier is affected by an increase of the (flexibility) need for flexibility of the client. In view of the limited number of skilled resources this development also becomes a true challenge. The third capability that is involved concerns program management. Clients in the industries of banking, retail, and telecommunications expect that to realize flexibility, suppliers have to prioritize, coordinate, and prepare the organization to anticipate the required needs.

Summary and conclusion

The key developments indicated above influence the greater part of the twelve capabilities described above, nine of them being affected. Challenging the supplier capability model, we draw two conclusions. First, we establish the importance of five capabilities to which suppliers have to pay attention: organizational design, process reengineering, leadership, domain expertise, and governance. Two of these, process reengineering and leadership, can be regarded as focal. Each of these is affected by three key client developments. We are of the opinion that suppliers first have to adapt their leadership capability, as their strategy toward clients needs to change. Subsequently, the process reengineering capability has to be adapted based on the new leadership capability. The well-known proposition "structure follows strategy" is also applicable in this respect.

Our second conclusion is based on the importance of supplier knowledge of the markets in which clients are operating, which confirms prior research by Kern and Willcocks (2001). Due to insufficient market knowledge, suppliers adopt an inadequate proactive attitude toward their clients. Therefore, we conclude that suppliers require a new capability: business market knowledge. We define this capability as follows: the ability to fathom business markets in which clients are acting and the capacity to translate market developments into business opportunities for both client and supplier. Viewing the capability model, we suggest that this business market knowledge capability is positioned on the interface between the relationship competence and the delivery competence.

Conclusion and further research

This, in essence empirical, research set out to learn more about client developments that occur during an IT outsourcing arrangement from a client perspective. The identified developments have been related to IT supplier capabilities and have been discussed. Research on five client organizations demonstrates that environmental, atmosphere, and exchange developments do affect client organizations. Therefore, we argue that these developments also cause a significant impact on supplier capabilities. For a better understanding of the relationship with suppliers, the explored key developments were compared with the supplier capability model developed by Feeny et al. (2005). Our research demonstrates that, from the perspective of the clients, (that) the capabilities mentioned need to be adapted by suppliers. Therefore, we may conclude that suppliers have to strengthen these capabilities to meet present and future client demands. We suggest that the new identified capability "business market knowledge" is added to the capability set of suppliers.

Our study shows that there is insufficient attention to supplier capabilities, while this topic is crucial for the success of an outsourcing arrangement (McFarlan et al. 1995; DiRomualdo et al. 1998). Instead, in the exchange of information between clients and suppliers, topics are discussed that are directly related to IT services. We observed an important lack in outsourcing arrangements, which leads to the need for further research. This research has established that the results of the empirical research by Lacity and Willcocks (2000a), with regard to client organizations that encounter severe problems, are still valid. Therefore, we argue that discussing supplier capabilities is a continuous subject of debate in outsourcing relationships. This observation certainly provides a valuable contribution to both the academic community and practitioners.

This chapter also contributes to the existing IT outsourcing research literature in particular by exploring client developments and their relation with the supplier side of an outsourcing arrangement. An additional contribution to the literature can be made by exploring the weighting of supplier capabilities. More insight into the weight of capabilities will enable suppliers to decide to what extent capabilities have to be governed. Although our study found interesting client developments, it is important to note its boundary conditions. First, the identified client developments are based on a limited number of five organizations. The insights can be enhanced by investigating more client organizations and conducting more interviews. Second, the study was carried out from a client perspective. More in-depth case research is required to include the perspective of the supplier. In particular, new research from a supplier perspective needs to establish the extent to which client developments affect supplier capabilities. Such work would advance academic understanding of the supplier side. The supplier capabilities based on the capability model of Feeny et al. (2005) are described from a strategic perspective and therefore they are more diffuse. Further research is necessary to specify the addressed capabilities to create a clearer view. We do not claim that our results are definitive or conclusive, but instead we intend to open up new research questions, such as: how suppliers cope with the explored client developments, and which capabilities are adapted. Longitudinal case studies are necessary to explain how suppliers manage these challenges over time and align their mutual relationship with the client organization. Future work will focus on an adaptation of the supplier capability model.

Acknowledgment

During the production of our paper for the First Information Systems Workshop on Global Sourcing our coauthor Prof. Dr. René W. Wagenaar passed away unexpectedly on Sunday, February 25, 2007. We will remember him as an inspiring research leader, a fine colleague with loyalty and integrity, and a warm personality. In particular, we would like to remember Prof. Dr. René Wagenaar for his valuable comments relating to this chapter.

In addition, we express our thanks to the organizations and interviewees involved in this study for their kind cooperation.

References

Alborz, Seddon, P.B., and Scheepers, R. (2003) *A Model for Studying It Outsourcing Relationships*. In 7th Pacific Asia Conference on Information Systems, 10–13 July. (Adelaide, South Australia).

Bensaou, M. and Venkatraman, N. (1996) Inter-Organizational Relationships and Information Technology: A Conceptual Synthesis and a Research Framework. *European Journal of Information Systems*, 5(2): 84–91.

Clark, T.D., Zmud, R.W., McCray, G.E. (1995) The Outsourcing of Information Services: Transforming the Nature of Business in the Information Industry. *Journal of Information Technology*, 10: 221–237.

Cunningham, C. and Tynan C. (1993) Electronic Trading, Interorganizational Systems and the Nature of Buyer–Seller Relationships: the Need for a Network Perspective. *International Journal of Information Management*, 13: 3–28.

Currie, W. and Seltsikas, P. (2001) Exploring the Supply-Side of It Outsourcing: Evaluating the Emerging Role of Application Service Providers. *European Journal of Information Systems*, 10: 123–134.

Denzin, N.K. (1978) *The Research Act: A Theoretical Introduction to Sociological Methods*, New York: McGraw-Hill.

DiRomualdo, A. and Gurbaxani, V. (1998) Strategic Intent for IT Outsourcing. *Sloan Management Review* Summer: 67–80.

Eisenhardt, K. and Martin, J. (2000) Dynamic Capabilities: What Are They? *Strategic Management Journal*, 21: 1105–1121.

Ethiraj, S. (2005) Where Do Capabilities Come from and How Do They Matter? A Study in the Software Service Industry. *Strategic Management Journal*, 26: 25–45.

Feeny, D., Lacity, M., and Willcocks, L. (2005) Taking the Measure of Outsourcing Providers. *Sloan Management Review*, 46(3) 41–48.

Hakansson, H. (1982) *International Marketing and Purchasing of Industrial goods: An Interaction Approach,* Chichester: John Wiley & Sons.

Henderson, J.C. (1990) Plugging into Strategic Partnerships: the Critical Is Connection. *Sloan Management Review*, 31(3) 7–18.

Holway, R. (1998) *Software and Computing Services Industry in Europe: Markets and Strategies, 1998–2002*. Munich: PAC Gmbh.

Kern, T. and Willcocks, L. (2000) Exploring Information Technology Outsourcing Relationships: Theory and Practice. *Journal of Strategic Information Systems*. 9: 321–350.

Kern, T. and Willcocks, L. (2001) *The Relationship Advantage: Information Technologies, Sourcing and Management*. Oxford: University press.

Kern, T. and Willcocks, L. (2002) Exploring Relationships in Information Technology Outsourcing: the Interaction Approach. *European Journal of Information Systems*, 11: 3–19.

Klepper, R. (1994) Outsourcing Relationships in Khosrowpour, M. (ed.), Managing Information Technology with Outsourcing: Idea Group Publishing, Harrisbury, PA.

Lacity, M. and Willcocks, L. (2000a) Inside It Outsourcing: A State-of-the-Art Report, Templeton Research Report 1, Templeton College, Oxford.

Lacity, M. and Willcocks, L. (2000b) *Global IT Outsourcing Search for Business Advantage*, Chisester: John Wiley & Sons.

Lacity, M. and Willcocks, L. (2001) *Global Information Technology Outsourcing: In Search of Business Advantage*, Chichester: John Wiley & Sons.

Leek, S., Turnbull, P., and Naude, P. (2000) Is the Interaction Approach of Any Relevance in an It/E-Commerce Driven World? In Proceedings of the 16th Annual International Marketing and Purchasing Conference, University of Bath, UK.

Levina, N. and Ross, J. (2003) From the Vendors Perspective: Exploring the Value Proposition in Information Technology Outsourcing. *MIS Quarterly*, 27: 331–364.

McFarlan, F.W. and Nolan, R.L. (1995) How to Manage an It Outsourcing Alliance. *Sloan Management Review* Winter: 9–23.

Oosterhout, E., Waarts, E., and Hillegersberg, J. (2006) Changefactors Requiring Agility and Implications for IT. *European Journal of Information Systems*, 15: 132–145.

Poppo, L. and Zenger, T. (1998) Testing Alternative Theories of the Firm: Transaction Cost, Knowledge-Based, and Measurement Explanations for Make-or-Buy Decisions in Information Services. *Strategic Management Journal*, 19: 853–877.

Quinn, J.B. (1999) Strategic Outsourcing: Leveraging Knowledge Capabilities. *Sloan Management Review*, 40(4): 9–21.

Teece, D., Pisano, G., and Shuen, A. (1997) Dynamic Capabilities and Strategic Management. *Strategic Management Journal*, 18: 509–533.

Yin, R.K. (1994) *Case Study Research. Design and Methods*, volume 5, 2nd edition. Thousand Oaks, CA: Sage.

Appendix 1 Interview instrument

The interview instrument is based upon Hakansson's Interaction Approach model, which consists of three categories.

Category: environment

Question 1: How does the environment affect your company?

Question 2: How do the market developments influence your company and which activities?

Question 3: How would you characterize the competitive climate in your industry and how is this related to IT?

Question 4: How does external legislation (e.g., Sarbanes-Oxley) affect your IT services?

Question 5: Do you review the "environmental" developments with your IT supplier on a regular basis?

Category: atmosphere

Question 1: How does the atmosphere affect the relationship between your company and your supplier?

Question 2: How does your outsourcing strategy (total, selective) affect your IT supplier(s)?

Question 3: How would you characterize your position toward the IT supplier: power or dependency?

Question 4: By what means does your company culture influence your IT supplier?

Question 5: Does innovation play an important role within your company and, if so, in what way will this influence the IT supplier?

Category: exchange

Question 1: What are the relevant exchange processes?

Question 2: What are the characteristics (e.g., regular vs. ad-hoc, generic vs. specific) of each of the exchange processes?

Question 3: What were some of the recent management difficulties you encountered in the relationship with your supplier?

Question 4: How would you describe the flexibility requirements toward your IT supplier related to the exchange process?

Question 5: How important is the relation between the demand manager (customer) and the delivery manager (supplier)?

CHAPTER 4

Operational capabilities development in mediated offshore software services models

Sirkka L. Jarvenpaa and Ji-Ye Mao

Introduction

Offshore outsourcing, or offshoring, involves crossing national boundaries to purchase services. Although offshoring includes both activities contracted to independent third parties abroad and international insourcing to foreign subsidiaries, here we will only consider the former. Offshoring of services is critically dependent on a supply of providers (vendors) that have operational capabilities to offer comparative cost advantage, satisfactory quality, and on-time delivery despite the distances involved, and the differences in time zones and cultures (Carmel and Tjia 2005). Yet the literature on information technology (IT) offshoring as well as on outsourcing of IT services more generally has largely focused on customers (particularly in the U.S. and Europe; e.g., Willcocks and Lacity 2000; Goles 2001; Willcocks and Lacity 2007). The vendor perspective has been much less studied (Levina and Ross 2003; Feeny et al. 2005; Borman 2006). In the context of offshoring, research is largely limited to India-based providers and the business models they use with their U.S. customers (e.g., Rajkumar and Mani 2001; Kaiser and Hawk 2004; Vashistha and Vashistha 2006; Oshri et al. 2007).

In software services offshoring, China represents an understudied setting yet an important one for several reasons. First, there are strong expectations of the Chinese software services industry's explosive growth in the coming years (Qu and Brocklehurst 2003). China's software services outsourcing reached RMB 2.6 billion (about US$340 million) in the first quarter of 2006. During the same quarter in 2007, the market increased to RMB 3.3 billion (about US$430 million) (Analysis International 2007). The development of the software industry is designated in China as a national priority with aggressive targets for export (Economic Daily 2007). Second, the Chinese providers use business models that are different from those presented in the offshoring literature. The software export firms based in China are largely small and medium-sized with heavy reliance on the *mediated offshoring business model*, whereby a Chinese vendor delivers offshore software services to a larger foreign-based IT contractor (vendor) that interfaces with the end-client firms.

The mediated business model has both theoretical and practical implications for the development of the operational capabilities in the Chinese software services firms. To survive and grow, these firms must be able to develop operational capabilities that go beyond the country-level comparative low labor costs that are shared by all the Chinese firms and by firms in many other low-cost countries (Qu and Brocklehurst 2003). Yet the development of these capabilities is impeded by the business model the firms deploy. Among the limiting factors are small-sized projects, low value-adding tasks, and limited opportunities to interface with the end-client.

This chapter focuses on the development of operational capabilities in the mediated business model. Operational capabilities are those involved in the provision of a service or a product. The previous literature on large vendors has identified three types of operational capabilities of critical importance to IT vendor success: client-specific capabilities, process capabilities, and human resources capabilities (Rajkumar and Mani 2001; Levina and Ross 2003; Ethiraj et al. 2005). Although some capabilities cannot be deliberately created due to their relative rarity or social complexities (e.g., culture), many capabilities reflect an evolutionary learning process in which an organization needs to invest financial, cognitive, and emotional resources (Zollo and Winter 2002). Deciding on what capabilities to build and how to build them are critical managerial choices for any firm, but the decision is particularly present for small and middle-sized offshore software services firms with limited resource bases. Capabilities development can sap critical resources without necessary returns and undermine not only firm growth but also survival (Sapienza et al. 2006). The current theories on the development of capabilities relate mainly to large firms or firms in mature economies (Zollo and Winter 2002; Zahra et al. 2006). Hence, the unique context of the current research can benefit both theory development and the practice of global services offshoring.

In this chapter, we advance theory by arguing that small and medium-sized Chinese firms face major hurdles in developing their operational capabilities, at least partly because of the mediated business model. Client-specific capabilities, process capabilities, and human resources capabilities are all affected by the small size of projects, low value-adding tasks, and lack of direct interaction with the end-client. We also build a theory of the mechanisms that Chinese firms use to overcome these challenges, and develop the three sets of capabilities to accomplish profitable growth in a highly competitive industry. Our theorizing is based on interviews and interactions with industry experts and consultants, as well as four case studies in Chinese firms where we conducted semi-structured in-depth interviews with knowledgeable informants, including owners, senior managers, project managers, developers, human resources managers, and quality managers.

In this chapter, we refer to the vendor as the firm supplying IT services and the client as the buyer of the IT services. The rest of the chapter is organized as follows. In the next section, we present the background to the mediated model in China, to operational capabilities in IT offshoring, and to the learning perspective of the development of capabilities. Then, we present the research approach and methods. In the fourth section, we present the case analyses on four vendors. Subsequently, in the last section we suggest some theoretical and practical implications from the cases followed by a conclusion.

Theoretical background: the mediated business model, operational capabilities, and capabilities development

The information systems literature on offshore outsourcing is recent but rapidly increasing. Much of the literature focuses on client capabilities to manage offshore vendors (e.g., Nicholson and Sahay 2001), client decision processes of what, how, and when to offshore (Carmel and Agarwal 2002; Aron and Singh 2005; Rottman and Lacity 2006), transforming the client–vendor relationship from a tactical to a strategic one (Kaiser and Hawk 2004), organizational form and location decisions (Aron and Singh 2005; Vestring et al. 2005), and the deployment of advanced software process approaches (Pries-Heje et al. 2005).

Although broad in the issues covered, the literature is narrow in its geographic coverage. The offshore studies are mostly limited to India-based vendors (Nicholson an Sahay 2001; Rajkumar and Mani 2001; Kaiser and Hawk 2004; Aron and Singh 2005; Levina 2006; Rottman and Lacity 2006; Oshri et al. 2007). Other regions, such as Russia (Pries-Heje et al. 2005; Levina 2006), China[1] (Qu and Brocklehurst 2003), and Taiwan (Wu 2006) have been much less studied.

Transaction cost economics has been the dominant theoretical paradigm in offshore sourcing (e.g., Qu and Brocklehurst 2003), although recently the theoretical frameworks have become more diverse, encompassing the systems dynamics approach (Dutta and Roy 2005), knowledge systems perspective (Garud and Kumaraswamy 2005), and the resource-based view of the firm (Wu 2006). The latter view (Penrose 1959; Barney 1991) is still debated, although it is largely an accepted theoretical lens in information systems research to examine how firm-specific capabilities are developed and how the capabilities contribute to firm performance (Gonzales et al. 2006).

Our focus is on capabilities development in a mediated business model. Only a few empirical studies have examined offshore vendor capabilities development, and largely from the vantage point of large India-based vendors who are independent players whose work is not contracted through other IT firms (e.g., Kaiser and Hawk 2004; Ethiraj et al. 2005). Hence, we break new ground by focusing on China and examining a mediated offshoring model.

Mediated business model in Chinese software services firms: drivers

The mediated business model is briefly mentioned in the literature (e.g., Rajkumar and Mani 2001; Ethiraj et al. 2005) but largely viewed as a transitory model during the early phases of a vendor's life. For example, Morstead and Blount (2003) associate the mediated model with Tier 2 vendors that have yet to mature to Tier 1 vendors.

The mediated model is common in the export business of Chinese software services to Japan (Qu and Brocklehurst 2003). Japan represents the largest market for Chinese firms (Hu et al. 2007). Similarly, China constitutes the main offshoring destination for Japan (OECD 2007). According to Qu and Brocklehurst (2003, 62), "China has at least managed to compete with India on an equal footing in the Japanese market."

In the Chinese-Japanese offshoring services, the mediated business model has developed over time. Initially, the Chinese firms provided on-site staffing to alleviate the cost pressures that Japanese firms faced in the early 1990s, but over time, the staff augmentation model was complemented or substituted with offshore development to deliver greater cost reductions to the Japanese firms. Expatriate Chinese who had worked in Japan started to set up offshore facilities in China.

In the mediated model, the *client* is not the end-user of the software, but a Japanese IT company (see Figure 4.1). The Japanese IT firm (client)

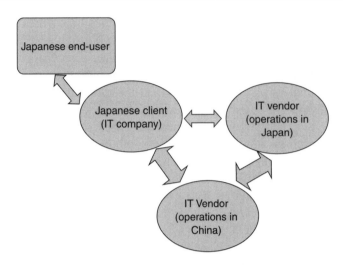

Figure 4.1   Business models in Chinese-Japanese software services offshoring

contracts work with the Chinese software services firm (vendor) to carry out tasks such as program design, coding, and unit-testing. The Japanese IT firm (client) performs the high-level functional design, and it might break the application into several different projects to be subcontracted to different Chinese vendors. It is also the client who integrates the different deliverables into a functioning system and manages the interactions with the *end-client* (end user of the software, such as a bank; Qu and Brocklehurst 2003).[2]

The mediated model competes primarily with country-level comparative low labor costs and less on the basis of skill or competence advantage (Carmel and Tjia 2005). Chinese firms face Japanese IT firms that maintain arguably the best quality control and most sophisticated process management in the world. Chinese process management capabilities lag behind in this. For example, in 2005 only 21.6 per cent of the software services businesses in Beijing had been certified as CMM/CMMI level 3 or above, and only one of them reached CMMI level 5.

Drivers of the Mediated Model. The drivers of the mediated model are multifold. Perhaps the primary ones are the lagging maturity in process capabilities and the fragmented market comprised of small sized firms (OECD 2007). The largest Chinese vendor, Neusoft, has only 9,000 employees (Neusoft 2006). The mediated model allows firms of small size and with limited process capabilities to enter the market. Indeed, the low entry barriers have triggered high levels of entry by new firms in China

(Vashistha and Vashistha 2006). The growth has occurred despite the limited supply of managerial resources with experience in the software industry or prior experience in the client industry (Ju 2001).

The mediated model also helps to overcome the lack of robust partnership networks overseas. Chinese software firms are found to have weak partnership networks compared to their Indian counterparts (Wu et al. 2005).

The mediated model overcomes some of the obstacles related to work culture and legal system. Although geographically, culturally, and linguistically, Chinese firms have an advantage with the Japanese clients compared to the Indian or Western firms, there are still major differences. The Chinese mentality of "cha-bu-duo" ("close enough is good enough") promotes ad hoc work practices. The mediated model lowers the client risk from these work practices. Gupta and Raval (1999) suggest that cultural issues can "make or break an offshore project."

Finally, the mediated model also increases the client's control over issues that pose legal risks. Chinese legal system, while improving, is an important impediment to China's growth as an offshoring destination (OECD 2007). The mediated model protects clients against what is characterized in the literature as a weak contract and intellectual property system in China (Kennedy and Clark 2006). Rottman and Lacity (2006) report that firms break projects into smaller ones to protect intellectual property. By distributing smaller segments among different suppliers, no one vendor sees enough of the project at any one time to understand it fully and exploit this understanding opportunistically.

Operational capabilities in software services firms

Although the mediated model accommodates the broader environment in which Chinese firms operate, little is known about operational capabilities that allow firms to succeed with the mediated model. The existing literature on IT outsourcing has identified three classes of capabilities with vendor success (Levina and Ross 2003): (1) client-specific capabilities (2) process capabilities, and (3) human resources (HR) capabilities.

Client-specific capabilities focus on relational routines and resources that align vendor activities with the client's goals and priorities on a short- and long-term basis (Levina and Ross 2003; Ethiraj et al. 2005). The vendor must develop an understanding of the client's business and design cost-effective communication and interaction patterns (Rajkumar and Mani 2001). The vendor must have sufficient knowledge of the business (e.g., banking), the functional domain (e.g., stock trading), and the specifics and idiosyncrasies of the client's operating environment. The vendor's interactions with clients must help clarify expectations and establish a sense of client trade-offs (user needs versus budget limits). Ongoing communication must clarify priorities, anticipate resource requirements, and report on issues and changes in project status.

Process capabilities relate to task delivery routines and resources that accomplish software design, development, and execution (Levina and Ross 2003; Ethiraj et al. 2005). The capabilities reflect technical competences, skills, and resources in systems and software development processes. The capability maturity model (CMM) developed by the Software Engineering Institute (SEI) at Carnegie Mellon University is commonly used to improve software development processes. However, CMM/CMMI requires substantial discipline and explicit learning investments in infrastructure, systems, and training programs (Ethiraj et al. 2005). This is likely to be the main reason for the relatively low percentage of Chinese vendors with higher levels of CMM/CMMI certification.

Human resources capabilities are associated with recruiting practices, training and mentoring programs, designing jobs with a balanced mix of specialization, exposure to a variety of project tasks, and developing performance appraisal and compensation systems (Levina and Ross 2003; Ferratt et al. 2005). Rotating employees across projects and tasks gives them opportunities to learn new skills and interact with different team members (Argote 1999). Individual career development plans, promotion from within, and alternative career hierarchies are all associated with beneficial effects on human resources capabilities (Levina and Ross 2003).

Levina and Ross (2003) found in a study of a large U.S. vendor that the three operational capabilities had to be simultaneously present and mutually reinforcing each other. Their findings suggest that making choices among the three capabilities might be misguided, as all three capabilities must be developed in concert.

In the offshoring context, Ethiraj et al. (2005) examined client-specific and process management capabilities in the context of a large Indian offshore vendor. They found both capabilities to be associated with firm performance. The project management capabilities helped to maximize internal operational efficiencies, and improve quality and profitability in the rapidly maturing Indian software industry that targets offshore markets. In the software development literature more broadly, many have found that the increased levels of formalized routines in systems development improve quality and productivity (e.g., Herbsleb et al. 1997; Krishnan and Kellner 1999).

For client-specific capabilities, Ethiraj et al. (2005) note the key role of personnel used by offshore vendors at the client site (the so-called on-site personnel). A similar finding was reported by Kaiser and Hawk (2004), who examined the development of vendor and client capabilities among a large Indian vendor and its U.S. financial services clients. The on-site personnel were critical to ensure robust communication channels and develop a long-term relationship between the firms. In her study of a small Russian and Indian provider, Levina (2006) found the boundary spanning practices of middle managers at the client organization to be more critical for effective collaboration than the middle managers at the provider organization. Outside the offshoring and outsourcing literature, such middlemen are often labeled as relationship managers, account managers, client executives, or consultants (Iacono et al. 1995; Brown 1999).

In terms of human resources capabilities, Ethiraj et al. (2005) only mention the need to invest in training programs in new technologies and software processes for both developers and managers. Others, not specific to the offshoring literature, have noted that human resources practices are closely aligned with firm strategy (Youndt et al. 1996). Ferratt et al. (2005) review two human resources archetypes. Archetype 1 has a short-term transactional orientation that puts lower emphasis on firm-specific investments in terms of formal training and mentoring. Archetype 2 has a longer-term relationship orientation that puts greater emphasis on worker participation in firm decisions, and on significant investment in formal training and mentoring. Following the notion of "fit" (see Ferratt et al. 2005), firms competing primarily on comparative labor cost advantage would be expected to emphasize Archetype 1.

Development of operational capabilities in the mediated offshoring model

The mediated model has implications for the development of operational capabilities. The mediated model is associated with *small project size*, *low value-adding tasks*, and *limited interaction with the end-client*. Qu and Brocklehurst (2003, 64) note that "most Chinese suppliers are not even aware who the end-users are." Others have noted that Chinese firms have little contact with the end-user's business except for at certain stages of project such as field support.[3] This limits the acquisition of client-specific capabilities, particularly business domain knowledge and the development of robust communication routines. The high-level and high-paying work is retained by the Japanese IT firms, which leaves low level work to the

Chinese vendors. The low level work demands low technical skills from the Chinese developers. Therefore, the mediated model can also impede the development of human resources capabilities. Small-sized projects, low-valued tasks, and limited end-client interaction limit the degree of employee specialization as well as the variety of tasks that they are exposed to. In such an environment, the firms are challenged to develop meaningful business career paths.

Although the mediated model can be constraining in terms of capabilities development, we counter-argue that Japanese-Chinese offshore outsourcing presents an environment in which Chinese vendors are able to overcome – at least partially – some of these constraints and develop their capabilities incrementally. Since the Chinese vendors work with Japanese clients (Japanese IT companies), which tend to possess strong process capabilities, it is an opportunity for the Chinese firm to learn and gain maturity. Also, the projects involve substantial knowledge transfer from the client to the vendors in terms of business knowledge and project management know-how. Japanese clients maintain a hands-on approach to project management, which allows them to assess quality, progress, and costs, and to take intervening actions if necessary, as they do in other industries (Liker and Choi 2004). The client's technical experts often remain on the vendor site for an extended period to introduce business requirements to the project team, perform design reviews, and monitor quality.

Learning Mechanisms for Developing Capabilities. How are Chinese firms exploiting these opportunities to develop their capabilities, despite the constraints of the mediated model? In the remainder of the chapter, we take a learning perspective of the development of operational capabilities (Zollo and Winter 2002). Zollo and Winter (2002) distinguish between two types of learning mechanisms in capabilities development in large firms: (1) deliberate and explicit firm-specific investments and (2) implicit "learning by doing." The deliberate investments involve explicit knowledge articulation and knowledge codification mechanisms and require greater managerial and financial resources than the passive experiential processes of learning by doing. The explicit investments involve the time and energy to engage in collective discussions, performance evaluation processes, and codification of knowledge in the form of manuals, blueprints, and project management software. The implicit learning by doing involves repeated and cumulative experiences. Both implicit and explicit categories of learning mechanisms result in improved performance, although the degree of improvement can be affected by a variety of factors, such as internal organizational processes and structures (Eisenhardt and Martin 2000).

The mix of learning mechanisms also depends on the characteristics of the capabilities to be developed (Zollo and Winter 2002). Ethiraj et al. (2005) argue specifically that implicit and tacit experience by doing is the dominant learning mechanism for client-specific capabilities, whereas improvements in process capabilities require explicit learning investments in infrastructure, systems, and training programs. By inference, Ethiraj et al. (2005) argue for explicit investments in human resources capabilities development.

Importantly, Ethiraj et al. (2005) focus on large firms. Zollo and Winter (2002) focused on large firms in mature economies and industries. We know of no study that has explicitly examined capabilities development in small- and medium-sized offshore software services firms, although studies exist on capabilities development in call centers (Pan et al. 2005) and IT hardware component sourcing (Wu 2006).

About this research

Data collection took place in two phases. During the summer of 2004, the two researchers conducted 12 interviews to obtain a broad view of the software services industry in China. A diverse group of interviewees included developers (team and project leaders), a user managers, senior managers, business consultants, the senior analyst of a research firm, and founders and CEOs of software firms. The interviews were all held in Beijing and involved Americans, Chinese, and expatriate Chinese, representing diverse enterprises that included a start-up, state-owned enterprise, foreign companies, and private Chinese firms.

The second phase took place during the summer of 2005 and involved case studies in four software services firms in Beijing, China. The four firms in Beijing were selected for three reasons. First, Beijing represents the largest base for software development and export, as well as the most rapid pace of growth in China. Second, the researchers had connections or could obtain referrals to the four firms in Beijing. Third, although all four firms were exporting software services, they varied in terms of background, size, and software services. Two of them were considered well-established services providers to Japan, whereas the other two were recent entrants to Japanese-Chinese outsourcing. One of the latter two was already established in American-European export markets. Three of them had been founded by Chinese entrepreneurs and were under the control of Chinese managers at the time of the study. The other one was a joint-venture of the Japanese IT firm and a Chinese research institution. Although the ownership and management of this Japanese joint-venture was quite different from the others, we decided to keep it in the analysis to provide a contrast to the other three firms (see Tables 4.1 and 4.2)

Table 4.1   Profile of the companies studied

Company	Primary services to Japan	No. of Employees	Starting time	Ownership	Market
A - high growth publicly held firm.	Testing, coding, design, architectural design.	1200+ (72)[a]	1995	Listed on Hong Kong Stock Exchange, initially held by management and Japanese clients with minority interests of less than 15%.	90+% to Japan.
B - Slow growth small firm.	Testing/ coding, some design.	130 (60)	2001	Management& Japanese minorities.	96% to Japan, 4% in China.
C - Established firm, new to Japanese market.	Staffing, some development.	700+ (20)	1995	Management, and strategic investors lately.	90% Euro-US, 10% to Japan.
D - Slow growth joint-venture.	Middleware software services.	576 plus 100+ contractors.	1994	Japanese parent-90%. Local partner-10%.	99% to Japan.

[a] All numbers in Table 4.1 were based on Summer 2005 data, and those in parentheses indicate the number of employees in Japan

Table 4.2   General background of the companies studied

Company	Background
A - High growth publicly held firm	Started up by two former university classmates, previously an experienced developer in Japan and a software sales representative in China for a multinational. Publicly listed on Hong Kong Stock Exchange in 2004. One of the largest vendors in China, with over 10 subsidiaries in China, and one in Japan, in 2006.

Table 4.2 Continued

Company	Background
B - Slow growth small firm	Founders previously worked in a Japanese joint-venture company in China, or Japan.
	Worked with many different clients and various types of projects.
	Much of the initial work had been at the lower end of the value chain but increasingly moving up to higher value-adding work.
C - Established firm, new to Japanese market	Ranked among the top ten offshore vendors in China, founded by four former university classmates.
	Outsourcing business to the Japanese market since 2003.
	Initially staffing by internal people, and after some setbacks replaced them with Chinese developers with Japanese work experience.
D - Slow growth joint-venture	The Japanese parent IT firm and a Chinese research institution held 90% and 10% of the stakes respectively. 90% of the business was in middleware and platform software, e.g., web server, database server, directory server, and storage server.
	Technological expertise spanned over 30 to 40 different middleware products, plus mobile application software, and quality control tools.
	The CEO emphasized, "we are a technology company."

Results

In our analysis, we organized the case studies around the three types of capabilities identified as critical for vendor success in the existing outsourcing and offshoring literature (Levina and Ross 2003; Ethiraj et al. 2005): client-specific capabilities, process capabilities, and human resources capabilities. Furthermore, we explored the learning mechanisms (Zollo and Winter 2002) in the development of these capabilities in the context of the mediated model of offshoring.

As synthesized in Table 4.3 and Figure 4.2, all of the four firms relied heavily on tacit knowledge accumulation in building the client-specific capabilities, although deliberate investments in firm-specific structures and processes were also evident in the case data but to a lesser extent. The accumulation of learning about the client's business domain and hence the development of client-specific capabilities were strongest at middle and top management levels. The top management brought years of experience in responding to clients' needs and their business networks, or lack thereof, in Japan. The repeated interactions had developed high levels of familiarity between the management of the vendor and the client. Staff at lower levels of the firms had many fewer opportunities to gain customer-specific capabilities including domain knowledge.

Table 4.3   Learning mechanisms of the capabilities

Capabilities	Learning mechanisms
Client-specific	Top management's overseas work experience, familiarity with the client culture, focus on long-term relationship with clients, and ability to creatively adapt client procedures to suit the Chinese context.
	Infrastructure development to cater to client needs in safety and security measures, separate venues and work units, and communication channels for client.
	Extensive use of onsite staffing and bridge engineers, including native Japanese; decentralized quality control (QA) function to cater to client needs.
	Having client expert onsite; participating in training sponsored by clients.
Process	ISO 9000:2000, CMM certification and related training; employee work report; standardized requirements documentation, templates, and design review procedures.
	Adopting the client company's procedures, tools, QA systems, and philosophy ("accounting approach" to process management, "quality first" and productivity).
	Deliberate effort in learning by doing, and then fixed as standard processes; extensive effort in "optimizing" ISO processes based on client needs.
	Learning from clients, e.g., by applying a U.S.-based major client's sophisticated testing procedures for Japanese clients; Managerial training.
Human resources	Middle managers received external training; hiring fresh graduates and providing training regardless of firm sizes, and experienced expatriates; systematic career development systems.
	Frequent visits by employees to the client firm; cultural blending activities; employees' self-driven learning.
	"People-oriented" philosophy; flat organizational structure and friendly work environment; Japanese language training, opportunity to work overseas on client sites, and pay rises to motivate employees.
	Adopting tools and platforms in Japanese language; team-building camps, and mandatory half a year's language training; employee development programs.

Similar to client-specific capabilities, process capabilities were developed from both deliberate investments and experience accumulation, although here, the explicit investments were more apparent than the development of client-specific capabilities. Most of the firms also made proactive investments in deliberate learning of project management tools and methodologies. The firms had pursued CMM process maturity competences to varying extents, and more importantly each firm had adapted the standard processes to their circumstances. The nature of the projects and the interface with the client, who possessed not only domain knowledge

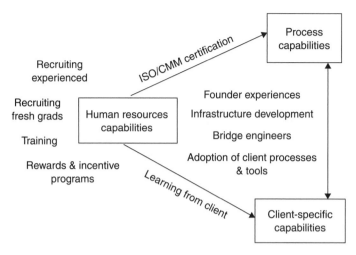

Figure 4.2   Learning mechanisms in the four cases

but also process capabilities and technical skills, appeared to be determining factors. This is a unique feature of the mediated model influencing the mix of learning mechanisms by the Chinese vendors.

The practice of developing human resources capabilities was a response to the constraints of limited firm financial and managerial resources as well as to the turnover of lower level staff, which were common in such a mediated business model. Skill development, promotional policies, encouragement, and incentives remained somewhat ad hoc, except in Company C. Most visible learning and improvements took place at middle levels.

Next, we discuss how the firms appeared to have overcome the constraints of the mediated model and have been able to develop their capabilities. It is worth noting that one of the four companies, Company D, was a 90 per cent Japanese subsidiary, therefore it was not representative of the China vendors in general and should be used as a reference only for comparison.

Company A – high growth publicly held firm

Client-specific Capabilities. To a large extent, Company A's capabilities development occurred implicitly via close coupling with its clients. The bulk of the company's business came from a couple of very large Japanese IT firms who served end-user clients in the banking and securities industry (e.g., electronic trading solutions).

Initially, the President of the firm and co-founder had brought with him years of experience in responding to the clients' needs and their business networks in Japan. These repeated interactions had developed high levels of familiarity with the business domain and practices of the client. According to the President,

> trust with Japanese clients has evolved to such a stage over time that I can sign a contract without looking at the financial details. If I lose money on a particular project, they will make it up with extra in the next contract to me. If I bid 100 man-months and ended up using 80 only, we'd do more on usability and user interfaces, so that we are not too far off. If my client has to cancel a project, and asks me to share some of the loss, I'd do it because I know they'll pay me back in the next project.

The President continued, "This is hard for the Indian companies to do, coming from a Western contract-based culture. This is at the root of eastern agricultural economies, which is something common between Chinese and Japanese culture." On an ongoing basis, much of the learning of client-specific capabilities occurred implicitly at the project level through the Japanese technical experts who the clients sent to the vendor site.

Company A had also made explicit investments to stay closely connected with the clients. But so did their clients. Company A's divisions and departments were structured with direct correspondence to the clients. In some cases, a client paid for a fixed charge to retain a department on long-term contracts for staff stability and guaranteed availability. This allowed the vendor to develop a workforce with a high level of domain knowledge in a client's business. The staff for different clients were housed in different geographic locations, as a way to manage security and protect customer confidentiality. In some cases, the technical development environments were physically disconnected from the company's infrastructure but connected with that of the client. Company A also had dedicated on-site personnel, so-called "bridge engineers," for major projects at the client sites. Bridge engineers handled the day-to-day interaction between the client and the offshore vendor site.

Process Capabilities. Company A's process capabilities originated from the President's creative adaptation of the methodology he had learned in Japan to the local culture and client needs. The company continued to develop process capabilities via learning from the technical experts sent to the vendor site and from "the bridge engineers." The project teams used the client's software design and building platforms. Estimates of potential workload were based on prior projects with the particular client.

Compared to learning from the clients via experience and adopting their sophisticated processes, it was less important for the firm to invest extensively in standard processes and quality standards beyond a certain degree. Two of the company's departments passed CMM 2 in 2002, but the company had made a conscious decision not to pursue CMM 3. One project manager remarked, "CMM is a reference point for us: the client requirements are our guiding principles." A developer remarked, "we do not practice quality here as a straightjacket." To be responsive to client needs, the quality assurance function was decentralized. Most of the quality personnel resided within the departments serving specific clients. There was only a small central quality assurance group.

Human Resources Capabilities. Naturally, the frequent changes in requirements and rigid process adherence featured in the mediated model were not always welcomed by the developers. One of them described how in one project, 90 per cent of the team quit because of fatigue and the lack of recognition of individual contributions. The developers also resented the fact that their development environments were constrained by the client's needs and that they had little opportunity to gain skills on new platforms. One described the work environment as "'blue-collar' style, equipped with basic furniture and crowded, and offices scattered in the city for cost-saving." The developers complained about the lack of challenging projects that involved new technologies. The task features imposed a challenge for human resources capabilities development to identify and train the people with the right skill set and attitudes. The company's strategy was focused on operational efficiency at the low level of coding and unit testing, which involved lower risks and required fewer capabilities. However, this meant low-level and low value-adding work for developers.

A key mechanism for human resources capabilities was recruitment. At the entry level, the company preferred to hire fresh college graduates as the main source of developers and then provide initial training for them. It was believed that people who had already worked for three to five years became hard to train and inculcate with the company values. Training was conducted in a centralized intensive mode for three months, consisting of Japanese language training and working on prior client projects. Through this explicit process, codified knowledge was shared and transferred to new employees. Much of the task-specific and client-specific training occurred on the job later on.

Company B – slow-growth small firm

Client-specific Capabilities. Similar to the case in Company A, a director of Company B attributed his firm's client-specific capabilities to "our senior management's experience in working with Japanese clients." The senior management had much tacit knowledge of the clients' operations and stayed in close daily contact with the client's project personnel. For middle and lower level personnel, developing client-specific capabilities was more challenging. Company B obtained disparate and relatively small projects from a diverse set of clients. A project manager described their work as "hard bones with little meat to bite."

Process Capabilities. Company B was still searching for the optimal mix of deliberate and experiential learning mechanisms to build its process capabilities. As the smallest and youngest company in our sample, Company B faced the biggest resource constraint. One of the examples given by a project manager was very telling of the reliance on ad hoc implicit learning. Many of his projects "came with tight schedules and changing objectives. As a result, there were many versions to manage, a modification might affect not only just one module, but all modules need to be inspected for the rippling effect." It was only through trial-and-error and gradual accumulation of experience that the project team figured out an approach in response. Their devised approach was to have full multirounds of internal discussion aimed at thorough understanding of the design. This approach was also used to deal with the client's desire for a joint discovery of requirements. As another example, an individual programmers' first reaction to technical challenges was to get on the Internet or follow other forms of self-learning, rather than use the formal institutional infrastructure for support.

As the company grew and projects became larger, the increasingly complex work put pressure on it to move away from ad hoc practices to developing a more disciplined approach. "Initially, we had no methodological guidance for estimation and resourcing but after many setbacks we developed our own system of project management," noted the quality manager. Some of the major clients, especially those who had developed closer relationships with the company through a history of successful past projects, had also sent their personnel to the company to train developers in process management.

To enhance its process capabilities, Company B augmented its learning from clients by investing in both standard processes and certification. The firm had achieved 1SO 9000 certification and was planning for CMM 3 at the time of our data collection. Part of the task of the central quality group was to optimize ISO processes, understand CMM requirements, and consolidate CMM and ISO into the firm's processes. This work was very hands-on. The quality manager reported: "Right now, Q/A is involved in the full process of product development, but once the processes are mature, we [Q/A] might just follow the key points." However, Company B struggled with finding the right balance between best-in-class processes and the client's tight delivery deadlines. A manager commented: "Indeed, we have improved our competence through doing outsourcing for Japanese clients. Our clients have strict quality processes. We follow their processes as much we can and in the process, improve our own abilities." One of the founders noted that

> *our Japanese clients do not care much about the level of CMM because Japanese companies have their own procedures and processes. We are building a quality system to develop our own processes, a uniformed system to respond to all kinds of requirements from Japan. It allows a common response to all scenarios.*

Human Resources Capabilities. The strategy to develop human resources capabilities was similar to that of Company A, especially in terms of recruitment practices. The company hired entry-level developers mostly from universities in Beijing, whereas the middle tier was recruited from job fairs. New staff were asked to attend new employee training programs and re-do a previously completed project to accumulate experience. As in Company A, Company B's human resource practices aimed to promote Japanese business customs that stressed the needs of the client company. Moreover, the company retained a large percentage of the team on-site. The opportunity to work in Japan was used as both a reward and employee development practice.

Company C – established firm, new to the Japanese market

Client-specific Capabilities. Having been used to conducting business with Western clients, Company C found that learning client-specific capabilities in the Japanese market had been challenging. The CEO noted that it took two to three years of work with Japanese customers before gaining their confidence. Technological know-how was not an entry barrier, but trusting relationships were important, as "steady business comes after trust is established." Because of the differences in business practices and customs, the firm was able to leverage little of its international reputation with European and U.S. clients in Japan. To overcome this constraint, the firm used its human resources practices to build client-specific capabilities. The firm had hired several seasoned Chinese managers with work experience in Japan to develop client relationships.

Process Capabilities. As in the other companies, process capabilities were also built via learning from the clients as well as deliberate investments in certification. Company C heralded its superior ability to learn from clients by sending its personnel to the client's training courses. One of the founders explained: "We send employees to our clients' project management training courses. We have adopted many procedures from our customers including their internal quality tools." Company C passed ISO 9000 quality certification in 2004 and CMM 3 certification in December 2006, partly because its U.S. clients valued the CMM certification. Regarding Japanese clients, a manager explained, "The Japanese have different methodologies, but still the general process thinking is the same. We can leverage our process management successes from the U.S. and European side in our Japanese business." In practice, this meant meeting the internal quality frameworks of Japanese clients using the CMM and ISO reference points internally.

Human Resources Capabilities. Company C had the most extensive and deliberate human resources capabilities among the four companies. The CEO's motto was, "great people come through good HR processes," which highlighted the central importance of human resources capabilities. The company had an extensive internal training program that focused not only on technical skills but also on cross-cultural and client management as well as process management. Such extensive training was exceptional in the software services industry in China. The company was known for its emphasis on learning and team-oriented culture. All of its senior managers had earned their EMBA degree on a part-time basis. After three years of service, employees were sponsored to study for a master's degree in software engineering from top software engineering schools.

Although the recruitment practice was similar to that of the competitors, Company C invested more in formal training of entry level and middle level employees. For example, fresh graduates were given three months of training, conducted by two outside companies. For a project manager hired from overseas, he or she would be brought back to Beijing for at least one week for orientation and cultural immersion.

To complement deliberate learning mechanisms, the firm also created an environment to facilitate experiential learning. When asked for examples, the General Manager of Japanese operations mentioned that despite the multimillion losses in his initial management responsibilities, he was still trusted by founders and given more opportunities. A junior employee compared his experience with his previous employer and noted how Company C went out of its way to assign work that leveraged his talents and strengths. Managers knew their employees well through social and training camps, which were exceptional among Chinese offshore firms.

Company D – slow-growth joint-venture firm

Client-specific Capabilities. Because Company D was a joint-venture of its client (a Japanese IT firm), developing firm-specific capabilities was less of a priority. The senior management had previously worked in the client company. Members of the core team for key projects visited the parent company to experience the culture and to get to know the client. The company also invested and participated in cultural exchange visits to Japan organized by third parties for selected employees. One of the project managers told us that she had visited Japan seven or eight times during the last five years.

Process Capabilities. Compared to the other three firms, Company D invested heavily in quality certification processes and formal training curricula. The firm was the first software company in Beijing to reach CMM 5, and the third or fourth in China. The strong emphasis on process capabilities and deliberate learning was consistent with the nature of project tasks, as Company D was specialized in software product development, mostly in complex middleware. According to the CEO, the reasons for CMM 5 certification included: (1) it was "considered important to outsiders, particularly as we try to enter the Chinese market;" (2) it could serve as "a reference point to the current quality system and help enhance the current process;" and (3) it could help improve an employee's pride in the company. Furthermore, by implementing explicit assessment of process capability, the company could gauge gaps and implement targeted improvements, and become the "No. 1 in quality and productivity in China" as a software services vendor. At the project level, the company claimed to have achieved deeper analysis and improved estimation skills. The CMM 5 had led to the development of a risk management capability.

Human Resources Capabilities. The general recruitment practices of the firm were similar to those of competitors (e.g., targeting fresh university graduates for entry-level jobs), but also varied to some extent. For example, consistent with the nature of project tasks, the company had a high ratio of advanced degree holders (25% had a masters or PhD). The company emphasized management training and preferred to promote from within. Developers interviewed by us also expressed a strong motivation and belief in continuous learning, and recognized its importance.

To recap across the four cases, different firms emphasized somewhat different capabilities and employed different mechanisms to suit the mediated business model. Some of the contingency factors that appeared to affect capabilities development and learning mechanisms were vendor scale, project tasks, and client relationships. What also surfaced was the necessary foundation of human resources capabilities.

Discussion

This study addresses an important issue for researchers and practitioners of offshoring of software services: how do offshore vendors develop their capabilities in a mediated offshoring business model? We used the three-part organizing framework for operational capabilities of the Levina and Ross (2003) study on outsourcing. The same capabilities have been studied by Ethiraj et al. (2005) in the offshoring context and found to relate to an offshore vendor's project success, but the vendor was a large established one in India providing offshoring services to the U.S.

Our study focused on small and medium-sized firms that do their business as subcontractors to Japanese IT firms to carry out tasks such as software testing and coding. In relation to the extant literature and theoretical background, we made three important arguments. First, we suggested that the mediated model can help overcome some of the challenges that small and medium-sized Chinese firms face, including their small size, low maturity of process capabilities, and the weak legal environment, although the mediated model can also constrain the development of certain operational capabilities. Second, moving beyond the prior literature on the three types of capabilities, we further examined their relationships in the mediated model and identified the pivotal role of human resources capabilities. Third, we have integrated the three types of capabilities and the contingency factors into a synthesized model (shown in Figure 4.3), and examined their two-way relationships between the capabilities and contingency factors. The latter are also seen as the outcome of capabilities development in a dynamic model.

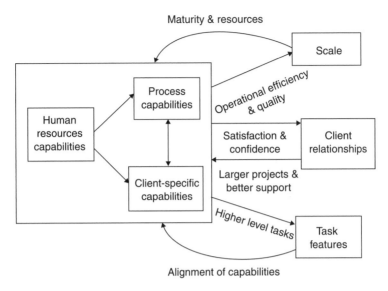

Figure 4.3   The full model of capabilities development

The mediated model

All four companies studied have been in existence for several years. All of them were considered financially solvent according to the industry experts. The mediated model has also allowed considerable growth and financial success in two of the firms, and strong performance in the other two. In particular, Company A was ranked among the top five Chinese firms providing offshoring software services to Japan (in terms of revenues). Company C was ranked among the top ten offshoring firms in China.

The more successful firms have managed to incrementally develop their capabilities following a successive path that allowed them to move from coding and unit-testing work, to functional design, conceptual design, and even architectural design. Moving to larger and higher-level projects allowed the Chinese firms to deliver greater cost advantage and reap higher profitability, provided that satisfactory quality and on-time delivery could be assured.

The case studies suggest that the mediated model affects capabilities development; but rather than constraining, the mediated model shifts the development of capabilities from the vendor's organizational boundaries to the "extended organizational forms" (Aron and Singh 2005). Long-term close relationships with clients facilitate the transfer of domain knowledge, IT technical knowledge, and process management.

Human resources capabilities appeared to be constrained by the mediated model. In some of the firms, only low level ("blue collar") work is assigned to the vendor. In such a model (as in manufacturing), scale and operational efficiency are important for the vendors. The work can be tedious and result in low morale. Some of the Chinese developers conveyed the sentiment that they feel that they are required to act passively, doing everything according to the design specifications, without any need to think for themselves.

The constraint on human resources put pressure on the firms to invest in recruitment, development, and appraisal processes that fit with their strategy. Whereas firms shared common recruiting approaches, they also exhibited different human resources practice archetypes in training and employee development. For example, Companies A and B followed Archetype 1: short-term orientation, reliance on recruiting rather than developing personnel, and lower emphasis on firm-specific investments in ongoing employee training. In contrast, Companies C and D were more of Archetype 2: longer-term orientation, promotion from within, significant investment in training, and development. The finding might appear surprising, given that the mediated model is seen to be primarily competing on efficiency and comparative low labor costs, which suggests Archetype 1. A closer examination of the cases reveals that the differences can be accounted for with the contingency factors such as project tasks, vendor scale, and client relationship.

Similar to the prevailing offshore models described in the literature (Kaiser and Hawk 2004; Ethiraj et al. 2005; Levina 2006; Oshri et al. 2007), the mediated model accommodated vendor personnel ("bridge engineers") at the client site. However, the bridge engineers' role was "narrowed" compared to what has been described with the nonmediated offshore models. For example, Kaiser and Hawk (2004) describe how the on-site vendor personnel accomplished requirements determination for new applications and even conducted performance reviews for the client technical personnel. In the mediated model studied here, the bridge engineers' role seemed to be more limited in terms of functions as well as client access. Particularly early on in the projects, the access was limited but widened as the project moved to testing and maintenance phases. The limited access was overcome by top management's prior experience in Japan and their ongoing close involvement in the projects.

The mediated model also required high levels of vendor flexibility and adaptive capability. With Japanese clients, requirements were specified at a high level at the start of the project. The requirements had to be further identified and specified while the software was being developed. This led to the client's sending their own technical personnel to the vendor locations to manage the discovery and identification process. The vendor visits promoted learning, but they also could lead to cultural conflict. China and Japan have different customer service cultures. This is not unique to software services firms but prevails more generally between China and Japan. While Japanese clients tend to strive for perfection in customer services, which leads to frequent changes in the requirements to satisfy their end-clients, Chinese developers are under the influence of their "cha-bu-duo" attitude ("close enough is good enough.") Human resources practices were needed to help employees to deal with these cultural conflicts.

Development of operational capabilities

As illustrated in the case analysis (e.g., see Figure 4.2), the development of client-specific capabilities involved a variety of implicit and explicit learning mechanisms. Client-specific relationships were built on the basis of repeated interactions and contracts, investments in organizational design, and training in the client's service culture. Process capabilities were built by exploiting both implicit and explicit learning mechanisms as were human resources capabilities.

The existing literature (e.g., Levina and Ross 2003) has noted the complementary relationships among the capabilities. Our case studies extend these findings by anchoring human resources as the foundation for the development of the two other capabilities (see Figure 4.2). In the mediated model, each company's success is tied to its capabilities development effort in recruiting various levels of talents, providing training in the client language, culture, technical skills, project management processes, and client-service mentality in the employees to cater to the clients' communication style, business requirements, and processes. The importance of human resources capabilities was stressed by all of the four companies and by interviewees at all levels.

Whereas the four companies exhibited varying degrees of reliance on formal process certification such as ISO and CMM/CMMI, they had a nearly identical approach to recruiting at the entry level and middle level. To some extent, process capability is developed and acquired via a combination of recruiting and training.

In the mediated model, client-specific capabilities are manifested in the effective adoption of the client process, processes and procedures, communication styles, and business knowledge. As one of the managers pointed out, the adoption of client processes and tools was important, and sometimes more so than ISO and CMM standards, because it could facilitate the mediating Japanese IT firm's effort to integrate the final systems, which may have been developed by several parties. In addition to training, client-specific capabilities gradually developed via bridge engineers, staffing on the client site (e.g., for system integration and support), client representatives' visits, and regular communication between the vendor and client personnel. The accumulation and retention of such capabilities also hinged on human resources capabilities. The four cases illustrated slightly different practices in retaining and motivating employees based on their circumstances.

In the mediated model, where the Chinese vendors operated at the low end of the value chain featuring mostly coding and unit-testing, the work was relatively portable and modular, and revenue and productivity were based on fixed estimated man-months. Therefore, cost control was important, which requires operational efficiency via process enhancement and quality assurance to stay within the project budget, schedule, and allowed bug rate. Scaling up was key for the vendors to obtain larger and more profitable contracts, which in return secures resources for explicit learning mechanisms such as CMM certification and richer forms of client engagement, for example, bridge engineers, visits to client sites, and video conferencing and phone calls. Interestingly, Company B had its multiyear projection of head-count growth on its website, as a management objective. Figure 4.3 illustrates these interdependencies among the operational capabilities.

Contingent nature of the learning mechanisms

We identified three factors that appeared to influence the adoption of learning mechanisms, and each of them will be elaborated below. First, the scale of the company is a factor. Larger ones possess more resources, greater bargaining power, and internal specialization of organizational units and individuals (e.g., dedicated QA personal), which led to larger and more profitable projects. Only after firms became larger could they afford the certification (CMM and ISO) and other forms of deliberate learning. Smaller firms such as Company B had to rely more on experience accumulation. For example, as mentioned in the previous section, one of the teams had many problems with the evolving client requirements, and it was only through trial-and-error method that gradually they figured out their own way to deal with this.

Second, the strong orientation to long-term client relationship was a key factor in capabilities development in the mediated model. Through repeated interactions with two to three of its largest clients over time in supplying software services, Company A had developed not only a better understanding of the client's business requirements and customer service culture but also efficient approaches to deal with clients' styles of communication and requirements specification. For example, the company had developed customer-specific development and review check lists. An interesting finding of the four case studies is that in these companies the client relationships tended to grow tighter for mutual gains, along with vendors' capabilities development and maturity. Tighter relationships might result in clients' financial investment in the vendor firm for minority interests, as in Company A and B.

Third, as predicted by Zollo and Winter (2002), a firm's task features (originating from its strategy) tend to exert influence on the learning mechanisms. A comparison between Company A and Company C lends support to this assertion. Company A was a low-cost and high-efficiency firm, achieving its high profitability via a combination of focus on financial services, working with few clients with many large projects, and effective cost control. Both client-specific and process capabilities resided primarily with senior and middle managers. In contrast, Company C had some unique capabilities in software product localization and a diverse range and levels of tasks, which required a more specialized workforce. Company C exhibited the use of extensive deliberate learning mechanisms, including human resources practices of Archetype 2 at all levels of the firm

It is worth noting that this chapter goes beyond Zollo and Winter (2002) by specifying the impact of the capabilities development on the contingency factors in an interactive relationship for the mediated business model. Viewed also as the outcome of capabilities development, the importance of the contingency factors is further emphasized.

Conclusion

Our findings contribute to the stream of research that emphasizes context-specific capabilities. The business model of the offshore vendor impacts its capabilities development. However, the learning mechanisms of capabilities can take on more generic mechanisms. Although the companies varied in the level and value of client-specific capabilities, interactions with clients were part of the mechanisms to develop the capability in the different firms. Of course, some mechanisms can be specific to firms as well. For example, Company A dealt with financial services firms that were particularly concerned with security and privacy. Security procedures that protected client confidentiality were a critical part of customer-specific capabilities.

Whereas this study focused on the offshore vendors' perspective and has obvious implications for them, our findings have implications for clients as well, especially for overseas IT firms seeking cost reduction. In managing relationships with vendors who lack both business domain knowledge and project management capabilities, deep relationships that embed knowledge transfer are critical. Deep relationships can evolve through escalation of project sizes via repeated interaction, to reach co-dependence to maximize mutual gains. However, at least initially, it is the client (the buyer of services) who must make implicit and explicit learning investments to help develop the vendor's capabilities.

Limitations and future studies

This research has several limitations. First, the sample is a convenient one, based on accessibility to vendors. All firms were headquartered in Beijing, where one of the authors is located and has industry contacts. However, our focus on Beijing-based vendors is appropriate, since Beijing is the largest base in China for software exports. Second, as an exploratory study, this research is aimed at identifying issues concerning capabilities development, not to prove or test any theory. Also, our study lacked a longitudinal perspective. Our next step will be to develop hypotheses and launch a survey of capabilities development by Chinese offshore software vendors. Moreover, the offshore outsourcing industry is undergoing a consolidation process involving many merger and acquisition deals to create the necessary scale to compete internationally. This certainly will impact on the firms' operational capabilities and learning mechanisms, and will be an interesting direction for future research. Future research also needs to attend to the financing structures and ownership that are undergoing rapid changes in China.

Notes

1. The literature on offshoring to China (e.g., Feenstra and Hanson 2005; Hsieh and Woo 2005; Kennedy and Clark 2006) focuses on manufacturing and product outsourcing, not services outsourcing.
2. The material was supplemented with interviews with various experts in the industry during July 2004.

3. The material is based on interviews with experts in the industry during July 2004.

References

Analysis International (2007) Analysis International Says China Offshore Software Outsourcing Market Reached RMB 3.315 in Q1 of 2007, http://english.analysys.com.cn/home/index.php, last accessed September 30, 2007.

Argote, L. (1999) *Organizational Learning: Creating, Retaining, and Transferring Knowledge,* Boston, MA: Kluwer Academic Publishers.

Aron, R. and Singh, J.V. (2005). Getting Offshoring Right. *Harvard Business Review,* 83(12): 135–140.

Barney, J.B. (1991) Firm Resources and Sustained Competitive Advantage. *Journal of Management,* 17(1): 99–120.

Borman, M. (2006) Applying Multiple Perspectives to the BPO Decision: A Case Study of Call Centres in Australia. *Journal of Information Technology,* (21) 99–115.

Brown, C.Y. (1999) Horizontal Mechanisms under Differing IS Organization Contexts. *MIS Quarterly,* 23(3): 421–454.

Carmel, E. and Agarwal, R. (2002) *The Maturation of Offshore Sourcing of Information Technology Work. MIS Quarterly Executive,* 1 (2): 65–78.

Carmel, E. and Tjia, P. (2005*) Offshoring Information Technology: Sourcing and Outsourcing to a Global Workforce,* Cambridge, UK: Cambridge University Press.

Dutta, A. and Roy, R. (2005) Offshore Outsourcing: A Dynamic Causal Model of Counteracting Forces. *Journal of Management Information Systems,* 22(2): 15–35.

Economic Daily (2007) Second Batch of Chinese Service Outsourcing Cities, 1/7/2007.

Eisenhardt, K. and Martin, J. (2000) Dynamic Capabilities: What Are They? *Strategic Management Journal,* 21: 1105–1121.

Ethiraj, S.K., Kale, P., Krishnan, M.S., and Singh, J.V. (2005) Where Do Capabilities Come From and How Do They Matter? A Study in the Software Services Industry, *Strategic Management Journal,* 26: 25–45.

Feenstra, R.C. and Hanson, G.H. (2005) Ownership and Control in Outsourcing to China: Estimating the Property-Rights Theory of the Firm. *Quarterly Journal of Economics,* May: 729–761.

Feeny, D., Lacity, M., and Willcocks, L.P. (2005) Taking the Measure of Outsourcing Providers. *MIT Sloan Management Review*, 46(3): 41–48.

Ferratt, T.W., Agarwal, R., Brown, C.V., and Moore, J.E. (2005) IT Human Resource Management Configurations and IT Turnover: Theoretical Synthesis and Empirical Analysis *Information Systems Research* 16(3): 237–255.

Garud, R. and Kumaraswamy, A. (2005) Vicious and Virtuous Circles in the Management of Knowledge: The Case of Infosys Technologies. *MIS Quarterly*, 29(1): 9–33.

Goles, T. (2001) The Impact of Client-Vendor Relationship on Outsourcing Success, Unpublished Ph.D. Dissertation, University of Houston, Houston, TX 2001.

Gonzales, R., Gasco, J., and Llopis, J. (2006) Information Systems Outsourcing: A literature Analysis. *Information & Management*, 43(7): 821–834.

Gupta, U. and Raval, V. (1999) Critical Success Factors for Anchoring Offshore Projects. *Information Strategy*, 15(2): 21–27.

Herbsleb, J., Zubrow, D., Goldenson, D., Hayes, W., and Paulk, M. (1997) Software Quality and the Capability Maturity Model *Communications of the ACM*, 40(6): 30–40.

Hu, W., Chen, Y., Fan, Y., and Cao, K. (2007) Software Outsourcing in Beijing: Fundamentals, Trends, and Implications, Working Paper, Renmin University of China.

Hsieh, C-T. and Woo, K.T. (2005) The Impact of Outsourcing to China on Hong Kong's Labor Market. *The American Economic Review*, December: 1673–1687.

Iacono, C.S., Subramani, M., and Henderson, J.C. (1995) Entrepreneur or Intermediary: The Nature of the Relationship Manager's Job. *International Conference on Information Systems*, 289–301.

Ju, D. (2001) China's Budding Software Industry. *IEEE Software*, May–June: 92–95.

Kaiser, K. and Hawk, S. (2004) Evolution of Offshore Software Development: From Outsourcing to Co-Sourcing. *MIS Quarterly Executive*, 3(2): 69–81.

Kennedy, G. and Clark, G. (2006) Outsourcing to China – Risks and Benefits. *The Computer Law and Security Report*, 22(3): 250–253.

Krishnan, M.S. and Kellner, M.I. (1999) Measuring Process Consistency: Implications for Reducing Software Defects. *IEEE Transactions on Software Engineering*, 25(6): 800–815.

Levina, N. (2006) Collaborating Across Boundaries in a Global Economy: Do Organizational Boundaries and Country Contexts

Matter? Twenty-Seventh International Conference on Information Systems, Milwaukee, 627–542.

Levina, N. and Ross, J.W. (2003) From the Vendor's Perspective: Exploring the Value Proposition in Information Technology Outsourcing. *MIS Quarterly* 27(3): 331–364.

Liker, J.K. and Choi, T.Y. (2004) Building Deep Supplier Relationships *Harvard Business Review*, 82(12): 104–113.

Morstead, S. and Blount, G. (2003) Offshore Ready: Strategies to Plan & Profit from Offshore IT-Enabled Services, ISANI Press, USA.

Neusoft, at http://www.neusoft.com/en/news/html/20060705/778123936. html (last accessed on December 15, 2006).

Nicholson, B. and Sahay, S. (2001) Some Political and Cultural Issues in the Globalization of Software Development: Case Experience from Britain and India. *Information and Organization*, 11: 25–43.

Organisation for Economic Co-operation and Development (OECD) (2007) Is China the New Centre for Offshoring of IT and ICT-enabled Services? March 29 2007, JT03224696.

Oshri, I., Kotlarsky, J., and Willcocks, L. (2007) Managing Dispersed Expertise in IT Offshore Outsourcing: Lessons from Tata Consultancy Services. *MIS Quarterly Executive*, 6(2): 53–65.

Pan, S., Pan, G., and Hsieh, M.J. (2005) A Dual-Level Analysis of the Capability Development Process: A Case study of TT&T. *Journal of the American Society for Information Science and Technology*, 57(13): 1814–1829.

Penrose, E.T. (1959) *The Theory of the Growth of the Firm*, Wiley: New York.

Pries-Heje, J., Baskerville, R., and Hansen, G.I. (2005) Strategy Models for Enabling Offshore Outsourcing: Russian Short-Cycle-Time Software Development. *Information Technology for Development*, 11(1): 5–30.

Qu, Z. and Brocklehurst, M. (2003) What will it Take for China to Become a Competitive Force in Offshore Outsourcing? An Analysis of the Role of Transaction Costs in Supplier Selection. *Journal of Information Technology*, 18(1): 53–67.

Rajkumar, T.M. and Mani, R.V.S. (2001) Offshore Software Development: The View from Indian Suppliers. *Information Systems Management*, 18: 63–73.

Rottman, J.W. and Lacity, M.C. (2006) Proven Practice Effectively Offshoring IT Work. *MIT Sloan Management Review*, 47(3), 56–63.

Sapienza, H.J., Autio, E., George, G., and Zahra, S.A. (2006) A Capabilities Perspective on the Effects of Early Internationalization of Firm Survival and Growth. *Academy of Management Review*, 31(4): 914–933.

Vashistha, A. and Vashistha, A. (2006) The Offshore Nation: Strategies for Success in Global Outsourcing and Offshoring, New York: Mcgraw-Hill.

Vestring, T., Rouse, T., and Reinert, U. (2005) Hedge Your Offshoring Bets. *MIT Sloan Management Review*, 46(3): 27–29.

Willcocks, L. and Lacity, M.C. (2000) Relationships in IT Outsourcing: A Stakeholder Perspective, in R. Zmud (ed.) *Framing the Domains of IT Management*, Pinnaflex Inc. Cincinnati, OH: 355–384.

Willcocks, L. and Lacity, M. (2007) *Global Sourcing of Business and IT Services*, Palgrave Macmillan, London.

Wu, L-Y. (2006) Resources, Dynamic Capabilities and Performance in a Dynamic Environment: Perceptions in Taiwanese IT Enterprises. *Information and Management*, 43: 447–454.

Wu, Q., Klincewicz, K., and Miyazaki, K. (2005) Sectoral Systems of Innovation in Asia: Partnership Networks of Software Companies in China and India. Working paper, Graduate School of Innovation Management, Tokyo Institute of Technology, December 16, 2005.

Youndt, M.A., Snell, S.A., Dean, J.W., and Lepak, D.P. (1996) Human Resource Management, Manufacturing Strategy, and Firm Performance. *Academy of Management Journal*, 39(4): 836–866.

Zahra, S.A, Sapienza, H.J., and Davidsson, P. (2006) Entrepreneurship and Dynamic Capabilities: A Review, Model, and Research Agenda. *Journal of Management Studies*, 43(4): 917–955.

Zollo, M. and Winter, S.G. (2002) Deliberate Learning and the Evolution of Dynamic Capabilities. *Organization Science*, 13(3): 339–351.

CHAPTER 5

Integrated collaboration across distributed sites: the perils of process and the promise of practice

Gary C. David, Donald Chand, Sue Newell, and João Resende-Santos

Introduction

In an era in which a strategic command of global resources is becoming a requisite for success, firms are struggling to successfully encourage collaboration across their onshore and offshore sites (Lipnack and Stamps 2000). This challenge centers on how to distribute work, responsibilities, and leadership across sites and then reintegrate them into a coherent whole, in which decision-making is well-coordinated and workers collaborate effectively to complete tasks. The literature on globally distributed teams generally frames the impediments to coordination and collaboration in terms of communication problems due to the divergent nationally based cultural attributes of the sites, language barriers, and the limitations of information and communication technologies (ICTs) (Kankanhalli et al. 2006–2007; Mihhailava 2007). As a consequence, firms are pursuing a dual strategy of improving the communication infrastructure (in terms of ICTs and formal global process standards) coupled with cultural training. However, in this chapter we consider how this approach only addresses part of the equation for achieving integrated collaboration. Ultimately, globally integrated collaboration requires an approach that allows both the managers and the workers to examine the multitude of shifting factors that are rooted in the *context* of work.

In seeking to explore this context in more detail, we focus on how collaboration is influenced by enacted (rather than espoused) organizational strategy. More specifically, we demonstrate how an enacted organizational strategy can create structural impediments even while this strategy is focused on facilitating collaboration between sites. We do this by drawing on World-systems theory (WS) (Wallerstein 1974, 2005) as a heuristic framework. This encourages a reorientation of the unit of analysis from the attributes of individual sites (and their particular national cultural characteristics) to the social dynamics across sites (and the structural and interactional factors that influence them). By viewing the distributed sites through the World-systems lens, the focus of the problem shifts from the individual work sites or grouping of sites according to national location to the relationships among the sites. In other words, the use of this lens demonstrates how it is important to look at *all* of the distributed sites and their relationships with each other. This allows for a comprehensive view of the factors that contribute to the formation of actual and perceived relationships between sites, groups, and individuals within the context of the broad organizational strategy.

We apply this World-systems framework, coupled with a focus on the use of ICTs, to examine the attempt to build collaboration in the distributed software development department of a financial services company, referred to as GLOBALIS (for "Global IS"). The case illustrates how tensions in social relationships across sites were influenced by the socio-politico-organizational context. Moreover, by focusing on emergent practices, the case also illustrates how some units in GLOBALIS were able to overcome these structural impediments to develop positive social relations that facilitated collaboration.

The rest of the chapter is organized as follows. The next section outlines the traditional approaches to global collaboration and summarizes the theoretical perspectives used in the chapter. This is followed by a description of the case study. We then explore the application of World-systems theory to global collaboration, bringing out the organizational factors that impact effective collaboration. This is followed by an analysis of a project in which the proactive socialization by the project manager enables the team to overcome the impediments of global collaboration. The last section elaborates on the implications of the findings and future directions of research.

Traditional approaches to global collaboration

As companies are attempting to transform themselves from being "multinational" to "global," they are facing the challenges of how to distribute, coordinate, and integrate work across sites. Although global work is not new, the extent to which companies are attempting to achieve cross-site collaboration constitutes a new model of global work. In looking at this issue we can draw on Thompson's (1967) seminal work on task interdependencies. This work identifies the processes through which task inputs are combined to complete a whole piece of work. Thompson identifies three forms of interdependence: sequential (where subtasks are completed in a specified sequence and the output of one task is the input of the next – as in assembly line manufacture); pooled (where subtasks are performed separately and outputs are pooled in an additive way); and reciprocal (where subtasks must continuously interact because the outputs and decisions from one will have a direct impact on the other). Many companies (like GLOBALIS) are attempting to distribute tasks across sites that need to be combined in a reciprocal way to successfully complete the project. This is because expertise is often distributed across sites in ways that do not align well with the various tasks that constitute a particular project and, moreover, because reciprocal interdependence is more likely to lead to innovative solutions. However, as Thompson indicates, this form of interdependency requires more extensive collaboration than would a pooled or sequential approach to task interdependencies. In other words, there needs to be extensive interaction and knowledge flow between members at the distributed sites to complete the project tasks.

Thus, a key challenge of global collaboration is how to effectively accomplish highly interactive project work virtually. Three key issues have been discussed in the literature as helping us understand such distributed collaboration: (1) overcoming cultural differences; (2) developing the ICT infrastructure; and (3) establishing standardized global processes. We next consider each of these issues in turn and illustrate how context is often under-theorized in relation to each area. We then turn to an examination of World-systems theory, which provides a heuristic framework for thinking about this context, and which we then apply to our case.

Culture and distributed collaboration

National and local cultures are seen to impact distributed work (Krishna et al. 2004). The most often-used conception of nationally based culture is provided by Gert Hofstede (1981, 1991). His model includes a national culture ranking across five traits and has been a crucial part of research on global work and cultural diversity training. For example, Søndergaard (1994, 448) found over 1000 citations of Hoftede's 1981 book alone in journal articles during the period from 1980 to September 1993. The traits identified by Hofstede are said to be implanted in the minds of culture members as a type of value programming, and they impact the mindsets, behaviors, and decisions of each cultural member.

Despite the popularity of Hofstede's conceptualization of culture, there has been a growing chorus that questions the validity of Hofstede's findings as well as the applicability of his model. Westrup et al. (2003, 19–20) note that his approach "promotes a static formulation of culture and can easily lead to treating culture as a causal agent." Ford et al. (2003, 9) summarize three main shortcomings of Hofstede's approach, including the points that cultures are: (1) assumed to fall along national boundaries; (2) viewed as static; (3) assumed to be homogeneous and devoid of subcultures. Given that Hofstede's research was conducted in the 1970s, there are concerns over whether the findings are generalizable to today. Avison and Myers (1995, 52) go so far as to say, "the prevailing taken-for-granted view of the culture concept within the IS research community needs to be abandoned." Despite these shortcomings, this conception of culture is often at the base of organizational "cultural training programs," as it is in training hosted by GLOBALIS.

Beyond the limits of the mainstream national cultures framework, Huang et al. (2003) and Galliers (2003) remind us that there are *organizational* cultures and subcultures to consider. Knorr-Cetina (2000) speaks of *epistemic cultures*, which refer to the localized practices expressed by professional cohorts. Van Maanen and Barley (1984) discuss the presence of *occupational communities* in which a group of people share in the same kind of work and derive their identity from that work. As Liberman (1995, 119) observes: "Analyses of intercultural communication too frequently read like they are rule-governed events; however, participants rarely perceive them that way." These studies remind us that greater emphasis needs to be placed on studying how culture and communication manifest themselves in specific *contexts*.

ICTs, global processes and distributed collaboration

In relation to the ICT infrastructure, systems, and databases provide the backbone for performing distributed work. The ICT first enables workers to communicate and engage in collective problem solving, and research has considered how ICT can best support this communication. For example, information systems research on global IT has examined the effective and innovative use of communications tools such as email (Sproull and Kiesler 1986), video conferencing (Meier 2003), and Instant Messaging (Hersleb et al. 2002) in distributed work. Second, since software projects require both application-problem-domain knowledge and technical software engineering expertise, it is also important for the ICT infrastructure to support knowledge management functions. Thus, the focus of knowledge management research in global IT work has been on knowledge transfer in relation to the application problem domain from the client to the vendor organization (Robillard 1999), and the knowledge of policies, processes, and systems from the onshore group to the offshore groups (Tiwana 2004). However, while ICTs are necessary for communication and knowledge sharing in distributed environments, they are by no means sufficient. It then becomes important to look at the social aspects of the context in which this knowledge sharing and interaction are taking place.

The ICT infrastructure will be combined with global processes to facilitate collaboration. That is, there will be formally defined workflows, policies, procedures, metrics, skills, and interfaces across the distributed work sites. Thus, research on process improvement models, such as the Software Engineering Institute's Capability Maturity Model and ISO standards (Bamford and Deibler 1993) and Spice (Dutta et al. 1998), demonstrate how adopting these standards can create improvements in requirements management, project management, configuration management, development methodologies, and testing and validation (Damian et al. 2002). In other words, organizations with matured business processes have well-documented global processes in terms of policies, procedures, workflows, and responsibilities (Hammer 2007).

These standardized processes, along with the accompanying ICT infrastructure, become the environment in which global collaborative work is supposed to take place. However, research also reminds us that technological use, whether of ICT or global processes, in the pursuit of collaborative work is not something that can be planned *a priori* but is something that is *ad hoc* and emergent. As Harper and Hughes (1993, 142) state: "Controlling actions are not then to be looked at simply as the following of procedurally defined rules but as the contingent outcome of processes of interpretation as to how the rules fit the case to hand." Thus, while rules and procedures may give the appearance of establishing order, that appearance often is illusionary. Bannon (1993, 8) echoes this sentiment: "Information-flow diagrams of office activities do not, in any literal sense, specify how work actually is accomplished." It is in the actual doing of the work that collaboration lies, and not the mandates of how work should be done: "people fill gaps in technology, and construe their action together with their peers in ways that are more or less in line with official organizational policy" (Koskinen 2000, 18).

This line of research indicates that while increased availability of communication technologies means that communication *can* take place; it does not mean that it *will* take place. Moreover, more communication does not automatically mean increased collaboration versus, for instance, increased conflict. Likewise, rules and production methodologies do not mean work will proceed in an orderly fashion. People are not "cultural dopes" (Garfinkel 1967) passively following rules and adhering to structural dictates. Rather, they are active participants in the creation of an emergent and situated social order. It then becomes important to understand the impact of organizational procedures and strategies, and how to facilitate collaboration in this global context. The key for organizations, thus, becomes how to provide the environment in which collaboration and cooperation can take place using the tools and processes provided. In other words, context matters, and to understand *how* context matters, we next turn to a consideration of the WS framework.

World-systems theory

Viewing the world as composed of discrete entities, with national boundaries creating the basis for separation, was the dominant perspective in social sciences until a fundamental shift occurred with the advent of World-systems theory by Immanuel Wallerstein (1974, 2005). Skocpol (1977, 1075) notes, "Immanuel Wallerstein's *The Modern World-System* aims to achieve a clean conceptual break with theories of 'modernization' and thus provide a new theoretical paradigm." This paradigm shift provides a lens through which global organizations can be viewed as continuous wholes rather than discrete entities. Doing so allows for attention to be paid to how the relationships between sites create the organizational "reality" of everyday work. Thus, our focus becomes centered on workplace interactions and how these interactions build the structure of the global organization.

There are different versions of World-systems analysis (Skocpol 1977; Evans 1979), and they are exceedingly complex in their totality. We do not intend the use of World-systems (WS) theory in this chapter to be a support for or a refutation of WS theory as it has originally been developed or applied. Rather, we draw inspiration from it as a heuristic device for understanding globally distributed collaborative work, namely that to fully understand the dynamic of collaboration within a distributed organization (especially globally distributed organizations), one must treat the organization as a system rather than focusing on the sites as discrete entities.

There are two foundational ideas in WS theory. The first is to treat the entire world as a self-contained social system, with its own internal logic, mode of operation, unified and complete division of labor, and internal exchange. Or, as Janowitz (1977, 1091) observes in his analysis of Wallerstein, in WS theory "it is necessary to analyze change in terms of the relations among nations, that is, the 'social system' that is created by the linkages among nations." In terms of what defines a world-system, Chase-Dunn and Hall (1993, 856) state, "We use the term *world-system* to refer to the actual social context in which people live and the material networks that are important for everyday life." It is the emphasis on the social context and material networks that we use as a basis for our analysis of globally distributed work.

The second key idea is the system's single division of labor, by which the world economy is functionally and hierarchically separated into core, periphery, and semi-periphery. Since production processes change and shift as a result of technology, the concepts of core and periphery properly refer to the location of production processes in the world economy, and not nation-states per se. At the same time, nation-states are often associated with their position in the world economy, whether it be as core, semi-periphery, or periphery nations. That is, some countries occupy a core-like production position, or periphery-like production position, and so on. While this suggests that countries can move up or down the ladder and change positions over time, such movement is not common and will only occur as the result of a qualitative shift in the production that takes place in that country.

Since profitability and level of technological innovation define and determine the type of production, core countries monopolize high-tech, high-profit enterprises, while the periphery countries are underdeveloped (McCormick 1990, 126). In practice, the core maintains control of technology up until the point that the technology becomes routinized. Furthermore, since core-like production organizations are highly profitable, and involve new technologies, innovation, and the like, they are quasi-monopolies and they *maintain a tight grip on technological innovation*.

However, over time the quasi-monopolies of the core become "self-liquidating." As such they exhaust themselves and their profitability drops. It is only after production becomes less profitable that production (technology) shifts to the periphery. It is at this point that existing technologies might be transferred from the core to the periphery to take advantage of the cheaper labor markets. Thus, while technology can move from the core to the periphery, the *technology typically only moves to the periphery after it has become routinized*, and savings are possible only from cheap labor. In summary, production moves to the semi-periphery, and eventually to the periphery in search of cost-savings from cheap labor.

As a heuristic device for framing our case analysis, WS theory thus focuses our attention on the system of social relationships across the distributed sites of an organization; it draws our attention away from a focus on the deficiencies (or strengths) of individual sites. Moreover, within this social dynamic across sites, we need to identify whether sites operate as core or periphery, and then consider how this pattern of relationships influences collaboration. We turn to explore these dynamics through our case study, presented next.

About this research

GLOBALIS' headquarters is in Boston, MA with multiple solution centers in the New England region. Almost 15 years ago GLOBALIS established solution centers in Texas and Utah, and it has been operating two wholly owned solution centers in Ireland for the last 10 years. Three years ago it launched its first solution center in Gurgaon, India, and a year and a half ago began a full-services solution center in Bangalore. Three years ago our team began observing the development of the GLOBALIS global delivery process in the U.S. (five sites), Ireland (two sites), and India (two sites). For a period of 12 months (July 2005–June 2006) our research team tracked four IT projects using a workplace studies paradigm. This included interviews, site visits, observations of video conferences and conference calls, and frequent discussions with and presentations to GLOBALIS personnel. Interviews were conducted with 40 employees of GLOBALIS, who included six senior management personnel, six project managers, and twenty-eight workers associated with the four projects. Visits to the onshore and offshore sites associated with the project also took place. During these visits, we also observed the nature of the work associated with the project, especially meetings and other situations where people from the various sites interact with one another.

Data analysis and findings

The espoused strategy: creating a unified work environment to support global collaboration

For a variety of reasons, GLOBALIS have explicitly shunned the idea of outsourcing because they want all work to be done in-house. Their stated rationale for going global is simply because they are seeking to find and use the best talent, at the best price. Thus, senior executives in the business have a very clearly stated offshoring strategy – to develop a unified business where work is undertaken collaboratively in globally distributed projects. In its attempts to establish collaboration, GLOBALIS is using approaches used by other organizations, which include implementing and diffusing its organization culture across sites, standardizing both production and communications technologies, cultural training, and occasional travel. We describe these first, and then explore the problems that surfaced despite these attempts to unify the work.

To generate a feeling of a shared community and organization culture, GLOBALIS has created a similar "feel" across sites through interior design, colors, and presence of company symbols. Company executives have repeatedly said, "You can be in Bangalore and you could think that you are in Boston." Although an oversimplification, this speaks to the company's interest in developing a unified workplace.

The methodologies, software, and systems used at the different sites of GLOBALIS are standardized as well. Three years ago when the Bangalore site was launched, GLOBALIS engineered a global delivery model built around an enterprise project planning and monitoring system to identify and allocate worldwide resources based on the time to market, quality, and cost attributes of the project. This enterprise system allows authorized users to track and monitor projects from initial leads to completion with defined templates and procedures to support the intermediate activities. All the sites use the same set of tools for requirements management, configuration management, applications development, testing, and reporting (although they may not use them in the same way). In addition, each site is equipped with a worldwide telephone service, standardized teleconferencing, video conference capabilities, SameTime group ware, email, and mobile devices. Recently, GLOBALIS has made available a variety of "social software," which is intended to facilitate communication and information exchange across and within sites. In summary, in terms of tools, methods, systems, and policies the GLOBALIS sites are essentially identical.

In terms of cultural training, GLOBALIS contracted with a consulting company to train their employees in how to do business with India. This training was a one-day program through which managers would attempt to learn about the traits and characteristics of Indian culture while developing an awareness of their own culture. The training program used the dichotomous cultural categories based on the work of Hofstede and found in much of the writing on national cultures in global organizations. Although efforts were made to caution attendees about overgeneralizing the categories attributed to India, these depictions were the basis of the training, and the basis for drawing attention to potential points of conflict between American and Indian workers. Even though there are GLOBALIS sites in Ireland, there was no training program on doing business with Ireland. Furthermore, Indian employees did not receive training in how to do business with the United States. Rather, the training experienced by Indian employees was more focused on how to work within the organization.

Finally, while travel does take place, it has become a more difficult proposition because of the entry restrictions for foreign nationals into the U.S., the cost of travel, the extensive geographic distribution of work, and also a general unwillingness of American workers to travel overseas (especially for a protracted period of time and to India in particular). Thus, travel has become more limited than most senior managers would like. In addition, when Indian workers do travel to the U.S. for extended periods, the exposure to their American counterparts generally is limited to worksite interactions focused on training.

Despite the best intentions of senior management, the implementation of the approaches outlined thus far has not yielded the intended consequence, with projects often not meeting deadlines or not fulfilling project goals. In many instances, as acknowledged by the managers and employees themselves, this is because collaboration is poor – communication is often slow, knowledge sharing is difficult, and tensions between sites are often high. Turnover is also very high at the Indian and Irish sites. In the next section, we examine why this has occurred, using the World-systems framework to explore how core–periphery relationships between sites developed despite the rhetoric of global unity. This allows us to see how, in some ways, it is the very approaches that the GLOBALIS management has used to try and create unity that have had the opposite effect to that intended, so making collaboration more, rather than less, challenging. Thus, we will examine how these approaches have contributed to creating the barriers they were trying to remove. The case of GLOBALIS demonstrates the potential shortcomings of these approaches.

The enacted strategy: creating core–periphery relationships between sites that undermined collaboration

We will present a series of observations that suggest that attempts to manage global relationships through a standardized, top-down strategy yielded limited positive outcomes, and resulted in social relationships of perceived inequality across sites, actually encouraging perceptions of a great social distance between sites. At the same time, there were positive examples of global relationship management that occurred in certain project teams. These successes had to overcome the core/periphery mentality that developed in GLOBALIS, and did so through the development of an interpersonal and collective (versus intergroup) orientation toward each other. In the final section, we consider how this shift in awareness is the key to facilitating globally distributed collaborative work.

Observation 1: Asymmetrical interactions in technologically mediated communication

We observed monthly video conferences and regular conference calls between New England and other distributed GLOBALIS personnel. For the most part, these meetings were observed at the main corporate offices in Boston. During these meetings, we observed numerous *asymmetries* in the interactions. One asymmetry concerns the times of meetings. The meetings generally took place at 8:00am Eastern Standard Time (EST), which meant that it was 1:00 p.m. in Ireland, 7:00 p.m. in India, 7:00 a.m. in Texas, and 6:00 a.m. in Utah. Thus, people in New England were beginning their workday with a meeting, while workers in Ireland were having their day interrupted and people in Texas, Utah, and India had to work outside their normal work hours.

These monthly video conferences were meant to provide senior managers with the opportunity to report on employee allocations, project status, and potential allocations of future work. However, more open discussions of future directions, organizational strategies, and general brainstorming regarding projects would take place. When a standard reporting format and agenda was followed, the allocation of speaking turns was based on who was next on the agenda. When the meetings took more of a free-form structure, turn allocation was centered on the Boston office, resulting in an asymmetry in which people at the distributed sites were not involved (even those with the technological capacity to be so). Gaze, which is an important component in next speaker selection (Goodwin 1980; Atkinson and Heritage 1984; Heath, 1984), would be directed at those sitting at the table in Boston. Given the way the video conference technology functioned, only the last person to utter an audible sound at a distributed site would appear on the monitor in Boston. If someone did not make any sound during the meeting, they would never be visible to people elsewhere. This resulted in people muting their speaker to avoid being on camera.

Another asymmetry was rooted in who "ran" the meeting, who was able to ask questions, and the nature of those questions. The meeting was "run" by a manager in Boston, meaning time was kept from Boston, the meeting began from Boston, the agenda was followed or altered from Boston, and so on. Questions asked from the distributed sites tended to be clarification questions, while the questions from Boston were accountability questions (why something was not done, project delays, employee allocations, etc.). We did not observe staff from the distributed sites asking accountability questions. Thus, accountability was a unidirectional practice originating from Boston.

Observation 2: Cultural training emphasizing difference

We attended one full-day training program on Indian culture that was designed and delivered by an external consultant to GLOBALIS employees in the New England region, and we were able to carefully review the training materials. The focus of the training was on how to manage the work of GLOBALIS employees at the Indian sites. Despite statements that one cannot generalize the traits of any culture, the training material presented highly stereotypical descriptions of Indian culture, such as the one given below on the lack of initiative in Indian culture:

> Because of the hierarchical nature of Indian society, the most senior or elderly male generally has the most authority in the workplace. There is little tradition in India of individual initiative or innovation. Employees generally wait for instructions and then do as they are told. They don't ask for or desire more responsibility. There is a strict adherence to the division of labor and acceptance of one's roles.

Beyond being stereotypical and condescending, this is also completely wrong. On our visit to India, we heard of the desire for higher-level work, for direct engagement with customers, for added responsibility, for greater research and development. The passage above also completely contradicted statements made by management when marketing the services of the India sites, with these portrayals emphasizing the skills and initiative of "Indian workers." Nevertheless, the cultural training that was provided often framed the interactions between Indian workers and their American counterparts who had received this training, with the Americans explaining problems that were encountered during collaborations with workers in India through the simplistic discourse of cultural differences. In many ways, then, the cultural training was legitimating "sophisticated stereotyping" (Osland et al. 2000).

During our visit to Bangalore and Gurgaon, we asked the Indian workers whether they had received any culture training program on working with their U.S. counterparts. Most of the Indian workers we interviewed barely remembered the training because it was a short three hours of training that focused on how to communicate in English. All they could remember was that they were told not to use the word "but" in their emails. Apparently this advice was meant to counteract the stereotype "Indians can't say no." The way the two training programs are framed, namely U.S. culture training focusing on how to manage work and Indian culture training focusing on how to communicate more precisely, actually establishes a hierarchical relationship between U.S. and Indian sites.

Observation 3: Unequal project and system ownership

Most projects and systems are owned by the Boston site. The Texas and Utah sites own systems that they manage to support their external customers. However, the sites in Ireland and India rarely own systems: during our research we only found two examples of temporary ownership. The Bangalore site owns an Enterprise Problem and Change Management tool used by the various business units within the firm to manage changes and problems in their IT environments. This vendor product was customized by GLOBALIS to fit its business requirements. It is now an eight-year-old enterprise system that has undergone significant enhancements. Although the Bangalore site is responsible for upgrade-type development work and back-end support, the Texas site owns the product and performs requirements gathering and front-line support.

The Ireland1 site owns a program that enables the management of access privileges and ensures security reporting compliance. Its users are all the global business units of GLOBALIS. The product is in "keep the lights on" phase, and there are only two business analysts at a New England site and ten developers and support personnel at the Ireland1 site. Moreover, we were told by those at Ireland1 that the program was handed to them because of too many customer complaints; in other words, the Ireland1 site took over the program when it had become highly problematic. On taking over this program, the Ireland1 site assumed the ownership to develop a center of expertise in computer security in Ireland. However, recently, a decision was made to build an entirely new security system; and the decision has been made that this new product will be owned by another New England site, not the Ireland1 site, much to the consternation of those in Ireland1.

Thus, once a program was moving from maintenance to development mode, it was transferred from outside the U.S. back to Boston.

Regarding the implementation of technology, at one of the monthly video conference meetings, we observed that the manager at the Gurgaon site recommended that GLOBALIS adopt an Instant Messenger tool that the Indian site felt would make communications more effective. This recommendation was quickly rejected. Later we learned that decisions regarding which technology to use and standardize on are initiated and made at the Boston site. Thus, decision-making power lies primarily in the Boston site, with distributed sites retaining less authority regarding what technologies will be used.

These three observations all demonstrate how approaches that were supposed to unify the sites in fact had the opposite effect to that intended. Applying the World-systems framework, we can see how these different approaches helped to generate core–periphery relationships across the sites – the Boston HQ site was able to control interactions through the use of ICT, emphasizing how this site was central or core relative to other sites; the cultural training emphasized differences and reinforced a client-vendor (or core-periphery) mentality; and project ownership was very difficult for remote sites to secure, emphasizing their periphery status. It is hardly surprising that these core–periphery relationships impeded genuine collaboration across sites. Before we turn to our discussion, we introduce two further observations that provide examples of how these core–periphery relationships can be overcome, where more personal relationships are given the opportunity to develop.

Observation 4: Rule-following versus ad hoc'ing

In one GLOBALIS project, we witnessed how rule-following disrupted global relations, while ad hoc'ing the process resulted in building relationships. A team in an Indian development center was assigned to work with a team in an Irish development center. The Irish workers had had prior experience with the customer for the project, while the Indian workers were new to the project and the customer. Because of time constraints, the Irish team wanted to build a prototype based on their knowledge and experience with the customer. They asked the Indian team to start coding from a general set of requirements that the Irish team provided. The Indian team did not want to start work until the requirements were formally specified. While the Irish team felt that Indians were being too process-oriented, the Indian team claimed that they were following the protocols laid out by the organization. The Indian team was following the organizational processes; the Irish team wanted to ad hoc the process.

The team manager of the Indian team happened to travel to Ireland for unrelated training. The manager of the Irish team found out about this visit, and was annoyed that he was not told of this visit, to arrange a possible meeting. The Irish manager invited the Indian visitor to stay for three more days to meet with him and other members of the team. This face-to-face meeting allowed the manager of the Indian team to appreciate the situation of the Irish team and understand that uncertainties needed to be resolved before the system requirements could be thoroughly specified. By the third day, the Indian manager and Irish team were making jokes and developing more of a personal relationship. This resulted in the team members in India and Ireland starting to converse and joke through email, signifying a break-through in the team relationship. The building of the personal relationships among the team members, together with an increased understanding of the project context by the Indian team manager, resolved the conflict and work began on the project. While following the rules disrupted collaboration, ad hoc'ing the process allowed the sides to build a relationship.

Observation 5: "Social engineering" and building relations

The last example also demonstrates the importance of personal relationships in facilitating distributed collaboration. One of the projects we tracked involved a nine-month long human resources and payroll application project, which was the largest attempted by GLOBALIS. The business analysts and systems testers were located in New England, the project management and half of the development team resided in Ireland, and the other half of the development team was in India. The Irish team, who had prior domain knowledge of the project and its requirements, were to recruit and work with the Indian team. The Indian employees, many of whom were new to the organization, had no domain knowledge. Thus, the issue of transferring knowledge and building up the Indian team's capacities became a paramount issue.

A focus of recruitment was the interpersonal skills of the team members. The Irish management team used conference calls to ascertain each Indian applicant's ability to communicate through technology. In fact, interactional competence was given greater importance than technical ability, which was believed to be more easily taught. The project started with a team kick-off, where members were asked to post their photographs, and say something novel or funny about themselves. The managers initiated a buddy system so workers could get to know one another and form a virtual workplace community. Also, some members of the Irish team were sent to India, during which time there was opportunity to exchange personal information, as might occur during a normal workday. Upon return, the Irish workers were able to facilitate relationship development between those who had never met face-to-face, as with the Indian manager in the previous example. By facilitating relationship transfer, the workers ultimately were able to facilitate collaboration.

Discussion and conclusions

Our case demonstrates how the strategic decisions made regarding how work should be done and who should do it can create a global hierarchical structure, even where managers espouse the ideal of a unified company (see Figure 5.1). Since all the strategic decisions concerning the selection of the production technologies, ownership of core programs, and IT alignment with the business are made at the headquarters site in Boston or the neighboring New England sites, from a World-systems framework we can locate the Boston and other New England sites as part of the core. Next, since the sites in Texas and Utah are allowed to own systems to better serve their local customers, these sites possess the full life-cycle development technology. As a consequence, the Texas and Utah sites can be positioned as belonging to the semi-periphery. The two sites in India

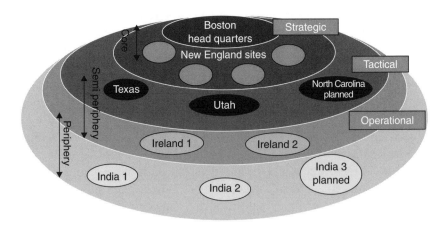

Figure 5.1   GLOBALIS decision-making hierarchy

with no system or product ownership role belong to the periphery. The remaining two sites in Ireland are somewhere between the semi-periphery and the periphery. The extent to which process standardization solidifies this structure makes integrative or reciprocal collaboration (Thompson 1967) exceedingly difficult to achieve.

Adopting a World-systems perspective of globally distributed organizations allows one to see the impact of core/semi-periphery/periphery relationships among the sites. First, such arrangements can impede the creation of trust among the sites. As von Krogh (1998, 136) has found, "Good relations purge a knowledge-creation process of distrust, fear, and dissatisfaction." Inversely, poor relations make it difficult to achieve knowledge sharing. If the relationship is marked by social distance, collaboration becomes very difficult. Second, since periphery sites typically do not get to own systems and products, there is little opportunity for workers at these sites to interact with the customers and develop domain knowledge. Since customer contact and domain knowledge is held by core sites, it is much more difficult for periphery sites to move up the production value chain. This lack of opportunity to develop domain knowledge increases attrition and thus reduces the ability to develop good relationships and collaborative work. Third, since the sites on the periphery are not included in direction setting and new technology selection, organizations miss out on the contributions of its global staff and the full benefits of creativity that diversity brings. Fourth, the World-systems perspective clarifies a variety of behaviors that are incorrectly attributed to national culture. For example, behaviors such as reluctance to push back, doing what one is told, showing little initiative and leadership, lacking sensitivity to deadlines, and the like, were often associated with "the culture of India" by their U.S. colleagues. However, the cause of these behaviors can also be traced to the core–periphery relationships (and client/vendor mentality) that frame global relations in GLOBALIS. Moreover, in GLOBALIS we found that workers in Bangalore and Gurgaon work more easily with the Texas and Utah sites compared with the Boston and New England sites. Furthermore, they were most comfortable working with the Ireland sites. This suggests that viewing the U.S. as one unified culture (as Hofstede 1981) for studying collaboration is inadequate.

Our case also shows, however, that there were examples where this core–periphery relationship was overcome. In these cases, it was the establishment of personal relationships that was key. In WS theory, power is postulated as being rooted in the global structure of production relations in which certain locations maintain control over the means of production and other locations are exploited for their possession of the raw materials for production. What we have found in our case study is that power is rooted in the everyday interactions that make up the basis for organizational structure. Even though the strategy of the organization was to have a "flat" organization, the actions of managers created a hierarchical organization. At the same time, certain managers and workers were able to overcome these structural barriers to achieve the organizational goals. These emergent personal relationships helped to facilitate a sense of commitment to shared practices, which became the fundamental element in establishing a "mutually intelligible social order" (Rawls 2005). However, our results also demonstrate that facilitating travel so that people can meet face-to-face does not necessarily create the social relationships that can overcome structural impediments. For example, when the Indian workers traveled to the U.S., we observed that there was little interaction after work hours or even during lunch breaks, unlike when the Indian manager travelled to Ireland, or when the Irish workers traveled to India. This meant that social relationship development was limited during these visits to the U.S., and actually created feelings of alienation and isolation, rather than shared commitment.

These findings lead us to postulate a new global collaboration model, which is shown in Figure 5.2. The figure illustrates the situated nature of distributed relationships, where nationality is not the deciding factor in

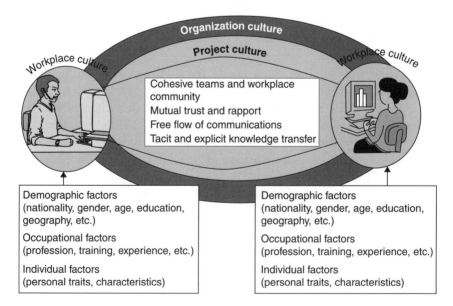

Figure 5.2   Integrated model of distributed work

the amount of social distance between sites. For example, despite being "U.S." sites, the type of decision-making power held by the U.S. sites can vary significantly. The "core" site possesses the ability to make "strategic" decisions regarding the ultimate direction of the organization and how its resources will be allocated and used. Distributed sites can possess tactical and operational decision-making power (in terms of system and product ownership, work allocation, etc.). Thus, being a U.S. site does not mean the site has power to control the direction of the organization. Furthermore, distance is not the determining factor in where a site resides in the global system. In GLOBALIS, the Irish and some U.S. sites share a similar position in the organization in terms of decision-making and evaluative authority. Likewise, the Indian sites typically are allowed to make operational decisions only. It also should be mentioned that this distribution can change based on the specific project, although the core site retains central authority.

We found that when sites occupied a similar stratum of the organization, they were able to use this position to develop social relationships. This was based on a feeling of "being in the same boat" vis-à-vis the core site. At the same time, occupying the same position could also create a feeling of competition. Thus, it became incumbent on the managers to facilitate an environment in which rapport could be developed. This was done through purposively creating opportunities to learn about one another and generally "humanize" coworkers at the distributed sites. It also was the case that relationships across strata of the organization could be problematic because of feelings of entitlement and resentment created by the structural arrangement of sites. Even though the organization was attempting to create integration through their global strategy, the impact often was quite different.

Figure 5.2 focuses on the interaction between workers as the foundation of workplace culture. In this milieu, national culture is but one of many variables that can impact these interactions. Too often, "misunderstandings between members of different cultures are assumed to be comprised of consciously remembered and constructed differences rather than relating to situational factors" (Miller 1995, 144). Our model reintroduces the importance of the situational context while retaining the impact of demographic, occupational, and individual factors. It also demonstrates that despite "obvious" differences, it is possible for people to create a shared identity and culture. As Seely Brown and Duguid (2002, 140) observe, "People with similar practices and similar resources develop similar identities." The goal of global managers is to create the space in which these shared practices can develop.

The points presented in this chapter have theoretical and managerial implications. Theoretically, we expand the pool of concepts in examining distributed collaborative work by including WS theory. This provides a link between social (political) science and management and IS literatures. While WS theory is more nuanced than presented here, it provides a heuristic to explore how social distance and organizational structure matter more than national boundaries, as well as indicating the importance of looking at the system-context, rather than isolated units. In terms of managerial implications, this chapter calls on decision makers to carefully consider how a hierarchical distribution impedes collaboration. As sites develop competencies, there will be a need for them to move up an organization's value chain and possess greater decision-making power. At the very least, organizations need to be aware of how these dynamics operate as they attempt to achieve distributed collaboration and virtual workplace communities.

For a global organization to establish a "flat," integrated, and collaborative workforce, they need to establish a collective orientation based on reciprocal relationships developed through joint work. While standardized processes can provide the parameters for this work, "human behavior (is) not based on plans or on cultural universals but on the *situatedness* that characterizes human acting" (also Suchman 1987; Salamon 1993; Spinelli and Taylor 2003, 1). This emergent ad hoc adherence to organizational protocols facilitates mutual reciprocity, establishes trust, and promotes the development of positive global relations. For organizations to adopt this approach, it would mean giving up the sense of control that comes from standardization. At the same time, organizations stand to gain from developing a workforce that is flexible, agile, and committed. Ultimately, it is up to organizations to determine whether the risk is worth the reward.

This chapter is limited in that it only examines how World-systems analysis can be applied to one organization. More work needs to be done with a broader representation of organizations to identify its ultimate utility. However, we can say that the model has resonated with organizational managers when presented during corporate training on how to encourage more reciprocal collaboration across distributed teams. This provides some anecdotal evidence that, while organizations are proclaiming themselves to be developing integrated sites, the actual enactment of this strategy can interfere with this goal. Ideally, a longitudinal analysis could be done of an organization or project team that has implemented changes based on the model. This would provide a better indication of how a change in policy can bring about the formation of integrated distribution in collaborative teams.

References

Atkinson, J.M. and Heritage, J. (eds) (1984) *Structures of Social Action: Studies in Conversation Analysis*, Cambridge, UK: Cambridge University Press.

Avison, D.E. and Myers, M.D. (1995) Information Systems and Anthropology: an Anthropological Perspective on IT and Organizational Culture, *Information Technology and People.* 8(3): 43–56.

Bamford, R.C. and Deibler, W.J.II. (1993) Comparing, Contrasting ISO 9001 and the SEI Capability Maturity Model. *IEEE Computer*, 26(10): 68–70.

Bannon, L. (1993) CSCW: An Initial Exploration. *Scandinavian Journal of Information Systems*, 5: 3–24.

Chase-Dunn, C. and Hall, T.D. (1993) Comparing World-Systems: Concepts and Working Hypotheses. *Social Forces,* 71(4): 851–866.

Damian, D., Maurer, F., and Sridhar, N. (2002) International Workshop on Global Software Development, *Proceedings of the International Conference on Software Engineering*, Orlando, FL.

Dutta, S., Van Wassenhove, L.N., and Kulandaiswamy, S. (1998) Benchmarking European Software Management Practices. *Communications of the ACM*, 41(6): 77–86.

Evans, P. (1979) *Dependent Development: The Alliance of Multinational, State, and Local Capital in Brazil*, Princeton, NJ: Princeton Press.

Ford, D.P., Connelly, C.E., and Meister, D.B. (2003) Information Systems Research and Hostede's *Culture's Consequences*: An Uneasy and Incomplete Partnership. *IEEE Transaction on Engineering Management*, 50(1): 8–25.

Galliers, R.D. (2003) Information Systems in Global Organizations: Unpacking Culture, in S. Krishna and S. Madon (eds) *The Digital Challenge*: *Information Technology in the Development Context*, Aldershot: Ashgate, pp. 90–102.

Garfinkel, H. (1967) *Studies in Ethnomethodology*, Englewood Cliffs, NJ: Prentice Hall.

Goodwin, C. (1980) Restarts, Pauses and the Achievement of a State of Mutual Gaze at Turn-Beginning. *Sociological Inquiry,* 50: 272–301.

Hammer, M. (2007) the Process Audit. *Harvard Business Review*, April: 111–123.

Harper, R. and Hughes, J.A. (1993) What a F-ing System! Send Em All to the Same Place and Then Expect Us to Stop Em Hitting: Making

Technology Work in Air Traffic Control, in G. Button (ed.) *Technology and Working Order: Studies of Work, Interaction and Technology,* London: Routledge, 127–144.

Heath, C. (1984) Talk and Recipiency: Sequential Organization in Speech and Body Movement, in J.M. Atkinson and J. Heritage (eds) *Structures of Social Action: Studies in Conversation Analysis,* Cambridge, UK: Cambridge University Press.

Hersleb, J.D., Atkins, D.I., Boywe, D.G., Handel, M. and Finholt, T.A. (2002) Introducing Instant Messaging and Chat into the Workplace, *Proceedings of Chi,* Minneapolis, MN.

Hofstede, G. (1981) *Culture's Consequences: International Differences in Work Related Values,* London: Sage Publications.

Hofstede, G. (1991) *Cultures and Organizations: Software of the Mind,* London: Sage Publications.

Huang, J., Newell, S., Galliers, R.D. and Pan, S.L. (2003) Dangerous Liaisons? Component-Based Development and Organizational Subcultures. *IEEE Transactions on Engineering Management,* 50(1): 89–99.

Janowitz, M. (1977) A Sociological Perspective of Wallerstein. *The American Journal of Sociology,* 82(5): 1090–1097.

Kankanhalli, A., Tan, B. and Wei, K-K. (2006–2007) Conflict and Performance in Global Virtual Teams. *Journal of Management Information Systems,* 23(3): 237–274.

Knorr-Cetina, K. (2000) *Epistemic Cultures: How the Sciences Make Knowledge.* Cambridge, MA: Harvard University Press.

Koskinen, I. (2000) Workplace Studies: an Ethnomethodological Approach to CSCW. Nordic Interactive Meeting. March 31. http://www.ncrc.fi. (last accessed on February 27, 2004).

Krishna, S., Sahay, S. and Walsham, G. (2004) Managing Cross-Cultural Issues in Global Software Outsourcing. *Communications of the ACM,* 47(4): 62–66.

Liberman, K. (1995) The Natural History of Some Intercultural Communication. *Research on Language and Social Interaction,* 28(2): 117–146.

Lipnack, J. and Stamps, J. (2000). *People Working across Boundaries with Technology.* 2nd edition, Chichester: John Wiley and Sons.

McCormick, T. (1990) World Systems. *The Journal of American History,* 77(1): 125–132.

Meier, C. (2003) Doing 'Groupness' in a Spatially Distributed Work Group: The Case of Videoconferences at Technics, in L.R. Frey (ed.) *Group*

Communications in Context: Studies of Bona fide Groups, Mahwah, NJ: Lawrence Erlbaum, 367–397.

Mihhailava, G. (2007) Virtual Teams: Just a Theoretical Concept or a Widely Used Practice? *The Business Review, Cambridge,* 7(1): 186–193.

Miller, L. (1995) Two aspects of Japanese and American Co-Worker Interaction: Giving Instructions and Creating Rapport. *The Journal of Applied Behavioral Science,* 31(2): 141–161.

Osland, J.S., Bird, A., Delano, J., and Jacob, M. (2000) Beyond Sophisticated Stereotyping: Cultural Sensemaking in Context. *The Academy of Management Executive,* 14(1): 65–79.

Rawls, A.W. (2005) *Epistemology and Practice,* Cambridge, UK: Cambridge University Press.

Robillard, P. (1999). The Role of Knowledge in Software Development. *Communications of the ACM,* 42(10): 87–92.

Salamon, G. (ed.) (1993) *Distributed Cognition: Psychological and Educational Considerations.* Cambridge, UK: Cambridge University Press.

Seely Brown, J. and Duguid, P. (2002) *The Social Life of Information,* Cambridge, MA: Harvard Business School Press.

Skocpol, T. (1977) Wallerstein's World Capitalist System. *American Journal of Sociology,* 82(5): 1075–1090.

Søndergaard, M. (1994) Hofstede's Consequences: a Study of Reviews, Citations and Replications. *Organization Studies,* 15(3): 447–456.

Spinelli, G. and Taylor, S. (2003) Ethnomethodological Reflections on Collaborative Work Practices in Simulation Modeling: a Short Journey to Elsewhere, *Proceedings 15th European Simulation Symposium.* http://www.scs-europe.net/services/ess2003/PDF/TOOLS16.pdf

Sproull, L. and Kiesler, S. (1986) Reducing Social Context Cues: Electronic Mail in Organizational Communication. *Management Science,* 32(11): 1492–1512.

Suchman, L.A. (1987) *Plans and Situated Actions: The Problem of Human-Machine Communication,* Cambridge, UK: Cambridge University Press.

Thompson, J.D. (1967) *Organizations in Action,* New York: McGraw Hill.

Tiwana, A. (2004) Beyond the Black Box: Knowledge Overlaps in Software Outsourcing. *IEEE Software,* September/October: 51–58.

van Maanen, J. And Barley, S.R. (1984) Occupational Communities: Culture and Control in Organizations. *Research in Organizational Behavior,* 6: 287–365.

von Krogh, G. (1998) Care in Knowledge Creation. *California Management Review*, 40(3): 133–153.

Wallerstein, I. (1974) *The Modern World System*, New York: Academic Press.

Wallerstein, I. (2005) *World-System Analysis: An Introduction*, Durham, NC: Duke University Press.

Westrup, C., Al Jaghoub, S., El Sayed, H., and Liu, W. (2003) Taking Culture Seriously: ICTs Cultures and Development, in S. Krishna and S. Madon (eds) *The Digital Challenge: Information Technology in the Development Context*, Burlington, VT: Ashgate Publishing Limited, 13–27.

CHAPTER 6

Successful knowledge transfer within offshore supplier networks: a case study exploring social capital in strategic alliances

Joseph W. Rottman

Introduction

This chapter highlights the efforts of a Fortune 100 manufacturing firm's five-year effort to achieve success with the offshore outsourcing of embedded software development. Despite stumbling initially, U.S. Manufacturing ultimately was able to engage a network of offshore suppliers to lower costs, reduce cycle time, increase quality, improve the work-life balance of developers, and meet stringent environmental requirements. For U.S. Manufacturing, a key to success offshore was a firm commitment to invest heavily in social capital and formalized knowledge transfer processes.

The U.S. Manufacturing was not alone in its initial struggles to exploit the perceived benefits offshore (cheaper wages, deeper talent pools, etc.). Researchers have cited a 50per cent failure rate offshore (Aron and Singh 2005) and decreased software quality (Carter 2006) when firms engage offshore suppliers. As this case shows, U.S. Manufacturing faced similar problems. In fact, their first attempt offshore failed to achieve success at any level other than the optimism that with a renewed effort, they may be able to make offshore work. In their second attempt offshore, U.S. Manufacturing initially went through a process of self-discovery and once internal development processes were understood and documented, they were able to effectively transfer that knowledge to suppliers. The knowledge transfer process was enabled by the creation and sustaining of social capital.

Social capital is the idea that shared experiences and relationships build an asset that will ultimately return dividends of cooperation, trust, efficiency, reduced reliance on project monitoring (Nahapiet and Ghosal 1998). The U.S. Manufacturing found that once social capital was established, team members (both U.S. Manufacturing teams and suppliers' teams) experienced better communication, shared similar goals, and trusted each other. For U.S. Manufacturing, it was necessary to understand that interpersonal relationships and the trust that comes from shared experience were as important to success offshore as the business rules and processes which dictated systems requirements.

The chapter proceeds with a review of the research on social capital, knowledge transfer, and strategic alliances and then details the efforts within U.S. Manufacturing's Software Center of Excellence (SCE) which was responsible for the development of embedded software used in U.S. Manufacturing's core products. The chapter highlights eight practices that the SCE used to effectively manage their strategic alliances by enhancing social capital and improving knowledge transfer while also protecting intellectual property and creating clear career goals for internal employees.

Literature review: social capital and knowledge transfer

The Inkpen and Tsang (2005) model represents the theoretical framework which we used to classify the practices that U.S. Manufacturing employed. This model, described below, is closely linked with many research areas. Namely, the bodies of literature related to trust, knowledge transfer, social capital, cross-cultural issues, and geographically dispersed teams are clearly relevant. Specifically, researchers have addressed the role of trust (Politis 2003; Chowdhury 2005), trust and geographically dispersed teams (Jarvenpaa et al. 1998; Trompenaars and Hampden-Turner 1998; Hofstede 2001), and knowledge transfer (Orr 1996; Tsoukas 1996; Hansen 1999; Argote and Ingram 2000; Levin and Cross 2004; Rottman 2006; Rottman and Lacity 2006a) While researchers have focused on various salient issues of group social capital (Oh et al. 2006), the effects of involuntary employee turnover (Shaw et al. 2005), voluntary turnover (Dess and Shaw 2001), the creation of knowledge at the individual level (McFadyen and Cannella 2004), absorptive capacity (Tsai 2001), and external knowledge acquisition (Anand et al. 2002), this chapter focuses on the creation of social capital and knowledge transfer within a strategic alliance.

Adapting Nahapiet and Ghoshal's (1998) model, which identified social capital and combinations and exchanges of intellectual influences on the creation of new intellectual capital, Inkpen and Tsang (2005) use three types of organizational groupings to describe the social capital dimensions and the facilitating conditions for knowledge transfer. They analyzed the structural, cognitive, and relational dimensions of social capital across three network types: intracorporate networks, industrial districts, and strategic alliances. To properly understand how the relationship between U.S. Manufacturing and its suppliers fits into the strategic alliance category, a brief description of the other network types is appropriate.

Inkpen and Tsang describe three types of networks: intracorporate networks, strategic alliances, and industrial districts. They define an intracorporate network as "a group of organizations operating under a unified corporate identity, with the headquarters of the network having controlling ownership interest in its subsidiaries" (2005, 148). The salient characteristics of this type of network are the clear hierarchies and centralization of decision-making. In contrast to the formality of the intracorporate network, an industrial district "consists of a network of producers, supporting organizations and a local labor market" (2005, 149). These firms would share a geographical area or market segment.

An industrial district consists of independent firms sharing similar goals and geographic areas who utilize similar producers, pull from the same labor pool, and target similar markets (Inkpen and Tsang 2005).

Strategic alliances, however, exist between firms that do not necessarily share a formal hierarchy or a geographical area and market segment. A strategic alliance "can be formed by firms located in different positions or in the same position in the value chain" Inkpen and Tsang (2005). Firms enter into a strategic alliance voluntarily with the idea of a common benefit resulting from the arrangement.

It is in the context of a strategic alliance that we adopt Inkpen and Tsang's definitions of both social capital and knowledge transfer. Based on both Inkpen and Tsang's definition of a strategic alliance and prior research related to alliances and outsourcing engagements, the relationship U.S. Manufacturing had with its suppliers constitutes a strategic alliance. As Table 6.1 shows, despite the relatively small scale of the SCE's relationship with its suppliers, prior definitions of alliances and strategic alliances validate the use of a strategic alliance framework in this case. In addition, as mentioned in the case discussion section below, the relationships between U.S. Manufacturing and its suppliers which continue

Table 6.1   Representative research studies utilizing strategic alliances

Author(s)	Support for use of strategic alliance in outsourcing relationships
Zineldin and Bredenlow (2003)	"Strategic alliances are viewed broadly as agreements among firms to work together to attain some strategic objective. This definition accommodates the myriad arrangements that can range from handshake agreements to licensing, mergers, outsourcing and equity joint ventures. Such cooperation may take the form of ... research and development partnerships."
	"Outsourcing is a typical form of strategic alliance. It is about 'make or buy'."
McFarlan and Nolan (1995)	"Alliances allow a firm to leverage a key part of the value chain by bringing in a strong partner that complements its skills."
Koka and Prescott (2002)	"Firms resort to strategic alliances to access capabilities necessary for competitive advantage."
Gulati (1995)	"Organizational members of the partner firms [in alliances] work together directly from their own organizational confines. Nonequity alliances include unidirectional agreements, such as licensing, second-sourcing, and distribution agreements, and bidirectional agreements such as joint contracts and technology exchange agreements."
Tiwana and Keil (2007)	"[Strategic alliances] allow outsourcing firms to specialize deeper in their domain of core competence without being distracted by non-core activities."
	"A related motivation for forming outsourcing alliances is to access specialized knowledge that is so removed from the outsourcer's core activities that it might simply not exist in the outsourcing firm."
Inkpen and Tsang (2005)	"A strategic alliance is a group of firms entering into voluntary arrangements that involve exchange, sharing or co-development of products, technologies or services. The last two decades have witnessed a proliferation of strategic alliances among firms as a result of technological development and globalization."

to increase in size and complexity, allowed U.S. Manufacturing to meet regulatory deadlines, develop new products more quickly and efficiently, manage its talent pipeline better, and reduce development costs.

Building on the work by Nahapiet and Ghoshal (1998), Inkpen and Tsang define social capital as "the aggregate of resources embedded within, available through, and derived from the network of relationships possessed by an individual or organization" (Inkpen and Tsang 2005). In the context of the U.S. Manufacturing case, the connection between U.S. Manufacturing and its suppliers represents a "social capital resource" belonging to both firms. It is this idea that the connection itself between a supplier and a customer has an exploitable value that was missing in U.S. Manufacturing's first offshore effort. The realization of the value and the practices employed to harness that value was a key success factor in U.S. Manufacturing's second offshore attempt.

Argote and Ingram define knowledge transfer as the "process through which one network member is affected by the experience of another. Knowledge transfer manifests itself through changes in knowledge or performance of the recipient unit" (Argote and Ingram 2000, 151). In the context of a strategic alliance, "alliances provide opportunities to create redeployable knowledge such as technical knowledge or market knowledge" (Inkpen and Tsang 2005). The next section of the chapter details the research method.

About this research

This research developed over two years. Initial contact with U.S. Manufacturing was made at a large Indian supplier's executive summit, involving their 20 largest and most prestigious clients. This initial meeting resulted in a site visit to U.S. manufacturing's world headquarters, tours of the manufacturing facilities, introductions to, and interviews with, on-site supplier personnel, site visits at the Indian supplier's development center in Bangalore, India, and follow-up interviews with U.S. Manufacturing after the supplier interviews.

Detailed case background

The U.S. Manufacturing is one of over 20 U.S. customer firms studied as part of a larger project that focuses on the lessons learned by U.S. firms who are engaged in offshore development of software (Rottman and Lacity 2004; Rottman and Lacity 2006b). Among the over 20 U.S. customer organizations studied in this project, U.S. Manufacturing showed the most strategic use of knowledge transfer. Before achieving strategic advantage with offshore outsourcing, however, U.S. Manufacturing failed in its initial offshore initiatives. After diagnosing the causes of its initial failures, U.S. Manufacturing remedied the supplier relationships with new structural, cognitive, and relational practices. These practices, which we have analyzed through the theoretical lens of social capital, highlight the importance of actively designing practices to build social capital to ensure successful strategic alliances.

U.S. Manufacturing is a Fortune 100 manufacturer of industrial equipment with over 75,000 employees spread across 20 countries. The successful knowledge transfer practices and attention to social capital highlighted in this article are centered within U.S. Manufacturing's Six Sigma certified

SCE. The SCE at U.S. Manufacturing employs approximately 150 people and has an annual IT development spend of approximately $32 million. The members of the SCE are responsible for the development and deployment of embedded software systems that are highly integrated into the manufacturing and operation of U.S. Manufacturing's core products.

The SCE began its offshore journey in late 2000 with the hope of taking advantage of the labor arbitrage available offshore. With the primary goal of saving money on development costs, they selected small projects to begin their offshore engagements. A small pilot project (two offshore employees) integrating a new Global Positioning System (GPS) steering system into one of their larger product lines currently in production is, as we shall see, indicative of the fact that in the first round of offshore outsourcing, U.S. Manufacturing failed to invest in the processes and practices needed to build social capital and improve knowledge transfer.

For this project, U.S. Manufacturing chose a large Indian supplier and placed all employees offshore to take greatest advantage of the labor rates. Specifically, this project required the offshore supplier to design and create the embedded software intended to control the steering systems and interface with the GPS satellites. The project involved new software tools, interface systems, and processes for both the SCE and the supplier. Primarily due to the fact that knowledge transfer was an afterthought, this project failed to produce any of the deliverables outlined in the statements of work and was ultimately pulled back in-house and completed well behind schedule and over budget.

According to the Engineering Supervisor:

> *It didn't succeed. We would get something back and it didn't do what we wanted it to do and we would have to redo the whole thing. We weren't very good at being outsourcers and the model of throwing a document over the wall and having a supplier magically give us what we want in the end- it didn't and doesn't work.*

The GPS project was indicative of the many failures U.S. Manufacturing encountered, which were in large part related to social capital knowledge transfer. Owing to the project delays, the need for extensive rework to correct inaccurate and incomplete applications, project timelines, and budgets were not met and business sponsors were disappointed in the process. Looking back, the manager of the SCE and his staff felt that they had underestimated the need for extensive domain knowledge transfer (product, process, and market) as well as their own expertise in managing an offshore project.

According to the Manager of the SCE:

We had to realize that our Indian vendors did not understand embedded software or even the equipment we manufacture. They didn't even know what our product looked like! Now we are spending considerable time on domain knowledge transfer and training.

Another indication that the first round failures could be traced to insufficient social capital and knowledge transfer occurred when the staff of the SCE compared those failed projects which engaged offshore suppliers with projects that utilized only onshore suppliers. The *post mortem* that staff undertook showed that domestic suppliers, due to their experience of working with U.S. Manufacturing, their proximity to business users, and their ability to see the products in action, lessened the need for social capital and *fundamental* knowledge transfer.

According to the Six Sigma Blackbelt:

We never considered how much knowledge our [onshore] suppliers brought to the table. Having worked with them for years, they already knew a lot about us and our systems. We underestimated the amount of interaction that took place between them and our users and other developers. There was a lot of information going back and forth that we did not see. When we went offshore, that couldn't take place, and we then realized its importance.

Despite the failures, U.S. Manufacturing did see some promise in offshore development. While the projects themselves were not completed, they were confident that the offshore developers might be able to reduce the project backlog if U.S. Manufacturing was able to share knowledge and expertise with the suppliers in a better way. Based on internal process improvements and some improvement of code late in the engagement, U.S. Manufacturing decided to move forward with the offshore model. According to the Manager of the SCE:

I must admit it was a tough sell, but we started to put in place much better systems to monitor our offshore resources as well as our internal teams. Our first few projects and the Six Sigma journey taught us: "if you can't count it, you can't improve it." So after some retooling, we tried again.

In January 2004, the SCE used the lessons it had learned and relaunched its offshore effort. Realizing the need for better knowledge transfer, the second attempt was more measured and thoughtful. The SCE realized that the knowledge transfer process for embedded software development was critically important. One way the SCE tried to meet this challenge relates to how the SCE structured the engagements. In the second attempt, most of the employees of the offshore suppliers would spend time on-site at U.S. Manufacturing's headquarters prior to working on the outsourced projects. According to the Manager of the SCE:

> *What we saw was the benefit and real value of actually bringing those people here for a short time to bring them up to speed. Let them see how an application works and work right next to the team doing the development. That is the real benefit to the teaming aspect.*

The first attempt showed U.S. Manufacturing that they needed to spend considerable time and resources on the knowledge transfer phase. The creation of embedded software requires a specialized skill set and manufacturing domain knowledge. Embedded software is very different from traditional software. Embedded software is found in many devices: thermostats, cell phones, cars, elevators, and the like. Embedded software is used when any device has to interact with its environment. The "rules" for traditional software do not apply to embedded software. For example, response time, speed, power consumption, and correctly interfacing with the external environment are paramount. In addition to "normal" coding skills, embedded software development requires additional skills not readily available in the offshore space. Inherent in the successful creation of embedded software is an intricate and detailed knowledge of the equipment that will house and interact with the software.

Considering the extensive knowledge transfer and training issues involved with embedded software development facing U.S. Manufacturing, they identified the risks associated with employee turnover and the need to ensure continuity of service. To mitigate these risks, U.S. Manufacturing arranged with their supplier to overlap the onshore presence of key personnel. The training sessions were initially delivered by U.S. Manufacturing's architects and project leaders to the supplier's project leaders.

These trained employees would typically remain on-site at U.S. Manufacturing for 6 to 18 months. However, the hourly onshore rates are typically 3–4 times as high as the offshore rates, and the labor arbitrage deteriorates the longer the employees are on-site. U.S. Manufacturing's ultimate goal was to have a 20/80 ratio of supplier employees who are onshore versus offshore, and to outsource no more than 30 per cent of the development. However, migrating the trained employees offshore to train offshore employees would create a talent and knowledge vacuum on-site and sever many professional and personal connections that had been created. To address this issue, U.S. Manufacturing overlapped the supplier's new on-site resource with the old one for between three and six months. While this approach is expensive, the two on-site employees were able to establish common frames of reference and transfer relationships and connections to the new employee. In addition, the new employee was trained by the old employee, freeing up U.S. Manufacturing's architects and project leaders to engage in higher level activities. Once the old employee had migrated offshore, they were then able to transfer the knowledge obtained during their on-site time to the offshore employees and capitalize and expand on the intense learning which took place on-site.

The supplier selection and engagement process was also very different in round two for U.S. Manufacturing. The failures in round one showed U.S. Manufacturing that it was critical to establish a long range plan with the offshore suppliers, and that the communication of U.S. Manufacturing's long range strategy was necessary during the due diligence phase of the engagement. Specifically, the members of the SCE targeted firms that were willing to begin the process slowly, knowing that the supplier would need to invest heavily in the knowledge transfer process to ensure success. In round two, U.S. Manufacturing selected two large Indian suppliers who had already exhibited expertise in the embedded software market, primarily in the automotive industry. In addition, they selected a boutique firm that specialized in embedded software in the manufacturing market. This prior experience of the embedded software development process was a critical success factor that was overlooked in round one:

> We really didn't understand how different we (embedded software development) were until we saw the failures in round one. We now know that our vendors need a very specialized skill set and we now know how to identify and test for those skills. We are much better at vendor selection and talent assessment.

The services of the two large suppliers and one boutique firm represented about $3.4 million or 10 per cent of SCE's annual budget. These suppliers provided about 15 people on-site and 35 people offsite. The three engagements are all increasing in dollar value and headcount.

The manager of the SCE summarized round two by stating:

> I think we are now doing it right and the data we are gathering support that idea. Our vendors are not only providing a lower cost talent

pool, but they are helping us strategically. We keep looking for ways to increase the engagements. Our costs are down, productivity is up, and the quality is as good, if not better than what we can do in house.

The successes found in round two were due in large part to the establishment of social capital and the benefits of social capital for successful knowledge transfer between U.S. Manufacturing and its suppliers. The next section details the dimensions of social capital and the practices U.S. Manufacturing employed.

Social capital dimensions and SCE practices

The practices utilized by the SCE at U.S. Manufacturing are listed in Table 6.2 as they correspond to the social capital dimensions. This classification was made using the transcripts of the interviews as well as Inkpen and Tsang's description of the various dimensions.

Each dimension affects knowledge transfer differently and has differing facilitating conditions. "The structural dimension of social capital involves the pattern of relationships between the network actors and can be analyzed from the perspective of network ties, network configuration and

Table 6.2 Social capital dimensions and SCE practices

Social capital dimension	SCE practice
Structural (Network ties and configuration)	1. Utilize multiple suppliers to enhance network ties and to increase social networks.
	2. Increase network utilization and frequency and maintain multiple connections by unitizing projects into small segments.
	3. Ensure knowledge retention and transfer by requiring supplier to have shadows for key supplier roles.
Cognitive (Shared goals and culture)	4. Strengthen cultural understanding by visiting the offshore supplier and project teams.
	5. Clarify goals by communicating the offshore strategy to all parties.
	6. Integrate the supplier's employees into the development team.
	7. Co-train internal employees and supplier employees to communicate goals and increase cultural awareness.
Relational (Trust)	8. Increase internal trust by understanding and managing the talent pipeline.

network stability" (Inkpen and Tsang 2005, 152). The structural dimension within social capital relates to the boundaries that must be spanned in order for knowledge transfer to take place (Levina and Vaast 2005). These boundaries may be spanned by network ties. "The fundamental proposition of social capital theory is that network ties provide access to resources" (Nahapiet and Ghoshal 1998, 252). However, in a strategic alliance, the amount of information passing through this boundary can lead to a divulging of proprietary intellectual property or an unbalanced relationship with one supplier. "Ties provide the channels for information transmission, but the overall configuration of these ties constitutes an important facet of social capital that may impact the development of intellectual capital" (Nahapiet and Ghoshal 1998, 252). This represents a significant risk for U.S. Manufacturing.

To mitigate these risks while enhancing the network structure, U.S. Manufacturing developed three practices for effective knowledge transfer.

Structural Dimension: Practice 1: Utilize multiple suppliers to enhance network ties and to increase social networks

The SCE distributed work among three suppliers (two large and one boutique). While maintaining engagements with multiple suppliers did increase transaction costs and management overheads, the benefits included protection of intellectual property and the creation of a competitive environment to keep costs low and quality high.

The use of multiple suppliers created larger social networks, thus increasing U.S. Manufacturing's ability to both create social capital and manage knowledge transfer. While it may seem counter-intuitive that increasing the number of suppliers would increase the social capital between teams, the SCE found that exposure to divergent engagement models, vendors with different work processes and styles, and vendors with unique expertise, broadened the outlook of the internal employees. Specifically, internal teams were able to enhance their own skill sets and increase their levels of expertise and confidence by working with developers from multiple vendors.

The manager of the SCE concluded:

> In our first try, we only used one vendor and we did not learn much from them and they did not help us. When we spread work out [across vendors], our processes improved, as did the exposure of our internal people to multiple viewpoints. It also helped us to "keep alive" multiple vendors – we were spreading the development around.

This practice is closely related to Structural Dimension Practice 2, in that intellectual property can be protected and the network enhanced by not only utilizing multiple suppliers but by also breaking the projects into units.

Structural Dimension: Practice 2: **Increase network utilization and frequency by breaking projects into small segments**

The first part of the practice involved the unitization of tasks to be sourced. These tasks were typically 5 to 7 business day activities that had clearly defined objectives and requirements. While the transactional overheads of this strategy were considerable, the Manager of the SCE claimed the transaction costs were more than recouped by such close monitoring:

> *In our first round [the failed attempt at offshore sourcing], projects were allowed to creep and the only people who saw the creep were the accounts payable people on our end and the accounts receivable people at the supplier. Now, each task has an owner and we watch the projects from a functional perspective, not an accounting perspective. By using this strategy, we are seeing much less re-work and the quality has improved considerably!*

Considering the proprietary nature of the software the SCE developed, they faced an interesting problem: how to transfer enough knowledge to enable successful product development while protecting their trade secrets. To mitigate this risk, the SCE (1) unitized projects into small segments of work, and (2) dispersed these segments among three offshore suppliers to effectively distribute the intellectual property. They viewed their intellectual property as a puzzle. By distributing small pieces among three suppliers, no one supplier could assemble the puzzle on their own (see Figure 6.1).

This model also created a system of both strong and weak network ties between teams. The strength of a tie is a continuum, and can be defined as "a combination of the amount of time, the emotional intensity, the intimacy (mutual confiding), and the reciprocal services which characterize the tie" (Granovetter 1973, 1361). In the case of U.S. Manufacturing, the strong ties facilitated trust, reciprocal information exchange, and performance, while the weak ties facilitated the generation of new information. For example, an internal team working closely on a project with Supplier One would develop strong ties. In addition, that team might also work peripherally with Supplier Two. This created a weak tie with Supplier Two, which exposed the team to new techniques, tools, and processes. While connections did not exist between suppliers, U.S. Manufacturing teams did interact simultaneously with multiple suppliers, thus increasing network

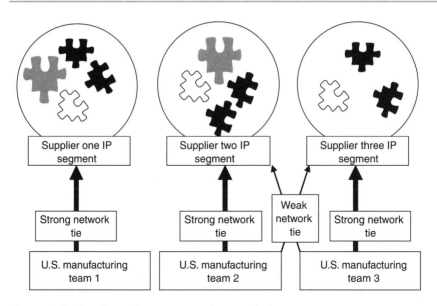

Figure 6.1 Intellectual property and network ties

utilization, network ties, and the opportunity for knowledge transfer. As Hagedoorn et al. (2006) noted, a combination of strong and weak network ties can have a positive impact on the firm, which was the case with U.S. Manufacturing.

This practice had important impacts on the knowledge transfer process. Specifically, by unitizing the work into small objects, the number of exchanges between U.S. Manufacturing and its suppliers increased, thus increasing the strength of each tie while creating multiple connections between them as well.

Structural Dimension: Practice 3: **Ensure knowledge retention and transfer by requiring suppliers to have shadows for key supplier roles**
To counteract the increased training costs associated with unitization of projects and the use of multiple suppliers, the SCE required suppliers to overlap key people in the engagement. This practice also helped to mitigate the risks associated with supplier employee turnover. Supplier employee turnover was as high as 75 per cent in some of the companies studied. Employee turnover can have a destabilizing effect on a social capital network. As Inkpen and Tsang found, "personnel turnover affects intracorporate knowledge sharing, which often takes place through formal or informal exchanges on an individual basis. Maintaining a stable pool of personnel within a network can help individuals develop long-lasting interpersonal relationships" (2005, 156).

To help maintain the stability of the network, the SCE required that trained supplier employees remain on the account for at least one year after training or the supplier would incur the costs of training a replacement. This facilitated knowledge transfer because relationships were maintained and network stability increased.

For key supplier roles such as project leaders or architects, the need to ensure continuity was even greater. The U.S. Manufacturing required suppliers to provide shadow employees for key on-site supplier roles. Depending on the role, the required shadowing period was three to six months. This overlap period had two major social capital and knowledge transfer benefits. First, the knowledge transfer was undertaken predominantly between the supplier's employees, thus freeing up the SCE's valuable architects and leaders. Second, the incumbents were able to ease the impending transition by introducing their replacements to U.S. Manufacturing's business units and staff and subsequently transferring more social aspects of the arrangement. This helped to maintain the social contacts and connections that had been created during the engagement. According to the engineering supervisor:

Once we started overlapping the liaisons, our customers felt much better about rolling people off the project. The outgoing liaisons made our job much easier since they took their initial training and subsequent learning and were able to convey it to their replacement much, much better than we can.

Figure 6.2 shows the relationship between the supplier's on-site project leaders and the offshore team. The shadowing allowed the social capital (both personal and professional) to be maintained when the supplier's employee then shared the knowledge with the offshore development team members.

Specifically, the Senior Project Manager for U.S. Manufacturing's large Indian supplier extolled the impacts of employee shadowing:

It was nice to share experiences both professional and personal with other managers who had been on-site. We would have meetings with each other and talk about projects and the people involved. Even though I never met [U.S. Manufacturing's] teams in person, talking to my counterpart here in India helped me learn processes and personalities.

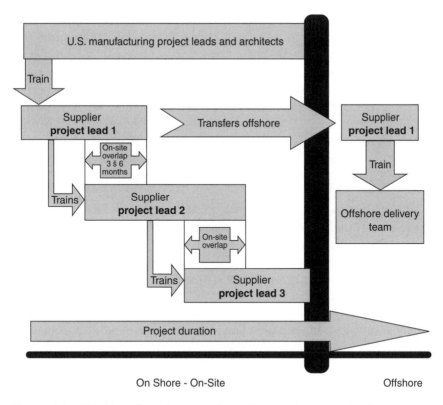

Figure 6.2   U.S. Manufacturing use of supplier employee shadowing

Cognitive dimension practices

The cognitive dimension of Inkpen and Tsang's framework encompasses the idea of shared cultural goals and vision. "Shared goals represent the degree to which network members share a common understanding and approach to the achievement of network tasks and outcomes" (2005, 153). Within a strategic alliance involving a U.S. customer and Indian suppliers, achieving a cultural understanding is key to successful knowledge transfer. Social norms and cultures can both positively and negatively affect the acceptance of a new idea or goal (Rogers 2006). Furthermore, "since partner firms usually have distinct cultures, strategic alliances are often formed on the basis of cultural compromise among the partners concerned. Cultural conflict will arise if certain partners rigidly push forward their own ways of doing things" (Inkpen and Tsang 2005, 153). To help avoid these conflicts, U.S. Manufacturing utilized four key practices, detailed below.

Cognitive Dimension: Practice 4: **Visit the offshore supplier and project teams to build personal connections and understand the offshore landscape**

While on the surface this practice seems obvious, it did not occur to the manager of the SCE for two years. The costs (financial, time, health concerns etc.) often prevent U.S. managers from visiting the Indian suppliers. When the manager of the SCE finally made the trip to Bangalore to visit the people he had worked with for two years but had never met face to face, he realized the high value of the trip. During his two-week trip, he visited both the large suppliers and the boutique firm:

> *I can't believe I waited two years to meet the people I have been only e-mailing and seeing in video conferences! What a difference this trip has made. Now I know my team. I should have done this at the very beginning. I now have faces, and more importantly personalities, to go with names and titles. This trip was worth every penny.*

It was not only the meetings themselves which created the connections. Rather, face-to-face interactions allowed for a level of social interaction that was impossible during teleconferences or email conversations. The individuals were able to have casual conversations about families, shared experiences, even personal goals. In addition, shared meals and social activities helped to cement the connection between U.S. Manufacturing and their suppliers. These interactions represented "informal socializing ties" (Oh et al. 2004) and, for U.S. Manufacturing, increased the level of social capital.

Not only did the trip help U.S. Manufacturing understand the culture of their suppliers but the reverse was true as well. U.S. Manufacturing was able to communicate their goals and culture to the supplier. This sharing of both culture and goals enhanced the social capital and subsequently eased knowledge transfer. In addition, it helped establish the groundwork for future negotiations.

According to the Head of Delivery Excellence for U.S. Manufacturing's large Indian supplier, *"It was wonderful to finally meet [the manager of the SCE]. So many things become clear when you meet face to face. Email and teleconferences don't let you get to know the person."*

Cognitive Dimension: Practice 5: **Clarify goals by communicating the offshore strategy to all parties**

The U.S. Manufacturing, like most of the U.S. client firms we studied, were using offshore outsourcing to "do more with less." They did not intend to reduce internal headcount through outsourcing, but planned to use offshore outsourcing to reduce the immense backlog of work.

This message was strongly communicated to the internal IT staff, which assuaged their fears and made them more willing to cooperate with offshore suppliers. In addition, this message was shared with offshore suppliers so they did not have to worry about replacing U.S. workers.

From the onset of its offshore effort, U.S. Manufacturing took a transparent and well-communicated approach regarding its offshore strategy. To combat the then vitriolic national atmosphere toward offshore outsourcing and to alleviate fears, U.S. Manufacturing was very deliberate in their communications to the development staff. Considering that U.S. Manufacturing did not intend to reduce internal headcount through outsourcing, but instead reduce workload, their message was more favorable than other outsourcing announcements. The plans to explore offshore outsourcing were met with optimism and relief by the internal staff of the SCE. Facing a three-year backlog and a flat staffing forecast, employees welcomed the possibility of a decreased workload. According to the manager of the SCE:

> *My people were tired of working 60 hour weeks. We communicated that offshore was a way to better manage our project pipeline since we were not going to add a bunch of expensive North American resources to meet the demand and then lay them off later, we had to find other ways of being able to add flexibility to our workforce. And so they are not worried about losing their job. They just see this as a way of getting back to some kind of normal 40 to 50 hour workweek, and even more importantly, as a way for them to move up in their level of responsibility.*

Communicating the goal of utilizing offshore as a way of managing the application backlog and not reducing development headcount helped the internal development staff to understand the goals of U.S. Manufacturing and how these would impact their own careers and employment (see Practice 8). This created an atmosphere that enhanced the knowledge transfer effort. For example, according to the engineering supervisor,

> *I was amazed at how open our developers were with the supplier's team. Once they realized that the quicker they [the offshore team] were up to speed, the sooner they could share the load, there was no "turf" to protect, or "secrets" to keep.*

This practice was also evident in the relationship between U.S. Manufacturing and the suppliers. The members of the SCE used an internally developed decision support system (described in detail in Practice Eight below) to actively manage headcount and inform the supplier of upcoming work. By being able to predict future revenue, the suppliers were able to focus developer efforts on production rather than revenue generation. According to the manager of the SCE:

Initially, the developers seemed to have one eye on the current project and one eye on "what is coming next." Once we were able to share our forecasts with them, the attention turned to the current tasks.

The suppliers shared in the benefits of this practice. According to the on-site engagement manager:

My job is made easier by having the project forecasts from [U.S. Manufacturing]. While the largest part of my job is the current engagement, there is an expectation from my superiors to look for additional opportunities. Since they share with me the plan, I can spend more time on what is to be done now.

The successful use of this practice also confirms the work of Inkpen and Tsang and the strategic aspect of the relationship U.S. Manufacturing had with its suppliers.

For strategic alliances we also expect that goal clarity reduces interpartner conflict by facilitating the negotiation and establishment of shared goals. When the objectives and strategies of an alliance are clearly stated, a foundation of common understanding and the means to achieve the collaborative purpose is established among the partners. (2005, 157)

Cognitive Dimension: Practice 6: **Integrate the offshore employees fully into the development team**

One way to encourage knowledge transfer is through the enhancement of social relationships (Oh et al. 2004). Many firms find it difficult to integrate the supplier's employees into the culture and social systems of their firms. Our research shows that offshore suppliers are often viewed with fear and even contempt. For example, the program managers at one Fortune 100 firm we investigated witnessed open hostility between offshore system administrators and business units who would have never engaged in such unprofessional behavior with internal employees.

The U.S. Manufacturing made a concerted effort to encourage and facilitate integration. This integration was not limited to training or knowledge transfer. It helped to create a team atmosphere that would last even after the supplier's employees are transferred offshore. According to the manager of the SCE:

> *When we bring these offshore people in for training, they sit with the people who will be doing the work just like them. They're in the meeting learning about all this stuff and being mentored by the leaders on a pretty personal basis for the most part. And I think the fact that we value diversity and try to encourage that, and that we try not to build walls among the people who are here, helped to foster the building of those relationships. We make sure that the vendor's employees are invited to birthday parties and happy hours. It helps for the teams to come together.*

This effort to increase the social capital between internal and supplier employees paid dividends at U.S. Manufacturing. The line between "us and them" blurred and the suppliers' employees (both on and offshore) were viewed by U.S. Manufacturing employees as team members, and they all shared in the successes and challenges of the projects.

According to the Group Project Manager at one of U.S. Manufacturing's large Indian suppliers:

> *Of all of our embedded systems clients, [U.S. Manufacturing] has worked the hardest to make our employees feel very much part of the team at [U.S. Manufacturing]. Our C-Sat (customer satisfaction ratings) from [U.S. Manufacturing] show the value of this integration. Our employees have internalized the mission and values of [U.S. Manufacturing]. It is a highly coveted assignment to work on the [U.S. Manufacturing] account.*

Cognitive Dimension: Practice 7: **Synchronize the training of offshore employees with internal training efforts**

While the co-training of internal employees with supplier employees creates significant trade secret and intellectual property risks, the SCE felt that it was necessary. Owing to the significant amounts of product and process knowledge the suppliers needed to successfully develop software, and to the need to foster common goals among all developers, the SCE chose to co-train both internal and supplier developers.

The SCE provided the key supplier employees with facility tours and training classes on engine architecture, production software, equipment simulation products, operating guides for various lines of equipment, quality assurance processes, and an overview of all of the various manufacturing products and platforms. They were introduced to various software development tools, the development environment, and embedded development tools.

These classes were delivered on-site and in person to the supplier's on-site employees. The SCE paid the supplier employees for the time spent in training, but it only paid offshore (versus the much higher on-shore) rates.

For the offshore developers, the classes were recorded and streamed offshore. According to the manager of the SCE:

> *We couldn't ship an engine or a piece of large equipment over to India, so we did the next best thing: we videotaped many equipment pieces in action and showed what the ECUs (Electronic Control Units) were designed to do.*

In addition, the SCE invited most of the employees of the offshore suppliers to spend some time on-site prior to working on the outsourced projects. According to the Manager of the SCE:

> *What we saw was the benefit and real value of actually bringing those people here for a short time to bring them up to speed. Let them see how an application works and work right next to the team doing the development.*

Relational Dimension: Practice 8: **Increase internal trust by demonstrating how offshore outsourcing will improve internal career paths.**

Trust has been discussed widely in the management arena. Specifically, the use of rewards (Ferrin and Dirks 2003), communication frequency (Becerra and Gupta 2003), trust factors related to offshore development success (Jennex and Adelakun 2003), electronic data interchange (Hart and Saunders 1998), and interorganizational trust (Zaheer et al. 1998) have shed light on various facets of organizational trust. In the context of this case, we focus on the role of trust in a network setting. It is vital that both parties in the alliance have sufficient trust to share knowledge and that the allies are not viewed as competitors (Inkpen and Tsang 2005).

To foster the trust internal employees had in upper management's sourcing plans, the SCE clearly communicated the effects that offshore outsourcing would have on internal career paths.

To understand and communicate how the use of offshore outsourcing would affect the career paths of internal employees, U.S. Manufacturing analyzed its internal human resource systems and project pipeline to better understand how to manage its workforce. This helped to create a positive "shadow of the future" at U.S. Manufacturing. From past experience, SCE managers knew that about one-third of programmers are promoted to higher-value roles. For example, if SCE managers project that they will need five architects in three years' time, they hire 15 new programmers internally. Even though these internal programmers cost considerably more than offshore equivalents, the SCE managers knew that they needed to provide entry level experiences to groom future IT leaders. According to the Engineering Supervisor:

> *We have made the business case to management that even though internal programmers are not as cost efficient as sourced programmers, we need to maintain a certain level of expertise internally.*

As suggested by this practice, the SCE needed an accurate forecast of future IT needs. To accurately predict the human resources (HR) demand requires significant knowledge of the HR environment, past HR trends, and the current staffing constraints. The U.S. Manufacturing created an intricate staffing model which used as inputs the current and past project staffing data, the current internal talent pool, and the projected demand. The rules for the system integrated 10 years of staffing history within the SCE and allowed for significant flexibility.

The staffing plan was openly communicated to both internal IT staff and *suppliers*. By communicating the plan to internal IT staff, U.S. Manufacturing's developers were not worried that they were "building their own guillotines" by working closely with the suppliers' teams. Instead, trust was established and enhanced by the internal employees seeing a clear and achievable career path. By communicating the plan to offshore suppliers, the offshore suppliers could better plan for their staffing needs and better predict their future revenue generation. Such predictability enabled suppliers to stop selling and start working.

This trust was also evident from the [supplier's?] perspective. According to the supplier's Group Project Manager for the U.S. Manufacturing account:

> *Of all of our clients in the embedded software space [U.S. Manufacturing] gives us the best picture of what is coming down the road. We use their forecasts to help us with our forecasts and can better predict how the account will grow.*

The open communication of the vibrant internal career path and long-term commitment to suppliers laid the foundation for trust among the parties. Both sides saw the benefit of the relationship. As predicted by theory, the atmosphere of trust contributed to the free exchange of knowledge between committed exchange partners (Lin 2007).

In addition, researchers have identified separate types of trust: namely, companion trust, competence trust, and commitment trust (Newell and Swan 2000). In the case of U.S. Manufacturing, *commitment trust*, which is "central in proprietary networks where financial, property, or intellectual rights of the network relationships are at least partly defined" (Newell and Swan 2000, 1295), represented the type of trust needed for fostering knowledge transfer. It was this type of trust which allowed the internal teams to fully engage the offshore teams without fear of damaging their own career goals. By reducing uncertainty, commitment trust was increased. The U.S. Manufacturing realized that if their second attempt was to succeed, internal employees needed to see and understand their future roles within U.S. Manufacturing.

The U.S. Manufacturing is not alone in its desire to understand and predict the career paths of their IT employees. The 2004 survey of CIOs by the Society of Information Management (SIM) cited "Attracting, developing and retaining IT professionals" as the second most important issue facing IS executives in 2004 (Luftman 2005). The facilitation of growth by internal employees was a key feature in the development of the offshore models in round two. The U.S. Manufacturing placed significant value on grooming their IT architects and project leads internally, and rewarding experience and loyalty. According to the Manager of the SCE:

> We are now looking downstream in our pipeline and asking, "Based on our projected demand and the projects we know we'll be undertaking, do we know how many architects, project leads and how many programmers will be needed in 3–5 years?" We then will use that data and determine, if we will need 5 architects in 3 years and we know from our past experience that one out of every 3 internal programmers makes it to architect, we know that we need to hire 15 programmers in order to "grow" enough architects, because we do not use the vendor's employees as architects. We have made the business case to management that even though internal programmers are not as cost efficient as sourced programmers, we need to maintain a certain level of expertise internally.

Implications for researchers and practitioners

While many researchers have studied both social capital and knowledge transfer, few have put forward specific practices which improved social capital and eased the knowledge transfer process. While additional research is needed to determine how various social capital and knowledge transfer practices are generalizable across firms and industries, the current study does show the importance of understanding both successful and unsuccessful offshore engagements through the lens of social capital. In the case of U.S. Manufacturing, while the nurturing of social capital was not a sufficient lever for success, it was a necessary one.

Practitioners, both on the customer and supplier sides of offshore engagements, should find evidence of the need to address both social capital and knowledge transfer issues within their engagements. While many suppliers place considerable weight on CMM and CMMi certifications and processes (Adler and Kwon 2002), this case shows that strong relationships and connections between the people involved are also critical to success. While transactions costs and intellectual property concerns do increase as both social capital and knowledge transfer increase, practitioners should develop a proper balance to ensure that cohesive and well-connected teams are able to form and pertinent knowledge and experiences are able to be transferred from customer to supplier.

Conclusion

The U.S. Manufacturing faced significant challenges in the offshore outsourcing of embedded software development. These challenges were significant enough that their first attempt failed to produce any acceptable deliverables. Moving forward from that failure, they developed eight practices that facilitated effective knowledge transfer. Using a social capital network model, this chapter posits that these practices were effective because they increased the social capital between U.S. Manufacturing and its suppliers. Managing the relationship at the structural, cognitive ,and relational dimensions allowed the partners in the strategic alliance to increase network stability, reduce cultural barriers, share and understand common goals, and strengthen network ties.

References

Adler, P.S., and Kwon, S-W. (2002) Social Capital: Prospects for a New Concept. *Academy of Management Review,* 27(1): 17–40.

Anand, V., Click, W., and Manz, C. (2002) Thriving on the Knowledge of Outsiders: Tapping Organizational Social Capital. *The Academy of Management Executive*, 16(1), Feb.: 87.

Argote, L. and Ingram, P. (2000) Knowledge Transfer: a Basis for Competitive Advantage in Firms. *Organizational Behavior and Human Decision Processes*, 82: 150–169.

Aron, R. and Singh, J. (2005) Getting Offshoring Right., *Harvard Business Review*, 8(12): 135–143.

Becerra, M. and Gupta, A. (2003) Perceived Trustworthiness within the Organization: The Moderating Impact of Communication Frequency on Trustor and Trustee Effects. *Organization Science*, 14(1): 32–44.

Carter, T. (2006) Cheaper's Not Always Better. *Dr. Dobb's Journal*, available on http://www.ddj.com/184415486 (accessed on 7/18/06).

Chowdhury, S. (2005) The Role of Affect- and Cognition-Based Trust in Complex Knowledge Sharing. *Journal of Managerial Issues*, 17(3): 310–326.

Dess, G. and Shaw, J. (2001) Voluntary Turnover, Social Capital, and Organizational Performance. *Academy of Management, The Academy of Management Review*, 26(3): 446–457.

Ferrin, D. and Dirks, K. (2003) The Use of Rewards to Increase and Decrease Trust: Mediating processes and differential effects. *Organization Science*, 14: 18–31.

Granovetter, M. (1973) The Strength of Weak Ties. *American Journal of Sociology*, 78: 1360–1380.

Hagedoorn, J., Cloodt, D., and Van Kranenburg, H.(2006) The Strength of R&D Network Ties in High-Tech Industries – A Multi-Dimensional Analysis of the Effects of Tie Strength on Technological Performance, Merit and Department of Organization and Strategy , DRUID Summer Conference 2006, Copenhagen, Denmark, June 18–20.

Hansen, M. (1999) The Search-Transfer Problem: the Role of Weak Ties in Sharing Knowledge across Organization Subunits. *Administrative Science Quarterly*, 44(1): 82–111.

Hart, P. and Saunders, C. (1998) Emerging Electronic Partnerships: Antecedents and Dimensions of EDI Use from the Supplier's Perspective. J*ournal of Management Information Systems*, 14(4): 87–112.

Hofstede, G. (2001) *Culture's Consequences*, 2nd edition, Beverly Hills: Sage.

Inkpen, A. and Tsang, E. (2005) Social Capital Networks and Knowledge Transfer. *Academy of Management Review*, 30(1): 146–165.

Jarvenpaa, S.L., Knoll, K., and Leidner, D.E. (1998). Is Anybody Out There? Antecedents of Trust in Global Virtual Teams. Journal of Management Information Systems, 14(4): 29–64.

Jennex, M. and Adelakun, O. (2003) Success Factors for Offshore Information System Development. *Journal of Information Technology Cases and Applications*, 5(3): 12–36.

Koka, B. and Prescott, J. (2002) Strategic Alliances as Social Capital: a Multidimensional View. *Strategic Management Journal*, 23: 795–816.

Levin, D. and Cross, R. (2004) The Strength of Weak Ties You Can Trust: The Mediating Role of Trust in Effective Knowledge Transfer, *Management Science*, 50(11): 1477–1490.

Levina, N. and Vaast, E. (2005) The Emergence of Boundary Spanning Competence in Practice: Implications for Implementation and Use of Information Systems. *MIS Quarterly*, 29(2): 235–363.

Lin, C. (2007) To Share or Not to Share: Modeling Tacit Knowledge Sharing: Its Mediators and Antecedents. *Journal of Business Ethics*, 70: 411–428.

Luftman, J. (2005) Key Issues for IT Executives 2004. *MIS Quarterly Executive*, 4(2) 269–285.

McFadyen, M. and Cannella, A. (2004) Social Capital and Knowledge Creation: Diminishing Returns of the Number and Strength of Exchange Relationships. *Academy of Management Journal,* 47(5): 735–746.

McFarlan, F. and Nolan, R. (1995) How to Manage an IT Outsourcing Alliance. *Sloan Management Review*, 36(2): 9–23.

Nahapiet, J. and Ghoshal, S. (1998) Social Capital, Intellectual Capital and the Organizational Advantage. *Academy of Management*, 23(2): 242–266.

Newell, S. and Swan, J. (2000) Trust and Inter-Organizational Networking. *Human Relations*, 53(10): 287–1328.

Oh, H., Labianca, G., and Chung, M-H. (2006) A Multilevel Model of Group Social Capital. *The Academy of Management Review,* 31(3): 569.

Oh, H., Chung, M-H., and Labianca G. (2004) Group Social Capital and Group Effectiveness: The Role of Informal Socializing Ties. *Academy of Management Journal*, 47(8): 860–875.

Orr, J. (1996) *Thinking about Machines*, London: Cornell University Press.

Politis, J.D. (2003) The Connection between Trust and Knowledge Management: What Are Its Implications for Team Performance. *Journal of Knowledge Management*, 7(5): 55–66.

Rogers, E.M. (2006) *Diffusion of Innovations,* 5th edition New York: Free Press.

Rottman, J. (2006), Successfully Outsourcing Embedded Software Development. *IEEE Computer,* 39(1): 55–61.

Rottman, J. and Lacity, M. (2004) Twenty Practices for Offshore Sourcing. *MIS Quarterly Executive*, 3(3): 117–130.

Rottman, J. and Lacity, M. (2006a) Knowledge Transfer is the Key to Successful Strategic Outsourcing. *The Outsourcing Project*, Vol. 4, Chapter 1, July, 2006. Available on http://www.cxoeurope.com/documents.asp?d_ID=87.

Rottman, J. and Lacity, M. (2006b) Proven Practices for Effectively Offshoring IT Work. *Sloan Management Review,* 47(3): 56–63.

Shaw, J., Duffy, M., Johnson, J., and Lockhart, D. (2005) Turnover, Social Capital Losses, and Performance. *Academy of Management Journal,* 48(4): 594–625.

Tiwana, A. and Keil, M. (2007) Does Peripheral Knowledge Complement Control? An Empirical Test in Technology Outsourcing Alliances. *Strategic Management Journal*, 28: 623–624.

Trompenaars, F. and Hampden-Turner, C. (1998) *Riding the Waves of Culture*, London: Nicholas Brearley.

Tsai, W. (2001) Knowledge Transfer in Intraorganizational Networks: Effects of Network Position and Absorptive Capacity on Business Unit Innovation and Performance. *Academy of Management Journal,* 44(5): 996–1005.

Tsoukas, H. (1996) The Firm as a Distributed Knowledge System: A Constructionist Approach. *Strategic Management Journal,* 17 Special Issue: 11–25.

Zaheer A., McEvily, B., and Perrone, V. (1998) Does Trust Matter? Exploring the Effects of Interorganizational and Interpersonal Trust on Performance. *Organization Science*, 9(2): 141–159.

CHAPTER 7

Risk, anxiety, and the production of comfort/trust in the context of globalized modes of working: the case of an Ireland-India IS offshoring relationship

Séamas Kelly and Camilla Noonan

Introduction

In this chapter, we explore the notion of anxiety and its management in the context of the development of an IS offshoring relationship between a small Irish financial services firm (NetTrade) and a large Indian software development company (IndiaSoft) with an extensive global presence. In particular, we focus on the "relationship work" required to produce and sustain a sense of emotional comfort on the part of the client in the context of, or what was constructed as, an extremely unfamiliar and risky venture. In so doing, we synthesize a novel theoretical perspective for illuminating key aspects of the phenomenon in question, by drawing mainly on Anthony Giddens' ideas on risk, trust, and globalization (Giddens 1990, 1991, 1994) supplemented by important contributions from other authors (e.g. Zucker 1986, Mayer et al. 1995; Misztal 1996). Although we employ the concept of "trust" as a key analytical device, we use this interchangeably with "comfort." This is an effort to emphasize the notion of trust as an "emotional commitment," which clearly distinguishes Giddens' analysis from the manner in which the concept has been generally used in the mainstream management literature.

While the management of risk has long been seen as a central problem in software development generally (Barki et al. 1993, Willcocks and Margetts

1994; Boehm and Demarco 1997), and IT outsourcing more specifically (Earl 1996; Willcocks and Lacity 1999; Willcocks et al. 1999), work in this area has focused mainly on rational strategies for dealing with risk (e.g., its identification, assessment, and management), rather than on the manner in which it is experienced and handled at an emotional level. Our aim here, then, is to broaden the discussion of risk, and its particular salience for IS offshoring initiatives, with a view to moving beyond purely cognitivist conceptions to consider important, yet often marginalized, emotional dimensions (c.f. McGrath 2006; Ciborra and Willcocks; 2006). In particular, we attempt to illustrate the central role of anxiety/insecurity in shaping the contours of organizational life and to examine the mechanisms used to produce the sense of comfort that is vital to active engagement with environments characterized by risk. Furthermore, we highlight the particular importance of such a perspective to the area of IS offshoring, by arguing that the globally distributed nature of such work alters the risk profile of systems development while simultaneously problematizing conventional mechanisms for producing comfort.

The theoretical contribution of the chapter is grounded in, and enhanced by, a detailed account of on an ongoing in-depth, longitudinal, interpretive study of the development of the offshoring relationship between NetTrade and IndiaSoft. The case focuses on a crucial 18-month period in NetTrade's commercial evolution, during which a decision was made to outsource the development of a replacement for their core technology to one of IndiaSoft's offshore development centers in India City. Specifically, we examine the ongoing implementation process as it unfolded: from NetTrade's initial decision to look for a suitable vendor, through the development of the NetTrade–IndiaSoft relationship, to the delivery of the first major component of the system. The notions of risk and anxiety had a special salience in this context due to the key strategic importance of the system, and the scale of the development project in relation to the size of NetTrade (the projected cost of the system actually exceeded the Net Asset Value of the entire firm at the time). Moreover, before IndiaSoft was suggested as a possible option to NetTrade, nobody in the firm had any awareness of, let alone given any consideration to, an offshore IT sourcing model. IndiaSoft, for its part, has no other Irish client of equivalent size to NetTrade.

In our analysis of the case, we argue that the development of the offshoring relationship to this point involved two distinctive, yet overlapping and mutually reinforcing, phases (Courtship and Cohabitation) that demanded different kinds of practices and skills for their successful negotiation. From the client's point of view, two salient forms of comfort/trust were important: trust in the qualities of the vendor; and trust in the stability and predictability of the collaborative social order (i.e., trust as "habitus"). In the Courtship phase, the emphasis was primarily on the client developing trust in the vendor's ability to deliver the system and in the latter's integrity and benevolence toward the former. This trust rested primarily on presentational (through the performances of vendor representatives at key access points) and reputational bases, although characteristic-based and institutional-based mechanisms also played a role. In the Cohabitation phase, by contrast, the emphasis shifted to a struggle to construct a stable collaborative order, where both parties had to come to mutual accommodations about key social practices (primarily communicative practices in this case). These practices contributed to the predictability of the social order and, importantly, their successful negotiation and institutionalization was dependent on the skilful balancing of "trust, tact and power" (Giddens 1990, 82).

The chapter is structured as follows. In the following section, we synthesize a distinctive theoretical perspective that illuminates the relationship between the emergence of new modes of global working, risk, and anxiety. In particular, we emphasize the important role of trust, as an "emotional commitment," for the production of a sense of existential comfort that facilitates the bracketing of risk and engagement with unfamiliar practices. We then go on to outline our research approach to the empirical fieldwork (i.e., the NetTrade-IndiaSoft case) upon which the chapter is based, before describing and analyzing the case study in some detail. We conclude by reflecting on the key conclusions that might be drawn from the work and their wider implications for research and practice.

Conceptual basis – globalization, risk, anxiety and the production of comfort/trust

In this section, we introduce some of Anthony Giddens' ideas on globalization, anxiety, and the production of comfort/trust, which we develop and supplement with reference to the work of a number of other scholars who have studied trust. We regard Giddens' work in this area as particularly relevant and insightful, in that it has a number of distinctive features by comparison with much of the extant literature on trust in management/ organization studies. Three issues are especially salient in this regard: his view of trust as a matter of "faith" or an "emotional commitment"; his distinction between personal and impersonal forms of trust and his theorization of the relationship between the two and; his observation that new modes of trust production (based on the interaction between personal and impersonal forms of trust) become especially important for securing a sense of emotional comfort (thus reducing anxiety and facilitating productive engagement) in the context of a more globalized world where interactions routinely span greater temporal-spatial and cultural distances. While these points are developed further below, it is important to explain briefly their significance with respect to the general trust literature.

Trust is seen as one of the most complex and difficult concepts to apply in social science research, due to the diversity of different ways it has been defined and the multiple social functions that it assumed to fulfill (Misztal 1996). Despite attempts to integrate competing conceptualizations that have been employed in the domain of management/organization studies (e.g., Rousseau et al. 1998), significant divergences and anomalies persist. In contrast to Giddens' view of trust as an emotional commitment, for instance, much of the literature regards trust as the product of a very calculative, deliberative, rational decision-making process (McAllister 1995; Ring 1996; Rousseau et al. 1998). This betrays a very "cognitivist" perspective (Chaiklin and Lave 1996, Dreyfus and Dreyfus 2005, Kelly 2005) that has been roundly criticized by those who would advocate a more holistic approach to understanding the human subject, one which avoids a dualism between the cognitive and the emotional (c.f. McGrath 2006, Ciborra and Willcocks 2006). Indeed, a key shortcoming of the notion of "calculative trust" is that it fails to adequately discriminate between trusting behavior and calculated risk taking. Giddens' perspective, then, is based on a richer conceptualization of the human subject, and to emphasize the distinctiveness of this approach, by comparison with the more usual use of the concept of trust in the literature, we employ the term "comfort/trust" in this chapter.

Giddens sees trust as an emotional commitment in the form of a continuous state, as opposed to a decision at a discrete point of time, and in this way, he sees it as intimately bound up with the maintenance of an agent's sense of psychological security. This emphasis on personal anxiety and insecurity opens up an important dimension of organizational life that has received very little attention in the mainstream management and IS literatures (for some notable exceptions, see Miller and O'Leary 1987; Knights 1990, 1992; Bloomfield and Coombs 1992; Knights and Murray 1994; Sturdy 1997; Knights and Willmott 1999; Wastell 2003). One notable contribution in the area of software development is Wastell's (1996) use of psychoanalytic theory to examine the unhelpful ways in which systems development methodologies may be used to combat insecurity and anxiety on the part of developers. While this insightful analysis opened up a very promising direction for the study of systems development practice, however, it has not been built upon subsequently. Moreover, that fact that such anxieties and insecurities are likely to be accentuated in a globally distributed context would suggest that this is an area in need of attention. The perspective developed here, which is particularly attentive to tensions between co-located and distributed forms of interaction, addresses this lacuna in a distinctive way.

Finally, a key strength of Giddens' work is that he enlarges the scope of the concept of trust to encompass impersonal forms of trust or trust in systems. While he is not alone in this (see, e.g., Luhmann 1979, 1988), much of the management/organization studies literature confines itself primarily to discussions of trust as an interpersonal phenomenon (Rousseau et al. 1998). Not only does Giddens illustrate the importance of trust in systems but he also demonstrates how this is linked to, and indeed grounded in, personal forms of trust.

In what follows in this section, then, we introduce some of Giddens' key ideas in relation to globalization, risk, anxiety, and the production of comfort/trust, before going on to supplement this perspective by drawing on the work of a number of other important scholars in the area. This synthesized theoretical perspective is then employed to make sense of the NetTrade-IndiaSoft case that is described subsequently.

Giddens on globalization, risk, anxiety, and the production of comfort/trust

The sociologist Anthony Giddens (1990, 34) argues that, in modernity, the nature of trust relations has been transformed and, indeed, takes on a new importance. Trust is inherently connected to *absence* (there is no need to trust what one can directly monitor), and is bound up with the organization of "reliable" interactions across time-space. He defines trust as

> ... confidence in the reliability of a person or system, regarding a given set of outcomes or events, when that confidence expresses a faith in the probity or love of another, or in the correctness of abstract principles. (Giddens 1990, 34)

Thus, he distinguishes between two types of trust relations prevalent in modern societies: *trust in abstract systems*[1] and *personal trust*. The former relations are based, to a large extent, on *faceless commitments* while the latter depend on *facework commitments* (trust relations that are sustained by, or expressed in, social connections established in conditions of copresence).

The investment of trust in abstract systems (especially expert systems) is a central feature of modern life. No one can completely opt out of the abstract systems involved in modern institutions yet, due to their diversity and complexity, our knowledge of their workings is necessarily limited. Therefore, trust (or faceless commitments) becomes a very important means of generating the "leap of faith" that practical engagement with them demands. Often, however, engagement with abstract systems involves encounters,[2] with individuals who "represent" or are "responsible" for them (e.g., in the case of visiting a medical doctor). Such contacts with experts are very consequential and take place at *access points*, which form the meeting ground of facework and faceless commitments.

In the case of some experts (e.g., a doctor) where encounters take place regularly over a period of years, these can take on the characteristics of trustworthiness associated with friendship and intimacy. However, in general, encounters with experts are much more irregular and transitory than this and, therefore, they have to be managed very carefully by the expert if he or she is to win or maintain trust of the laypeople involved. Drawing on Goffman (1956), Giddens argues that facework commitments are dependent on the demeanor of operators and, therefore, such encounters often involve displays of "manifest trustworthiness and integrity, coupled with an attitude of 'business as usual' or unflappability" (Giddens 1990, 85). Access points remind people of the fallible nature of system operators and, therefore, reassurance is called for, both in terms of the reliability of the individuals involved and the knowledge or skills upon which their expertise relies. Thus, experts must make a strict division between "frontstage" and "backstage" performance at access points, and the control of the threshold between the two is the essence of professionalism. Attitudes of trust are strongly influenced by experiences at access points, as well as by updates of knowledge provided by mass communications media and other sources.

Thus, facework commitments are an important means of generating continued trustworthiness in the abstract systems of modernity with which we routinely interact. In this way, trust in impersonal abstract systems is anchored in the trustworthiness and integrity of colleagues. Of course, regular encounters and rituals are required to sustain such collegial trustworthiness: that is, trust rests on a "presentational base." Furthermore, in Giddens' terms trust is not a cognitive/calculative phenomenon but, rather, is based on an *emotional* commitment to things being as we expect them to be. Trust, therefore, may be understood as a sense of emotional comfort; a device that can be used to "bracket out" potential risks (Giddens 1990) and generate the "leap into faith" that cooperative engagement with others demands (Gambetta 1988).

From this perspective, then, trust is a continuous state, rather than a discrete decision, and a key mode of trust production are stable institutionalized routines; what Misztal (1996, 127) terms *trust as "habitus."* Having stable and well-recognized rules of interaction gives a sense of predictability, reliability, and legibility to social life, thus reducing the anxiety caused by the ambiguity and openness of many social situations. The construction of a shared set of stable social practices among people who are strangers or mere acquaintances, however, can be problematic and calls for the balancing of "trust, tact and power" (Giddens 1990, 82). As Giddens (1990, 82–83) puts it:

> Tact and rituals of politeness are mutual protective devices, which strangers or acquaintances knowingly use (mostly at the level of practical consciousness) as a kind of implicit social contact. Differential power, particularly where it is very marked, can breach or skew norms of tact and politeness rituals.

The implications of this are twofold. First, it emphasizes the importance of a stable social order for the production of trust and reduction of anxiety.[3] Second, it emphasizes the important role of tact and rituals of politeness, in the absence of marked differential power, in helping to bring about the mutual accommodations required to develop the shared social practices required to sustain any stable collaborative order. In other words, attention is drawn to the micro-politics of trust production.

Supplementing Giddens' ideas – exploring the nature of, and bases for, personal trust

Despite the emphasis Giddens places on personal trust, he does not explore its constitution in any great detail. In a review of the literature, however, Mayer et al. (1995) identify three characteristics of a trustee that appear consistently: ability, benevolence, and integrity. Ability is defined as

> the group of skills, competencies and characteristics that enable a party to have influence within some specific domain. The domain of

the ability is specific because the trustee may be highly competent in some technical areas, affording that person trust on tasks related to that area. However, the trustee may have little aptitude, training or experience in another area, for instance, in interpersonal communication. ... Thus, trust is domain specific.

Benevolence, on the other hand, is defined as the extent to which a trustee is believed to want to do good *to the trustor*, aside from an egocentric profit motive (suggesting that the trustee has some specific attachment to the trustor). Finally, the relationship between integrity and trust involves the trustor's perception that the trustee adheres to a set of principles that the trustor finds acceptable.

If the dispositions and characters of a collection of people are individually well-known to each other then cooperative relations may be founded on what Williams terms as *thick trust* (Williams 1988, 8). In other words, cooperation among a group of individuals is greatly facilitated if they have established personal bonds and know one another very well. However, where thick trust does not exist, other means of establishing or producing trust are required as a basis for cooperation. Zucker identifies three key modes of trust production in the modern world (Zucker 1986): *process-based* (information based on personal experience), *characteristic-based* (information based on ascribed characteristics), and *institutional-based* (formal protection against default).

In modes of process-based trust production "a record of prior exchange, often obtained second hand or by imputation from outcomes of prior exchange, provides data on the exchange process" (Zucker 1986, 60). Therefore, process-based trust is based on the availability of large quantities of person- or group-specific information which can often be in the form of positive reputations.[4] This is the most commonly identified mode of trust production in sociological and anthropological work, and most of the early work in the area focused on gift-exchange (c.f. Mauss [1925] 1954). In such cases, trust is required due to the time lapse between the gift and the counter-gift and the possible ambiguity surrounding accepted conceptions of what constitutes a fair exchange. One possible mechanism for developing such trust involves "restricting exchanges to those whose prior exchange histories are known or to those with some guarantee concerning the nature of future exchanges" (Zucker 1986, 62). Information about prior exchange histories can be obtained by engaging in repetitive exchanges with a party and, therefore, such informal trust-producing mechanisms "require extensive interaction over long periods of time and/or produce trust between a small number of individuals involved in a limited set of exchanges" (Zucker 1986, 62). Such exchange relationships are generally highly specific to the parties involved in the exchange and involve idiosyncratic understandings and rules. Thus, trusting relationships are built in successive stages, tentatively and conditionally over time (Good 1988).

A more formal mechanism for the production of process-based trust involves the use of reputation (or, brand name in the case of products). As Misztal puts it:

> Reputation permits us to trust another person by providing us with some information regarding the sort of person we are dealing with, before we have had a chance to have contact with that person. (1996, 120–121)

Thus, reputation serves as a warrant for trust and can, therefore, be seen as valuable social capital (Misztal 1996, 121). The establishment of a favorable reputation requires significant investments of time and resources and is, thus, something which individuals and groups will be very careful to maintain. Therefore, a reputation not only provides information about the trustworthiness of an individual or group but also serves as a device for restricting the behavior of those who have invested in it (Misztal 1996, 98). Moreover, as Casson (1991, 16) has pointed out, "[l]oss of reputation is particularly serious for people who are locked into a group where barriers to exit are high. In fact it can be shown that reputation effects succeed quite well in sustaining trust in small, compact, and isolated social groups." Reputation, therefore, promotes cooperation by increasing the possibility of carrying out promises, thus helping to facilitate efficient contractual relations by allowing economic agents to reduce transaction costs and overcome limited information (Dasgupta 1988; Lorenz 1988, 198–202). Misztal (1996, 127) also underlines the importance of reputation by pointing out that "the absence of cooperation is a result not so much of bad reputation as of the lack of reputation. In other words, the existence of reputation is an important social capital which facilitates people's willingness to cooperate by helping to overcome a scarcity of information."

The second basis for trust, according to Zucker (1986), is individual characteristics. Such characteristics may be ascribed to individuals through labeling or stereotyping mechanisms:

> When there is scarcity of information, particularly when we have more information about the group than an individual member, there is a tendency to simplify the perception of the social environment

by identifying all individuals with the groups to which they belong. (Misztal 1996: 126)

Thus, characteristics such as gender, ethnicity, family background, or age may be used as an index of trust in a transaction, as they "serve as indicators of membership in a common cultural system, of shared background expectations. In general, the greater the number of social similarities (dissimilarities), the more interacts assume that common background expectations do (do not) exist, hence trust can (cannot) be relied upon" (Zucker 1986, 63). Furthermore, as in the case of reputations, stereotypes or preconceptions are not easily changed, even in the face of challenging evidence. New information about an individual will tend to be interpreted in accordance with existing preconceptions, thus serving to reinforce those preconceptions (Good 1988, 41).

The third basis of trust production, institutional, is more generic in its application, in that it extends beyond a specific transaction or set of exchange partners (Zucker 1986, 63). Two types of institutional-based trust are identified: person-specific (or firm-specific) and intermediary mechanisms. Person- or firm-specific trust depends on membership of a social group "within which carefully delineated specific expectations are expected to hold, at least in some cases based on detailed prior socialization" (Zucker 1986, 63). The professionalization of occupations (see Reed 1992, 206–213) provides a very clear illustration of how this type of trust can be signaled. Thus, for example, the attainment of specific educational or professional certifications can signal one's trustworthiness within a particular social sphere. The second type of institutional trust, intermediary mechanisms, involves insuring against potential losses in the event of a transaction not being completed or not producing the expected results. Intermediary institutions such as courts of law or insurance companies specialize in protecting parties involved in an exchange in this way.

In summary, then, we have attempted to synthesize a distinctive perspective on the production of comfort/trust based largely on the ideas of Anthony Giddens and supplemented by the contributions of other key scholars in the area. This illustrates the importance of comfort/trust in people and systems, how this is problematized in modern contexts marked by increased interaction over temporal-spatial and cultural distance, and the mechanisms through which it might be produced. Comfort/trust is seen as a key means of "bracketing" risk, thus allowing productive engagement with an inherently insecure world. By highlighting the importance of comfort/trust, however, we do not wish to downplay that of more conventional means of control as a risk management strategy. Following Das and Teng

(1998), we see trust and control as playing mutually supplementary roles in the production of an overall sense of confidence. As Hart (1988) felicitously puts it, trust exists "at the interstices of control."

About this research

The empirical research described in this chapter is the result of an ongoing, in-depth, longitudinal, interpretive study of the establishment and development of the offshoring relationship between NetTrade and IndiaSoft. We followed the project from its inception in the latter part of 2005, when we were introduced to the case by the joint CEO of NetTrade. We also managed to secure the cooperation and involvement of IndiaSoft. We established contact with their local office in Dublin and negotiated further access to the development center (IndiaCity) in India. Data collection consisted informal chats with the CEO, a number of visits to the NetTrade offices in Dublin, a week visit to IndiaCity development center during which we conducted interviews, observed activities, and reviewed various documents associated with this project. Overall, we interviewed the 14 key players involved in the project, in formal and informal settings, many of them repeatedly and for extended periods of time. This amounted to approximately 35 hours of formal interviews, and at least this much time again was spent observing in the workplace and attending informal outings. Furthermore, key personnel at NetTrade were requested to keep a written journal, reflecting on their interactions with IndiaSoft, particularly during their early visits to India.

Distance and the production of comfort in the NetTrade-IndiaSoft case

NetTrade, a small Irish financial services firm, was established in 2001 by its joint CEOs, John and Niall. They described themselves as *a small unknown company with the standard start-up mentality* (John, Joint CEO, NetTrade). After four very successful years in operation, they began to plan for future growth. The key strategic issue related to their IT system, which was core to their business. Up to that point, NetTrade had leased the software from a small U.K.-based supplier but the attraction of having their own bespoke system was always apparent. In addition to the risk associated with over-reliance on a supplier, two additional factors influenced their decision to develop their own bespoke system. First, as the business grew, their requirements for additional system functionality were also growing. Second, under the current arrangement, they owned the license for this system but not the code. Consequently, they felt that a bespoke trading system would *put us [them] on a different planet entirely* (John, Joint CEO, NetTrade).

In Autumn 2005, NetTrade set out to formally identify a partner to develop the system for them. As this was the key strategic system upon which future prosperity depended, the quality of the delivered product was paramount. Consequently, it was with some trepidation that NetTrade approached the development project:

> *It was difficult because we didn't know what we were doing ... we were shooting in the dark and did not know who would be even interested in doing business with us* (John, Joint CEO, NetTrade)

The firm was very conscious that it would be financially exposed should anything go wrong (the projected cost of the system was greater than the Net Asset Value of the entire firm at that point in time). They decided to manage this risk by insisting to potential vendors that the project be structured in stages (or *bite-sized chunks*). This meant that NetTrade would pay for each deliverable and would reserve the right to pull back from the other stages of the project in the event of dissatisfaction or changing financial circumstances.

After meeting with a number of *singularly unimpressive* local consulting firms, a personal friend of John and Niall's suggested that they might explore an offshoring model and introduced them to IndiaSoft, a major Indian software vendor with a base in Dublin. After an initial meeting with Ajit (the Indian General Manager of IndiaSoft's Irish operation) and Stephen (an Irish Business Development Manager for IndiaSoft), NetTrade were extremely impressed and, despite some significant apprehension about their unfamiliarity with this mode of development, decided that an offshoring approach was worth exploring further. Throughout their initial interactions with IndiaSoft, NetTrade were very honest about their anxieties, their inexperience, and their need for guidance through the process that lay ahead:

> *We knew what we wanted but we were not "deal" savvy. We were not through the RFP process, which was the first thing we told everybody. Don't expect us to tell you, you need to tell us. We didn't know but we knew we didn't know. We did make a big deal about that.* (John, Joint CEO, NetTrade)

In addition to stated concerns about their inexperience, and consequent dependence on the vendor, another major issue concerned NetTrade. They were very conscious of the fact that in IndiaSoft's eyes, they might be viewed as a small, relatively unimportant and insignificant Irish company in the context of the firm's overall client portfolio. They feared that this imbalance could be problematic going forward:

> *That was a big deal because the first question (and one that we kept coming back to) was, what happens when Ford or GM or whoever calls, will we get screwed? ... it is engrained in us, people will value you less because you are smaller.* (John, Joint CEO, NetTrade)

As is evident from our discussion below, the Indian firm went to considerable lengths to address these fears, thereby laying the foundations for a successful relationship that developed over the 2005–2007 period under study. In late December 2005 and in line with the "bite-sized chunks" philosophy of the firm, an agreement was reached that IndiaSoft would be engaged to do an initial requirement specifications and scoping exercise. NetTrade were extremely satisfied with the resulting document and decided to contract with the Indians for delivery of the system.

Key events over this time period include:

December 2005:	First meeting with IndiaSoft and signing of the initial agreement for requirements specification.
January 2006:	First visit by John (Joint CEO, NetTrade) and Paul (Head of Finance) to IndiaSoft's development center in IndiaCity, India to commence the requirements gathering and scoping process.
March 2006:	Representatives from IndiaCity visit Dublin to complete requirements gathering.
April 2006:	Functional Specification completed and negotiations take place around the signing of the contract for the development work. Work commences.
August/September 2006:	John (Joint CEO, NetTrade) and Deborah (Head of IT) visit IndiaCity to view prototypes. Issues around live data feed requirements surface.
December 2006:	Paul (Head of Finance) and Deborah (Head of IT) visit IndiaCity to monitor progress. NetTrade receive invoice for cost overruns.

January 2007:   New IndiaSoft Business Relationship Manager (Ajay)
                joins the project.
                Representatives from IndiaSoft visit Dublin to ensure
                smooth delivery.
                Installation difficulties at NetTrade.

These events will be returned to in the subsequent analysis.

One of the notable aspects of this case is that, for the most part, the offshore development project ran relatively smoothly and was not beset by any major crises. This is not to say that frustrations and anxieties were not encountered along the way, but these were addressed and repaired in a relatively calm and mature manner. Here, we argue that a key factor in understanding this smooth running of the project was the way in which a sense of comfort was produced and sustained over time. The careful cultivation of this sense of comfort, although costly and resource intensive, played a key role in the success of the project. Here, we draw on some of the theories of trust introduced earlier, in an attempt to trace some of the mechanisms by which this comfort was produced, enhanced, undermined, and reestablished over time.

Following Giddens, we suggest that a key source of anxiety in the offshoring project was the difficulty in establishing trust in the expert systems of technical and professional knowledge upon which IndiaSoft drew (i.e., to provide "guarantees" with respect to the "correctness" of the technological solution that would be delivered across distanciated time-space (from India to Ireland)). Of critical importance here, then, was the manner in which this abstract system was "re-embedded" in the concrete context of the NetTrade–IndiaSoft relationship.[5]

We argue that within the time frame outlined above, two distinctive, yet overlapping and mutually constitutive, phases are discernible. In the Courtship phase, the emphasis was on establishing a sense of trust in IndiaSoft as the suitor of choice, thus allowing NetTrade to bracket the associated risks and comfortably proceed with the project.[6] In the Cohabitation phase a new emphasis emerged, that focused on the joint construction of a stable collaborative order. In what follows, we examine and compare the social practices that underpinned these important processes.

Stage 1: Courtship – establishing trust in IndiaSoft
With respect to becoming comfortable with the notion of an offshoring arrangement, John identified three different components with which he, and his colleagues at NetTrade, needed to reconcile themselves: the generalized offshoring model; the idea of offshoring to India specifically; and

IndiaSoft as the vendor of choice. The fact that John had only vaguely heard of software offshoring prior to the initial suggestion by a friend in August 2005, illustrates the distance he had to travel before committing to this route:

> *To me now it seems like an easy decision. But then I knew very little about the whole outsourcing area...it was a real dark place that we were trying to figure out...I asked myself whether this made sense, how did it work? Were we just looking for a cheap option? Were we crazy?* (John, Joint CEO, NetTrade)

The initial comfort that created the impetus to explore the offshoring model and aligning with IndiaSoft specifically was based mainly on established trust relations, that is, **process-based trust**. Both direct and indirect forms of such trust were apparent. Direct forms are observed in the case of recommendations of friends and friends of friends. John and Niall approached IndiaSoft in the first place on the recommendation of a close personal friend with experience of the IT industry. Furthermore, and perhaps more importantly, on approaching a very senior manager in a large global IT consulting firm, who was a friend of a fellow NetTrade board member, for advice on the subject, they received a *big thumbs up* with respect to the offshoring model and IndiaSoft's capability in the area. A final example was seen in April 2006, when the two firms entered into negotiations around the contract. Niall talked about how reassured he was by the minimalist nature of IndiaSoft's contract:

> *I am still surprised by their template contract that they had for us in terms of how short it was. I was totally taken aback that, for a company like IndiaSoft, it was not more comprehensive and did not cover more areas. Even from their point of view, I thought there would be more protections in there for themselves. Even perceiving it like that was quite reassuring – they were obviously not out to screw anybody.* (Niall, Joint CEO, NetTrade)

The initial awareness of the offshoring possibility was followed by the commencement of what John described as a *demystification process*, where he began to notice and actively seek out articles about outsourcing in, what he considered, trusted sources such as "The Economist." The reputational effects (indirect process-based trust) of such sources, supplemented by testimonies from IndiaSoft reference clients, contributed to a growing sense of comfort with the overall offshoring model.

A more **firm-specific, institutional basis** for establishing trust and creating comfort was drawn on as IndiaSoft outlined and explained their CMM level 5 certification in their presentations to NetTrade.

The first major **access point** to the IndiaSoft offshoring model came with the initial face-to-face meeting with Ajit and Stephen in NetTrade's office in Dublin. This meeting appears to have been very consequential for the development of the relationship, as John and Niall were left feeling extremely impressed and reassured.

> *I remember vividly the meeting with Ajit and Stephen and I just found them incredibly impressive – very, very impressive – particularly Ajit. From a cultural point of view, I am used to Anglo-Saxon meetings; everyone is fairly machismo and everybody makes themselves heard... he was a GM and everyone around the table knew that he was very senior and he said almost nothing. And then at the end he said four or five sentences and they were so pithy and so... I personally like people like that that do not talk too much. He finished it off, summarized the meeting, and he was very impressive.* (Niall, Joint CEO, NetTrade)

> *They wowed us in terms of their apparent ability to deliver quality and this on top of what appears to be an unbeatable proposition from a cost perspective.* (John, Joint CEO, NetTrade)

Reflecting on their early meetings when representatives presented information about IndiaSoft and the offshoring models employed, John was clearly impressed by their apparent ability. He described the presentations as *extremely slick and professional* and he was struck by their *systematic approach to software development*. This professional manner and slickness was reinforced by references to IndiaSoft's CMM level 5 certification (even though neither John nor Niall had previously heard of CMM, they were able to find out more about it subsequently). Interestingly, however, it was not the apparent professional ability of the IndiaSoft representatives that made the greatest impression; rather, it was their **general demeanor** and their **care and attentiveness**, which was to become a recurring feature of subsequent interactions.

A number of qualities seemed to set IndiaSoft apart from the other software firms that they had approached. First, there was the overall sense of **integrity** which was largely born from a sense of value congruity with NetTrade. Of crucial importance here was NetTrade's conception of their own values and sense of identity, which had been the subject of lively ongoing reflection and discussion since the inception of the company. In particular, a set of five core values had been agreed upon and, perhaps unusually for a financial services company, two of the principal ones were *humility* and *basic honesty*. The former emphasized the importance of a low-key, unfussy and modest style, while the latter emphasized the value of integrity in dealing with people. In this respect, then, IndiaSoft were viewed as fellow-travelers with whom NetTrade's guiding values were very well aligned, and their humility and integrity seemed to indicate a kind of dependability:

> *Bottom line – It was their humility. It is a value that we very genuinely hold and when we are selecting people to work with… if they don't have it and are more on the arrogant side, they are not for here. IndiaSoft definitely have it.* (Niall, Joint CEO, NetTrade)

This apparent **value congruity** generated a kind of **characteristic-based trust** that both John and Niall generalized to, what they saw as, the distinct cultural affinities between Ireland and India. Memorably, John subsequently remarked how the Indian people he interacted with at the outset, and throughout the project, reminded him of Irish software engineers he had worked with on graduating with a Computer Science degree, nearly 20 years before. They were, he claimed, *modest, hard working, and hungry* before the more recent Irish economic success enjoyed on the back of the so-called "Celtic Tiger" made them *too complacent and brash*. In IndiaSoft, then, John and Niall saw values that they could identify with, and were trying to foster in their own company; values that they nostalgically associated with an apparently bygone "golden" age of Irish economic development.[7]

The **care and attentiveness** that they received from IndiaSoft came as a very pleasant surprise and was greatly welcomed by NetTrade. John and Niall were both greatly impressed by IndiaSoft's thoroughness in responding to points and requests made by NetTrade:

> *they responded to everything on our list – they wanted us; they loved us and we like being loved… they seemed to want our business – they showed an interest in our business in a way that others didn't… When you meet somebody that you are impressed with, it is just a good experience and you want to proceed… we (had) a connection here and we like(d) them… we were constantly getting good vibes.* (John, Joint CEO, NetTrade)

> *IndiaSoft had such a huge capacity to listen and respond to this – it is absolutely brilliant, they are great listeners.* (Niall, Joint CEO, NetTrade)

While this level of attentiveness was quite unexpected on the basis of their dealings with other agencies and companies in Ireland (*it is engrained in us, people will value you less because you are smaller*: John), it was instrumental in allaying one of their key fears: that of their project being so small and insignificant that it would *get lost* within a big organization like IndiaSoft. This apparent **benevolence** on the part of IndiaSoft toward NetTrade was reinforced by John's relationship with Stephen who, importantly, was based in IndiaSoft's Dublin office (located only a short distance from NetTrade's office). Stephen *did a good job initially in selling IndiaSoft as IndiaSoft Ireland* and so reassuring John that whatever fears he might have of NetTrade *getting lost* in IndiaSoft, that there was no way this would happen in IndiaSoft Ireland (another relatively small, but growing, Irish company), or indeed in the IndiaCity development center (again a small, but growing, business entity). Here again we see an example of IndiaSoft "mirroring" NetTrade and, in so doing, strengthening the sense of trust and mutual affiliation.

IndiaSoft's care and attentiveness was also manifested in the numerous ways in which they appeared to go the extra mile to accommodate NetTrade's needs thereby making them feel valued as a client. Key events here included Stephen making a trip to the delivery center in IndiaCity to coincide with John's and Paul's initial visit there; the attentiveness and personal hospitality afforded by Pratima (the head of the IndiaCity Delivery Centre) to John and his colleagues during his visits to India (the fact that someone so senior was taking an interest in the project made a very big impression on John); the fact that IndiaSoft appeared to be very sensitive to NetTrade's anxieties about the project and did everything they could to accommodate their *bite-size chunks* risk management philosophy (for instance the fact that they agreed to break the total cost of the system into four manageable staged payments was seen as a very significant gesture by NetTrade and provided some welcome relief from the financial burden that they were undertaking to develop the system); and the fact that IndiaSoft went to great lengths to take the unusual step of providing ongoing remote access to a working prototype of the system, at John's behest.

One interesting observation about this process of comfort building was that the steps taken to ease NetTrade's anxiety appeared to appeal to both cognitive and emotional elements of John's and Niall's personalities. The "bite-sized chunks" approach, for example, was a very rational and sensible strategy for risk management. By contrast, however, both John and Niall spoke often about the (much less tangible) *good vibes* that they constantly got from IndiaSoft and the important role that this played in their decision-making. In this regard, we are reminded of Giddens' assertion that trust is always blind and that it involves an emotional, as opposed to a cognitive, commitment to a given set of outcomes. The comfort established in this case, then, involved both trust (an emotional commitment) and calculation (more of a cognitive sense of assurance).[8]

Stage 2: Cohabitation – constructing a stable collaborative order
Despite the excellent and reassuring early impressions as to the ability, benevolence, and integrity of the IndiaSoft representatives, and the reliability of their software delivery systems and processes, it was clear that increasing levels of trust were developed only tentatively over time. In other words, the mechanisms for developing trust discussed above were not confined to one identifiable period of the project, but extended throughout the duration of the relationship. As the project progressed, process-based trust again came to the fore as NetTrade became more comfortable with the IndiaSoft offshore development model. Key to this was the quality of the intermediary deliverables and, more importantly, the deepening personal relationships between key actors in both companies. In particular, these relationships gave the project a new robustness, which allowed issues to be dealt with in a more open and direct manner.[9]

In the Cohabitation phase, however, a new emphasis emerged: that of constructing a **stable collaborative order**. While a good basis for trust had been developed in the earlier period, both parties now had to collectively establish communal social practices to enable them to work closely together. Of critical importance here, from the point of view of producing trust, was the stability and predictability that such practices would confer on the project interactions. Once activities around the project commenced, incongruent **communication practices** quickly surfaced and presented a number of challenges. The first evidence of tension in the relationship emerged during John's initial visit to India. Together with his Head of Finance (Paul), John spent eight days in intensive meetings meticulously explaining their requirements to the Indians. He became immediately concerned that the process lacked direction and input from the Indians:

> *I'm concerned that there is not a strong leader outlining the process and stepping us confidently through it.* (John, Joint CEO, NetTrade)

> *One negative aspect would be that they seem a bit too accommodating. I would prefer if they sometimes disagreed and instead gave their views as alternatives.* (Paul, personal journal)

On several occasions, John repeatedly asked the then project sponsor (Suran) to send him copies of the Indian team's rough notes from the requirements sessions. He wanted these to ensure that the Indians understood NetTrade's needs around the new system. This was new to IndiaSoft – they had never received such a request from a client and they were reluctant to comply, preferring instead to complete a draft of the requirements document that might then be reviewed by John[10]:

> *... sometimes we wanted things that were not planned for as a deliverable and I don't think their processes allow for it...and this was frustrating because they did not tell us this explicitly...we were not getting a straight answer.* (John, personal journal)

At later stages, further frustrations were evident around the directness of communication:

> *I remember I got into a very bitter discussion around the issue of volume testing. ... We asked what they planned to do around volume testing ... he would not answer the question ... even if the answer was "we don't know" – that would have been an honest answer – but getting the other response was annoying.* (John, Joint CEO, NetTrade)

These communication deficits were even acknowledged on the Indian side, as one informant confided how sometimes *things tend to go from green to red with no amber light!*

Despite weekly status meetings and ongoing contacts, John felt that *there are big silences in the process*, and these silences made him very uncomfortable.[11] A good example of this was seen toward the end of 2006 when a dispute ensued about the acquisition of the data feed to test the software. After an initial delay around selecting and reaching an agreement with a data provider that would feed the live data into Dublin, NetTrade were surprised to learn that IndiaSoft also needed a live feed link into the development site in India:

> *There was one deliverable from the NetTrade site – the live data feed. There was a delay on NetTrade's side as to the provider...For us to proceed with our work, we needed this basic information. The delay had an impact. This was discussed at status meetings. The dash board/ status report went to Dublin and there was a traffic light on the report in terms of the effort, costs, schedule etc. We communicated it explicitly enough but John thought we did not communicate it correctly. He*

realised that this would have a schedule impact but said that we were not explicit on the cost impact. This reflected the lack of project experience on NetTrade's side. (Suresh, Project Sponsor, IndiaSoft).

This was later confirmed by Ajay (the new Business Relationship Manager (BRM), who joined the project in January 2007):

Ahmed must have mentioned it about five times on the status reports and got no response and when you get no response you tend to ignore it ... and we should not have done this. (Ajay, BRM, IndiaSoft(Irl.))

John notes how this came as a big surprise to NetTrade:

... it wasn't there earlier in the summer when we setting up. I kept saying ye are the experts, tell us what you want, tell us how it works ... you are supposed to have done this many times in many different ways – so guide us. (John, Joint CEO, NetTrade)

John claimed that IndiaSoft had casually alluded to this in August 2006, but the issue was hardly raised again. They sent the Application Programmer Interfaces (APIs) of potential data providers, assuming that this would enable IndiaSoft to proceed with development. It took a few weeks for NetTrade to sign a contract with a provider and once this was secured, an additional problem arose – IndiaSoft could not read the live data at their development site and, considering it *out of scope*, were reluctant to engage directly with the provider to find a solution. John notes that this caused a lot of anguish for NetTrade's IT manager (Deborah):

There was always reluctance to do this, which is very frustrating because we have no expertise. (John, Joint CEO, NetTrade).

We provided this for them – they could not read it ... so we had to go back to the provider and figure it out ... it was very difficult dealing with the provider. For us (i.e. Deborah), being in the middle was actually the most frustrating part of it all ... and I could see the guys getting frustrated ... but it was a shared problem. (John, Joint CEO, NetTrade).

It resulted in significant upheaval and delays in the project and IndiaSoft made a demand for an additional payment of €80,000.[12] NetTrade were very aggrieved about the manner in which this communication was managed and, on this occasion, responded angrily and forcefully:

> *I was livid…* (John, Joint CEO, NetTrade)

> *It was extremely disappointing from a project management point of view. We were very genuinely angry, and justifiably angry with Stephen. The fact that it was totally out of the blue was just crazy and we communicated it to them hundreds of times. It was bad project management on their side and this should not have got through their controls.* (Niall, Joint CEO, NetTrade)

This invoice was delivered at a particularly anxious and tense time in the project and served to further strain interfirm relations. However, neither firm was tempted to resort to the terms of the contract, or to refer to minutes of meetings or status reports in support of their position. Drawing attention to his emotional commitment to his relationship, John later talked about the precarious nature of the situation that they found themselves in:

> *… the contract is useless in many respects isn't it? If you are a small contract up against IndiaSoft… its almost unimaginable that we will really go down the legal path… somehow the contract is not what it's about. …*

Ajay joined the project and insisted that the issue be pushed to one side so that full attention could be devoted to the critical task at hand. John was happy with this arrangement:

> *Nobody is trying to screw anybody. We are all honourable and we will come to an agreement.* (John, Joint CEO, NetTrade)

This indicates the important role of the social capital which had been so painstakingly created, and contributed to an extraordinary resilience in interfirm relations. However, despite this resolution, the project was beset by further problems throughout the month of January:

> *There was an awful lot of tension around the installation. It has gone from the one day that they predicted to the three days that we allowed for. … then it was 5 days and now it's ten days and we are still not finished. There was a big blame game going on… .* (John, Joint CEO, NetTrade).

Suresh claimed that his people (though our opinion is that this was his opinion) were saying that installation and issues like this was outside scope for them… the tone was really wrong…the suggestion was that there was no solution… Or at least that he could be part of the solution… I got angry…that kinda stuff can make you really annoyed… and I'm goin'. you're kidding me! We need to get this thing solved, we need to come together. (John, Joint CEO, NetTrade).

John noted how Ajay seemed to be visibly perturbed by this conversation and he felt that even Suresh realized that this was not the correct approach. After this meeting, another conference call took place between Stephen, Suresh, and Ajay, following which the project was judged to be back on track:

We have all hands on deck. And the team in India is delighted. They want to stop with the politics and get in there and solve problems and they are great. (John, Joint CEO, NetTrade)

Throughout this cohabitation phase, we see ongoing negotiation of appropriate communicative practices, which proved to be most challenging as it involved difficult processes of finding mutual accommodations between Irish and Indian cultural norms. This process was complicated by the temporal/geographical separation. Moreover, the deeply embedded nature of such practices meant that attempts to alter them required significant skill, as well as the balancing of "trust, tact and power" (Giddens 1990, 82). In what follows, we explore these *micro-political processes* in more detail, by illustrating how agents attempted to balance trust, tact, and power in the course of their strategic actions. In so doing, we introduce three concepts that emerged from our grounded analysis of the data: namely, ***tactical signaling***, ***brokering***, and ***the third man***. Ironically, while NetTrade bemoaned the fact that IndiaSoft were less than direct in some of their modes of communication, the former often made use of similarly indirect modes themselves as they tried to shape the project by appropriately balancing trust, tact, and power.

The first example of tactical signaling was seen during the first visit to the delivery center. John recalls how less than impressed he was by the project manager (Sumeet) who had been assigned to the project. In contrast, he was very impressed and enthusiastic about Sunil, the younger functional requirements person. This played heavily on John's mind throughout his stay but he found it difficult to raise the point directly with

IndiaSoft. In an effort to subtly deliver this unpalatable message, he opted for a different strategy:

> *The other guy was the yes, yes, yes, he hadn't a clue. I made a point of praising Sunil and did not say anything about the other guy so he disappeared from the team, which was a good thing.* (John, Joint CEO, NetTrade)

The message was understood, it seems, as Sumeet was promptly moved from the project. On the other hand, even though John privately admitted to being a little concerned about the extent to which he seemed to be driving the initial requirements gathering process in India, he tactfully decided against raising these issues directly with IndiaSoft at the outset, for fear of being seen to question their professionalism.

These subtle and very careful forms of signaling were also helpfully used in other contexts. On the advice of friends, John made it very clear to IndiaSoft at the outset that he was keen to inspect the résumés of all staff assigned to the project. He later confessed that, despite the fact that he found it difficult to make sense of them, his main intention was to signal to IndiaSoft that he was being very vigilant and watching things closely:

> *They sent us CVs. I glanced through them .it was hard to decipher them... Indian colleges etc. I asked for them and there was a bit of posturing around wanting to get good guys etc. We couldn't really read them, but they looked grand.* (John, Joint CEO NetTrade)

The symbolism associated with making regular trips to India was also seen as important:

> *We went back over in December... it was really to show them that we were taking things seriously and even just to enhance the relationship... to reaffirm it. (Paul, Head of Finance NetTrade)*

Brokering was another vital means of facilitating productive communication while minimizing damage to the integrity of important relationships. The importance of brokers (or *boundary spanners*) has been highlighted in the Knowledge Management literature. Typically, these are described as individuals who facilitate the sharing of expertise between groups of people who are separated by location, hierarchy, or function (Allen and Cohen 1969; Tushman 1977; Wenger 1998; Pawlowski and Robey 2004; Levina 2005). Much of the emphasis is placed on the importance of translating/decoding idiosyncratic domain knowledge. The theoretical perspective that we developed earlier would suggest that a broker's role might extend beyond translating/communicating, embracing an enlarged remit of reassurance, and comfort creation.

Stephen, who had cultivated very strong relationships with people at NetTrade (especially John) and at the IndiaCity delivery centre, was a particularly good example of a broker. John described Stephen as someone who *appeared to have a foot in both camps* and was very receptive to, and understanding of, any issues raised by NetTrade. The fact that Stephen was Irish and of a similar age and background to John, meant that both parties found it very easy to communicate with one another. As the project progressed, Stephen was replaced by Ajay, John found himself not only increasingly using Stephen (and then Ajay) to broker important issues that needed to be communicated to India but also as a vehicle through which frustrations could be vented. For example, John talked about *regularly thrashing Suresh to Stephen (and Ajay)... and I (he) had a sympathetic audience.*

Stephen appeared to align with NetTrade's perspective on various issues. This was nicely articulated by Niall when he reflected on a meeting that was held to iron out the penalty fee imposed on the firm in December 2006:

> ... *it was very interesting from a cultural perspective watching Stephen and Ajay – both representing the same company but they were not singing from the same hymn sheet ... Stephen ended up being a little more on our side and Ajay was very much protecting IndiaSoft – his heart and mind were back in IndiaCity whereas Stephen was looking at it from our perspective ... Stephen ended up agreeing with us on almost everything and he probably should not have.* (Niall Joint CEO, NetTrade)

This perception of having like-minded allies on the Indian side served to allay concerns and anxieties and uphold NetTrade's position on various issues that arose. For example, as noted earlier, John was concerned about the silences in the process at various junctures – at a later stage, he was very frustrated at how NetTrade were being blamed for delays in the project. Stephen's appreciation of NetTrade's viewpoint and position seemed to reassure John that his anxieties and frustrations with the Indian firm were well founded. In turn, this seemed to instill confidence around his judgment:

> *Even Stephen would say that they need to do more to speak up.*
>
> *If you think about it, what they are saying here is that their development environment is dependent on the successful setting up of the UAT and production environment in order for them to finish the development... and I'm going ... that's just daft! ... and Stephen agreed.*

As noted earlier, Ajay's introduction to the project in January 2007 immediately served to diffuse tensions and re-instill a sense of comfort about relations going forward. John recalled how Ajay told them that Stephen would sort out the dispute at a later stage. He told them that he would not *get into that 80,000 thing* but that he would *make it his business to flag things well in advance going forward.* Niall recalled: *When Ajay came, he said he would tell us everything (...) and (our meetings) are very frank.* Consequently, John spoke about a renewed sense of optimism around the project.

The other key broker between NetTrade and IndiaSoft was Sunil (an Indian). From the very early stages of the project Sunil and John began to form a very good relationship. As noted above, John was initially very impressed by Sunil's ability and by the extent of his domain knowledge. Moreover, he appreciated Sunil's style of interaction, which was much less diffident than some of the other IndiaSoft team members: *Sunil was like a dog with a bone; he was constantly pursuing problems and issues and in the end he knows much more about our systems than we do ourselves!* The two months that Sunil spent in Dublin during the on-site requirements gathering phase facilitated the blossoming of this relationship with John. The two found that they had a lot in common and spent significant time together discussing the system and broader business and cultural issues.

The formation of these kinds of strong relationships, however, did not come without a cost. Sunil sometimes found that his relationship with John put him in a difficult position with respect to his loyalties within the project. For instance, while Sunil was on-site in Dublin during the deployment phase in January 2007 he was caught inadvertently in a minor dispute over the release of source code to NetTrade. John was keen to have access to the code so that his technical staff could inspect it and familiarize themselves with it. Unbeknown to him, however, Suresh (the project sponsor in India) had explicitly instructed Sunil not to release the code, without publicly making this known. At one particularly tense project meeting in Dublin when John kept asking Sunil for the code, Sunil had to ask John for a private word outside of the meeting, whereupon he disclosed that Suresh had vetoed this.

John seemed very sensitive to the difficulties that Sunil faced, and even described an incident where he used a combination of signaling and brokering to deliver a message to India. In the course of the dispute over the implications of the data feed delay, John complained that problems were poorly communicated by Suresh, thus contributing to their escalation. Following this criticism, John received an email from Suresh that went into great detail about ongoing issues. In full knowledge that Sunil was seated close by, John loudly and angrily complained about the fact that Suresh had suddenly *gone from giving no information about what's going on to giving way too much* in the hope that his annoyance would be relayed back to India by Sunil.

A further tactic that was used by NetTrade, often inadvertently, might be termed the ***third man***. This involved introducing a third party who did not have a close relationship with IndiaSoft, and who could consequently be more ruthless in their dealings with them. Two brief examples can be cited to illustrate this. First, during the contract negotiations between John and IndiaSoft in April 2006, John made regular reference to the importance of reaching an agreement that would be acceptable to NetTrade's board. Indeed, in the end, one of the major reasons IndiaSoft reduced their price substantially was on the basis that if it exceeded a certain critical amount the board had decreed that the contract should be submitted to public tender:

> *We went back to IndiaSoft that the non-executive board was a weight upon which everything hung … what would board think? … it was a useful entity … we probably overplayed it …* (John, Joint CEO, NetTrade)

Second, NetTrade hired a specialist software firm (TestCo) in September 2006 to help them develop their User Acceptance Testing plan. One of the TestCo consultants sat in on a User Acceptance Testing (UAT) meeting at which we were present in January 2007, and proceeded to aggressively question Sunil about the way IndiaSoft were prioritizing problem reports, in a manner that John or his colleagues would have found difficult. At the conclusion of this meeting (which was attended by one of the researchers), Sunil looked visibly upset at the tenor and tone of the questioning, despite the fact that he appeared to handle the substantive issues raised very competently. Without a *third man* this kind of robust interaction would have been almost impossible at this stage of the project. The imperatives of trust and tact would simply not have allowed it.

Discussion and conclusions

In this chapter, we have explored the notion of anxiety and its management in the context of a model of offshore software development that is becoming increasingly common in the contemporary world. In particular, we have focused on the important question of how comfort/trust is produced in circumstances that may involve high risk and a very opaque development process that is inherently difficult to monitor, not least because of issues associated with geographical and cultural separation. By so doing, we draw attention to the, often invisible, "relationship work" that is required to develop and sustain the crucial social infrastructure that underpins project relationships, lending them an important robustness.

The chapter makes empirical and conceptual contributions. With respect to the former, the case study presented is particularly interesting for a number of reasons. First, the existence of strong personal relationships between members of the research team and some of the key players involved in the project facilitated an unusually high level of access to the research site. This provided a rare window on the intimate workings of key social processes as they unfolded over time, allowing us to explore the "... ebbs and flows of the evolution of relationships" (Lacity and Willcocks 2001, 290). In the context of an accepted dearth of published in-depth accounts of the development and dynamics of offshoring relationships (Sahay et al. 2003), then, the study provides a basis for a relatively nuanced and granular understanding of such activities. A further interesting feature of the study is the Ireland-India connection. Whereas other studies have focused on global software alliances spanning such locations as USA-India (Kumar and Willcocks 1996), USA-Caribbean (Abbott 2004), Canada-India (Sahay 2003), U.K.-India (Nicholson and Sahay 2001; Nicholson and Sahay 2004), Norway-Russia (Imsland and Sahay 2005), and so on, we know of no study that has specifically explored cultural aspects of an Ireland–India relationship. Finally, the study offers an unusual example of offshoring practice, in that it involves a very small and young firm that has entered into a sourcing relationship with a large and well established vendor of IT development services (see Nicholson and Carmel 2003).

From a conceptual point of view, the chapter attempts to introduce a language that enables us to problematize and shed light on some crucial, yet intangible and often overlooked, aspects of offshoring practice. As such, the emphasis has not been on "theory generation," where this enterprise is conceived of as the development or refinement of a set of testable propositions. Rather, our aim here has been to synthesize, in a grounded manner, a sophisticated theoretical lens that illuminates important features of the dynamics of offshoring relationships (see Walsham 1995 for a discussion of this notion of theory as a "sensitizing device"), and of its importance in the context of interpretive studies in the IS field). Specifically, we have drawn on a diverse range of writers on trust (in particular Anthony Giddens, Lynne Zucker, and Barbara Misztal) to synthesize a rich and novel conceptual lens, with a view to making sense of our experiences in the field.

This synthesized perspective has provided us with the means to explore the process by which comfort/trust was produced within the context of, what was for NetTrade, a very risky and anxiety-provoking journey into the unknown. The distinctiveness of the conceptual lens developed here offers the possibility of opening up a number of novel theoretical directions for research on software offshoring. In particular, the emphasis on anxiety and its management offers fresh perspective on the challenges associated with managing such global work arrangements. Not only does it draw attention to important mechanisms by which comfort/trust is produced and anxiety contained, but it illustrates how these processes become especially problematic in an offshore model where interaction routinely spans temporal-geographical and cultural distance. We have argued that the production of confidence involves both cognitive/calculative (i.e., the adoption of rational strategies for reducing risk exposure) and emotional (comfort/trust) components, which enabled a (partial) bracketing of risk and associated anxiety, thus facilitating productive engagement with the project at hand. This emphasis on the emotional dimension of organizational life constitutes a significant departure from much of the mainstream literature in the management/organization studies area thus opening up new research vistas. Specifically, it provides an enlarged, non-cognitivist, perspective on the supposed role of, *inter alia*, interorganizational routines (Zollo et al. 2002) and brokers/boundary spanners (Levina 2005), which indicates that these are more than mere mechanisms for facilitating information exchange/sharing or communication; their importance might also be due to the manner in which they offer reassurance and help produce a sense of psychological security/comfort. Furthermore, the perspective on trust developed here broadens the scope of much of the extant literature by explicitly considering impersonal forms of trust (system trust), while linking these with forms of personal trust.

We drew on the synthesized theoretical lens to explore two distinctive kinds of comfort/trust production that appeared especially important in the NetTrade-IndiaSoft case. First, there was the establishment of comfort/trust by NetTrade in IndiaSoft as a suitable offshoring partner and, second, there was trust as "habitus" – the struggle to establish a stable, predictable, and productive collaborative order (consisting of a set of well understood and mutually acceptable social practices, especially communicative practices).

In the course of our analysis of the case, we attempted to illustrate how these different modes of trust production operated and complemented one another. In so doing, we considered two distinctive phases of the relationship to date (Courtship and Cohabitation), where one mode appeared to take precedence over the other. While these kind of distinctive phases have been used as analytical devices elsewhere in the outsourcing literature (e.g., Cartwright and Cooper 1993; Klepper 1995; McFarlan and Nolan 1995; Lacity and Willcocks 2001; Marshall et al. 2005), the work presented here attempts to go beyond mere categorization to provide a more in-depth analysis of the key functions of each stage and the practices required to support them (c.f. Ring and Van de Ven 1994; Kern 1997; Willcocks and Kern 1998). Furthermore, we were careful to point out that these were not strictly linear sequential stages. The trust generating practices that predominated in each stage were not absent in the other, it was merely a question of emphasis: both sets of concerns endure throughout the lifetime of a project and, indeed, are mutually constitutive, but at different points the emphasis tends to be on one over the other.

In the Courtship phase, in the early part of the relationship, the emphasis was primarily on "manifest displays of trustworthiness" at key meetings/interactions (i.e., access points), on reputational effects (i.e., indirect forms of process-based trust), and on apparent value congruence between Indian and Irish graduates (characteristic-based trust). Of critical importance was the establishment of trust in the reliability of the expert system of knowledge/practices employed by IndiaSoft, which was grounded in personal interactions with IndiaSoft representatives at access points to the system. With a view to enlarging Giddens' perspective, we focused on perceptions of ability, integrity, and benevolence as constitutive features of personal trust. With respect to the latter quality specifically, a key feature appeared to be the extraordinary care and attentiveness lavished upon NetTrade by IndiaSoft.

In the Cohabitation phase, the emphasis shifted to other kinds of strategic action that involved the balancing of trust, tact, and power in the construction of a stable collaborative order (trust as "habitus"). Here, we identified a number of micro-political tactics that were employed in attempts to establish mutually acceptable working practices, especially communicative practices. These were essentially indirect and tactful ways of dealing with important issues so as not to cause offence, and they included "signaling," "brokering," and "the third man." The aim here was to draw attention to the complex micro-politics of trust, in the context of the development of secure, stable, and predictable practices that would keep anxiety at bay.

A striking feature of this analysis it the amount of effort, care, and attentiveness that was required to establish productive social relations, notwithstanding the apparent value congruity of the two firms involved. These efforts, however, contributed to the creation of important social capital that gave the project a new robustness which sustained it during difficult periods. The dispute concerning the data feed was perhaps the most significant problem that beset project relations in the process to date, but what was remarkable was the manner in which the potential damage was managed and repaired. Neither party referred back to contracts or written records but, rather, decided to push the issue to one side, to proceed with the project and to revisit the issue at some future point.

> *Nobody is trying to screw anybody. We are all honourable and we will come to an agreement.* (John, Joint CEO, NetTrade)

This last quotation indicates the extent of the social capital that had been developed between these two firms in such a short period of time; John felt obligated to act honorably in relation to IndiaSoft and, perhaps more importantly, he was confident that IndiaSoft would behave honorably toward him.

Finally, and to extend this theme, there is evidence to suggest that this NetTrade-IndiaSoft relationship may run for some time yet. The current plans to extend and deepen the relationship might suggest the transition to a new, more stable phase (Marriage) marked by an explicit mutual commitment to a longer-term, ongoing strategic relationship (thus leveraging the social capital and mutual understanding that has been so painstakingly built. Should this happen, it will be interesting to compare and contrast the challenges associated with this phase with subsequent ones, and to explore the practices required to sustain and enhance the relationship for mutual benefit.

We hope that practitioners may find value in the depth and richness of the case material presented. By addressing the dearth of detailed accounts of the dynamics of such relationships in the IS literature to date (Sahay et al. 2003), we aim to contribute to the formation of enhanced levels of practitioner expertise in the area of software offshoring (Flyvbjerg 2001; Dreyfus and Dreyfus 2005). In keeping with our philosophy of the distinctive strengths of interpretive case study research (see Flyvbjerg 2006), we have resisted the temptation to attempt to distil the richness of the empirical material presented here into a small number of highly generalized prescriptions for practice. Furthermore, we hope that the theoretical perspective that has guided our analysis will provide managers with a productive way of seeing and engaging with, the world of practice.

In conclusion, we envisage a number of promising future directions for this research work. As well as continuing to follow the NetTrade–IndiaSoft relationship as it unfolds over time, we might also broaden our theoretical perspective to incorporate psychoanalytic perspectives on anxiety and its management (see, e.g., Wastell 1996, 2003). Moreover, the richness of the empirical data available offers us the opportunity to develop complementary analyses, drawing on alternative theoretical perspectives (e.g., learning, power/politics, surveillance, and management control) to illuminate other important aspects of the case.

Notes

1. Giddens uses the term "abstract systems" to collectively refer to two distinct types of disembedding mechanism that allow social interactions/relations to be "lifted out" of the particularities of specific locales and restructured across indefinite spans of time-space:
   - *Symbolic tokens*: these refer to media of exchange that have standard value, and thus are interchangeable across a plurality of contexts. Money is an important example of symbolic tokens, which can be passed around regardless of the specific characteristic of the individuals or groups that handle them at any particular juncture.
   - *Expert systems*: these bracket time and space through deploying modes of technical knowledge which have a validity independent of the practitioners and clients who make use of them. Thus, like symbolic tokens, they provide "guarantees" of expectations across distanciated time-space.

   The reorganization of time and space and the disembedding mechanisms prise social relations free from the hold of specific locales, recombining them across wide time-space distances. These radicalize and globalize the preestablished institutional traits of modernity and act to transform the content and nature of day-to-day social activity.
2. In his analysis of "encounters," Giddens draws heavily on the work of Erving Goffman.
3. Zollo et al. (2002) have also drawn attention to the importance of stable routines in facilitating productive interorganizational relations. Specifically, they draw on evolutionary economics to argue that such routines facilitate "... information gathering, communication, decision-making conflict resolution, and the overall governance of the collaborative process" (p. 709). Moreover, they draw an explicit distinction between the development of interorganizational routines and trust,

because they view trust rather narrowly as an "interpersonal" (p. 709) phenomenon and as the result of "... deliberative efforts to assess the likelihood of opportunistic behaviour" (p. 709). While we would agree with these authors' conclusions that interorganizational routines are extremely important, we would argue that the view of comfort/trust synthesized here is more insightful, in that it does not confine the importance of such routines to mere "information gathering" and "communication." Rather, "trust as habitus" also emphasizes the important anxiety-reducing functions of such routines.

4. Although Zucker's emphasis on information and deliberation clearly has cognitivist leanings that would sit uncomfortably with the perspective synthesized here (i.e., we would view interaction as consisting of much more than mere information exchange), we nonetheless believe that the broad mechanisms that she identifies are a very helpful supplement.

5. More precisely, building on the notion that any such abstract system will be interpretively flexible and may be enacted or embedded differently in different contexts, we argue that the key issue at stake is the expert **system-in-use** (i.e., the specific way such abstract principles are instantiated in the practices that constitute this project). The fact that systems **always** have to be re-embedded underscores the importance of making the connection between forms of system trust and personal trust, between the rule and its application (Wittgenstein 1953). It is not merely trust in "abstract principles" that needs to be reestablished at access points but also trust in the manner in which these principles are appropriated and applied.

6. We could, indeed, countenance a further stage immediately prior to this Courtship one. At the Dating stage, NetTrade explored a number of options and had some brief liaisons with a number of other vendors. (They had to kiss a few frogs before finding their Prince!) In fact, these encounters were very important in framing their subsequent relationship with IndiaSoft. Here, however, we believe that the comfort producing mechanisms at play were essentially the same as those in the Courtship phase, and so we rejected the idea of analyzing them separately.

7. Whether this was an "accurate" impression of IndiaSoft or not is, perhaps, beside the point. While we are conscious of the danger of resorting to cultural stereotypes here, the key issue is that John formed and sustained this impression of them, and acted on that basis. One point worth considering in this respect is the extent to which IndiaSoft staff were "mirroring" (perhaps unconsciously) particular traits of their

client. It would be interesting, for instance, to observe how their "presentation of self" (Goffman 1956) would differ with a very different kind of client. On the evidence of our interaction with IndiaSoft staff, however, both in Ireland and in India, we could also clearly recognize the kind of traits to which John drew attention, and broader social values appear to be a very important feature of life in the firm. Furthermore, there are some good bases for making cultural comparisons between Ireland and India. Not only do both countries share a similar British colonial history (indeed India adopted a modified version of the Irish constitution postindependence and even a modified version of the Irish national flag!) and an emphasis on familial and community ties, but comparisons might also be drawn between recent modes of economic development based on engineering and high technology (see, e.g., Foley and O'Connor 2004). Indeed, as John Stuart Mill once pointed out, "[t]hose Englishmen who know something about India, are even now those who understand Ireland best" (Cook 1993, 53).

8. Of course, we would be sympathetic to the general idea that even ostensibly rational/cognitive exercises are often enacted in ritualistic ways as a means of facilitating a more emotional type of commitment. This illustrates the difficulties associated with making a clean separation between the "cognitive" and the "emotional."

9. At the same time, however, the trust also had a brittle quality. In September 2006, one of the researchers met an Irish software developer who had worked with IndiaSoft in India for a short, and unhappy, period. His experience of working with IndiaSoft was not very positive, and was dramatically at odds with NetTrade's impression of them. John, on hearing this story, became extremely worried about the project, and for a short time began to seriously question his own judgments.

10. This kind of interaction became a familiar theme in the project and might be understood as involving the negotiation of the boundary between front-stage and back-stage (Goffman 1956). Such was John's anxiety that he was always trying to "peep backstage." In his view, however, IndiaSoft did not want to show him their *dirty laundry*. The fact that trust rests on a presentational base, where front-stage impression management is vital, would suggest that IndiaSoft's reluctance to accede to John's wishes was well founded.

11. Cramton (2001) notes how physical separation and reliance on communications technologies can exacerbate uncertainty when trying to interpret the meaning of silence.

12. Demonstrating their irritation over the issue, the €80,000 bill that they received was always referred to as a *penalty* by NetTrade but as *cost overrun* IndiaSoft.

References

Abbott, Pamela Y. (2004) Software-Export Strategies for Developing Countries: a Caribbean Perspective. *Electronic Journal of Information Systems in Developing Countries (EJISDC)*, 20(1): 1–19.

Allen, T.J. and Cohen, S.I. (1969) Information Flows in Research and Development Laboratories. *Administrative Science Quarterly*, 14(1): 12–19.

Barki, H., Rivard, S., and Talbot, J. (1993) Towards an Assessment of Software Development Risk. *Journal of Management Information Systems*, 10(2): 203–225.

Bloomfield, Brian and Coombs, Rod (1992) Information Technology, Control and Power: The Centralization and Decentralization Debate Revisited. *Journal of Management Studies*, 29(4): 459–484.

Boehm, B.W. and Demarco, T. (1997) Software Risk Management: Principles and Practices. *IEEE Software*, 14(3): 17–19.

Cartwright, Susan and Cooper, Cary L. (1993) The Role of Culture Compatibility in Successful Organizational Marriage. *The Academy of Management Executive*, 7(2): 57–70.

Casson, M. (1991) *The Economics of Business Culture*, Oxford: Clarendon Press.

Chaiklin, Seth and Lave, Jean (eds) (1996) *Understanding Practice: Perspectives on Activity and Context*, Cambridge: Cambridge University Press.

Ciborra, Claudio and Willcocks, Leslie P. (2006) The Mind or the Heart? It Depends on the (Definition of) Situation. *Journal of Information Technology*, 21(3): 129–39.

Cook, S. B. (1993) *Imperial Affinities: Nineteenth Century Analogies and Exchanges between India and Ireland*, Delhi: Sage.

Das, T.K. and Teng, Bing-Sheng (1998) Between Trust and Control: Developing Confidence in Partner Cooperation in Alliances. *Academy of Management Review*, 23(3): 491–512.

Dasgupta, Partha (1988) Trust as a Commodity, in Diego Gambetta (ed.) *Trust: Making and Breaking Cooperative Relations*, Oxford: Basil Blackwell: 49–72.

Dreyfus, Hubert L. and Dreyfus, Stuart E. (2005) Expertise in Real World Contexts. *Organization Studies*, 26(5): 779–792.

Earl, Michael J. (1996) The Risks of Outsourcing IT. *Sloan Management Review*, 37(3): 26–32.

Flyvbjerg, Bent (2001) *Making Social Science Matter: Why Social Inquiry Fails and How It Can Succeed Again*, Cambridge: Cambridge University Press.

Flyvbjerg, Bent (2006) Five Misunderstandings about Case-Study Research. *Qualitative Inquiry,* 12(2): 219–245.

Foley, Tadhg and O'Connor, Maureen (eds) (2004) *Ireland and India, Colonies: Culture and the Empire – Proceedings of the fourth Galway conference on colonialism*, Dublin, Ireland: Irish Academic Press.

Gambetta, Diego (ed.) (1988) *Trust: Making and breaking of Cooperative Relations*, Oxford: Blackwell.

Giddens, A. (1990) *The Consequences of Modernity*, Cambridge: Polity.

Giddens, A. (1991) *Modernity and Self-Identity: Self and Society in the Late Modern Age*, Cambridge: Polity.

———— (1994) Risk, Trust and Reflexivity, in Ulrich Beck, Anthony Giddens, and Scott Lash (eds) *Reflexive Modernization: Politics, Tradition and Aesthetics in the Modern Social Order*, Cambridge: Polity, 184–197.

Goffman, E. (1956) *The Presentation of Self in Everyday Life*, London: Penguin.

Good, David (1988) Individuals, Interpersonal Relations, and Trust, in Diego Gambetta (ed.) *Trust: The Making and Breaking of Cooperative Relations*, Oxford: Blackwell, 31–48.

Hart, Keith (1988) Kinship, Contract and Trust: The Economic Organization of Migrants in an African City Slum, in Diego Gambetta (ed.) *Trust: The Making and Breaking of Cooperative Relations*, Oxford: Blackwell, 176–93.

Imsland, Vegar and Sahay, Sundeep (2005) Negotiating Knowledge: The Case of a Russian-Norwegian Software Outsourcing Project. *Scandinavian Journal of Information Systems,* 17(1): 101–130.

Kelly, Séamas (2005) New Frontiers in the Theorisation of ICT-Mediated Interaction? Exploring the Implications of a Situated learning epistemology, in William R. King and Reza Torkzadeh (eds) *Proceedings of the International Conference on Information Systems (ICIS)*, Las Vegas, USA.

Kern, Thomas (1997) The *Gestalt* of an Information Technology Outsourcing Relationship: An Exploratory Analysis, *Eighteenth Annual International Conference on Information Systems (ICIS)*, Atlanta, Georgia, USA.

Klepper, Robert (1995) The Management of Partnering Development in I/S Outsourcing. *Journal of Information Technology,* 10: 249–258.

Knights, David (1990) Subjectivity, Power and the Labour Process, in David Knights and Hugh Willmott (eds) *Labour Process Theory*, London: Macmillan, 297–335.

———— (1992) Changing Spaces: The Disruptive Impact of a New Epistemological Location for the Study of Management. *Academy of Management Review,* 17(3): 514–536.

Knights, David and Murray, Fergus (1994) *Managers Divided: Organisation politics and Information Technology Management,* Chichester: John Wiley & Sons).

Knights, David and Willmott, Hugh (1999) *Management Lives: Power and Identity in Work Organizations,* London: Sage.

Kumar, Kuldeep and Willcocks, Leslie P. (1996) Offshore Outsourcing: a Country Too Far? *Fourth European Conference on Information Systems (ECIS),* Lisbon, Portugal, 1309–1326.

Lacity, Mary C. and Willcocks, Leslie P. (2001) *Global Information Technology Outsourcing: In Search of Business Advantage,* Chichester: John Wiley & Sons.

Levina, Natalia (2005) The Emergence of Boundary Spanning Competence in Practice: Implications for Implementation and Use of Information Systems. *MIS Quarterly,* 29(2): 335–363.

Lorenz, Edward H. (1988) Neither Friends Nor Strangers: Informal Networks of Subcontracting in French Industry, in Diego Gambetta (ed.) *Trust: Making and Breaking Cooperative Relations,* Oxford: Basil Blackwell, 194–210.

Luhmann, Niklas (1979) *Trust and Power,* Chichester: John Wiley & Sons, 208.

———— (1988) Familiarity, Confidence, Trust: Problems and Alternatives, in Diego Gambetta (ed.) *Trust: Making and Breaking of Cooperative Relations,* Oxford: Blackwell, 94–107.

Marshall, Donna, Lamming, R.C., Fynes, B., and de Búrca, S. (2005) The Development of an Outsourcing Process Model. *International Journal of Logistics: Research and Applications,* 8(4): 347–359.

Mauss, M. ([1925] 1954) *Essay on the Gift: An Archaic Form of Exchange,* trans. I. Cunnison, London: Routledge & Kegan Paul.

Mayer, Roger C., Davis, James H., and Schoorman, F. David (1995) An Integrative Model of Organizational Trust. *Academy of Management Review,* 20(3): 709–734.

McAllister, Daniel J. (1995) Affect- and Cognition-Based Trust as Foundations for Interpersonal Cooperation in Organizations. *Academy of Management Journal,* 38(1): 24–59.

McFarlan, F. Warren and Nolan, Richard L. (1995) How to Manage an It Outsourcing Alliance. *Sloan Management Review,* 36(2): 9–23.

McGrath, Kathy (2006) Affection Not Affliction: the Role of Emotions in Information Systems and Organizational Change. *Information and Organization,* 16: 277–303.

Miller, Peter and O'Leary, Ted (1987) Accounting and the Construction of the Governable Person. *Accounting, Organizations and Society,* 12(3): 235–265.

Misztal, Barbara M. (1996) *Trust in Modern Societies,* Cambridge: Polity, 296.

Nicholson, Brian and Carmel, Erran (2003) Offshore Software Sourcing by Small Firms: an Analysis of Risk, Trust and Control, *Ifip Tc8 & Tc9/WG8.2 & WG9.4 Working Conference on Information Systems Perspectives and Challenges in the Context of Globalization,* Athens, Greece, 211–222.

Nicholson, Brian and Sahay, Sundeep (2001) Some Political and Cultural Issues in the Globalisation of Software Development: Case Experience from Britain and India. *Information and Organization,* 11(1): 25–43.

Nicholson, Brian and Sahay, Sundeep (2004) Embedded Knowledge and Offshore Software Development. *Information and Organization,* 14: 329–365.

Pawlowski, S.D. and Robey, Daniel (2004) Bridging User Organizations: Knowledge Brokering and the Work of Information Technology Professionals. *MIS Quarterly,* 28(4): 645–672.

Reed, M.I. (1992) The Sociology of Organizations: Themes, Perspectives and Prospects, in W.M. Williams (ed.) *Studies in Sociology,* Hemel Hempstead: Harvester Wheatsheaf, 301.

Ring, Peter S. and Van de Ven, A.H. (1994) Developmental Process of Cooperative Interorganizational Relationships. *Academy of Management Review,* 19(1): 90–118.

Ring, Peter Smith (1996) Fragile and Resilient Trust and Their Roles in Economic Exchange. *Business and Society,* 35(2): 148–175.

Rousseau, Denise M., Sitkin, S., Burt, R., and Camerer, C. (1998) Not So Different after All: A Cross-Discipline View of Trust. *Academy of Management Review,* 23(3): 393–404.

Sahay, Sundeep (2003) Global Software Alliances: The Challenge of Standardization. *Scandinavian Journal of Information Systems,* 15(1): 3–21.

Sahay, Sundeep, Nicholson, Brian, and Krishna, S. (2003) *Global IT Outsourcing: Software Development across Borders,* Cambridge: Cambridge University Press.

Sturdy, Andrew (1997) The Consultancy Process – An Insecure Business? *Journal of Management Studies,* 34(3): 389–413.

Tushman, M. L. (1977) Special Boundary Roles in Innovation Processes. *Administrative Science Quarterly,* 22(4): 587–605.

Walsham, Geoff (1995) Interpretive Case Studies in IS Research: Nature and Method. *European Journal of Information Systems,* 4: 74–81.

Wastell, David G. (1996) The Fetish of Technique: Methodology as a Social Defence. *Information Systems Journal,* 6: 25–40.

Wastell, David (2003) Organizational Discourse as Social Defence: Taming the Tiger of Electronic Government, in Eleanor Wynn, et al. (eds) *Global and Organizational Discourse about Information Technology,* Boston, MA: Kluwer Academic Publishers, 179–195.

Wenger, Etienne (1998) Communities of Practice: Learning, Meaning and Identity, in Roy Pea, John Seely Brown, and Jan Hawkins (eds) *Learning in Doing: Social, Cognitive, and Computational Perspectives,* Cambridge, UK: Cambridge University Press.

Willcocks, Leslie P. and Kern, Thomas (1998) IT Outsourcing as Strategic Partnering: The Case of the UK Inland Revenue. *European Journal of Information Systems,* 7, 29–45.

Willcocks, Leslie P. and Lacity, Mary (1999) It Outsourcing in Insurance Services: Risk, Creative Contracting and Business Advantage, *Information Systems Journal,* 9, 163–80.

Willcocks, Leslie P., Lacity, Mary, and Kern, Thomas (1999) Risk Mitigation in IT Outsourcing Strategy Revisited: Longitudinal Case Research at Lisa. *Journal of Strategic Information Systems,* 8(3): 285–314.

Willcocks, Leslie P. and Margetts, H. (1994) Risk Assessment in Information Systems. *European Journal of Information Systems,* 4(1): 1–12.

Williams, Bernard (1988) Formal Structures and Social Reality, in Diego Gambetta (ed.) *Trust: Making and Breaking Cooperative Relations,* Oxford: Basil Blackwell, 3–13.

Wittgenstein, Ludwig (1953) *Philosophical Investigations,* Oxford: Blackwell.

Zollo, Maurizio, Reuer, Jeffrey J., and Singh, Harbir (2002) Interorganizational Routines and Performance in Strategic Alliances. *Organization Science,* 13(6): 701–713.

Zucker, Lynne G. (1986) Production of Trust: Institutional Sources of Economic Structure 1840–1920. *Research in Organizational Behaviour,* 8: 53–111.

CHAPTER 8

Requirements analysis in offshore is development: remote bridging of differences in understandings

Paul C. van Fenema, Vinay Tiwari, and Paul W.L. Vlaar

Introduction

Intensified competition and advances in telecommunications, accompanied with increasing maturity of offshore IT vendors (Carmel and Agarwal 2002; Gartner and Marriot 2003; Hirschheim, et al. 2005), have resulted in the proliferation of Information System Development (ISD) outsourcing. Perceived cost advantages, flexibility, and the availability of a competitive labor pool have compelled various organizations to outsource work to "offshore" countries (Carmel and Agarwal 2002; Robinson and Kalakota 2004). Although traditional ISD outsourcing projects already face challenges related to the notorious complexity of systems development (Brooks 1987; Keil and Mann 2000), to users' inability to accurately specify requirements (Boland, 1978), and to developers' inability to elicit requirements from users (Davis 1982; Salaway 1987), offshoring further exacerbates these problems. The distinct backgrounds, experiences, and cultures of participants in offshore relationships (Carmel 1999; Carmel and Tjia 2005) give rise to differences in perceptions, assumptions, and understandings among stakeholders, which tend to be particularly significant during requirements development (Sommerville and Sawyer 1997; Damian and Zowghi 2003). For such projects to become successful, it is imperative that multiple stakeholders develop sufficiently similar understandings of requirements so that the software that is eventually developed by offshore vendor teams is valued by clients and on-site team members.

In contrast to other types of distributed work, where professionals with more or less equal expertise levels participate in a project (e.g., student teams) (Cramton 2001), offshoring ISD entails delivering value to external customers by having professionals with different expertise levels cooperate with each other (i.e., members of on-site and offshore teams showing strong asymmetries in experience and knowledge). This renders it difficult to develop congruent (i.e., logically interrelated) and actionable (i.e., opportunity to transform them into artifacts and deliverables) understandings, particularly between stakeholders who are not co-located. Although communication and knowledge transfer between on-site client representatives and on-site vendor team members sometimes involves strenuous efforts and friction, communication challenges between on-site and offshore vendor liaison staff and team members are generally much more pronounced, due to a lack of face-to-face contact, limited informal and synchronous communication, and restricted immediacy of feedback (Herbsleb and Mockus 2003; Carmel and Tjia 2005).

We therefore focus on the relationship between on-site and offshore vendor teams, to obtain insights into the strategies that team members use to bridge differences in their understandings. Although most observers would subscribe to the idea that incongruent and inactionable understandings are detrimental to offshore performance, it has hitherto remained unclear which strategies are used by members of on-site and offshore vendor teams to overcome differences in understanding with their counterparts. Our objective is to gain a better understanding of the nature of such strategies, the motives behind these strategies, and the conditions under which they operate most effectively.

To investigate these issues, we adopt a socio-cognitive perspective on requirements analysis, focusing specifically on the micro-level aspects of communication and understanding that are considered to be critical for IS offshoring (see, e.g., Herbsleb and Moitra 2001; Prikladnicki et al. 2003). Based on the existing literature, we distinguish two dimensions of understanding, consisting of its domains (i.e., indicating whether understanding pertains to the content of requirements and/or the contexts in which requirements originate and to which they pertain) and levels (i.e., lower levels of understanding versus higher levels of understanding within a particular domain). We conducted 18 interviews with on-site and offshore members of an offshore ISD project involving one of India's largest offshore outsourcing vendors. Analysis of the interviews and documents pertaining to this project provided us with rich and in-depth accounts of the challenges that participants in the project faced, and the strategies that they pursued to arrive at more congruent and actionable understandings.

Our data analysis is based on a conceptualization of differences in understanding along two dimensions – domains and levels of understanding. It reveals that at least three generic strategies are used by vendor team members to bridge these differences: (1) translating requirements; (2) raising the level of understanding within a specific domain (specialization); and (3) shifting attention from one domain of understanding to another domain (generalization). We found specific reasons for these strategies and elaborate on the conditions under which they may be used.

These findings contribute to the literatures on social cognition and ISD offshoring by providing more fine-grained insight into the dynamics of understanding in offshore outsourcing than hitherto available. They allow practitioners in offshore settings to better assess and appropriate the options they have for developing sufficiently similar understandings among the members of their vendor teams. Although our findings stem from ISD offshoring, with due consideration they may be applied to other types of offshore activities such as global R&D and business process outsourcing. Offshoring such activities will introduce similar issues due to common constraints, such as large geographical distances, time zone differences, and a diverse workforce.

In the following section, we discuss the theoretical background to our inquiry. Subsequently, we elaborate on the methods that we use to examine requirements analysis in a recent offshoring project. Following this, we present our empirical findings. The chapter concludes with a discussion of the theoretical and practical implications of our findings, along with the limitations of our study and avenues for future research.

Background

A socio-cognitive perspective of requirements analysis

Requirements development is considered both critical, because it has a pivotal role in determining the success or failure of software projects (Vessey and Conger 1993; Hoffmann and Lehner 2001), and complex, because it involves multiple stakeholders with their own perspectives on requirements and software systems (Curtis et al. 1988; Davidson 2002). It frequently entails high levels of ambiguity and uncertainty. This complicates the interpretation, analysis, and structuring of requirements (Weber and Weisbrod 2003; Gorschek and Wohlin 2006), and contributes to their chaotic nature (Walz et al. 1993). Although approaches to requirements development are very varied, consensus exists that requirements development activities at least include: gathering and eliciting requirements; analyzing those requirements for consistency and completeness; and, deciding which requirements to focus on given particular project constraints (Davis and Zowghi 2006).

Several IS researchers have focused on analyzing requirements analysis from a social-interaction perspective (Newman and Robey 1992; Davidson 2002), building on the premise that requirements are socially constructed through interactions among ISD participants. Following such a perspective, we define requirements development as the framing and gauging of the expectations related to the functional and technical aspects of information systems held by various stakeholders. These processes direct operational development activities and determine the value of the final software product in the perception of the customer. In this process, multiple stakeholders provide their viewpoints and opinions to enrich, focus, and correct requirements understanding (Aurum and Wohlin 2005).

Challenges in offshore outsourcing

In offshore relationships, users and business analysts usually reside at the client site, and technical analysts and developers tend to perform their work from offshore locations (Robinson and Kalakota 2004). Large geographic distances substantially accentuate the complexity of coordination in such global set-ups, and they demand strategies for working efficiently (Lee et al. 2006). Some of the most common challenges faced in global outsourcing projects relate to communication, organizational structures, language barriers, time separation, and cultural differences (Carmel 1999; Herbsleb and Mockus 2003; Krishna et al. 2004). Specifically, communication between on-site and offshore staff tends to be characterized by misunderstandings and ineffective knowledge transfer. Members of these groups have limited opportunities for developing common ground (Cramton 2001) or common understanding (Lawrence 2006). In particular, vendor team members find it difficult to develop sufficiently similar and consistent understandings in these circumstances (Damian and Zowghi 2003; Bhat et al. 2006). Recently, several empirical studies have touched upon this problem (Prikladnicki et al. 2003; Sinha et al. 2006). Sinha et al. (2006), for instance, advanced the view that communicating and managing requirements was a primary issue for participants in offshoring relationships.

Zooming in on cooperation between on-site and offshore vendor teams, we exclude factors such as interorganizational communication issues and cultural diversity. We are interested in the extent to which the developer has clearly *understood* – without doubt and ambiguity – what needs to be developed (Boland 1978). The general contention appears to be that, to establish such an understanding, initially divergent views and understandings need to be reconciled and deepened; something which depends heavily on the communication skills of stakeholders and the use of commonly understood terms and languages (Cramton 2001; Bechky 2003; Zowghi and Coulin 2005). Although on-site team members may believe that they have clearly defined and explained requirements, offshore team members may develop understandings of such requirements that differ from those intended by the on-site team members. To assess how such differences in understanding arise and which strategies can be used to overcome them, we need to better comprehend the concept of understanding. We identify two dimensions – domain and level – along which understanding can be categorized.

Domains of understanding

The first dimension of understanding captures potential variation in the domains to which understanding pertains. Broadly speaking, understandings can relate to the content of requirements (i.e., technical aspects) and the contexts from which these originate (i.e., business aspects). Requirements analysis depends to a large extent on documents sent by the on-site team to offshore team members, and vice versa (Krepchin 1993; Meadows 1996). Recipients of these texts need to be able to construct literal, "face-value" understandings of these documents, implying that they interpret the "cold, dead numbers" and symbols (Boland 1991, 453, cited in Lee 1994). The identity of the author and the nature of the contexts in which requirements originated and to which they apply do not play a role here. Instead, parties use generic conventions which are used to construct their understandings (Bowker and Star 2002).

Understanding the context of requirements is regarded to be essential to arrive at a "warm" and "subjective" reality (Boland 1991, 453, cited in Lee 1994), in addition to a generic understanding of the content of requirements. This tends to be particularly crucial when situational opportunities and constraints may shape the meaning underlying the behavior and requirements of organizational members (Orlikowski 1996, 2005; Kirsh 2001; Johns 2006). In this respect, Bechky (2003, 313) proposes that "even when knowledge is made explicit in a codified routine, [and] when it is communicated across group boundaries, some organizational members may not understand it because they apply and interpret this knowledge within different contexts." In this case, members of on-site and offshore vendor teams develop distinct interpretations and understandings as compared to what their counterparts intended.

Levels of understanding

The second dimension of understanding concerns its degree of detail or abstraction (e.g., see Boisot 1998). Several studies on requirements analysis refer to the level of detail in which requirements are formulated to explain why software developers and programmers have been able or unable to execute certain requirements (e.g., Battin et al. 2001; Weber and Weisbrod 2003; Gorschek and Wohlin 2006). However, these studies do not explicitly discuss the level of detail or abstraction regarding the *understandings* that are maintained by participants in ISD projects. Focusing on the latter, we follow the literature on qualitative data analysis (e.g., Van Maanen 1979; Miles and Huberman 1994) to conceptualize differences in understandings among participants in offshoring relationships. We do not wish to imply that different stages of qualitative data research have a one-to-one relationship with various levels of understanding among members of on-site and offshore vendor teams. However, we draw upon the analogy between both phenomena to explicate our point that members of on-site and offshore vendor teams may differ in terms of their levels of understanding of the content and context domains related to requirements.

The literature on qualitative data analysis generally distinguishes various levels of data and data-analysis. First-order concepts arise from ideas, comments, views, or facts as mentioned by informants in their own language, or observed by researchers in documents or events (Corley and Gioia 2004). Second-order themes emerge from the search for relationships between bundled and labeled data pieces, so as to discover higher-order themes (Van Maanen 1979). These themes are then further grouped into higher-order categories or aggregate dimensions based on the relations between them and the themes that they represent (Gioia et al. 1994; Riessman 2002). When researchers iterate and migrate – usually recursively – across these levels, they gain "a clear grasp of the emerging theoretical relationships" (Corley and Gioia 2004, 184).

In offshore ISD, some developers – particularly in early stages of a project – may have a very detailed understanding of certain programming languages and technical jargon, whereas others may be almost ignorant about these factors. Let us imagine employees who have just been hired, or who have not worked with a specific program language or information system before. By reading, studying, and discussing aspects of these programming languages, experiencing the use of technical jargon by others and through building software code themselves, these novices gradually move from understandings that resemble first-order concepts to understandings incorporating second-order concepts and aggregate dimensions. To conclude, understanding of an initial order implies that data are not considered from an integrative, conceptual point of view, but are rather seen as isolated elements. In this case, interpretation does not move beyond initial generic framing. Higher levels of understanding are more abstract, characterized by an awareness of the positioning of data in terms of a broader "meta" story (Riessman 2002) and context (Cherry and Macredie 1999). These higher levels of understanding underpin more intelligible and customized forms of value creation.

Bridging differences in understandings

Bridging differences in understandings across global distances requires deliberate efforts to enhance understandings beyond a status quo, so as to construct a better (i.e., more accurate and comprehensive) picture of the world (Putnam 2001, 107). Business organizations particularly focus on advancing and developing understanding when change is required or when the creation of new products and services demands a revision of employees' orientations and focus of attention. This tends to occur, for instance, when organizations merge, implement new technology, develop a new product, hand off a task, or develop and implement a new business strategy (Edmondson et al. 2001; Kumar et al. 2005). Members of on-site and offshore vendor teams also advance their understandings to envision comparable behaviors and outcomes (Donnellon et al. 1986). They thereby become better prepared for action that matters to their customers, as they have constructed a clearer account of the information and resources that are required to perform their task, and as they arrive at a more comprehensive conception of the organizational and contextual constraints impinging on that task (Hull et al. 2005; Johns 2006). In analyzing the case study, we therefore focus on the strategies that members of on-site and offshore vendor teams use to cope with differences in understandings – in terms of levels and domains – to enable the efficient and effective development and execution of requirements in offshoring projects.

About this research

We selected a project with an on-site-offshore set-up, based on the following criteria. First, we chose India as the offshore location, as this country represents the world's leading offshore outsourcing destination (Mehta et al. 2006). Additionally, one of the authors had worked for a major offshore organization in India (working on projects for a U.S. retail-store chain and a major U.S. insurance firm for more than two and a half years). Hence, the author had the experience of working within an offshore team in various roles (starting as a junior programmer, but soon becoming a module leader).

Second, we decided to focus on an on-site partner who was active in the financial services industry, as organizations from this industry were the first to experiment with the concept of offshore outsourcing. Finally, we selected a project that was in a comparatively mature state – that is, it had been in operation for more than two years – and consisted of several modules and instances of requirements sharing between on-site and offshore teams. After discussing with the project managers of a large Indian offshore firm about various projects involving three distinct financial services firms, the FINANCE project (for reasons of confidentiality, we have adopted a fictitious name) was selected. Initial interviews with on-site team members revealed that, on average, each project module consisted of around 7–10 requirements sharing instances between on-site and offshore teams, making it an ideal setting for our study.

Findings from the finance project

In discussing our findings, we concentrate on three generic strategies that members of on-site and offshore vendor teams appeared to use to cope with and capitalize on differences in their understandings. When presenting these strategies – translation, specialization, and generalization – we elaborate on the specific reasons on-site and offshore team members mentioned for deploying them.

Translation strategy: relating mindsets

First, participants in on-site teams made use of anticipatory translation techniques, translating requirements from a business point of view into technical language to accommodate and relate with the mindsets of offshore team members. On-site and offshore team members stressed the necessity of comprehensive translation to understand dependencies:

> *The understanding of the offshore to carry out the requirements themselves is not sufficient. We give them certain instructions to do the work in the following manner. They can't always see the reper-cussions of what will happen to the system.* (Interview with GK, On-site)

With offshore team members lacking insight into the background of requirements, they expected "foolproof" instructions:

> *For most of the programs in this module, they [onsite] analyzed and studied the entire requirement and prepared one design document. In this document, everything was there. So if I make a small change in one program, how is that going to impact the module and in which file it will be populated and all that.* (Interview with RK, Offshore)

Commonly, these teams deploy junior professionals and suffer from high turnover rates. Translation compensates for the offshore team's lack of experience.

> *Because the offshore team was quite new and they had no under-standing of what FOCUS means. So everything had to be written in such a way so that they can understand the FOCUS command from the document itself without looking at the report.* (Interview with SK, Onsite)

Instead of explaining the context of requirements in fuller detail to bridge the knowledge gap, offshore appreciated detailed instructions.

> *I feel that whenever they [onsite] sent anything offshore it is important that they write in a programmatical way rather than business way, i.e. rather than writing in business logic because definitely even if we have a lot of experience at offshore the business knowledge at offshore will not be equivalent to business knowledge at onsite – always there will be a gap. This gap can be filled by writing the requirements in programmatical way like write a program that takes this field and puts in that file rather than giving us business requirement.* (Interview with NK, Offshore)

It is not just that the offshore team lacks knowledge: they may bring a different perspective to the project. This increases risks of misinterpretation.

> *The offshore team is good technically speaking, and they do deliver what they are asked for, but since they don't carry the same perspective, you have to very specifically ask them to deliver things. You cannot expect them to interpret your answers [correctly], because the way you think is not necessary the way that offshore thinks, and normally they think differently* (Interview with GK, On-site).

Finally, the offshore team valued a translation strategy to circumvent the negative implications of assumptions from the on-site team with respect to offshore's understandings of requirements:

> *In one case, we were sent a requirement with code already pasted in it .... We thought that since it was written in the requirement document, we had to cut and paste it into the program .... Onsite's view was that we would write similar kind of lines. Not exactly these lines, but similar kind of lines and insert those lines at the end of the code. We thought that the lines in the requirement had to be inserted in the program. It is better to follow some kind of template for writing such things, so that the same standards are followed. If we follow some template, problems of interpretation and pinpointing can be solved* (Interview with NP, Offshore).

Translation directly enables the offshore team to act in a manner that delivers results according to on-site's expectations. The drivers of this strategy include the use of a common language, standardization, or analogies and metaphors. It is a strategy that aims to advance understanding by selecting a channel or "wavelength" with which offshore team members feel comfortable. By using this strategy, offshore's expertise is activated despite its limited understandings in a specific domain. Components of this strategy include the use of a common language, standardization, or analogies and metaphors.

Specialization strategy: deepening understanding within a domain

A second strategy used to reduce problems emanating from differences in understanding consisted of deepening members' understandings within a specific domain. These domains included the actual requirements communicated, the technology, and programming language adopted in a project, experience with the focal project, knowledge of a client's business, and generic know-how of working in an IT offshoring setup. This strategy was used to explore certain issues in depth, conforming to traditional learning strategies (Leidner and Jarvenpaa, 1995). In this case, the focus of learning is rather task-specific and narrow. On-site highlighted the limitations of a document-based approach which would call for a comprehensive translation of requirements into self-explanatory instructions.

> *If someone has been working for 2–3 yrs [in offshore projects] then he must be knowing all the technical things, so in that case we won't go too much in detail but if he is a trainee then we have to explain in detail level to them. There is a limitation in design – you can't write every single step in the document so we have to stop somewhere.* (Interview with NS, On-site)

Requirements documents in use left room for interpretation and assumptions. Feedback loops between on-site and offshore synchronized understandings on a particular topic and addressed offshore's uncertainties:

> *We go through the requirement and if there is some problem of understanding, we call the person concerned at onsite. First we put our understanding to them, that this is what I have understood regarding how to proceed and we put our doubts in front of them. If he thinks that my understanding is completely wrong, then he guides me from the start and if he thinks that I am missing just a small point, then he will just comment "don't do this but do that."* (Interview with RK, Offshore)

Finally, specialization served to make the motives and arguments behind thoughts and actions explicit. This enhanced the quality of software development, since the match with customer expectations increased. One of the interviewees vividly described specialization as

> *... a web you have to go in-in-in-in and at some point of time it will finish and then you nearly understand what they were expecting. It happens like one day after we have sent whatever they asked us to do, they will say that this is not the thing and during this they explain.* (Interview with Rahul, Offshore)

Specialization was achieved by constant feedback on offshore's queries, shifting communication from correspondence in emails to interactive forms (e.g., teleconferences), providing detailed accounts of the complexities in requirements. Once offshore reached a similar level of understanding of a specific domain to that on-site, discussions amongst equals ensued. While this strategy leads to improvement in a particular domain, it does not allow offshore team members to broaden their scope and advance understandings concerning other domains, as does the third strategy.

Generalization strategy: advancing understanding across domains

Finally, the third strategy for advancing understanding consists of shifting one's own or one's counterpart's attention to a domain of understanding that needs to be developed further. This strategy echoes repeated calls for generalization and redundancy in training team members (e.g., Hutchins 1991; Grant 1996; Nonaka 2000). On-site team members pointed to business and technical dependencies to motivate investments in broadening the offshore team's understanding. The former concerns the impact of software changes for business processes:

> ... they cannot test the global picture ... that what is the aim of the business ... what will be the impact upstream and downstream ... whether it is fulfilling business requirements or not ... these things they cannot assess ... that is why there are gaps. So, then we have to review and tell them the problems again ... these things are taken care by daily interaction, by calling them and clearing the whole picture (Interview with AK, On-site).

The latter refers to cross-dependencies between parts of the software application.

Both on-site and offshore stressed the role of understanding the business context of requirements. They invested in updating this understanding, sometimes even on a daily basis. Broadening offshore's understanding then coincided with increasing the levels of participation of offshore team members.

> Basically, in the first phase they just know a part of the entire project. They have just a narrow idea of what has to be done, but the picture is not clear in their mind during the initial phases. But as the project

passes, they understand everything and take active participation by the end. (Interview with SK, On-site)

By shifting attention to other domains offshore can come to operate more intelligently and more in tune with the on-site team and customer expectations.

We cannot directly go to the design document and directly code, we need coordination between onsite and offshore team. Only if that is there we get a clear understanding of what the requirement is and how we can implement those changes in the coding. (Interview with SK, Offshore)

Deployment of this strategy required – maybe more than average – engagement from both on-site and offshore. It also reflected a mixture of the project leader's interest in developing the capabilities of the offshore team, and the offshore team's initiative and interest in the on-site team's thinking.

'I used to call him [SK] and ask him lots of questions. He then explained how the system looks like, how things are working and other details which are not fully related to this particular requirement. That helps us a lot now to understand new requirements. (Interview with YP, Offshore)

In conclusion, this strategy focuses on advancing the understandings of offshore team members by providing input on domains in which they do not have sufficient understanding yet. This helps offshore in becoming aware of the interdependencies inherent in requirements and it allows them to keep the entire picture in mind while trying to develop their understanding of particular requirements.

Discussion and conclusion

Contributions

This chapter addresses the problem of bridging differences in understandings in the context of ISD offshore outsourcing. It thereby continues a long tradition of research on specialization and coordination (e.g. Grant, 1996; Hutchins, 1991; Nonaka, 2000). Following current literature (e.g., Cramton and Orvis 2003; Hinds and Mortensen 2005; Vlaar et al. 2006), we asserted that variation in culture, assumptions, expectations, and experiences among members of on-site and offshore vendor teams may create problems of understandings among team members. Building on a socio-cognitive perspective, we distinguished between different domains and levels of understanding. To explore how members of offshore and on-site vendor teams cope with such differences, we conducted a case study of an offshore project involving an Indian vendor and a U.S. client firm. Our results highlight three generic strategies used by vendor team members to bridge differences in understanding among on-site and offshore teams: translation, specialization, and generalization.

Our findings contribute to the literature on both social cognition and ISD offshoring by offering a detailed conceptualization of the dimensions and dynamics of understanding and the specific reasons for deploying various strategies for bridging differences of understanding. First, we answer calls for more empirical research on the micro-processes that affect the performance of offshoring initiatives (Rottman and Lacity 2004). More particularly, by focusing on differences in understanding between members of on-site and offshore teams, and the strategies they use to cope with those differences, we shift attention in the offshoring literature from macro and strategic levels to a micro-level perspective (Levina and Ross 2003; Aron and Singh 2005). Second, we address the need for inquiries into communication and interaction for distributed ISD projects (Damian and Zowghi 2003). By distinguishing different domains and levels of understanding and by focusing on various strategies for bridging differences in understanding among vendor team members, we extend research on understanding (e.g., Donnellon et al. 1986; Cramton 2001; Bechky 2003) with a more fine-grained conceptualization of a significant problem faced by cooperating organizations (see Vlaar et al. 2006) and the means they use to cope with these problems. Third, our work complements research on distributed student teams where team members start off with similar levels and domains of understanding (e.g., Jarvenpaa and Leidner 1997; Cramton 2001).

Implications for research

Our case provides insights into a compact organization in which on-site team members had high levels of understanding concerning the business domain, whereas most offshore team members only possessed low levels of understanding in this area. Offshore, in turn, sometimes had a better understanding of certain systems and programming languages. Current research provides ample evidence of the problems associated with these and similar situations in which misunderstandings, conflict, and faulty assumptions distort cooperation and cause a deterioration of performance (Cramton and Orvis 2003; Hinds and Mortensen 2005). Our study suggests that recognizing these problems (Scheibe et al. 2006) is not enough. Organizations need insight into strategies for dealing with the amalgamation of various domains and varying levels of understandings, and the situations in which they should be deployed. The strategies found in this study – translation, specialization, and generalization – represent alternatives for cooperating across sites and investing in capabilities.

Translation stands for a transactive interaction pattern, aimed at the correct execution of comprehensively defined requirements by offshore team members. In this case, onshore adds value in an exploratory manner – interacting closely with the customer – whereas offshore follows an exploitative strategy (Kang et al. 2007). As work moves from on-site to offshore, the value-adding process follows a transition between these modes. Offshore's exploitative value creation process implies that its roles and capabilities do not change. Moreover, its commitment and involvement remains minimal. This strategy would match situations of high time pressure (with no time to explain), high precision (with no room for interpretation), or high levels of turnover.

Specialization is likely to fit best with projects calling for great depth of expertise. In this case, on-site does not possess the (sometimes expensive) resources to instruct offshore. Instead, expertise from on-site and offshore must be combined and integrated to generate customer value (Oshri et al. Forthcoming; Galunic and Rodan 1998). On-site engages the offshore team members not so much for executing predefined tasks but for collectively understanding customer problems and the complexities of the development process. Specialization calls for offshore to invest resources in developing technical expertise among on-site team members, who are encouraged to remain involved in a project for a prolonged period of time.

Generalization further extends the need for offshore to actively participate in the global team. In the light of this, recent work on cooperation emphasizes the value of emotionally involved workers (Quinn and Dutton 2005) and active dialogues for innovation (Tsoukas 2005). For offshore outsourcing, such an approach requires considerable investments in communications, and possibly sacrifices in the area of work-life balance because of U.S. – India time zone differences (Boland and Citurs 2001; Carmel and Tjia 2005). When such a strategy is deployed, customers are expected to pay a premium which enables on-site and offshore team members to enhance value creation by jointly exploring new opportunities

(Kang et al. 2007). Innovative, high-profile projects for commercial and public organizations seem candidates for this strategy.

Implications for practice

Our findings allow practitioners in offshore settings to better assess the options they have for developing sufficiently similar understandings among members of on-site and offshore vendor teams – an extremely critical aspect in offshore ISD (Bhat et al. 2006; Scheibe et al. 2006). They also provide managers with a task and time dependent approach for developing such understandings along with a useful distinction between domains and levels of understanding. Furthermore, our findings reveal several task and team member characteristics which serve as contingency factors. For instance, if the task or requirement is complex and constantly changing, it is better for on-site to invest in advanced understandings of offshore team members across multiple domains. In contrast, if the task is simple and well structured, and if it must be completed within a short time span, it pays to only enhance offshore understanding within a particular domain (specialization). In addition, when on-site and offshore vendor team members possess experience and knowledge concerning fundamentally different domains, the translation strategy may be more cost-efficient and effective than the other two strategies. After all, increasing on-site and offshore team members' levels of understanding will be very costly, due to a lack of basic knowledge and experience in the respective domains. Moreover, shifting the attention from one domain to another domain will not allow partners to understand each other, unless high costs are incurred, because parties have insufficient experience with and knowledge of the other member's field of expertise.

Finally, our model serves as a basis for developing instruments that measure understandings and pinpoint asymmetries (see also Vlaar et al. 2007). Our conceptualization of the dimensions and dynamics of understanding also applies to other contexts in which asymmetrical understandings – that is, when one person's understanding differs in level and/or domain from that of another person or group – play a significant factor. This is the case, for example, with on-site-offshore transition projects, work hand-offs, socialization practices for newcomers in organizations, parties that need to accommodate to each other after engaging in alliances and joint ventures, and people starting to work abroad.

Limitations and future research

This study entails certain limitations. First, our data consist of accounts of past events experienced by informants. Event-based approaches or participant observation in which changes in understanding over time can be tracked may shed more light on the pace, scope, and rhythm at which understanding matures in offshore ISD projects. Second, as we base our findings on just one offshore relationship, further research is required to assess the generalizability of our findings. We have attempted to reduce this concern by providing sufficient variation in the experiences and understandings of individual team members participating in the study, and by selecting four development modules with different characteristics in terms of the size and complexity of requirements. A third concern is our focus on on-site–offshore communications, which constitutes only part of the full communication cycle in offshore projects. This choice derives from the fact that the absence of co-location is a key characteristic of offshoring relationships. Ideally, one would also investigate to what extent organizational, industrial, and cultural differences between clients and on-site vendor teams prohibit the development of congruent and actionable understandings, and which strategies clients and on-site team members deploy to cope with these problems.

Several avenues for future research can be identified. First, showing that offshore outsourcing set-ups provide an interesting and extremely rich context, we urge researchers to adopt a micro-perspective of offshoring arrangements, to advance our knowledge of organizational concepts such as understanding. Specifically, we encourage such a perspective for studying other elements of the client-on-site-offshore communication cycles. Second, we define two dimensions – domain and level – of understanding, but future researchers may be able to extend these ideas. For instance, they may want to consider the scope of understanding. Third, researchers could also look into how progressive ratings for the capability maturity model (CMM) are associated with the extent to which participants in offshoring relationships experience problems of understandings regarding IS requirements. Higher CMM levels may, for example, run in parallel with better developed understandings. Fourth, researchers may focus on problems related to the development and progression of understandings in more complex scenarios or knowledge intensive set-ups such as offshore R&D centers. In such task environments, developing higher levels of understandings between distributed teams is not only a precondition for success but also an objective of the relationship.

References

Aron, R. and Singh, J.V. (2005) Getting Offshoring Right. *Harvard Business Review, 83*(12): 135–143.

Aurum, A. and Wohlin, C. (2005) Requirements Engineering: Setting the Context, in A. Aurum and C. Wohlin (eds) *Managing and Engineering Software Requirements*, New York: Springer.

Battin, R.D., Crocker, R., Kreidler, J., and Subramanian, K. (2001) Leveraging Resources in Global Software Development. *IEEE Software, 18*(2): 70–77.

Bechky, B.A. (2003) Sharing Meaning across Occupational Communities: The Transformation of Understanding on a Production Floor. *Organization Science, 14*(3): 312–330.

Bhat, J. M., Gupta, M., and Murthy, S.N. (2006) Overcoming Requirements Engineering Challenges: Lessons from Offshore Outsourcing. *IEEE Software, 23*(5): 38–44.

Boisot, M. H. (1998) *Knowledge Assets: Securing Competitive Advantage in the Information Economy*, New York: Oxford University Press.

Boland, R.J. (1978) The Process and Product of System Design. *Management Science, 24*(9): 887–898.

Boland, R.J. (1991) Information Systems Use as a Hermeneutic Process, in H.-E. Nissen, H.H. Klein, and R. Hirschheim (eds) *Information Systems Research: Contemporary Approaches and Emergent Traditions*, New York: North-Holland, 439–458.

Boland, R.J. and Citurs, A. (2001) Work as the Making of Time and Space (Vol. 2 Winter). Sprouts: Working Papers on Information Environments, Systems and Organizations, available on http://weatherhead.cwru.edu/sprouts/2002/020101.pdf

Bowker, G.C. and Star, S.L. (2002) *Sorting Things Out: Classification and its Consequences*. Cambridge, MA: MIT Press.

Brooks, F.P. (1987) No Silver Bullet: Essence and Accidents of Software Engineering. *Computer, 20*(4): 10–19.

Carmel, E. (1999) *Global Software Teams: Collaborating Across Borders and Time Zones*. Englewood Cliffs, NJ: Prentice Hall.

Carmel, E. and Agarwal, R. (2002) The Maturation of Offshore Sourcing of IT Work. *MIS Quarterly Executive, 1*(2): 65–77.

Carmel, E. and Tjia, P. (2005) *Offshoring Information Technology Sourcing and Outsourcing to a Global Workforce*, Cambridge: Cambridge University Press.

Cherry, C. and Macredie, R.D. (1999) The Importance of Context in Information System Design: An Assessment of Participatory Design. *Requirements Engineering, 4*: 103–114.

Corley, K.G. and Gioia, D.A. (2004) Identity Ambiguity and Change in the Wake of a Corporate Spin-off. *Administrative Science Quarterly, 49*(3): 174–208.

Cramton, C.D. (2001) The Mutual Knowledge Problem and its Consequences for Dispersed Collaboration. *Organization Science, 12*(3): 346–371.

Cramton, C. D. and Orvis, K. L. (2003) Overcoming Barriers to Information Sharing in Virtual Teams, in C. B. Gibson and S. G. Cohen (eds) *Virtual Teams that Work: Creating Conditions for Virtual Team Effectiveness*, San Francisco, CA: Jossey-Bass, 214–230.

Curtis, B., Krasner, H., and Iscoe, N. (1988) A Field Study of the Software Design Process for Large Systems. *Communications of the ACM, 31*(11): 1268–1286.

Damian, D.E. and Zowghi, D. (2003) Requirements Engineering Challenges in Multi-site Software Development Organizations. *Requirements Engineering Journal, 8*: 149–160.

Davidson, E.J. (2002) Technology Frames and Framing: A Socio-Cognitive Investigation of Requirements Determination. *MIS Quarterly, 26*(4): 329–358.

Davis, A.M. and Zowghi, D. (2006) Good Requirements Practices are Neither Necessary nor Sufficient. *Requirements Analysis 11*(1): 1–3.

Davis, G. B. (1982) Strategies for Information Requirements Determination. *IBM Systems Journal, 21*(1): 4–30.

Donnellon, A., Gray, B., and Bougon, M.G. (1986) Communication, Meaning, and Organized Action. *Administrative Science Quarterly, 31*(1): 43–55.

Dougherty, D. (1992). Interpretive Barriers to Successful Product Innovation in Large Firms. *Organization Science, 3*(2): 179–202.

Galunic, D. C. and Rodan, S. (1998) Resource Recombinations in the Firm: Knowledge Structures and the Potential for Schumpeterian Innovation. *Strategic Management Journal, 19*(12): 1193–1201.

Gartner, I. and Marriot. (2003) *Offshore Sourcing: What Does the Future Hold?* Paper presented at the Outsourcing and IT Services Summit, London.

Gioia, D.A., Thomas, J.B., Clark, S.M., and Chittipeddi, K. (1994) Symbolism and Strategic Change in Academia: The Dynamics of Sensemaking and Influence. *Organization Science, 5*(3): 363–383.

Gorschek, T. and Wohlin, C. (2006) Requirements Abstraction Model. *Requirements Engineering, 11*(1): 79–101.

Grant, R.M. (1996) Toward a Knowledge-based Theory of the Firm. *Strategic Management Journal, 17*(Winter): 109–122.

Herbsleb, J.D. and Mockus, A. (2003) An Empirical Study of Speed and Communication in Globally-Distributed Software Development. *IEEE Transactions on Software Engineering, 29*(3): 481–494.

Herbsleb, J.D. and Moitra, D. (2001) Global Software Development. *IEEE Software, 29*(1): 16–20.

Hinds, P. and Mortensen, M. (2005) Understanding Conflict in Geographically Distributed Teams: The Moderating Effects of Shared Identity, Shared Context, and Spontaneous Communication. *Organization Science, 16*(3): 290–307.

Hirschheim, R., Löbbecke, C., Newman, M., and Valor, J. (2005) *Offshoring and its Implications for the Information Systems Discipline.* Paper presented at the International Conference on Information Systems (ICIS), Las Vegas.

Hoffmann, H. and Lehner, F. (2001) Requirements Engineering as a Success Factor in Software Projects. *IEEE Software, 18*(4): 58–66.

Hull, E., Jackson, K., and Dick, J. (2005) *Requirements Engineering* 2nd edition, London: Springer.

Hutchins, E. (1991). Organizing Work by Adaptation. *Organization Science, 2*(1): 14–39.

Jarvenpaa, S.L., and Leidner, D.E. (1997) Do You Read Me? The Development and Maintenance of Trust in Global Virtual Teams. INSEAD Working Paper.

Johns, G. (2006) The Essential Impact of Context on Organizational Behavior. *Academy of Management Review, 31*(2): 386–408.

Kang, S.-C., Morris, S.S., and Snell, S.A. (2007) Relational Archetypes, Organizational Learning, and Value Creation: Extending the Human Resource Architecture. *Academy of Management Review, 32*(1): 236–256.

Keil, M., and Mann, J. (2000) Why Software Projects Escalate: An Empirical Analysis and Test of Four Theoretical Models. *MIS Quarterly, 24*(4): 631–664.

Kirsh, D. (2001) The Context of Work. *Human-Computer Interaction, 16*: 305–322.

Krepchin, F. (1993) When Offshore Programming Works. *Datamation, 39*(14): 55–56.

Krishna, S., Sahay, S., and Walsham, G. (2004) Managing Cross-cultural Issues in Global Software Outsourcing. *Communications of the ACM, 47*(4): 62–66.

Kumar, K., van Fenema, P.C., and Von Glinow, M.A. (2005) Intense Collaboration in Globally Distributed Work Teams: Evolving Patterns of Dependencies and Coordination, in D. L. Shapiro, M. A. Von Glinow and J.L.C. Cheng (eds) *Managing Multinational Teams: Global Perspectives*, Oxford: Elsevier/JAI, 127–154.

Lawrence, K.A. (2006) Walking the Tightrope: The Balancing Acts of a Large e-Research Project. *Computer Supported Cooperative Work, 15*(4): 385–411.

Lee, A.S. (1994) Electronic Mail as a Medium for Rich Communication: An Empirical Investigation Using Hermeneutic Interpretation. *MIS Quarterly, 18*(2), 143–157.

Lee, G., DeLone, W.H., and Espinosa, J.A. (2006) Flexibility and Rigor: Ambidextrous Coping Strategies in Globally-Distributed Software Development Projects. *Communications of the ACM,* 49(10): 35–40.

Leidner, D.E. and Jarvenpaa, S.L. (1995) The Use of Information Technology to Enhance Management School Education: A Theoretical View. *MIS Quarterly, 19*(3): 265–291.

Levina, N. and Ross, J.W. (2003) From the Vendor's Perspective: Exploring the Value Proposition in Information Technology Outsourcing. *MIS Quarterly, 27*(3): 331–364.

Meadows, C.J. (1996) *Globework: Creating Technology with International Teams (PhD Thesis)*, Boston, MA: Harvard University.

Mehta, A., Armenakis, A., Mehta, N., and Arani, F. (2006) Challenges and Opportunities of Business Process Outsourcing in India. *Journal of Labor Research, 27*(3): 323–338.

Miles, M.B. and Huberman, A.M. (1994) *Qualitative Data Analysis: An Expanded Sourcebook* 2nd edition, Thousand Oaks, CA: Sage.

Newman, M., and Robey, D. (1992) A Social Process Model of User-analyst Relationships. *MIS Quarterly, 16*(2): 249–266.

Nonaka, I., von Krogh, G., and Nishiguchi, T. (2000) *Knowledge Creation: A Source of Value*, New York: St. Martin's Press Inc.

Orlikowski, W.J. (1996) Improvising Organizational Transformation Over Time: A Situated Change Perspective. *Information Systems Research, 7*(1): 63–92.

Orlikowski, W.J. (2005) Material Works: Exploring the Situated Entanglement of Technological Performativity and Human Agency. *Scandinavian Journal of Information Systems, 17*(1): 183–186.

Oshri, I., van Fenema, P. C., and Kotlarsky, J. (Forthcoming). Knowledge Transfer in Globally Distributed Teams: The Role of Transactive Memory. *Information Systems Journal.*

Prikladnicki, R., Audy, J.L.N., and Evaristo, R. (2003) Global Software Development in Practice Lessons Learned. *Software Process Improvement and Practice, 8*: 267–281.

Putnam, H. (2001) *Representation and Reality*, Cambridge, MA: MIT Press.

Robinson, M. and Kalakota, R. (2004) *Offshore Outsourcing: Business Models, ROL, Best Practices*, available on www.mivarpress.com: Mivar Press.

Salaway, G. (1987) An Organizational Learning Approach to Information Systems Development. *MIS Quarterly, 12*(2): 245–264.

Scheibe, K.P., Mennecke, B.E., and Zobel, C.W. (2006) Creating Offshore-Ready IT Professionals: A Global Perspective and Strong Collaborative Skills are Needed. *Journal of Labor Research, 27*(3): 275–290.

Sinha, V., Sengupta, B., and Chandra, S. (2006) Enabling Collaboration in Distributed Requirements Management. *IEEE Software, 23*(5): 52–61.

Sommerville, I. and Sawyer, P. (1997) *Requirements Engineering: A Good Practice*, New York: John Wiley & Sons.

Tsoukas, H. (2005) How is New Knowledge Created in Organizations? A Post-Rationalist Account. ICOS Presentation http://www.si.umich.edu/ICOS/Presentations/ and working paper.

Van Maanen, J. (1979) The Fact of Fiction in Organizational Ethnography. *Administrative Science Quarterly, 24*: 539–550.

Vessey, I. and Conger, S. (1993) Learning to Specify Information Requirements: The Relationship between Application and Methodology. *Journal of Management Information Systems, 10*(2): 177–201.

Vlaar, P.W.L., Van den Bosch, F.A.J., and Volberda, H.W. (2006) Coping with Problems of Understanding in Interorganizational Relationships: Using Formalization as a Means to make Sense. *Organization Studies, 27*(11): 1617–1638.

Vlaar, P.W.L., van Fenema, P.C., and Tiwari, V. (2007) Achieving Congruent and Actionable Understandings of ISD Requirements among Onsite and Offshore Vendor Teams. *Working Paper,* Free University Amsterdam.

Walz, D. B., Elam, J. J., and Curtis, B. (1993) Inside a Software Design Team: Knowledge Acquisition, Sharing, and Integration. *Communications of the ACM,* 36(10): 62–77.

Weber, M. and Weisbrod, J. (2003) Requirements Engineering in Automotive Development: Experiences and Challenges. *IEEE Software,* *20*(1): 16–24.

Zowghi, D. and Coulin, C. (2005) Requirements Elicitation: A Survey of Techniques, Approaches and Tools, in A. Aurum and C. Wohlin (eds) *Engineering and Managing Software Requirements*, New York: Springer, 19–46.

CHAPTER 9

Global expertise and quality standards in ICT offshore projects

Esther Ruiz Ben

Introduction

With the growth of employment demand in the 1990s and the boom in the software industry, outsourcing became crucial and helped sustain an already existent wave of offshoring. The economic crisis at the start of the new millennium had precipitated this wave, which was also supported by processes of production standardization that allowed tasks to migrate to lower-cost countries. This migration process, called IT off- or nearshore, has changed the definition of technical and managerial areas in the IT industry and in expertise development and management. In the case of the IT industry, we should emphasize the importance of the multinational enterprises that have built up their international capacities in IT services in recent years based on their presence in hardware markets and related sectors since the 1980s. The IT organizations have disaggregated into smaller functional units that can also be geographically relocated. Outsourcing developed in the 1990s not only in production but also in the emerging IT services fields, which now represent one of the most important segments of the German IT sector (Deutsche Bank 2005; EITO 2006).

Spatial concentration and dispersion are common in the internationalization process of every segment of the IT industry. Both phenomena are closely linked to modularization processes of work that allow for the adaptation of work processes to the needs of particular enterprises at a particular time and that mostly emerge from concrete projects. Modularization allows mobility and, at the same time, entails a loss of the spatio-temporal control of work and the immediacy of work processes. To recover this loss, companies use various mechanisms, such as global tools like ITIL and quality management systems based on globally recognized standards such as ISO. Systematization of processes and making knowledge explicit are needed to implement such mechanisms in day-to-day practices. Thus, expertise or the ability to act knowledgeably in a determined context (Oshri et al. 2007, 54) drawing on contextual practice, knowledge, experience, and qualifications can be made explicit through formalized practices like documentation. Expertise that emerges from projects developed across dispersed teams must be synchronized and coordinated to reach a given goal in a timely fashion. Moreover, generated knowledge must be stored to improve new products and to be applied in upcoming projects. Global implementation of common tools plays a crucial role in both synchronization and coordination of expertise among disperse groups and in enabling knowledge transfer. Moreover, global tools allow the rotation and succession of staff (Beulen, van Fenema, Currie 2005). However, the results of our research indicate that global tools and knowledge transfer systems are developed and implemented very differently in large companies practicing IT offshoring. Particularly in Germany, experiences with IT offshoring began later than in other countries, such as the U.S.A. or India. As a result, the transformation of many large IT companies into global players has not been established. Furthermore, the few large IT companies existing in Germany have deeply bureaucratic roots and in some cases civil servants among their staff. The corresponding work culture of such companies must dramatically change in a global environment requiring high flexibility and dynamism. The implementation of quality management tools represents a medium of transforming work habits and formalizing work processes that not every employee is willing to follow. Language and cultural differences among cooperating teams represent additional challenges for employees and are highly relevant risks for the success of IT offshore projects. Whereas U.S. American multinational IT companies can operate in many English-speaking regions – although the involvement of non-native speakers in IT offshore projects also hinders delivery processes – German is spoken in a far more limited spectrum of regions. Thus, many German IT companies tend to focus their offshore activities on Eastern European countries, particularly on those where some German is spoken, such as Poland or Romania. With this focus on Eastern Europe, IT companies hope to reduce the linguistic and cultural risks that can delay IT offshore projects. However, synchronization of expertise in dispersed locations still represents a challenge.

The question is how expertise can be timed in a highly dynamic and competitive environment in which project work represents the most extensive work form. Which mechanisms do large German IT enterprises and networks use to control expertise over time? Workaday practices in organizational settings embedded within national and international regulation patterns of qualification and educational paths are important factors to consider answering these questions, as I explain below.

In my view, quality standards and global tools represent forms of governing IT offshore projects, and they are also the basis for timing and structuring expertise in organizations. To support this thesis, I use key findings of my research into the internationalization of the German ICT branch. The chapter is structured in three sections. In the first section, I focus on the concept of expertise from an institutional perspective and its relation to knowledge. In this section, I also explain the characteristics and methodology of the research. In the second section, I refer to the key empirical results of my research into global expertise and quality standards. In this section, I also explain how expertise, standardization, and knowledge transfer are linked to each other. In sum, I show how quality standards in internationalized arenas of software development work as relational and multidimensional factors that influence patterns for standardizing knowledge, skills, and working practices, as well as the institutionalizing expertise.

Theoretical background

Expertise and knowledge in IT offshore projects

As I explained above, I draw on Oshri et al. (2007: 54) and Gasson (2005: 2) to understand expertise as the ability to act knowledgeably in a determined context. To act knowledgeably employees must possess some degree of knowledge that they have acquired through experience and qualification paths. While acting knowledgeably, actors share concepts and experiences. They apply their skills within the framework of stories that connect the application of knowledge to the particular context (Cook and Brown 1999) of working with other actors in projects for a given period of time (see Table 9.1). This is the level of *know-how knowing* as I show in Table 9.1, following the classification of Cook and Brown (1999). Thus, expertise relates to past experience (or embodied knowledge and skills, Fitzpatrick 2003), to present knowledge sharing and application in the context of project practices (or expertise development, Lave and Wegner 1991), and also to future knowledge transfer for coming projects and expertise integration in organizations. Depending on the organizational experiences with particular projects and products, knowledge sharing would be more or less formalized in its contribution to the structuring of expertise. In particular, the more complex the projects are, the more important formalization of knowledge sharing becomes (Herbsleb and Moitra 2001). Expertise is also related to the *know-what knowing* (Cook and Brown 1999) or the explicit knowledge related to organizational conventions (Gasson 2005, 5). Individuals use concepts that they share in the group and combine with genres as shared conventions and practices (Cook and Brown 1999). At the organizational level, such conventions crystallize into quality standards that serve as rationale for the practice and also legitimize particular forms of work. Moreover, global management tools serve to coordinate dispersed expertise in distributed work environments. Both quality standards and global management tools capture organization practices and conventions and serve as a socialization basis for newcomers in the organization, so that continuous training on such tools is very important to support knowledge transfer (Lam 1997; Newell et al. 2006). At the same time, depending on the degree of employees' engagement in the development of both quality standards and global management tools, professional autonomy and discretion will be considered as supported or threatened by employees. On this basis, and through claims of expertise from particular communities, institutionalized forms of work and domains of expertise can crystallize into professionalism.

Many studies have focused on knowledge sharing in group-work (Stork 2000; Herbsleb and Moitra 2001; Kobitzsch 2001). In particular, several authors have emphasized the importance of knowing *who knows what* – also known as transactive memory (Wegner 1987) with regard to globally distributed work. These authors construe transactive memory as a key for successful knowledge sharing (Faraj and Sproull 2000; Herbsleb and Moikra 2003). Wegner (1987), for example distinguishes between internal memory, as the knowledge of each team member, and external memory, which consists of knowledge located and retrieved when team members need it. Alavi (2001) adds that external memories can reside in other team members or in documents or databases. Some authors have shown that effective transactive memory systems contribute to enhanced knowledge sharing and task performance (Moreland 1999; Faraj and Sproull 2000; Lewis 2000). Global IT consultancy enterprises play an especially important role in providing particular domains of expertise and offering an overview of available expertise on an international scale.

In addition, *knowing why,* or the explicit knowledge of global rules and behavior patterns and tacit knowledge of local and social normative practices, constitutes a fourth type of knowledge in collaborative work (Gasson 2005, 5). The history of the organization is a kind of recording or organizational memory that gives identity and meaning to the organization and serves as reference point for contextual practices and future plans (Schein 1985; March 1991; Walsh and Ungson 1991; Martin 1992). In IT enterprises in particular and in relation to the growing internationalization of the sector, consulting firms play a crucial role in creating an organizational identity in a global economy. They also play a key part in managing expertise externally. Table 9.1 presents an overview of the relation between the types of knowledge, expertise, and professionalism at different levels of action.

Time plays a crucial role in the dynamic process of expertise institutionalization. Time is related to the history and future of the organizations, to the IT projects (group level) within the organizations, and also to the professional biographies of the experts. Expertise can be structured in network- and organization-related work-time practices and regulations, and through project-related time norms (deadlines). These practices become routinized and constitute a rule for the software developers' work. At the same time, software developers draw on these within their ongoing interactions. In software development projects, project team members negotiate practices and adapt them to the demands of new clients based on previous project experiences. Thus, experts act knowledgeably and with a certain level of autonomy in IT project work within organizations. However, dispersed work in IT offshore projects requires growing formalization of work processes through particular institutionalized norms in the form of, for example, quality management systems. This process shapes the constitution of expertise, or in other words the transformation of structural principles. I argue that quality management systems enable the coordination of multiple and dispersed groups in IT offshore projects while at the same time constraining the autonomy of experts. This means a conflict

Table 9.1 Types of knowledge and links to expertise and professionalism. On the basis of Gasson (2005); Cook and Brown 1999

	Individual	Group	Organization/communities of practice
Know-how	Qualifications (explicit) and skills (tacit)	Sto ries	Quality standards
		Expertise	**Professionalism**
Know-what		**Transactive memory systems**	
	Explicit	Genres	Global management tools
	knowledge rel. to organizational facts and conventions Concepts		Continuous training
Who knows what	Explicit knowledge about who has a particular expertise	Locally and globally	Claims of expertise consultancy
Know-why	Sensemaking of one's task	Sensemaking of project	Sensemaking of domain

between different work cultures in diverse organization environments and in different countries with different socialization trajectories regarding qualifications and transitions from education to working life. I argue that the *know-why* component of expertise must be understood regarding time in relation to professional biography, to projects, and to domains of practice within organizations. To achieve social cohesion and collaboration in IT offshore projects, organizations need formal mechanisms of communication and project management rules within the time scope of the projects. In my view, time influences IT offshore expertise, as practices in projects tend to be habitualized and institutionalized over time through formalization tools such as quality management systems. Expertise is knowledgeable and reflexive in action, situated in organizational contexts and emergent in projects. Expertise is related to organizational rules and norms that give sense not only to the concrete tasks and actions within projects but also to particular domains of practice in the long run in which quality standards serve as a collective pattern of timed action. Thus, the analysis of expertise in IT offshore projects needs, in my view, to consider the types of knowledge related to expertise in different levels of action and their relation to time, as I have explained above. In the next section, I present some empirical results of my work to illustrate my thesis.

About this research

In the DFG[1] project (INITAK), we analyze the transformation of tasks and related categorization of qualification and skill demands in relation to the internationalization of the German IT sector. In this study, we conduct case studies in six enterprises (three parent enterprises and three subsidiaries). We conduct a longitudinal analysis of quantitative data on the workforce in IT organizations. Furthermore, we consider qualitative materials from expert interviews (personnel managers, project and quality managers, software developers, labor council delegates, and external consultants), such texts as web-based homepages and job announcements on the internet, and group discussions and observations at the workplace on the principle of triangulation (Flick 2004). I used an open, semi-structured questionnaire that focused on thematic blocks and reflected the perspectives of the groups of experts I considered (personnel and project managers as well as quality managers and software developers in ICT organizations, and moreover external consultants). In this paper, I will focus on the questions relating to expertise in global IT projects and to the importance of quality standards and project management in IT offshore projects.

Key empirical results

Expertise in international software development teamwork

In our current research relating to the transformation of tasks and qualifications in the framework of the internationalization of the German IT sector (INITAK) we have conducted interviews with personnel and quality managers in several IT enterprises (see description above) that are expanding their activities in foreign countries and especially in Eastern Europe. The preliminary analysis regarding qualification and expertise requirements relates to one of our case studies in a large software development enterprise (F3). This enterprise is affiliated with a large multinational enterprise with multiple establishments around the world. According to the typology suggested by Beulen et al. (2005, 134), this enterprise would qualify as a *native service provider* that offers services from local operations in diverse countries and maintains its headquarters in developed countries. The German company, which has actually been a subsidiary of a native service provider for six years, was founded in the early 1980s by people from the academic field. The company has not shed its academic origins, as reflected in its links to academically based professional federations (GI – Gesellschaft für Informatik) or the majority of academic personnel that constitute its staff (90%). During the 1980s and 90s, the company expanded and established six additional locations in Germany, Switzerland, and more recently, in Eastern Europe. In particular, the availability of infrastructure in diverse countries provided by the parent company represents an important advantage in acquiring projects or offering favorable prices in comparison with other service providers. Thus, the motivation for off- and nearshore business is at once to reduce costs to stabilize the demand for projects and to expand the firm's market scope. Moreover, the company wants to remain innovative in the rapidly internationalizing environment of the ICT sector.

In particular, the German establishment F3, where we conducted our interviews in 2006, has had experience of nearshore in Eastern Europe since 2004, as well as in offshore regions like India and South Africa.

Focusing on a particular nearshore project in Poland, during the first phase the company could use the platforms of the multinational enterprise they belonged to, which brought advantages in terms of the availability of adequate personnel and infrastructure. It also gave the company an edge in the knowledge management of the enterprise. Nearly 50 staff were working in F3's nearshore establishment in 2006. The standard integration procedure for these staff members involves a visit to Germany for a training period of one year, during which they learn the project and quality standards of the enterprise.

Regarding the tasks that the F3 firm retains in Germany during its current internationalization, the first specification phases of software development projects, in which the contact with the customers is very intensive, remain in the German headquarters. However, some nearshore workers sometimes participate in discussions with the customers as a part of their integration training. The architecture phase also remains in Germany, whereas developers in the nearshore center conduct the detailed design of the architecture. Therefore the recruitment strategy of the firm F3 in its nearshore center is not only oriented toward hiring very young university graduates but it also targets experienced personnel who can rapidly adapt to the growing present project demands and can train and help to integrate young newcomers. The long-term internationalization perspective of F3 in its nearshore location is to expand their market opportunities in the country, building an increasingly autonomous center with highly qualified personnel. Apart from high qualification requirements in computer science, strong communication skills represent a prerequisite for recruitment. Candidates must also speak fluent German.

Personnel managers in F3 expect newcomers in the nearshore center to posses similar skills to German graduates. German standards thus represent the evaluation criteria for nearshore candidates. Personnel managers complain about the university system in the nearshore country and portray the system as more restrictive and regulated than the German system. They claim that graduates do not learn to take the initiative on their own or how to work autonomously. As a personnel manager in the nearshore establishment of the firm F3 points out:

> ... regarding the theoretical education I cannot find any difference, but mmm there is less project work or if they do it, it is only in small tasks. This means that there is less pure programming practice, and it also means that the education is much more regulated ("schooled"). They are guided throughout their undergraduate studies and the working method is much more like doing what you have been told to do. In German universities is somehow more like a research impulse, which means that you have to work more autonomously .... I say ... the workers here are not dependent, but until now, they didn't need to be autonomous. It is still very important that they learn these skills during the time they spend in Germany.

Work autonomy is crucial in software development, constituting a "professional attitude," an internalized work responsibility, and corporate loyalty. In other words, personnel managers in the F3 firm consider the German university system as more capable of transmitting work autonomy values and habits to the students compared to the nearshore country. Work autonomy constitutes a dimension of professionalism and also a very important source of control in software development environments. As Larson (1977, 199) argued, "professionalism ... functions as an internalized mechanism for the control of the subordinate expert." Moreover, the team functions as a kind of example of supervision, since team members are highly interdependent and are commonly oriented through time demands (in projects through deadlines as a structural principle, and from a long-term career-oriented perspective). Project managers work between both German and nearshore locations, but as a personnel manager in the firm F3 comments, in the future they will work only from Germany. As a result, project teams in the nearshore center must learn to work autonomously to prevent distance related difficulties:

> *... the project manager will reside then normally later in Germany and the project team workers in the nearshore center must be able to work much more autonomously otherwise there will be difficulties with the distance.*

Therefore, the composition of software development teams with young computer science graduates and developers with experience in Germany plays a very important role to establish the corporate professionalism in the expanding nearshore center. Personnel managers view the local language of the nearshore country as very difficult to learn. They also believe that developers in the nearshore center must integrate into the corporate culture and independently run all software development phases, including those involving customer contacts. The expertise specialization of the software developers in the nearshore center is not guided in advance, but emerges from the experience in the different phases that the workers undergo in the firm. As a personnel manager points out:

> *it is so that every developer (in the nearshore center) must preferably undergo and take part in every project phase and then it crystallizes with the time where he in fact has his strengths; if he for instance has his strengths in the technique then it can remain much better in technical design or if it is programming, or it is more the technical assessment in the collaboration with customers.*

However, for coordinating international teamwork between German and the software developers in the nearshore center, due to the differences in work habits in Germany and in the nearshore country perceived by personnel managers, the firm F3 use as common background the German institutionalized professionalism and especially a strong hierarchical quality management system that goes beyond the firm through the core multinational owner enterprise. This system has been developed and institutionalized in the enterprise through the years, taking internationally recognized quality standards as a basis, and functions as an internal control system for the whole organization and for teamwork. However, a quality manager in the firm F3 argues that this kind of system sometimes makes the organization "self-blind," if it does not permit acting in a reflexive way from the ground floor, reflecting the workaday problems within projects. Thus, according to the quality manager, communication and social skills are especially important, for two main reasons: first, to understand the problems of the software developers as well as the technical and management problems within a project; and second, to solve these problems according to three basic quality principles or, in the words of a quality manager, "the magical triangle for decision making: budget, timing and quality."

The quality manager in the firm F3 emphasizes the importance of the "social component" in teamwork and especially of reaching high quality in production. Thus, in contrast to offshore projects in India, nearshore projects in Eastern Europe, the quality manager points out, are easier to coordinate because the team members and the quality and project managers know each other and can more easily establish a communication basis:

> we need the social component. We have observed this precisely in our nearshore center; the nearshore center people were first here and thus we could build a social relationship. You know each other, you get out together for a drink and then, when we telephone it is like if he were in the neighbour room.

The firm plans to expand in the nearshore center country market, so that the autonomy requirements for software developers in the nearshore country will grow and they will have to act as mediators between different cultural backgrounds. It is important to note that although the German-based corporate professionalism dominates the expectations of the personnel managers, due to some reported misunderstandings in teamwork practices between the nearshore center and German software developers, the firm F3 has reacted by initiating the design of common "corporate rules" for the nearshore projects that sometimes are developed "ad hoc" within the project, but also take international quality standards as a basis. Quality standards serve as a basis for the practice of distributed work and managing emerging expertise in IT offshore projects. However, project experience among employees with a longer perspective beyond the particular end of one project enable the building of a group identity and also the improvement of professionalism in the different cooperating locations through the establishment of domains of practice. Whether the German-based corporate professionalism will prevail, or will coexist with local habits in the international software development environment of the firm F3, or, in other words, how expertise in both locations will be institutionalized, is yet an open question. But as an operative basis, ITIL, the management system used in the mother enterprise, is being extended to the daughter firms and, at the same time, project and quality mangers develop together particular ground-rules for the practice of offshore distributed work differentiated for near- and offshore locations, which they combine with the ITIL recommendations. Moreover a repository has been built up for encoding, updating, storing, and retrieving codified project-related information such as documentation, quality management patterns, coding standards and reviews, or intercultural collaboration recommendations. The particular development of such tools for managing global expertise are too extensive to be explained in this chapter. It is important to emphasize in this case that the success of IT offshore projects in this enterprise has not only depended on the development of quality management systems and tools emerging from practice but also especially on the engagement of the project and quality managers in the different locations and on the strong motivation of the employees supported by intense interpersonal exchange, face-to-face and technology-mediated, and by long-term perspectives and autonomy in the decisions relating to their own professional paths.

The second firm about which I report in this chapter, F1a, is an operative segment of a multinational company operating in the telecommunication and software areas of the ICT branch. The F1a was recently established as an operative segment and has had since its origins experience of off- and nearshoring in India and Eastern Europe. As a part of a multinational company, F1a is tied to the cultural identity of its owner and particularly rooted in the tradition of the German industrial culture with a strong "Beamtentum" influence.

The experiences of off- and nearshoring of F1a remain linked to the long internationalization tradition of the core owner company. The F1a is not a *native service provider* in the sense that they do not sell the service resources of the offshore locations to other companies. Internationalization constitutes for F1a not only a basic resource for reducing production costs but a long-term strategy for establishing the company in the global market. Nevertheless, the experience of offshoring is not very old and the change of work habits due to more formalization of practices is still flowing. Resistance to change, and the lack of existence of a corporate identity because of continuous restructuring and consequent fear of job losses, lead to implementation problems of offshore projects and to difficulties in building long-term IT offshore strategies and in establishing effective knowledge transfer among partners. Thus, face-to-face communication is much more needed in IT offshore projects in F1a. Some team workers and especially the team coordinators often travel to the home or host locations of the nearshore projects to maintain face-to-face contacts, which is highly valued to improve the communication and interaction of the team members. In particular, F1a currently has offshore projects in several countries such as India, Poland, Romania, and Slovakia. The programming phases and also tasks like testing of ICT projects have been delivered to these countries, sometimes with the help of external consultancy firms and sometimes in cooperation with partner companies. The consequences for the organization of work processes is that tasks, work modules, and deliveries must be clearly defined as well as the interfaces between work modules. These strong definition requirements in off- and nearshore projects are the main difference from locally based projects, in the opinion of one project manager. This means a stronger standardization of processes and documentation practices, as was the case in the past, and a rapid adaptation to current needs by selecting just some aspects of past documented processes. Documentation represents at this point a double-edged sword, since on the one hand, it is needed to identify possible process failures and to find solutions as well as to check the processes with quality standards, but on the other hand, it retards the working process and, moreover, it is sometimes not clear what is relevant to be documented. As a project manager in the enterprise F1a remarks, definition of modules and tasks, documentation, and process adaptation run parallel in successive constant iteration moments.

Quality management systems live and develop together within this process, and they are extremely important for the improvement of the working process in internationalized software development environments. However, in the case of F1a, such systems did not exist in the past years or they were only available on call, and were moreover not documented.

In the case of F1a, the supervision of the projects is in some cases conducted by an external consulting enterprise, which in the particular case of the project to which the interviewed project manager belongs, is extremely important due to its huge volume and complexity. As the consultant of this project comments, quality standards are crucial in off- and nearshore projects, both for coordination and also as a basis to find solutions in the event of work process problems. Quality standards are important for the external consultant also, as a legitimating basis for possible changes in work processes that the consultant has to achieve and implement in the "client" enterprise, in which somehow he plays a twofold role as an external worker and also interacting in the day-to-day practice of the project with the employees' "clients" as a colleague and supporter within the project. Thus, quality standards are the instrument to legitimate decisions relating to the work processes. However, the knowledge of such standards and also of the quality management systems of the company are also important for the team workers, since they have to implement them in the day-to-day project life. Thus, quality standards as well as quality management become more and more institutionalized in the company, which is reflected in the increasing number of courses that the company offers to the employees. Moreover, employees can only learn about quality standards and their implementation as well as about quality management within the company, since, first, it is not usual to get training in these issues at the universities and second, even if the employees have some knowledge having studied IT or mathematics, they do not have the particular knowledge of their implementation in such a complex environment of a multinational company. As the project manager puts it:

> What we do here you cannot learn at the university. Either I know it from my studies, if I learn IT or mathematics and there also especially software development and I know what documentation and test as a whole means or I do not know. And even if I know it, I have never known it in such an environment like this.

Thus, continuous internal training in quality standards and quality management is crucial for the employees working in off- and nearshore projects, and this means both in the home and host countries. However, quality standards must be also developed and timed in line with the different internal improvement of quality management systems in different companies. The language used for communication among partners is crucial here, since English knowledge, which is needed for understanding international quality requirements and for communication among offshore groups, is in many cases very deficient. In particular, the communication with Indian offshore partners is a problem in many projects, so that to avoid added costs related with such communication problems, IT offshore projects are increasingly implemented with partners in Eastern European countries with which they can communicate in German and for which the travel expenses for eventual face-to-face encounters are less.

Both cases, F3 and F1a, show that the improvement of quality management systems, particularly through the continuous knowledge feedback from different offshore locations, is very important to build a basis for understanding and for legitimizing particular work practices. At the same time, it is important to take into account the expertise differences among teams and among team members, which also means not to focus only on given standards dictated by the quality management systems, but to build flexible platforms to learn from ad hoc practices to use and transfer organizational knowledge. This means, first, to take into account the concrete local and project related systems of practice, social interaction and sensemaking, and second to engage in the externalization, reification, and explicitation of contextual knowledge or expertise. (Weick 1995; Nonaka and Kono 1998; Johnson et al. 2002; Gasson 2005).

Summary of findings and discussion

In this chapter, I have shown how knowledge and expertise are related to quality management systems and time in ICT offshore projects. The results of my research suggest that temporal norms and regulations are related not only to working practices but also to project deadlines as essential links to customers in software development. Thus, temporal norms constitute important dimensions of expertise definition. Moreover, it is important to emphasize the influence of quality standards to structure expertise. Quality management systems are developed in an iterative internal process within organizations, but must at the same time take into account the development of quality standards in the ICT branch toward which ICT organizations must orientate to remain competitive in the market.

Thus, quality standards also play an important role in timing expertise as an additional resource that large ICT organizations use to institutionalize innovation and also to control its rhythm. The significant role of large companies in the international standard setting organizations illustrates the importance of quality standards as strategic activity (Tate 2001).

In sum, from the perspective of the organization of work, quality standards play a very important role as internal controlling and timing instruments of knowledge, working, and communication processes, as well as an external mechanism beyond the ICT network to gain market advantages (Ruiz Ben 2007).

According to Cook and Brown (1999), *know-what knowledge* is related to organizational facts and conventions. In IT offshore projects global management tools such as ITIL are used, as I showed above, collecting and bringing together cross-organizational conventions and serving in combination with quality standards as a basis for establishing professionalism across organizations in IT offshore processes. As the results of my research show, it is very important to create domains of practice in a dynamic collaborative and integrative environment supported by the experts at different work areas and locations for the permanent improvement of quality management systems and global tools. Such domains of practice constitute a kind of meaning framework of tasks and projects. Whereas in the first case study, F3, the employees are involved in the different stages of domains of practice and also in the improvement of working norms from a long-term perspective of IT offshore, in F1a quality management systems have a shorter history in the organization and they still need time to be established in the day-to-day practices. However, in F1a, IT offshore projects are not organized in domains of practice within long-term strategy. This means that IT offshore project members must negotiate practices for every new project and must adapt to new group environments. Thus, they need time to build a project identity. In addition, communication problems, expertise divergences, and conflicts among working teams are common during the first phases of projects in this case. In particular, in distributed teamwork long-time perspectives for integration of expertise in domains of practice are needed to make sense of tasks and professional biographies.

As the case of F3 shows, the long-term development of domains of practice reinforces the *knowing-why* component of expertise regarding tasks and projects within organizations and beyond the time limits of projects. Within such domains of practice, quality systems, and global management tools support group cohesion from the beginning of the projects, in which employees from different locations become involved. Thus, such established mechanisms legitimate work practices and give sense to day-to-day practices while, at the same time, project and quality managers are engaged with employees in the improvement of the tools. Both, participation of the different actors in the improvement of quality standards as well as the offer of professional development perspectives within the organization contribute to the motivation of the employees.

In sum, I have analyzed expertise in IT offshore projects, adapting the typology of Cook and Brown (1999) regarding knowledge and considering quality management systems and time as crucial components of expertise development and integration in interrelated levels of organization. The results of my research suggest that the establishing of domains of practice from a long-term perspective in the organization supports the expertise transfer in offshore projects and the engagement of experts in the improvement of quality management systems.

Implications for research

My research has focused on expertise and knowledge in IT near and offshore processes within German multinational organizations. Further investigation is needed into expertise in the intersection of occupational communities within organizations, as well as additional empirical studies regarding networks of practice that extend beyond organizational boundaries. In particular, the analysis of situated work practices of IT experts in different cultural locations from a long-term perspective would help us understand the complex relationship of knowledge, work, expertise, professionalism, occupations, and organizations. Furthermore, we could better understand the meaning of quality standards for IT experts in workaday practices and in different contexts and in different times of their biographical trajectories. This means that future research should put more emphasis on the *know-why* component of knowledge related to time factors and regarding how occupational communities across organizations use organizational artifacts (such as quality management tools) to demarcate occupational domains beyond project limits and organizational innovation strategies.

Note

1. Deutsche Forschungsgemeinschaft: German Research Foudation.

References

Abbott, A.D. (1988) *The System of Professions*, Chicago, IL: The University of Chicago Press.
Ballard, D.I. and Seibold, D.R. (2003) Communicating and Organizing in Time: A Meso Level Model of Organizational Temporality. *Management Communication Quarterly*, 16: 380–415.

Baukrowitz, A. and Boes, A. (1996) IT-Fachkräfte auf dem Weg in die „Informationsgesellschaft" – Konzeptionelle Anregungen zur Neuordnung des Berufsfelds, in Schwarz, H. (eds) *Computerberufe im System der dualen Berufsausbildung und die Zukunft der DV-Kaufleute*, Wissenschaftliche Diskussionspapiere des Bundesinstituts für Berufsbildung (BiBB), Heft 20, Berlin und Bonn, 35–47.

Baukrowitz, A., Boes, A., and Schmiede, R. (2000) Die Entwicklung der Arbeit aus der Perspektive ihrer Informatisierung, in *Kommunikation@ Gesellschaft* Jg. 1, Num. 1. (www.kommunikation-gesellschaft.de).

Berg, P., Appelbaum, E., Bailey, T., and Kalleberg, A.L. (2003) Contesting Time: International Comparisons of Employee Control Of Working Time. *Industrial and Labor Relations Review,* April 2004, 57(3): 331–349.

Beulen, E., van Fenema, P., and Currie, W. (2005) From Application Outsourcing to Infrastructure Management: Extending the Offshore Outsourcing Service Portfolio. *European Management Journal*, 23(2): 133–144.

Boes, A. (2002) *Zukunftsprojekt Mitbestimmung? Empirische Untersuchung des Wandels der Arbeit und der Arbeitsbeziehungen in der IT-Industrie*, Dissertation, Darmstadt.

Boes, A. and Trinks, K. (2005) *Theoretisch bin ich frei*. Berlin: Sigma.

CDI (2002) CDI Deutsche Private Akademie für Wirtschaft GmbH: CDI-*Stellenmarktanalyse 2002*.

Constantine, L.L. and Lockwood, L.A.D. (1999) *Software for Use: A Practical Guide to the Methods of Usage-Centered Design*. New York: Addison-Wesley Professional.

Cook, J. and Brown, J.S. (1999) Bridging Epistemologies: The Generative Dance between Organizational Knowledge and Organizational Knowing. *Organization Science,* 10(4): 381–400.

Cusumano, M.A. and Selby, R.W. (1995) *Microsoft Secrets: How the World´s Most Powerful Software Company Creates Technology, Shape Markets, and Manages People*, New York: The Free Press.

DeSanctis, G. and Poole, M.S. (1994) Capturing the Complexity in Advanced Technology Use: Adaptive Structuration Theory. *Organization Science*, 5: 121–145.

Dierkes, M., Alexis, M., Berthoin Antal, A., Hedberg, B., Pawlowsky, P., Stopford, J., and Vonderstein, A. (eds) (2001). *The Annotated Bibliography of Organizational Learning and Knowledge Creation*, 2nd edition, Berlin: Sigma.

Dostal, W. (2000) Informatiker gesucht. *Informatik Spektrum*, 23(4) S: 258–263.

Dostal, W. (2001) Turbulenzen im IT-Arbeitsmarkt. *Informatik Spektrum*, 8: 35–52.

Dostal, W. (2002) IT Arbeitsmarkt. Chancen am Ende des Booms. *IAB Kurzbericht*, Ausgabe Nr. 19/21, 8: 9–13.

Dostal, W. (2006) *Berufsgenese*. Nürnberg: Institut für Arbeitsmarkt und Berufsforschung der Bundesagentur für Arbeit.

Endres, A. (2003) Softwarequalität aus Nutzersicht und ihre wirtschaftliche Bewertung. *Informatik Spektrum*, 18: 20–25.

Friedson, E. (1994) *Professionalism Reborn. Theory, Prophecy and Policy*, Cambridge: Cambridge University Press.

Gasson, S. (2005) The Dynamics of Sensemaking, Knowledge and Expertise in Collaborative boundary-spanning Design. *Journal of Computer-Mediated Communication,* 10(4): 1–23.

Giddens, A. (1984) *The Constitution of Society*, Berkeley, CA: University of California Press.

Hartmann, M. (1995) *Informatiker in der Wirtschaft: Perspektiven eines Berufs*, Springer Verlag: Berlin Heidelberg.

Huber, B., Reiff, I., Ruiz Ben, E., and Schinzel, B. (2002) *Frauen in IT- und ausgewählten technischen Ausbildungen und Berufen in Baden-Württemberg*. Stuttgart, Akademie für Technikfolgenabschätzunge in Baden-Württemberg.

Jones, M. (1997) Structuration Theory and IT, in W. Currie and B. Galliers (eds) *Rethinking Management Information Systems: An Interdisciplinary Perspective*, Oxford: Oxford University Press, 103–135.

Johnson, B., Lorenz, E., and Lundvall, B.A. (2002) Why All This Fuzz about Codified and Tacit Knowledge? *Industrial and Corporate Change,* 11(2): 245–262.

Klein, H.K. and Myers, M.D. (1999) A Set of Principles for Conducting and Evaluating Interpretive Field Studies in Information Systems. *MIS Quarterly, Special Issue on Intensive Research*, 23(1): 67–93.

Lamont, M. and Molnár, V. (2002) The Study of Boundaries in the Social Sciences. *Annual Review of Sociology*, 28: 167–195.

Larson, M.S. (1977) *The Rise of Professionalism*, Berkeley, CA: University of California Press.

Licht, G., Steiner, V., Bertschek, I., Falk, M., and Fryges, H. (2002) *IKT-Fachkräftemangel und Qualifikationsbedarf*, Mannheim: Nomos.

MacDonald, K.M. (1995) *The Sociology of the Professions*, London: Sage Publications.

March, J.G. (1991) *Entscheidung und Organisation*, Wiesbaden: Gabler.

March, J.G. and Olsen, J.P. (1975) The Uncertainty of the Past – Organizational Learning under Ambiguity. *European Journal of Political Research*, 3, 147–171.

Menez, R., Munder, I., and Töpsch, K. (2001) *Qualifizierung und Personaleinsatz in der IT-Branche.* Stuttgart: Publications of the TA, 200.

Meuser, M. and Nagel, U. (1991) ExpertInneninterviews – vielfach erprobt, wenig bedacht, in D. Garz and K. Kraimer (eds.) *Qualitativ-empirische Sozialforschung*, Opladen, Westdeutscher Verlag, 441–471.

Meuser, M. and Nagel, U. (1994) Expertenwissen und Experteninterview, in R. Hitzler, A. Honer, and C. Maeder (eds) *Expertenwissen,* Opladen: Leske+Budrich. S. 180–192.

Nonaka, I. and Konno, N. (1998) the Concept of ´Ba: Building Foundation for Knowledge Creation. *California Management Review,* 40(3): 40–54.

Nonaka, I. and Takeguchi, H. (1995) *The Knowledge-Creating Company,* New York and Oxford: Oxford University Press.

OECD (2002) OECD *Information Technology Outlook: ICTs and the Information Economy*, Paris: OECD.

Orlikowski, W. and Baroudi, J.J. (1991) Studying Information Technology in Organizations: Research Approaches and Assumptions. *Information Systems Research*, 2: 1–28.

Orlikowski, W.J. (1992) The Duality of Technology: Rethinking the Concept of Technology in Organizations. *Organization Science*, 3(3): 398–427.

Orlikowski, W. and Yates, J. (2002) It's About Time: An Enacted View of Time in Organizations. *Organization Science*, 13(6) November–December: 684–700.

Oshri, I., Kotlarsky, J., and Willcocks, L. (2007) Managing Dispersed Expertise in IT Offshore Outsourcing: Lessons from Tata Consultancy Services. *MIS Quarterly Executive,* 6(2): 53–65.

Plicht, B. and Schreyer, F. (2002) Ingenieurinnen und Informatikerinnen. Schöne neue Arbeitswelt. *IAB Kurzbericht*, 11: 1–8.

Pongratz, G. and Voß, G.G. (2003) *Arbeitskraftunternehmer. Erwerbsorientierungen in entgrenzten Arbeitsformen,* Berlin: Sigma.

Powell, W. (2001) The Capitalist Firm in the Twenty-First Century: Emerging Patterns in Western Enterprises, in P. DiMaggio, *The Twenty-First-Century Firm: Changing Economic Organisation in International Perspective,* Princeton, NJ: Princeton University Press.

Rammert, W. (2000) *Technik aus soziologischer Perspektive 2. Kultur – Innovation – Virtualität*, Opladen: Westdeutscher Verlag.

Rohde, G. (2004) Weltweite IT-Services. Berlin, Budapest oder Bangalore. *Mitbestimmung,* 50(3): 42–45.

Rothenwaldt, T. (2001) Computer werden Professionalisierung erzwingen, in *Informatik – Zeitschrift der schweizerischen Informatikorganisationen, Present and Future of the Informatics Profession,* 4, August: 16–18.

Ruiz Ben, E. (2002) Qualifikation, Erfahrung und Geschlecht. *FiFFKo,* 9: 37–41.

Ruiz Ben, E. (2003) Looking beyond the Software Boom. Gendered Costs and Benefits? in U. Pasero (ed.) *Gender from Costs to Benefits,* Opladen, Westdeutscher Verl. 236–253.

Ruiz Ben, E. (2005) *Professionalisierung der Informatik. Chance für die Beteiligung von Frauen?* Wiesbaden: DUV.

Ruiz Ben, E. (2007) Quality Standardization Patterns in ICT Offshore Projects, in Raisingiani, M. *Handbook of Research on Global Information Technology.* London: IGI Global, pp. 312–328.

Ruiz Ben, E. and Claus, R. (2005) Offshoring in der deutschen IT-Branche: Eine neue Herausforderung für die Informatik. *Informatik Spektrum,* 1: 75–84.

Schein, E.H. (1985) *Organizational Culture and Leadership. A Dynamic View,* San Francisco and London: Jossey-Bass Publishers.

Schön, D.A. (1983) *The Reflective Practitioner: How Professionals think in Action,* New York: Basic Books.

Skoddow, J. (2003) Die Entstehung der Berufe in der Datenverarbeitung, unter: www.ik.fh-hannover.de/person/becher/edvhist/berufe/computer-berufe.htm#1980, Stand: 12.05.03

Stelzer, D. and Mellis, W. (1998) Success Factors of Organizational Change in Software Process Improvement. *Software Process: Improvement and Practice,* 4(4): 227–250.

Tomaskovic-Devey, D. and Skaggs, S. (1999). An Establishment Level Test of the Statistical Discrimination Hypothesis. *Work and Occupations,* 26: 422–445.

Voß, G.G. (1998). Die Entgrenzung von Arbeit und Arbeitskraft. Eine Subjektorientierte Interpretation des Wandels der Arbeit. *Mitteilungen aus der Arbeitsmarkt und Berufsforschung,* 31: 473–487.

Walsh, J.P. and Ungson, G.R. (1991) Organizational Memory. *Academy of Management Review,* 16(1): 57–91.

Walsham, G. (1993) *Interpreting Information Systems in Organisations,* Chichester: John Wiley & Sons.

Walsham, G. (2001) *Making a World of Difference: IT in a Global Context.* Chichester: John Wiley & Sons.

Walsham, G. (2002) Cross-Cultural Software Production and Use: A Structurational Analysis. *MIS Quarterly*, 26(4): 359–380.

Wallmüller, E. (2001) *Softwarequalitätsmanagement in der Praxis*, Berlin: Carl Hansen Verlag.

Watson, T. (2002) Professions and Professionalism: Should We Jump off the Bandwagon, Better to Understand Where It Is Going? *International Studies of Management and Organization*, 322: 93–105.

Weick, K.E. (1995) *Sensemaking in Organizations*, Thousand Oaks, CA: Sage.

Werle and Iversen (2006) Promoting Legitimacy in Technical Standardization. *STI Studies*, 2(March): 19–39.

Yates, J. and Orlikowski, W. (1992) Genre of Organizational Communication : A Structurational Approach to Studying Communication and Media. *The Academy of Management Review*, 17(2): 299–326.

CHAPTER 10

Step by step: the development of knowledge transfer and collaboration in a nearshore software development project

Michaela Wieandt

Introduction

During recent years, Information and Communication Technology (ICT) companies with global practices have begun to build near- or offshore software delivery centers all over the world (Ruiz Ben and Claus 2004; Aspray et al. 2006). Nationally focused software enterprises tend to be more hesitant, concentrating rather on nearshore strategies (DB Research 2005; DB Research 2006; EITO 2006). For ICT firms focused on the German market, geographical proximity (which implies short flight hours), perceived cultural similarities, and the availability of German language skills, presumably make nearshoring a good alternative (Kearney 2004; Ruiz Ben and Wieandt 2006; DB Research 2006). This is also mirrored by high growth rates in IT services exported from the new EU-member states to the old Europe-15, which saw an annual average of 13 percent between 1994 and 2004 (DB Research 2006; see also Carmel and Abbott 2007). According to the literature, the shorter distance in nearshore contexts alleviates problems related to communication, control, and coordination (Abbott 2007), but the investigation of nearshore collaboration has drawn comparatively little attention so far (Carmel and Abbott 2006; Abbott 2007). So, a nearshore case was chosen to shed more light on the effectiveness of this kind of collaboration.

According to research on globally distributed or virtual work, a key issue is the constant and mutual exchange of business and technological knowledge between the different organizational units (Sole and Edmondson 2002; Ardichvili et al. 2003). This is particularly challenging when employees have to delegate sophisticated individual software development tasks to offshore workers, which requires constant communication and adjustment processes (Marks and Lockyer 2004; Boes and Trinks 2006). However, work relations between on-site and off- or nearshore employees are exacerbated by the fact that on-site employees are often reluctant to work with their foreign counterparts (Boes and Schwemmle 2004). Introduced by the management, off- and nearshoring are supposed to fulfill cost-cutting objectives, which often entail downsizing and dismissal (Boes 2005), and create a stressful environment of uncertainty, fear, and distrust among employees (Empson 2001).

The research presented here focuses on a nearshoring case, addressing the development of constructive relationships between on-site and nearshore location members in a medium-sized German software development company: *How is knowledge transfer established and organized in a nearshore context and what are the important factors in regard to the collaboration of on-site and nearshore employees?*

In the theoretical section, I will first introduce the concept of "knowledge" as used here. Based on the distinction between explicit and implicit knowledge the specific modes of transmission required for geographically distributed software development projects are also indicated. In the second part, I will introduce two concepts of off- or nearshoring collaboration derived from research into IT off- and nearshoring. Encompassing specific divisions of labor, these concepts indicate the importance of knowledge transfer and patterns of collaboration. They also demonstrate some of the intricacies concerning personal and organizational context factors. The data section illustrates the establishment of knowledge transfer and collaboration in a German software development company. It is shown how employees of both sites establish a transactive-memory-oriented knowledge base in an incremental manner, and that important factors of collaboration include the arrangement of the division of labor, a high social and organizational integration of the nearshore workers, as well as equal control mechanisms for all sites. The conclusion will contain some remarks on possibilities for future research as well as for sourcing practices.

Theoretical background: knowledge transfer and collaboration in dispersed software development projects

The nature of knowledge

The research on knowledge transfer broadly refers to two main approaches concerning the nature of knowledge (i.e., Lam 1997; Dyer and Nobeoka 2000; Sole and Edmondson 2002; Newell et al. 2006). The first approach considers knowledge to be a commodity possessed by individuals (Blackler 1995; Nonaka and Takeuchi 1995). From this viewpoint, knowledge can be expatiated and codified in an abstract and de-individualized form (i.e. in a database). It is easily transferable across projects, teams, and individuals. The second approach considers knowledge as situational, embedded and deeply linked to daily practice (Lave and Wenger 1991; Lam 1997; Tsoukas and Vladimirou 2001). Embedded in cultural, social, and organizational contexts as well as in social practices and relationships, knowledge is assumed to be implicit and tacit (Polanyi 1966), and thus difficult to transfer (Empson 2001; Sole and Edmondson 2002). As it is impossible to fully articulate tacit knowledge, this form of knowledge is only learnable through experience and social interaction (Empson 2001; Walsham 2002). Based on the views of Cook and Brown (1999) and Newell et al. (2006), it is assumed here that some knowledge can be possessed independently of practice, making transfer via learning over distances possible, while other types of knowledge are embedded in practice and require social contact to be learned. Nevertheless, possessable knowledge is also actively acquired and learned by individuals while being meaningfully interpreted against a certain context of the individual's tacit knowledge and biographical experience (Alheit and Dausien 2000; Walsham 2002). Thus, the transfer of knowledge is a form of individual knowledge acquisition and learning which encompasses (1) learning through networking and personal dialogue (i.e., knowledge as embedded practice); and (2) learning through databases and documents (i.e., knowledge as a commodity) (Lam 1997; Newell et al. 2006).

To further categorize knowledge concerning software development, Empson (2001) proposes a useful concept by distinguishing between technical and client knowledge. Technical knowledge encompasses (1) sectoral knowledge, which is generic, widely shared among software development firms and formally codified by the curriculum of universities (i.e., in programming languages); (2) firm-specific organizational knowledge consisting of either formalized or socialized products and processes; and (3) individual technical knowledge based on work experience and education, which is partly collected through exchange and knowledge dissemination and is more tacit in nature. Second, client knowledge refers to (1) the general understanding of a certain industry; (2) detailed knowledge of a client firm; and (3) personal knowledge of key individuals within the client firm, and encompasses elements of implicit and explicit knowledge as well. This kind of knowledge is created through interaction with the client throughout the software development process, which requires a comprehensive understanding of the clients' business processes, closer cooperation, and knowledge exchange being required for more individual software (Markus 2004; Gillard 2005). Therefore, software developers must also learn about the tacit and embedded structures of their client firms via social interaction and reflection processes.

Collaboration in software development projects

Software development is mainly performed in projects coordinated by means of project management including the setting of milestones and "packages" of work (Marks and Lockyer 2004; Latniak and Gerlmaier 2006). As a temporary confluence of experts (Guzzo and Dickson 1996; Sydow et al. 2004), these project groups are not necessarily teams (Newell et al. 2002; Koch 2004). To achieve cohesion and collaboration, team development requires some general mechanisms such as the common understanding of company-based rules and procedures for project management, integration mechanisms such as access to communication channels, social coordination through agreed norms, individual role responsibility, and the assignment of authority and control, as well as incentive systems (Newell et al. 2002). Software developers must exercise the social skills necessary for teamwork, including frequent interaction and collaboration with others (Marks and Lockyer 2004). Project managers must have team developing skills, that is in creating mutual dependency between tasks to swiftly generate collaboration and trust (Koch 2004). However, in dispersed work contexts the establishment of successful collaboration seems to require even more effort (Martins et al. 2004), as it is aggravated by off- or nearshoring settings implying communication problems, distance, and cultural differences.

Off- and nearshoring

Near- and offshoring refers to the fact that some of the duties belonging to a software project's life cycle are sourced out to a lower-wage country (Aspray et al. 2006).

Whether the term off- or nearshoring is used for sourcing activities seems to be a matter of distance (Carmel and Abbott 2006). Offshoring is associated with countries being "far away," referring to a distance of more than 1000 kilometers (c. 621 miles) (Scherf et al. 2005): for example, from a European viewpoint, China or India. The term nearshoring is used for activities which are closer to the homeland, more or less a few hours' flight away (Carmel and Abott 2006), that is East European countries are near-shore for Western European countries. A broader definition independent of the location of the outsourcing company refers to the term "international sourcing" (OECD 2004, 6).

Looking at the literature on off- and nearshoring (Amberg and Wiener 2004a, 2004b, 2005; Boes and Schwemmle 2004; OECD 2004; Aspray et al. 2006; EITO 2006), we can broadly distinguish two main concepts: a high-end and a low-end concept of sourcing activities, differing in regard to the division of labor. Both have different knowledge transfer requirements and collaboration patterns within software projects (Table 10.1). The concepts are analytical, so in practice they may be combined.

The clarity of task definition, coordination requirements (which imply instructions as well as adjustment processes to specify the programming

Table 10.1   The high-end and the low-end sourcing concept

Sourcing concept	High-end sourcing	Low-end sourcing
Division of labor	–	–
Task characteristics	More dependent, complex	More independent, simple
Tasks sourced out	Software-architecture, product design, project management, programming	Coding, testing, software maintenance
Delivery model characteristics	–	–
Project duration	Long-term, one year or more	One-off or short-term, possibly under a year
Clarity of task-definition	High	High
Coordination requirements, "adjustment"	High	Low
Communication requirements	High	Low
Required control	Throughout the process	Before acceptance
Knowledge transfer	Throughout the process, both sides exchange knowledge, at best developing a TMS	Information transfer to the sourcing organization at the beginning and in case of changes
Type of collaboration	Ranging from shared work between two teams to teamwork	Contractor

work), communication requirements, and control, depend on the distribution and complexity of tasks (Amberg and Wiener 2004a, 2004b; Boes and Schwemmle 2004; Aspray et al. 2006): lower qualified, more independent, and repeatable tasks like software-testing, software maintenance, or application management (i.e., help desk functions) encompass a more easily explained sectoral form of knowledge and are definable in terms of firm-specific demands. Here, short-term or one-off projects are also possible. Accomplishable via given instructions, coding and programming is considered to be low-end work if it is clearly and explicitly specified regarding firm- and client-specific demands (Slama and Kaefer 2005). In this case, coordination and communication efforts are rarely required after the initial transfer of knowledge in the form of comprehensive instructions and information on tasks and thorough specification of the software at the beginning of the project. Control by the sourcing organization only concerns results at the final acceptance stage (Amberg and Wiener 2004a). Within the project, only new instructions have to be transmitted. At the end of the project, the contractor has to deliver the software documentation as well. Therefore, collaboration between the two sites can be characterized as a contractual relationship in which the customer (the outsourcing organization) orders a specific software-related service from the contractor. This form of collaboration is therefore similar to outsourcing (Riedl and Kepler 2003).

High-end services such as software-architecture, product design, project management, or programming are difficult to define clearly. Tasks are more complex and dependent. They require comparatively more communication, coordination, and control throughout the working process, even if processes are formalized and standardized (Hysell 2000; Edwards and Sridhar 2002; Amberg and Wiener 2005; Oshri et al. 2006). High-end sourcing in software development processes requires intensive collaboration within and between teams and constant knowledge transfer, which entails explicit and tacit knowledge of technology and client firms (Boes and Schwemmle 2004; Amberg and Wiener 2005; Laser and Heiss 2005). This is also supported by the research on distributed knowledge-based development work (i.e., Lam 1997; Dyer and Nobeoka 2000; Sole and Edmondson 2002). According to Oshri et al. (2006), collaboration effectively relies on a collective knowledge base characterized as a transactive memory system (TMS), summarizing knowledge of different forms and enabling the encoding, storage, and retrieval of information in a codified and personalized form (see also Wegner 1987; Moreland 1999). Encoding refers to explicit knowledge collected in the form of a shared "cataloguing" system (ibid., 6). Access to this system encourages employees to develop a shared understanding of context and work-related processes, terminology and language, all of which are a precondition for, and part of, the exchange of tacit and embedded knowledge, including firm and client specific, as well as individual, knowledge. Storing refers to the way in which information is organized physically (e.g., in a database with cross references and key words) and in the memories of the staff involved. Retrieving implies that individuals know where and in what form information is stored within the team and that they are able to find required information. This suggests that they should be able to find information in the database. Team members have to develop "interpersonal channels" through which they can find out who has the information (Oshri et al. 2006). In this regard, a TMS is also concerned with the embeddedness of knowledge, indicating individual experience and competencies (Sole and Edmondson 2002).

In this sense, in a codified directory, encoding, storing, and retrieving knowledge requires a shared set of rules encompassing the labeling and categorization of what has been done, as well as who could do what, in a common database, including information such as subject and location of expertise, documents and up-to-date records To create a personalized directory showing how and why something has been done and "who knows what" and "who is doing what" (Oshri et al. 2006, 6), the teams have to develop a shared understanding of context and work-related processes, terminology and language, which includes the exchange of tacit and embedded knowledge in a collective learning process. This requires personal contact (Sole and Edmonsdon 2002; Ardichvili et al. 2003) or at least some additional information (Crampton 2001), that is, in the form of the rotation of team members, joint training programs, team-building exercises, and social activities as well as systematic and frequent contact via electronic devices (Oshri et al. 2006). Personal contact also enhances trust and group cohesiveness, which are assumed to be important factors for the success of distributed collaboration (Martins et al. 2004). In other words, the development of the two directories implies two main strategies for knowledge transfer: (1) the creation of networks and use of personal dialogue for the development of a personalized directory containing tacit and embedded knowledge; and (2) the creation of a common database and documents to set up a codified directory including explicit knowledge. So, this kind of sourcing requires much effort, and is therefore only efficient if it is a long-term project or work relationship.

Important subjective factors in regard to the creation of a TMS and close collaboration are the motivation and willingness of employees to share knowledge (Empson 2001), which is influenced by the company's infrastructure and incentive systems (McKinlay 2002) as well as by the organization's culture of knowledge sharing (Dyer and Nybeoka 2000; Ardichvili et al. 2003). In the context of sourcing activities, this may be impeded by the reluctance of employees to cooperate with their foreign counterparts

(Boes and Schwemmle 2004). Also, employees could employ strategies of resistance such as refusing knowledge transfer or hiding information to delay a project (Empson 2001; McKinlay 2002; Koch 2004), as off- and nearshoring policies are often part of a cost-cutting policy which can also include downsizing and therefore ultimately dismissal (Boes 2005), increasing the distrust and uncertainty of employees (Empson 2002).

Coming back to the research questions, how is knowledge transfer established and organized in a nearshore context and what are the important factors in regard to collaboration between on-site and nearshore employees? It can be suggested that the transfer of knowledge has to consider explicit as well as tacit knowledge and is linked to contextual factors regarding the general mechanisms of teambuilding, encompassing organizational culture, infrastructure, and underlying nearshore concepts as well as personal and subjective factors. Collaboration should not only be considered in terms of the division of labor, but must also take into account team processes and political factors, as illustrated by the following case study.

About this research

The case study was conducted as part of a broader research project on the internationalization of the German ICT industry, focusing on the impact of job profiles and qualifications on categorization (INITAK). We selected SW company (SWC), a pseudonym name of a software vendor from Germany, because it was conducting long-term nearshore relationships and had acquired extensive experience in managing outsourcing relationships. Within this company, we have focused on a long-term sub-project (sub-project C, SPC) which was for a large automobile company. We conducted 10 semi-structured interviews from February to July 2006.

Nearshoring and the development of knowledge transfer and collaboration

The SW company: organizational culture and working context

Representing a typical German software company (Friedewald 2004; Boes and Trinks 2006) SW company produces large, complex individualized software systems for business solutions for customers in the private (automobile, banking, insurance, logistics, health, and telecommunications) and public sectors, including consulting services. Founded in 1982, the company has expanded step-by-step, founding six subsidiaries, five of which are situated in different parts of Germany and one in Switzerland. In 2006, the company employed approximately 1100 employees, 96 percent of whom were highly educated (with a university degree or PhD). At the end of the 1990s, the company was bought by an international IT consulting and service company, but remained legally independent with its own organizational culture and identity.

In terms of customers, emphasis is given to high quality service due to the broad expertise, experience, and competence of its employees. Thus, education and on-the-job learning is highly accepted and desired by the management. The employees have internalized the norm of high quality service, regarding it as part of their job identity and characteristic of the organization's culture. This picture also includes the reliability of their systems as well as a high flexibility regarding customer requirements, including learning about the customer's branch, specific firms, and working processes, here referred to as client knowledge.

The organization is structured around several business and administrative divisions. The business divisions are led by a division leader (Geschäftsbereichsleiter). Subordinate to this person is a division manager (Geschäftsbereichsmanager), responsible for projects in a division and coordinating the project managers who are responsible for project management in this area and also for contracting. The next layer is formed by the project leaders who manage the project operations independently. They only delegate problems if they cannot solve them by themselves. Depending on the project size, they supervise some sub-project managers and/or the software developers.

The working culture at SW company was characterized in the interviews by a high degree of informal social contact, knowledge exchange and an open, communicative, supportive, and constructive working atmosphere where conflicts are openly resolved. Owing to the project-based nature of the work, a high emphasis was given to team building and motivation of workers. To socialize its employees and create a commonly shared identity and work practices, the company developed a training program which is compulsory for new entrants. It consisted of "lessons" on soft skills (i.e., communication, presentation, teamwork) securing a "homogeneous presentation of the company" and a unique "style of communication" with customers (human resources manager). Training in technical competency (i.e., programming, testing) was conducted to communicate the basic norms of work practice, quality, and processes. The program included different levels in regard to work experience and career prospects so that employees were systematically and continuously integrated into the organization's culture.

Owing to the subsidiary structure of the organization , in a part of the project, tasks were already distributed among different locations. Therefore, in the nearshoring context, employees had to collaborate with foreigners, experiencing language, social and cultural differences which added a new dimension to their work.

Nearshoring to Poland at SW company

The nearshore-center in Poland was founded in 2004 as part of a cost-saving strategy. According to the management, nearshoring had been necessary to meet price pressures in the branch (due to the IT crisis) and keep the German workforce stable. Therefore, the nearshore capacities are a means through which the company can "gain projects which we wouldn't have gained before," as a manager stated. Hence, it was legitimated by being "a job producing machine" (manager). This argument was internalized by all employees (including Polish employees), who referred to it in the interviews when asked for the company's reason for sourcing. So, the company's management offers an indisputable justification for nearshoring. Moreover, project management tasks and qualifications are offered to the employees as incentives, which they either found to be attractive or inevitable because of the necessity of nearshoring.

Poland, as a location, offered several advantages: being a favorable nearshore destination for German ICT companies (Ruiz Ben and Wieandt 2006), Poland provides infrastructural conditions including a considerably large ICT sector, IT skills, and a highly qualified work force (see also Piatkowski 2004). Neighboring Germany, distances are short (the flight duration to Warsaw is one hour). German language skills are available too, which is very important to realize cost saving and to avoid misunderstandings due to translation. Communication, software conception, and specification with the customer are all done in German. Thus, the working language is German and the Polish employees of the nearshore-center have to speak German very well. This was also felt to be an important factor of collaboration on both sides.

The SW company has developed four models of distributed work with different proportions of work to be done in the nearshore-center, depending on the complexity of the project and the project's duration. The first model is an introductory approach to prepare the distributed work: nearshore employees work on-site, supporting the German developers in the programming phase and becoming familiarized with the organization and the work. The second model represents a low-end approach: specification and architecture are done in Germany, programming is carried out by nearshore employees at the nearshore site, and implementation work is done by the Germans at the customer's site. The third model is designed for long-term projects with follow-up releases and is also applicable to offshore contexts. Supported by off- or nearshore employees, the first release is done in Germany while follow-up work will be transferred to the off-/nearshore site with a few Germans in supporting and instructing roles. The fourth model is an integrated approach: specification work is carried out in Germany by on-site and nearshore employees, programming is shared and situated at two locations, and implementation work as well as maintenance are also distributed. The aim is to gain entry to the Polish market, with the Polish subsidiary acquiring its own projects after having established work relations and socialization processes. The development of knowledge transfer and collaboration is best observed by studying a project. The example of subproject C illustrates how these models were applied and what consequences followed.

The worldwide purchase order (WPO) project and subproject C (SPC)

Subproject C is part of a worldwide purchase order project (WPO), representing one of the largest projects in SWC and involving 90 employees. The WPO was started ten years ago in 1996, with its first release in 1997. The client is a large automobile company situated in town B, where SWC has one of its subsidiaries (see Figure 10.1). The instructions involved developing a customer relations management system which enables the client's customers to order a car via the internet, giving the price and the exact time of delivery. At the same time, the order is booked into the production program of the car plant, which confirms the delivery date. Therefore, WPO integrates all programs and systems of the customer order process, that is sales planning, order management, or dealer management systems.

Sub-project C encompasses the development of the billing processes and started in 2001. It entails five steps with the first already live. The subproject organization consists of one project management at SWC headquarters and one at the customer's company in town B.

The customer's project management transfers the requirements of the software, containing explicit and tacit knowledge on the branch and the firm, to the SWC project management, who then coordinate the development teams onshore and nearshore. For specification, an SWC on-site team works with the customer's team at the customer's company, recording detailed knowledge on firm-specific working processes and on the

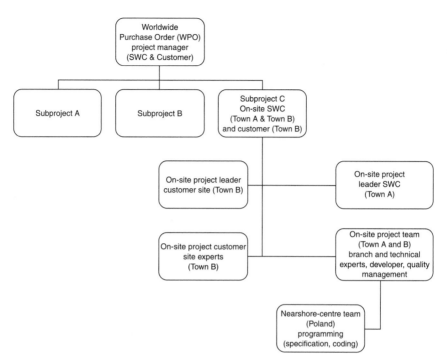

Figure 10.1   Organizational structure of the WPO project

experiences of individuals. The SWC-team consists of a team in town A, a team in town B, and a team at the nearshore-center in Poland.

Knowledge transfer development

In analyzing how knowledge transfer was established and organized at SWC, we discovered an incremental approach based on the four models constructed by the company's management, which resulted in the creation of a TMS. The integration of the nearshore-center began with the introduction model, which was converted into a low-end nearshore concept and then transformed into a high-end concept. Each phase of the nearshore activity implied certain measures of knowledge transfer which supported the establishment of the TMS.

Looking at the SPC-context, the German project manager developed three phases of collaboration incrementally increasing the integration of the Polish employees, starting with the introduction model in 2004, as summed up in Table 10.2.

Table 10.2 Development of the TMS in phase 1 of nearshoring

Phase of nearshoring	State of transactive memory system	Measures of knowledge transfer by project management	Part of transactive memory system
Phase 1 Introduction	Encoding	• Initial on-site job training entailing pair work • Company training program • Social events	Personalized directory • Shared understanding of contexts and work-related processes • Adoption of the companies' working processes, quality standards, and documentation procedures • Adjustment to working styles and routines • Exchange of cultural specifics
		• Establishment of a common data base "the repository"	• Codified directory

The personalized directory of the TMS was built up via direct contact. The Polish developers had to work in Germany during their first months in the company doing mainly programming work, which served to create a shared understanding of contexts and work-related processes. This was organized in a pair-constellation: each Polish developer had a German mentor who instructed him or her. This procedure was the same for new German entrants in order for them to study and adopt the company's software development processes, quality measures, and detailed documentation standards. Coordination and communication was performed directly and informally through floor-talks, coffee breaks, and "over the table" discussions. So, the Polish workers obtained detailed embedded knowledge on working styles, routines, and cultural differences, as well as on the company's organizational culture, supported by joint social events organized by the company. In addition, they attended the company's training program for new entrants.

For encoding and updating codified information in the project context, a commonly used data base called "repository" was built up in this phase, where information on the functional requirements of software, coding

Table 10.3 Development of the TMS in phase 2 of nearshoring

Phase of nearshoring	State of TMS	Knowledge transfer processes	Part of TMS
Phase 2 Transformation/ nearshore	Storing and retrieval	• Virtual contact (telephone, e-mail, video conferencing, internet) • Rotation of team members • Teaching functionality nearshore • Usage of the repository for exchange and correction	Storing and retrieval processes in the personalized directory • Further development of interpersonal, informal communication channels • Storing and retrieval processes in daily routines

standards, detailed specification, and documentation of software parts, code reviews, reports, and some additional information on collaboration (such as cultural differences between Polish and German people), were stored according to a certain system which also entailed a keyword system for searching. Additionally, parts of the codified directory included handbooks on quality management and project procedures, encompassing the project teams' knowledge on how to organize work with the nearshore-center. This attempt to capture (and to disseminate within the company afterwards) tacit and embedded knowledge on working processes and nearshoring was initiated by the company's management. The quality managers were required to keep these up to date.

In Phase 2, the Polish employees went back to Poland. During the SPC project, communication and knowledge transfer, including storing and retrieving processes, were mainly ICT-based, as shown in Table 10.3.

The German team did the rough design on its own and the detailed specification together with some Polish employees. After having finished the specification, the Polish employees returned to their team in Poland where they realized the programming. This was backed by weekly information sessions on the customer's processes and functional requirements performed by the Germans via video conference in Poland. However, communication beyond these meetings was still needed. The establishment of an ongoing knowledge exchange continued to provide challenges in finding ways to transmit informal communication:

> *Communication via telephone or e-mail is very important because it is important to receive all relevant information. Many things are*

exchanged in talks at the coffee kitchen, for example, "oh, keep in mind, the password changed." That is okay, but the people who are not there don't hear it and you cannot claim to make protocols of the break conversations. (Polish software developer)

To facilitate this informal information exchange via telephone (up to three hours a day), telephones were equipped with headsets. Equipment for telephone and videoconferencing was made available so that these conferences could take place once a week. A net meeting tool was installed, and they also developed a correction system for the coding work using the repository for exchange. These coordination and communication requirements between the teams were high and time consuming. A Polish software developer explained:

There is no possibility of asking a question over the table, that's why we spent a lot of time on the phone and wrote a lot of e-mails. That's very time consuming.

So, to accelerate communication processes and to intensify personal contacts, the company organized some rotations: Polish employees came to Germany for certain milestone-meetings and a German team leader went to Poland to accompany testing procedures and to further introduce the Polish employees to the functional requirements of the SPC-project. This was a prerequisite for their integration in technical specification tasks. In terms of a TMS development, they further developed fast interpersonal channels for information acquisition and exchange. Additionally, the repository was used for the storing and retrieving of documents from both sides. For example, it served as a depot for the exchange of code reviews where one employee enters the review and another retrieves it.

In the third phase, a concept of shared labor was established so that the Polish employees were increasingly integrated in specification work and technical construction (see Table 10.4).

During the first and second phase, they had built up sufficient knowledge and experience to carry out the development of simpler software components on their own while using the personalized and codified directory of TMS which was built up in the phases before. At the beginning of a development process, they were integrated into the definition of user requirements and specification of the software as well as in the technical construction, so they had the background knowledge to perform larger parts of the project on their own.

Table 10.4   Development of the TMS in phase 3 of nearshoring

Phase of nearshoring	State of TMS	Knowledge transfer processes	Part of TMS
Phase 3 Integrated teamwork	Storing and retrieval	• Usage of interpersonal channels for knowledge exchange • Usage of repository	• Establishment of TMS finished: usage of personalized and codified directory is part of work routines and further developed through work in progress

Important factors of collaboration

An overall prerequisite for the establishment of this incremental integration of the Polish developers was the conviction of the project managers that nearshoring is important for the company. Stressing the necessity of nearshoring, the company did not create any more incentive systems for the management of nearshore projects. So, the order to practice nearshoring caused some doubt among project managers, creating skepticism which needed to be addressed. Therefore, project managers needed to be convinced either by management or by their fellow colleagues to accept that nearshoring was a useful approach. This was said to be a prerequisite for their dedication to putting the concept into practice, which included, for example, the organization of collaboration efforts or the definition of adequate working packages. A project manager described this:

> In the middle of the year it came out that my management and my boss wanted to push that [nearshoring] through and it was clear that I couldn't get out of this. I accepted it and I said to my project leaders, okay, if it has to be, then I want it to work out. And then we sat down and discussed how the processes should turn out and how communication processes and know-how transfer would have to be structured and how tasks should be distributed.

Therefore, project managers transmitted and defended the idea of nearshoring within their projects. If they were convinced and willing to establish a successful collaboration by motivating colleagues as well as project leaders, an adequate setting could be established and software developers were generally receptive to the concept as well.

Looking at the phases of nearshoring, important factors of collaboration were introduced by the project managers. In the first phase, they organized

Table 10.5 Important factors of collaboration in phase 1

Phase of nearshoring	Measures by project management	Factors of collaboration
Phase 1: Introduction	• Conviction of all project leaders Common socialization: • On-site job training • Company training program • Social events	• Dedication to put nearshoring into practice • Spatial and social integration as basis for understanding rules and procedures • Teambuilding processes: trust, cohesiveness, social relationships • Shared identity: identification of the Polish workers as "colleagues" • Common language (German) and terminology • Networks among Polish workers

a comprehensive socialization process for the Polish employees. Table 10.5 sums up the main factors found.

Phase 1, including joint job training, company training program and social events, appeared as a socialization process of the Polish employees. During this process, they were spatially and socially integrated into the project teams, building the basis for a common understanding of rules and procedures in the organization. They improved their German language skills as well. It also encouraged team-building characteristics such as increasing trust and cohesiveness, as well as a shared identity among employees. This was also facilitated by the fact that the Polish employees were young university graduates perceived as learners rather than competitors. As a result, the Polish employees were identified as "colleagues" by the Germans, though different in culture and (native) language but belonging to the company and team. The on-site and nearshore teams felt like teams on their own but also embedded in the larger context of SPC. A project manager emphasized the importance of team collectivity:

> It is very important to avoid the colleagues from Poland feeling like they are an extended workbench or second class employees. They are part of the team, even if they are dispersed.

The personal contact in the first phase was very important in this regard, as a software developer stated:

> I find it very important to have a feeling of togetherness and team spirit. For that, it was very good to have the Polish colleagues here,

we have met, we had some time together and now it's not only the work level when we're on the phone, that is a big difference.

This socialization process served as basis of collaboration for both nationalities as well, so that they communicated on the same linguistic level by using the same terminology:

It's good that everyone who starts working at SW company has to do the same training, that creates a basis and everybody knows the same basic rules, which eases communication later on. (Polish software developer)

To the German employees, this first phase did not mean large changes in comparison with the previous situation, in which the teams of town A and B worked together in a dispersed setting. However, this situation changed in the second phase, with the Polish employees going back to Poland into the nearshore-center. Table 10.6 sums up the important points.

High task specification and detailed instructions of interpretative and contextual information were required to facilitate the dispersed collaboration and avoid misunderstandings due to cultural and linguistic differences. The interview partners mentioned that the larger distance between the Polish nearshore-center and towns A and B demanded the careful definition of adequate working packages to reduce time and cost efforts.

We had to define eligible work packages on the project management level, which you can, let's say, handle autonomously without having too much communication effort. (German software developer)

Table 10.6 Important factors of collaboration in phase 2

Phase of nearshoring	Measures by project management	Factors of collaboration
Phase 2: Transformation/nearshore	• High task specification, detailed instructions	• Facilitation of dispersed collaboration, avoidance of misunderstandings
	• Control by communication and exchange	• Sustained trust and team feeling
	• Rotation of team members	• Sustained team feelings, supported direct problem solving
		• Networks among Polish employees

Control was exercised through communication and exchange as well as through the software test at the end of a term, enhancing team cohesion because this was perceived as a common task. The formerly established networks among Polish workers served as supportive factors for the Polish employees, as well the option of communicating in the Polish language. At the same time, rotation of team members sustained team feelings and eased dispersed work by directly resolving problems on the site.

During the third phase, the Polish employees were integrated into more complex tasks such as specification and technical construction. Important factors of collaboration are shown in Table 10.7.

According to our interviewees, doing tasks that are more complex motivated the Polish employees, who felt unmotivated when only performing simple coding tasks. They perceived low-end tasks as unchallenging and too simple. As university graduates, they wished to develop their competencies and perspectives as well. As a Polish software developer stated:

> *It is more fun for us if we get larger packages of work and then take part in the work on specification and construction – not only the programming parts, but also the more interesting ones.*

During our interviews, we also heard that in another project Polish developers were already more integrated. They took part in the specification of customer requirements at the customer's site. Meetings with customers were supported by video-conferencing to integrate the Polish employees and give them direct access to client knowledge. Clients' acceptance of them was largely increased by their German language skills. An advantage of this strategy was seen in the reduction of coordination and control

Table 10.7   Important factors of collaboration in phase 3

Phase of nearshoring	Measures by project management	Factors of collaboration
Phase 3: Integrated teamwork	• Integration of the Polish employees in specification and technical construction • Career prospects • Equal quality measures and control • Clearly defined, more complex work packages	• Increase of motivation of the Polish employees • Avoidance of feeling inferior to German workers • Reduction of communication efforts • A more autonomous Polish site

for online cooperation (Wenger 1998; Ardichvili et al. 2003). This build-up of knowledge on "who knows what" and "who is doing what" supports the finding that on-site proximity facilitates the development of TMS (Wegner 1987; Moreland 1999). This intensive exchange consisted not only of work-based information but also of cultural differences, and resulted in reflection on how to treat the other side adequately (see also Maletzky 2006). During the second and third phase, this system of knowledge exchange was completed through work in progress, and was extensively used by the employees. We also found that the networks previously set up were the basis for virtual communication and knowledge sourcing (Sole and Edmondson 2002; Ardichvili et al. 2003). Looking at the difference compared to offshore settings we can assume that the geographical distance of the teams was problematic as well, but that this was easier to overcome because of short flight hours (and lower costs), and that the absence of time zone differences facilitated direct contact and journeys.

Looking at the second part of the research question – "What are the important factors in regard to the collaboration of on-site and nearshore employees?" – we found that team formation carried out on-site, implying the development of trust and cohesiveness, was a decisive factor in the success of distributed work (Martins et al. 2004). These close relationships were also the basis for fulfilling the communication needs in Phase 2 (Empson 2001; Sole and Edmondson 2002; Ardichvili et al. 2003). Having the same language and terminology was also perceived as being an important factor, most notably having German as a basis. A major challenge was to define the specific project targets and adequately specified tasks that could be properly performed by the nearshore team (Amberg and Wiener 2004b; Boes and Schwemmle 2004). This implied encouraging a particularly high interdependence of tasks to enhance trust and cohesiveness in the second phase (Newell et al. 2002; Koch, 2004), while re-separating them in the third phase. So, less coordination was needed because the Polish team received independent tasks, that is small but definable mini-projects, which they could solve more independently by using networks in their home country (Sole and Edmondson 2002). For them, involvement in high-end work meant a promotion, because they felt more independent from their German colleagues and more challenged by sophisticated tasks. This integration was possible because their German language skills were well developed. Thus, they felt increasingly motivated and committed. If this is not the case, frustration and a constant turnover of personnel can ensue, putting at risk the stability and efficiency of the project. Consequently, it can be stated that integration into high-end work may function as an incentive (McKinlay 2001) but that language is an important prerequisite for this. A considerably new concept is that quality standards are not only used for the control of tasks (Amberg and Wiener 2005) but also in encouraging trust and helping the near-/offshore employees.

The problem of the employees' resistance to nearshoring due to their fear of job losses (i.e., Empson 2001; Boes and Schwemmle 2004) was countered by the efforts of the company management to legitimize their decision, claiming nearshoring to be necessary and good for creating jobs, which was later internalized by the employees, who accepted and supported this strategy. An important role has to be attributed to the project managers as agents of change (Friedberg 1995) convincing their fellow colleagues, project leaders, and in the end, the employees. Therefore, the Polish workers were considered "colleagues," which led to a teacher–learner relationship between the German and the Polish employees, easing knowledge transfer and collaboration. Therefore, in this case, the perception of the relative value of knowledge is less determined by differences in the form of the knowledge (Empson 2001) but more by the position of the transfer partners, as displayed in the organizational constellation of the transfer context. This context should be analyzed in further studies because it is undoubtedly the case that for the Polish workers, knowledge accessibility and task designation were both selectively controlled by their German colleagues. On the other hand, this power may be limited by the fact that the Polish workers (1) gain more insight into projects and work, as they are able to claim more sophisticated tasks; or (2) may resign in search of new challenges (Marks and Lockyer 2004). To further analyze these constellations the concept of networks of power could be a useful approach (Constantinidis and Barret 2006). Moreover, according to the company's plans, the Polish employees are supposed to acquire projects in the Polish market. Therefore, the strategic perspective followed by the management seems to avoid any feelings of harassment or competition among the German and Polish colleagues as the Polish employees also benefit from the project.

Concluding remarks

A well-organized and well-conducted system of knowledge transfer from the onshore organization to the nearshore organization seemed to be an essential condition for successful collaboration between the employees of both sites in regard to software development environments. Company socialization, tight personal relations, social contact, as well as language skills improve collaboration immensely. Of course, the results of the case reported here are limited to the specific cultural setting of German–Polish relationships, the organization members' experience in regard to distributed work, and to one project being a large project situated in the automobile sector. This may imply some specific characteristics of nearshoring in this firm, which are only visible by comparing this project to others in different organizations and branches to obtain a more general picture. Therefore, confirmation and differentiation is needed through further research. This case study is only a first step in gaining more detailed information on collaboration and knowledge transfer in off- and nearshore settings. Several issues for further research emerge within this context: comparing off- and nearshore projects to gain more information on the impact of cultural differences, geographical distance, and organizational issues such as the division of labor, the implementation of quality standards, and control of work. A micro-political approach might be useful in investigating relations between team members of different sites, as well as the role of the management (Wieandt 2006) to explore what impact power relations have on work relations and knowledge transfer. The issues of communication and the translation of customers' demands in software development projects would also be an interesting area to investigate, particularly when comparing different customer branches. Furthermore, the role of the project management in the context of nearshore implementation should be further explored.

For practitioners, it could be concluded that it is more useful when a company's management communicates the nearshore concept to its employees. This includes underlying views on the division of labor, instructions for implementation and provision of sufficient means, particularly in the case of a high-end concept. Some incentives for the on-site employees could be useful to raise their dedication to putting the concept successfully into practice. In particular, project managers play a key role and should be adequately supported. Their ability to structure work, to lead and motivate employees, may be a basic factor for the success of a nearshore project. Furthermore, the establishment of a TMS appears to be very important in supporting high-end nearshoring because it eases knowledge transfer and communication. Similarly, it helps to support team-building processes in dispersed working situations (see also Oshri et al. 2006). This is effectively supported by an integration of the nearshore employees through a comprehensive socialization into the organizational context, work procedures, and routines, encompassing on-site on-the-job-training, joint company training programs, and team rotation. Moreover, in feeling integrated and equally treated, nearshore employees appear more motivated and committed. To secure a stable workforce in their nearshore locations, companies would also be wise to offer their nearshore employees some career incentives consisting of interesting work and career possibilities, particularly if they employ young university graduates.

References

Alheit, P. and Dausien, B. (1999) "Biographicity" as a Basic Resource in Lifelong Learning Conference Proceedings of the European Conference on *Lifelong Learning Inside and Outside Schools*, University of Bermen, 25–27 February.

Amberg, M. and Wiener, M. (2004a) Projektmanagement im Rahmen des IT-Offshoring: Planungsphase. Working paper No. 10 [WWW document] http://www.wi3.uni-erlangen.de/61.0.html (accessed 10th January 2005).

Amberg, M. and Wiener, M. (2004b) Formen des IT Offshoring, Working paper No. 2 [WWW document] http://www.wi3.uni-erlangen. de/61.0.html (accessed 10th January 2005).

Amberg, M. and Wiener, M. (2005) Kritische Erfolgsfaktoren für Offshore-Software-Entwicklungsprojekte [WWW document] http://www.wi3. uni-erlangen.de/61.0.html (accessed 23rd March 2005).

Ardichvili, A., Page, V., and Wentling, T. (2003) Motivation and Barriers to Participation in Virtual Knowledge-Sharing Communities of Practice. *Journal of Knowledge Management*, 7(1): 64–77.

Aspray, W., Mayadas, F., and Vardi, M.Y. (eds) (2006) Globalization and Offshoring of Software. A Report of the ACM Job Migration Task Force. Association for Computing. [WWW document] http://www.acm. org/globalizationreport/summary.htm (accessed 15th March 2006).

Blackler, F. (1995) Knowledge, Knowledge Work and Organisations: An Overview and Interpretation. *Organization Studies*, 16(6): 1201–1241.

Boes, A. (2005) Auf dem Weg in die Sackgasse? Internationalisierung im Feld Software und IT-Services, in. Boes, A. and Schwemmle, M. (eds) Bangalore statt Böblingen? Offshoring und Internationalisierung im IT-Sektor, Hamburg: VSA-Verlag, 13–65.

Boes, A. and Schwemmle, M. (2004) Herausforderung Offshoring. Internationalisierung und Auslagerung von IT-Dienstleistungen. Düsseldorf: Edition Hans Böckler Stiftung.

Boes, A. and Trinks, K. (2006) „Theoretisch bin ich frei!" Interessenhandeln und Mitbestimmung in der IT-Industrie, Berlin: Edition Sigma.

Carmel, E. and Abbott, P. (2006) Configurations of Global Software Development: Offshore versus Nearshore. Paper presented at GSC 2006, May 23, Shangai, China [WWW document] http://delivery.acm.

org/10.1145/1140000/1138509/p3-carmel.pdf?key1=1138509&key2=810297611&coll=&dl=acm&CFID=15151515&CFTOKEN=6184618 (accessed 17th July 2006).

Carmel, E. and Abbott, P. (2007) Why "Nearshore" Means That Distance Matters, Article Accepted for ACM Communications [WWW document] http://auapps.american.edu/%7Ecarmel/papers/nearshore.pdf (accessed 5th September 2007).

Constantinidis, P. and Barrett, M. (2006) Large-Scale ICT Innovation, Power, and Organizational Change: The Case of a Regional Health Information Network. *The Journal of Applied Behavioral Science*, 42(1): 76–90.

Cook, S.D.N. and Brown, J.S. (1999) Bridging Epistemologies: The Generative Dance between Organizational Knowledge and Organizational Knowing. *Organization Science*, 190: 381–400.

Crampton, C.D. (2001) The Mutual Knowledge Problem and its Consequences for Dispersed Collaboration. *Organization Science*, 12(3): 346–377.

DB Research (2005). Offshoring-Report 2005. Ready for Take-off. Frankfurt am Main: Deutsche Bank Research.

DB Research (2006) Offshoring an neuen Ufern. Nearshoring nach Mittel- und Osteuropa. Frankfurt am Main: Deutsche Bank Research.

Dyer, J.H. and Nobeoka, K. (2000) Creating and managing a High-Performance Knowledge-Sharing Network: The Toyota Case. *Strategic Management Journal*, 21: 345–367.

Edwards, H.K. and Sridhar, V. (2002) Analysis of the Effectiveness of Global Virtual Teams in Software Engineering Projects, in: Proceedings of the 36th Hawaii International Conference on System Sciences (HICSS '03) [WWW document] http://ieeexplore.ieee.org/iel5/8360/26341/01173664.pdf?arnumber=1173664 (accessed 17 EITO (2006). Report 2006. European Information Technology Observatory.

Empson, L. (2001) Fear of Exploitation and Fear of Contamination: Impediments to Knowledge Transfer in Mergers between Professional Service Firms. *Human Relations*, 54 (7): 839–862.

Friedberg, E. (1995) Ordnung und Macht. Dynamik organisierten Handelns, New York/Frankfurt am Main: Campus Verlag.

Friedewald, M. (2004) Benchmarking National and Regional Policies in Support of the Competitiveness of the ICT Sector in the EU. Interim report, prepared for European Commission, Directorate-General Enterprises.

Gillard, S. (2005) Managing IT-Projects: Communication Pitfalls and Bridges. *Journal of Information Science*, 31(1): 37–43.

Guzzo, R.A. and Dickson, M.W. (1996) Teams in Organizations: Recent Research on Performance and Effectiveness. *Annual Review Psychology*, 47: 307–338.

Hysell, Deborah (2000) Global Teamwork for a Global Resource, in Proceedings of 2000 Joint IEEE International and 18th Annual Conference on Computer Documentation. [WWW-document] http://ieeexplore.ieee.org/servlet/opac?punumber=7114 (accessed 17th July 2006).

Kearney, A.T. (2004a) Making Offshore Decisions. A.T. Kearney's 2004 Offshore Location Attractiveness Index. [WWW document] http://www.atkearney.de/content/misc/wrapper.php/id/49103/name/pdf_making_offshore_s_1081956080c0df.pdf (accessed 22nd February 2006).

Koch, C. (2004) The Tyranny of Projects: Teamworking, Knowledge Production and Management in Consulting Engineering. *Economic and Industrial Democracy*, 25(2): 277–300.

Lam, A. (1997) Embedded Firms, Embedded Knowledge: Problems of Collaboration and Knowledge Transfer in Global Cooperative Ventures. *Organization Studies*, 18(6): 973–996.

Laser, S. and Heiss, M. (2005) Collaboration Maturity and the Offshoring Cost Barrier: The Trade- Off between Flexibility in Team Composition and Cross-Site Communication Effort in Geographically Distributed Development Projects, in Proceedings of the IEEE International Professional Communication Conference (IPCC 2005), Limerick, Ireland, 718–728.

Latniak, E. and Gerlmaier, A. (2006) Zwischen Innovation und alltäglichem Kleinkrieg. Zur Belastungssituation von IT-Beschäftigten. IAT-Report 6(4). Gelsenkirchen: Institut Arbeit und Technik.

Lave, J. and Wenger, E. (1991) *Situated Learning: Legitimate peripheral Participation*, Cambridge: Cambridge University Press.

Maletzky, M. (2006) Teamwork in a Globalised Context – Influencing Factors on Achievement in German Mexican Collaboration. Paper Presented at the 10th International Workshop on Teamworking (IWOT 10), Groningen, Netherlands.

Marks, A. and Lockyer, C. (2004) Producing Knowledge: The Use of the Project Team as a Vehicle for Knowledge and Skill Acquisition for Software Employees. *Economic and Industrial Democracy*, 25(2): 219–245.

Markus, M.L. (2004). Technochange Management: Using IT to Drive Organizational Change. *Journal of Information Technology*, 19: 3–19.

Martins, L.L., Gilson, L., and Maynard, T.M. (2004) Virtual Teams: What Do We Know and Where Do We Go From Here? *Journal of Management*, 30(6): 805–835.

McKinlay, A. (2002) The Limits of Knowledge Management. *New Technology, Work and Employment*, 17(2): 76–88.

Moreland, R.L. (1999) Transactive Memory: Learning Who Knows What in Groups and Organizations, in L.L. Thompson, J.M. Levine, and D.M. Messick (eds) *Shared Cognitions in Organizations*, Hillsdale, NJ: Lawrence Erlbaum Associates, 3–31.

Newell, S. Bresnen, M., Edelmann, L., Scarbrough, H., and Swan, J. (2006) Sharing Knowledge across Projects. *Management Learning*, 37(2): 167–185.

Newell, S., Robertson, M., Scarbrough, H. (2002). *Managing Knowledge Work*, London, Palgrave Macmillan.

Nonaka, I. and Takeuchi, H. (1995) *The Knowlegde-Creating Company: How Japanese Companies Create the Dynamics for Innovation*, New York: New York University Press.

OECD (2004). OECD Information Technology Outlook: 2004 edition. Summary, OECD & Dev.

Oshri, I., van Fenema, P., and Kotlarsky, J. (2008). Knowledge Transfer in Globally Distributed Teams: The Role of Transactive Memory, *Information Systems Journal*, Online Early Articles, Published article online: 17-Feb-2008, doi: 10.1111/j.1365-2575.2007.00243.x, http://www.blackwell-synergy.com/action/doSearch, accessed March, 27th 2008.

Piatkowski, M. (2004) Factors and Impacts in the Information Society. A Prospective Analysis in the Candidate Countries. Report on Poland. Tiger, Transformation, Integration and Globalization Economic Research, Leon Kozmizski Academy of Entrepreneurship and Management (Publication No. EUR 21276 EN), Warschau.

Polanyi, M. (1966) *The Tacit Dimension*, London: Routledge & Kegan Paul.

Riedl, R. and Kepler, J. (2003) Begriffliche Grundlagen des Business Process Outsourcing. *Information Management & Consulting*, 18(3): 6–10.

Ruiz Ben, E. and Claus, R. (2004) Offshoring in der deutschen IT Branche. Eine neue Herausforderung für die Informatik. *Informatik Spektrum*, 28(4): 1–6.

Ruiz Ben, E. and Wieandt, M. (2006) Growing East: Nearshoring und die neuen ICT Arbeitsmärkte in Europa, FifF-Kommunikation 23(3): 36–42.

Scherf, Schütt and Partner, Beratungsozietät für effektives Ressourcenmanagement (2006) Voraussetzungen für erfolgreiches

Outsourcing von Software-Entwicklungs-Projekten, [WWW document] www.ssp-beratung.de (accessed 23rd November 2005).

Slama, Dirk and Kaefer, Wolfgang (2005) Model Driven Offshoring [WWW document] http://www.sigp.de/publications/os/2005/06/kaefer_slama_OS_06_05.pdf (accessed 29th November 2005).

Sole, D. and Edmondson, A. (2002) Situated Knowledge and Learning in Dispersed Teams. *British Journal of Management*, 13(S17–S34).

Sydow, J., Lindkvist, L., and DeFilippi, R. (2004) Project-based Organizations, Embeddedness and Repositories of Knowledge. *Editorial, Organization Studies*, 25(9): 1475–1489.

Tsoukas, H. and Vladimirou, E. (2001) What is Organizational Knowledge? *Journal of Management Studies*, 38: 973–993.

Walsham, G. (2002) What Can Knowledge Management Systems Deliver? *Management Communication Quarterly*, 16(2): 267–273.

Wegner, D.M. (1987) Transactive Memory: A Contemporary Analysis of the Group Mind, in B. Mullen and G.R. Groethals (eds) *Theories of Group Behaviour*, New York: Springer, 185–208.

Wenger, E. (1998) *Communities of Practice: Learning, Meaning and Identity*, Cambridge, UK: Cambridge University Press.

Wieandt, M. (2006) Teamwork When Implementing off-Shoring: Exploring the German ICT Sector. Paper presented at the IWOT X Workshop in Groningen, Netherlands, September 6th–8th.

CHAPTER 11

Managing dispersed expertise in IT offshore outsourcing: lessons from Tata Consultancy Services

Ilan Oshri, Julia Kotlarsky, and Leslie Willcocks

Introduction

Information Technology offshore outsourcing means using an offshore provider to handle some of an enterprise's IT work. Offshore outsourcing now has a track record, so it has become an option that IT leaders need to consider. But the practice has raised the issue of how to manage expertise dispersed across sites. Both clients and providers now realize that knowledge management is an important contributor to successful offshore outsourcing.

Tata Consultancy Services (TCS) is a large IT services provider with headquarters in Mumbai, India. Much of its work is IT offshore outsourcing. We identified the following eight practices that TCS uses to manage dispersed expertise. (1) Implement an organizational structure that is a mirror image of the client's structure; (2) Implement a knowledge transfer methodology; (3) Implement a knowledge retention methodology; (4) Monitor expertise development and retention at project and organizational levels; (5) Make expertise development a key organizational value; (6) Offer mechanisms to search for expertise at project and organizational levels; (7) Implement a reuse methodology at the global level; (8) Continuously measure the contribution of reusable assets.

Based on our research, we believe that over the next five years, offshore providers will need to develop a system for managing knowledge and expertise, just as TCS has done, to compete and deliver on client expectations. We also see the experiences and practices of TCS as valuable to clients as well at IT offshore outsourcing providers.[1]

Managing dispersed expertise

When the IT industry started it was more like a cottage industry, very much a people-dependent industry. It is now changing from people-dependent to process-dependent. When it becomes process-dependent, knowledge management becomes a part of the process itself. (Project Leader, TCS Offshore Team Mumbai)

Based on our estimates, revenues from offshore outsourcing of ITs will exceed $US 25 billion by 2008, and will experience a compound annual growth rate averaging 20 percent over the next five years.[2] For IT executives, this means that offshoring – either directly or through a captive company or indirectly through a domestic supplier – has become a serious option. Indeed, many IT executives have already embarked down this path. For outsourcing providers, this growth means an increasing number of clients will offshore their IT systems, and expect the providers to maintain, and in some cases continue to develop, their IT applications from remote locations.

However, client executives are already pondering a major question: Where do we draw the line on outsourcing our knowledge and expertise? How can a provider that we select develop the knowledge and expertise of our domain, systems, and practices, to not only maintain continuity of service but also achieve our much-vaunted targets of innovation and transformation?[3]

At the same time, IT outsourcing provider executives are asking themselves: How can we quickly develop expertise in new areas, particularly where our teams are remote and dispersed? And how can we retain knowledge when our people who have it move on?[4]

By *expertise*, we mean the ability to act knowledgeably in a specific domain. Expertise relates to achieving skillful performance, including applying knowledge to develop and improve products and processes. Expertise is a specific type of knowledge. It is dynamic, it evolves, and it consists of embodied knowledge and skills possessed by individuals. For our purposes, it refers to "knowing in practice."[5] How expertise is created, maintained, and leveraged is of critical importance to outsourcing providers and clients alike.

We explore expertise management in offshore IT outsourcing by describing the practices that TCS is using in one offshore outsourcing project.

Tata Consultancy Services

Tata Consultancy Services is part of the Tata Group. The TCS was founded in 1968 as a consulting service firm for the emerging IT industry. Since then, TCS has expanded to become a global player with revenues of over $US 2 billion in 2006.[6] With over 74,000 associates and 50 service delivery centers, TCS has established a presence in 34 countries. It provides various services, including business process outsourcing (BPO) and IT maintenance and development, to hundreds of clients around the globe.

Tata Consultancy Services has developed a global delivery model in which projects are handled mainly by teams located remotely from clients, but often with a small team also at the client site. Generally, TCS's on-site and offshore teams transfer work packages back and forth to each other until a task is completed. The project teams of TCS – based on-site, onshore and nearshore – therefore depend on expertise and knowledge that reside within TCS, at various locations. Thus, TCS has developed expertise management practices to leverage expertise globally, regardless of the physical location of either the expert or the expertise seeker.

The relationship and organizational challenges of managing expertise

Management of expertise is not without its challenges. We discuss the two main challenges in the context of TCS's work with ABN AMRO Bank. In late 2005, Netherlands-based ABN AMRO Bank announced a $US 1.2 billion outsourcing contract with five providers. Tata Consultancy Services is one of the five. It is to provide support and application enhancement services.

The outsourcing project organization of the ABN AMRO-TCS contract consists of three arrangements across three continents. Each arrangement type has an on-site component at the client site, and a remote component somewhere else.

1. In The Netherlands, *on-site* TCS teams at ABN AMRO's Amsterdam locations work with corresponding *offshore* TCS teams in Mumbai, India.

2. In Brazil, *on-site* TCS teams at ABN AMRO Sao Paulo locations work with corresponding *onshore* teams at TCS's delivery center in Campinas, 100 kilometers away.

3. In several countries (e.g., Switzerland, Germany, Monaco, and others), *on-site* TCS teams communicate with an onshore TCS delivery center in Luxembourg and a *nearshore* TCS delivery center in Hungary.

Typically, TCS team members reside in one location throughout a project, either on-site, onshore, nearshore, or offshore. Only a small number of TCS staff travel between locations for short visits. An on-site TCS team includes project members, project leaders, portfolio managers, program managers, a transition head, a relationship manager, and other functionaries – mainly quality assurance, human resource, and organization development personnel.

The ABN AMRO-TCS offshore outsourcing project was divided into two phases: transition and steady state. In the transition phase, the on-site TCS team was to learn about ABN AMRO's systems and transfer this knowledge to its corresponding offshore TCS team. In the steady state phase, the offshore TCS teams provide the main support for the bank's systems and services as well as develop applications. This multisite mode of working requires the on-site, onshore, nearshore, and offshore teams to overcome two expertise-management challenges.

Challenge #1: The Relationship Challenge. The relationship challenge deals with the client-provider relationship. With respect to managing expertise, the provider needs to answer the question: How can a client's knowledge be captured and retained at both on-site and remote locations to ensure uninterrupted service to the client and to further develop services for the client? This challenge requires the provider to assimilate the client's knowledge quickly and effectively.

Tata Consultancy Services views success in meeting this challenge as having no expertise gaps between its corresponding teams, that is the pairs of on-site-onshore, on-site-nearshore, and on-site-offshore teams. The TCS addresses this challenge by requiring the remote TCS team to develop the same level of expertise as its corresponding on-site TCS team.

Eliminating expertise gaps between on-site and remote teams is particularly important for offshore service companies, like TCS, because they need to demonstrate to clients that offshoring application maintenance and development will not reduce service or application quality. As one TCS delivery manager on the offshore team in Mumbai notes:

> When I had my initial discussion with the bank's portfolio managers, they asked, "How are you going to take care of the knowledge base? We have 10, 15, 30 years of experience at the bank, yet you are going to join afresh. You are just going to have a knowledge transfer for a short time" They asked, "So how do you ensure that you have this knowledge with you? And how are you going to retain this knowledge?"

Challenge #2: **The Organizational Challenge**. The organizational challenge concerns the provider's mechanisms for managing expertise within its own organization. It answers the question: How do we turn local learning and expertise into global assets? The challenge is to capture expertise from an on-site TCS team, then refine and reuse it globally, on other teams that may need it. The TCS addresses this challenge by developing expertise-coordination competencies to ensure that knowledge is reapplied across the company.

Tata Consultancy Services, and other outsourcing providers are exposed to vast amounts of knowledge through their numerous outsourcing relationships. However, this knowledge often becomes just the asset of a single project. It is rarely shared with other projects, which will likely confront similar challenges. The head of the learning and development department at TCS explains this challenge by saying:

> How do we create a kind of customer-focused experience? How do we share this knowledge? How can we enhance our learning about banking and insurance so that we can say that we know technology and we also know about the banking industry? Basically, I need to develop specific domain knowledge and link it to other value activities, share it with the entire workforce so our employees can talk to the customer in their own language and in their own domain of expertise as an expert. That is a challenge for me to create this kind of expertise.

Eight practices at TCS for managing dispersed EXPERTISE

We identified eight practices that TCS uses at ABN AMRO (and other outsourcing relationships) to address the two challenges just described. The first four practices address the relationship challenge of absorbing expertise from clients. The next four deal with the organizational challenge of sharing and leveraging expertise within TCS.

Practice #1: Implement an organizational structure that is a mirror image of the client's structure

One challenge that a client's in-house staff and a remote provider's staff face is identifying the corresponding expert on the other team. Knowledge needs to move from the client to the provider, and that knowledge generally needs to be at a specific organizational level, say, a client project manager to a provider project manager.

To address this challenge, TCS uses an organizational structure that ensures that client personnel and offshore TCS personnel can easily identify their counterpart: TCS mirrors the client's organizational structure on the remote team. Figure 11.1 illustrates this practice on one ABN AMRO-TCS team.

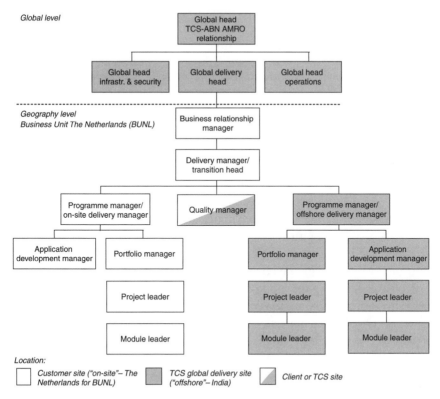

Figure 11.1 The organizational Structure of one ABN AMRO-TCS project team

Tata Consultancy Services adopted the bank's structure by including a number of portfolio managers, which TCS normally does not have. One TCS portfolio manager in Mumbai explains how TCS dealt with this challenge:

> *The way we have segregated these teams here adapts to the way they work at ABN AMRO. We wanted synchronicity in the sense that the way business teams are divided there, at ABN AMRO, we'd have a similar structure here also. Portfolio manager is a term that ABN AMRO uses. We said, "Okay, we will also have similar portfolio managers so that they can interact one-to-one, and these portfolio names will be similar to the way they are using them onsite."*

Our research into offshore outsourcing arrangements found three major types of organizational structures. The first is the *funnel*. It relies on a single point of contact and control between client and provider. The second is the *network*. It has multiple, diverse points of contact. The third is the *mirror*. It has multiple contacts created by replicating the structure on both sides of the relationship. Each type has its advantages and disadvantages. We have found, though, that the mirror structure has proven the most effective in organizing knowledge assimilation and transfer.[7]

Practice #2: Implement a knowledge transfer methodology

Knowledge transfer means transferring knowledge from client staff to on-site provider staff and then to offshore provider staff. It is often perceived as an activity that the provider must carry out to "get a grip" on the outsourced systems. But treating knowledge transfer as such emphasizes documenting the knowledge about the outsourced applications. And it sets the expectation that when service cannot be properly provided, the provider need only to go back to the documentation to find the needed information, or consult the client about the specific issue.

However, in using this approach to knowledge transfer, a provider may miss the opportunity to leverage the expertise learned about a client's systems. That knowledge can be used not only for those systems but also in contracts with other clients.

This opportunity to leverage existing expertise led TCS to create a knowledge transfer methodology, to ensure that its teams can define, capture, transfer, and absorb the critical knowledge required for application maintenance and development. More importantly, TCS's all-encompassing knowledge transfer methodology was designed to ensure that it can be replicated across numerous relationships, and thereby allow global sharing of knowledge captured and retained by local outsourcing teams. The TCS delivery head in Amsterdam explains this philosophy:

> *The activities within the TCS methodology would be the same whether I'm working here in the Netherlands or in Brazil. At the end of the day, when I look at my organization from a high level, we should not find any differences in the approaches used. From an overall organizational viewpoint, this single framework helps us achieve what we want to achieve.*

For knowledge transfer, TCS uses standardized templates and forms based on a glossary of terms that the client team and TCS's on-site and remote teams agree on. The on-site team of TCS is responsible for codifying and documenting the knowledge on the templates, with support from TCS's digitization group in Mumbai. By the end of this knowledge codification phase, the on-site team has also transferred the codified knowledge to its corresponding remote team.

The remote team then studies this documentation to be sure it is clear and it identifies areas where knowledge is missing. To ensure that this remote team has actually absorbed the knowledge and can use it in problem-solving scenarios, the team "plays back" its know-how to TCS's on-site team in the form of a presentation, explaining the functionality of the application as they understand it from learning the documents provided by the on-site team. The team not only demonstrates its knowledge by solving problems generated by the client during training but also when TCS provides service under the client's supervision.

This knowledge transfer methodology has proven vital to TCS teams, and it has allowed TCS to develop codified knowledge for reuse by other TCS teams. The TCS recognizes, though, that codified knowledge can only take team performance so far. To close the knowing-doing gap requires building experience and tacit knowledge on the job.[8]

Practice #3: Implement a knowledge retention methodology

In 2007, IT providers, particularly in India, have faced relatively high employee turnover in their offshore locations. High turnover can lead to knowledge loss between on-site and remote provider sites. Tata Consultancy Services realized it needed to ensure that the knowledge transferred and captured at its remote teams would be retained even if staff members went elsewhere. In short, it wanted its success to depend as little as possible on individual subject matter experts (SME) on it teams.

Tata Consultancy Services thus developed a knowledge retention methodology, which is based on a succession plan that combines both the process and people dimensions of expertise. In the process dimension, TCS managers select their successors by identifying the individuals who can replace them in case they need to leave the project or decide to leave the company. This process ensures that successors are trained to replace their managers and are prepared for their future roles. Furthermore, these successors back up the manager's knowledge in their respective areas of expertise.

Consider any major IT project. One of the hidden, and serious, reasons for delay is one or more key players leaving.[9] In our research, we found that such losses are inevitable in all major IT outsourcing arrangements – be they three, five, seven, or ten years in length. When clients and providers do not plan for the knowledge-loss implications of such departures, service speed and quality can be damaged, as can the provider's ability to innovate and add value.[10]

Practice #4: Monitor expertise development and retention at project and organizational levels

In monitoring expertise, a main challenge is linking the project and organizational levels. In most companies, expertise is managed and monitored at the project level. This means that project managers are responsible for identifying the expertise required to accomplish their project's objectives. They are the ones who must request that a team member's expertise needs to be upgraded, perhaps through training.

While this local approach may satisfy local project needs, the enterprise probably does not know the pool of expertise at its disposal. Therefore, it cannot take advantage of having centralized resources and the economies of scale centralization can bring. For these reasons, TCS links project and organizational levels of expertise monitoring.

Centers of Excellences (CoEs) at TCS play a role in monitoring. They indicate the expertise that should be upgraded when they see a gap between existing and required expertise on a project. The CoEs are actually networks of experts who have advanced know-how and experience in a particular market or technological domain. The CoEs of TCS are based on technologies (including Oracle and Java), industries (such as finance and banking), and services for the various service practices (such as IT and BPO services) provided by TCS. A member of the Oracle CoE describes how he monitors expertise:

Every month, I do a technical health check review of some projects… Our quality reviews are done against the quality check lists and quality guidelines. But these additional CoE reviews are done from a technology perspective. For example, if I am doing a project review, I try to find out whether the project is using the most advanced solutions.

In cases where projects do not use best practices, members of the appropriate CoEs make sure that those teams receive the know-how to properly execute their project according to TCS best practices. Therefore, CoEs were responsible for acquiring know-how from internal and external sources and then sharing that know-how with project teams. The member of the Oracle CoE adds:

All those aspects might lead to a risk from a technical perspective. We also look at the skill sets required for the project. If there are any gaps, we bridge them, either through training or consultation or by inviting in an alliance partner.

Another member of a CoE describes the expertise development process:

We have an internal learning and development group that conducts various training programs, depending on a project's requirements and to support individual learning plans. We do a gap analysis of individuals to find the areas that need further development. With that, the system tells us, "Okay, he needs to do this, this and this to reach the appropriate level." At that stage, the person has to undergo the training. We give him or her a particular timeframe in which to do all the knowledge acquisition activities to build up their personal knowledge.

The CoEs develop an overview of the pool of expertise in each community and the location of expertise. In a way, the CoEs therefore acted as repositories of knowledge concerning particular technologies or markets. They also act as directories that can point to an expert's location.

Practice #5: Make expertise development a key organizational value

The five values that matter most to TCS are integrity, respect for the individual, excellence, learning, and knowledge sharing. The TCS puts expertise development high on its value list. To ensure that learning and knowledge sharing take place across the company, its learning and development department oversees training and knowledge sharing activities. The head of this department in Mumbai explains:

> *The six enablers to success that we continuously invest in are: competency enhancement, leadership enhancement, being the custodian of the cultural climate of the company, strategic alignment, motivation of the employees and team integration. In our kind of company, we all work in teams. Individual excellence is fine, but we look at the cumulative excellence when people collaboratively work in teams.*

To support learning within and across teams, TCS uses an organizational structure that places the relationship at the center of knowledge sharing (see Figure 11.2).

Each project, which is the box in the middle of Figure 11.2, is supported by several groups. From a learning and expertise development viewpoint, the following groups contribute to the continuous development of know-how and skills:

- Centers of Excellence: Provide technical and business solutions. The CoEs are organized around technical solutions (i.e., technologies) and business silos (i.e., industries).
- Quality Assurance: Provides standard templates for the best practices used in TCS and also harvests best practices from each relationship project.
- Digitization and Codification: This group, based in Mumbai, codifies knowledge developed within relationships and makes this knowledge available to the rest of TCS.

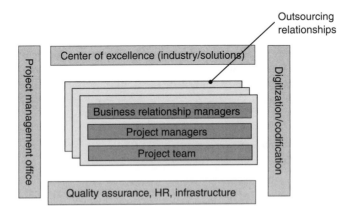

Figure 11.2 The structure of outsourcing relationships and supporting groups

This structure is replicated for all relationships, and the support provided is similar, regardless of the location or the size of the outsourcing contract. But expertise development is much wider than support from the specialist groups. Tata Consultancy Services staff also expand their expertise with continual improvements in TCS's methodologies and processes.

In addition, employees receive training during different phases of their career. New employees, for instance, receive induction training to introduce them to TCS, its available resources, and how to access expertise and know-how. New TCS employees in Sao Paolo, for example, whom we visited, knew who to contact in Mumbai for either technology or market support. They were also familiar with TCS's portals. One contains induction manuals, a welcome kit, and cultural awareness programs.

Even though they are remote from Mumbai, these Sao Paulo staff feel familiar with TCS because of the induction program and the on-site support from veteran TCSers. These new TCS staff also have access to the portal for the ABN AMRO relationship. It is used to capture and share learning within TCS and with the bank.

Practice #6: Offer mechanisms to search for expertise at project and organizational levels

Bringing expertise to bear in a timely manner is a challenge for most organizations. To address this challenge in its ABN-AMRO work, TCS has adopted similar management processes and systems in Amsterdam, Mumbai, and Sao Paulo.

One example is mechanisms for finding expertise. Some organizations use a search engine that provides pointers either to subject matter experts (e.g., Yellow Pages system) or to documentation about a domain (e.g., a knowledgebase). These mechanisms can be useful in solving problems, but they do not address the management of expertise in a global organization. In particular, search engines do not necessarily keep up with the evolution and changes in expertise.

To address this challenge, TCS links its search process for locating expertise with its vehicles for developing and sharing expertise. The resulting process is carried out at the project level (on-site and remote) and at the company level.

At the project level, the on-site and remote teams create an expertise directory, with pointers to where knowledge resides – that is, *who knows what* and *who does what*. Using TCS's knowledge transfer and knowledge retention methodologies, the pointers are created and constantly updated during the transition and steady state phases of each outsourcing project, as on-site and remote counterparts interact with each other to transfer knowledge and develop their expertise.

In addition, ABM AMRO and TCS created a project portal (internally called the knowledge base) that contains links to experts involved in the project as well as project and system documents created during the knowledge transfer phase. By tightly managing the knowledge transfer methodology, TCS not only ensures the transfer of knowledge between on-site and remote teams but also updates the directory of expertise.

At the company level, TCS has developed a broad memory system, which it updates regularly, so that expertise outside a project can be brought to bear on the project in a timely manner.

In addition to their role of monitoring the level of expertise, CoEs bring together information seekers and subject matter experts. One manager from Mumbai describes the role of one technological CoE:

> *These are the people who can solve the problems in certain areas, so we have a team of certain virtual members, anywhere between 30 and 50. These are the people who try to address the problem if the technical support team cannot.*

The CoEs also facilitate reapplying existing solutions from the beginning to the end of projects, by connecting experts with project teams to ensure that project teams are aware of and apply TCS best practices. One project leader from a Mumbai offshore team provides an example in the context of the ABN AMRO program:

> *I'm also part of a center of excellence for ABN AMRO, where we identify the kinds of training and the different environments for various technology requirements at ABN AMRO. We trained our people before they started their transition, and adopted a "best practice" of ensuring that the knowledge that we gained in the first six months was passed on to the people coming into this ABN AMRO engagement or those working on the technologies.*

Members of CoEs who are based within a project act as links between the project level and an organizational level unit, such as a technology, practice, or a market CoE. Through this web of connections, experts become aware of *who knows what* within other projects or CoEs.

However, TCS has found that relying solely on the organizational structure and information systems to support the web of connections is incomplete. So, on a regular basis, it organizes knowledge-exchange events and seminars at different locations for CoEs and other experts. The goal is to help remote counterparts stay in touch. For instance, at a technology fair in Mumbai in May 2006, experts from different technology domains demonstrated uses of their technologies at different booths. The TCS employees walked from booth to booth to learn about the applicability of existing solutions to their projects.

The importance of these processes becomes apparent when they are not in place. For example, we found considerable disappointment in two major customer relationship management projects involving clients and providers because neither project managed expertise or knowledge well.[11] As a result, knowledge did not flow easily between or within the organizations. In fact, knowledge silos developed, that is, knowledgeable people only shared knowledge with other knowledgeable people who had something to trade ("gurus" only talked to "gurus"). No knowledge accumulated, so there was nothing to leverage to the benefit of the overall projects. And none of the organizations could claim major learning from the projects.

Practice #7: Implement a reuse methodology at the global level

Search mechanisms are a beginning to systematically reuse information, knowledge, practices, and even software components. Increasingly firms strive to reuse best practices, templates, and software modules and components. In the 1990s, the major IT outsourcing providers in India took great interest in the IT methodologies, standards, and processes used in North America. So it is not surprising to find reuse high on TCS's agenda. But reuse by providers can be difficult because practices are often specific to a client, not generic. Some providers therefore promote standard solutions in the form of templates, tools, or component-based software development.

Component-based development involves developing software components and building software systems by integrating components. *Components* are units of independent production, acquisition, and deployment that interact with each other to form a functioning system. Being self-contained and replaceable, they can be reused across any number of products, and can be replaced by more recent and advanced versions in a "plug-and-play" manner, as long as the interfaces are compatible.[12]

Tata Consultancy Services has implemented a component-based methodology globally, developing and testing components by using expertise at different sites. To manage the development process as well as the interdependencies between components, though, has required a high degree of coordination among the sites. The TCS's pursuit of a globally distributed component-based design has had the effect of ramping up expertise across the involved sites because the experts have needed to constantly interact and exchange component, product, and market knowledge.

The TCS staff use the company's intranet to access the database of reusable components. The components come from various projects but have been stripped of their confidential client data. A specific team checks the entries, filters them, and makes sure that the most appropriate keywords were assigned to each component.

The TCS's reuse methodology has resulted in reusable components, but has also led to information about which staff members are experts in particular technologies. So component-based design has supported the search mechanisms in Practice #6. Staff can contact the expert for consultation prior to using a reusable component. Staff also have access via the intranet to a database of business history that contains brief overviews and lessons learned from past projects. This database has proved useful for finding out information about projects and contacting individuals involved in these projects for advice.

Reuse is highly dependent on systematic and accurate collection from projects. At TCS, such practices have become part of the culture – that is, "how things are done around here." Tata Consultancy Services has cultivated this culture through systematic training, from induction onwards, and through its collection practices in its methodologies and processes. All are applied routinely throughout the organization.

In our research, we have all too often found organizations failing at knowledge management by being overly dependent on software and not shaping their culture. As a result, staff do not understand or own, or feel motivated or capable of contributing to knowledge creation, collection, and reuse.[13]

Practice #8: Continually measure the contribution of reusable assets

Our research has found that many companies that reuse components do not assess and measure the contribution of their reusable assets to project and product success.[14] According to a Gartner report,[15] firms that have achieved a high capability maturity level, as defined by The Software Engineering Institute's Capability Maturity Model (CMM), are more likely to reap the benefits from building a pool of reusable components. This is because the foundation required to support reuse (i.e., proper design, thorough testing, and appropriate documentation) has been institutionalized in high CMM levels. Through continuous improvements in methodologies and processes, companies at CMM Level 5, the highest level, have optimized their processes, generally by applying metrics.

The TCS, which operates at CMM Level 5, uses metrics to assess the contribution of reuse and reusable assets to project and product success. The quality assurance group assesses usage rate, nature of the application and the destination project. Therefore, TCS collects information about the contribution of a reusable asset as well as its applicability in specific markets. As one quality assurance specialist from Mumbai describes:

> *We have something called Mighty, which is accessible to all. Associates can check for a reuseable competence. We in quality assurance track the competence sharing, how often it has been used, and which of our teams have used it. We are now encouraging teams to start using Mighty for all reusable competencies by making it a single repository.*

Therefore, TCS measures internal processes, such as reuse, and continues to seek ways to improve its reuse process by centralizing its competence and component repository through the introduction of the Mighty system.

These eight knowledge expertise practices contribute to TCS's success as an IT offshore outsourcing provider.

How expertise is managed in IT offshoring

As noted earlier, IT offshore providers face two challenges in managing expertise: the relationship challenge and the organizational challenge. Figure 11.3 depicts these challenges graphically. The inner circle represents the relationship challenge and shows the processes a provider must implement to absorb knowledge from clients. The outer circle represents the organizational challenge and shows the processes a provider must implement to coordinate expertise within its own organization.

The two circles do need to interact and depend on each other for providers to assimilate new knowledge from clients and reapply it. As noted, we have found that the management of expertise at TCS (and other IT providers) depends on having a system that captures and updates directories of *who knows what* and *who does what*.

Through interviews, discussions, and observations, it became clear to us that TCS has focused on developing an enterprise-wide expertise system to bring solutions to teams in a timely manner. The company does not expect its staff and teams to research and develop their own solutions. We also learned that managing expertise requires more than mapping

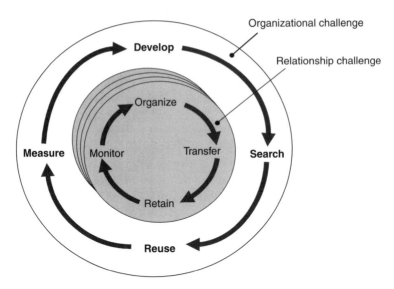

Figure 11.3 Expertise management processes at the relationship and organizational levels

the pool of available in-house expertise (e.g., the traditional Yellow Pages approach). In fact, it requires the entire organization to think and act from a managing-expertise lens.

Figure 11.3 can thus be viewed as the two processes that TCS uses to build and maintain its system that not only supports continuous absorption of knowledge and expertise but also dynamically updates the location of expertise and knowledge.

Addressing the relationship challenge. Providers need to introduce "boundary spanning" mechanisms to enhance their on-site and remote teams' ability to absorb new knowledge. The first stage – *organize* – is the time to do this, when the organizational structure of the teams is put in place. Selecting individuals with knowledge of the client's market and technologies can significantly enhance the on-site team's capacity to assimilate client's knowledge.

The *transfer* stage addresses moving the new knowledge from the provider's on-site team to the remote team. A needed mechanism is a clear transfer methodology, with communication protocols and channels. The IT outsourcing providers often rely on codification of on-site knowledge, which is "boundary spanning" because it can include standardized templates and a glossary of terms that defines a shared on-site-offsite language. This stage is also enhanced with a *who knows what* directory.

The *retain* stage is about ensuring that the expertise is indeed assimilated in the teams. With dispersed teams, this assimilation is greatly enhanced with a succession plan for every team member at every location.

Finally, the *monitor* stage involves continually examining the expertise in the relationship with two aspects in mind: (1) does the team's expertise meet the client and industry standards, and (2) which expertise needs to be enhanced to meet such standards? The provider should monitor its ability to absorb knowledge from the client, close any gaps between the client, on-site and remote teams, and also improve its knowledge absorption organizational process.

Addressing the organizational challenge. Providers need to develop competencies in expertise coordination, which includes four activities: develop, search, reuse, and measure.

The *develop* stage at TCS and other organizations we have researched[16] involves acquiring know-how and making *who knows what* and *who does what* entries into a directory. So this stage involves class training or on-the-job training as well as codification and storage of the knowledge and processes to make this know-how available to the entire organization.

The *search* stage relies on the expertise directories to locate solutions in a timely manner. Staff seek solutions through interpersonal networks and databases. The TCS undertakes massive codification of know-how, and its CoEs have proven just as efficient as the databases in locating experts and fostering solutions.

The *reuse* stage reapplies solutions and know-how from one client relationship to others, usually by adjusting and modifying the original solution. Therefore, part of reuse often involves locating the expert who originally created the component or template.

The *measure* stage uses metrics to assess the effectiveness of expertise utilization by measuring the degree to which a component has been reused and in what contexts.

As noted throughout this article, expertise management involves assimilating new knowledge and coordinating existing expertise. Developing these two competences addresses the relationship and organizational challenges, but only so far. Our parallel research leads us to believe that clients and providers need a broader vision to manage expertise and knowledge in a relational way. In short, both should consider future developments, as discussed in the next section.

Four challenges for the future

Developing and managing expertise requires considerable sustained investment by both provider and client in the eight practices over the lifetime of the outsourcing contract. To make such investments, both parties will want to know the costs and the benefits.

Large, global IT outsourcing providers are now competing to develop global strategies. We predict that they will replicate the low-cost structures of their Indian competitors, thereby eroding the Indian providers' relative cost advantages. To remain competitive, the major Indian providers will replicate the high-value, high-touch service of their global competitors.[17]

We see two keys to vendor competitiveness. One is "bestshore" policies. Thus, TCS has sites at Mumbai, Amsterdam Sao Paulo, Luxembourg, and Hungary, among others, to provide the best cost-service arrangement for its client ABN AMRO. The second is a global service delivery model. Both are already easily visible at TCS. Creating a strategy for developing and managing expertise is less visible, but equally vital, we believe. To gain an edge, providers must be able to absorb and coordinate expertise across company boundaries and among dispersed teams. In fact, we believe providers with global aspirations must **be seen by their existing and potential clients as competing on knowledge and expertise,** if their value proposition is to be seen as credible in the emerging global marketplace.

Nevertheless, pursuing expertise management as described here raises four challenges for clients and providers.

Challenge #1: **Clients must understand the benefits they will receive from a provider's expertise management strategy.** In the precontract stage, clients need to get a detailed statement, in financial terms as far as possible, of benefits to themselves of their provider's expertise management practices. Benefits could include a speedier improvement in service performance, faster availability of expertise at lower rates, and the provider's commitment to a higher level of innovation in processes, services, and technologies, resulting in observable performance improvements. Such benefits, though, must be agreed, documented and signed off in the contract, with money or credits going to the client where they do not materialize.

Challenge #2: **Clients must understand their costs of a provider's expertise management strategy.** Generally, these costs involve helping the provider coordinate knowledge transfer and making people available for knowledge transfer activities, such as seminars, interviews, and offshore visits. Clients should agree to these costs contractually. They should also know and agree contractually to the net benefits they will receive versus the net benefits the provider will receive. As we have observed in other work, when there is a large difference between the two, the deprived party's commitment to delivering on the expertise management strategy falls off.

Challenge #3: **Clients must safeguard their intellectual property**. Serious intellectual property issues can arise when there is any talk of transferring knowledge and expertise across company boundaries – and across countries. Our research suggests that organizations rarely know the value of the knowledge they possess, let alone how to systematically collect, store, grow, and leverage this knowledge. The natural inclination of modern outsourcing providers, however, is to go through the client's knowledge trove with a fine-tooth comb, uncovering the nuggets. It is therefore important that clients make intellectual property issues transparent at contract stage, and arrive at precise agreements about what is and is not allowable, at what price, and what penalties arise from noncompliance with agreements or misappropriation of knowledge.

Outsourcing can force clients to conduct a knowledge and expertise audit, so that they can hold informed discussions with providers and legal advisors. The audit should aim to sharpen management's understanding of core knowledge that needs to be retained – historically one of the weakest areas of client decision-making when outsourcing.[18] The audit should also help the parties arrive at more collaborative practical agreements. As one example, to retain intellectual property rights, a client may choose to fund client-specific expertise management activities in exchange for gaining ownership of the consequent expertise management systems.

Clients should also safeguard their intellectual property rights in the event of early termination or material alteration in the terms and scope of the contract. Outsourcing agreements must now deal with major business changes, even in three-year or five-year contracts. For example, during the first half of 2007, ABN AMRO was the subject of major purchase bids by the Royal Bank of Scotland, Barclays, and Bank of America. A pre-emptive contract that deals with intellectual property fall-out from a successful bid mitigates a potentially costly headache.

Challenge #4: **Leverage the relational advantage**. If TCS and other major IT outsourcing providers do go down the expertise management route, clients could reap one significant, but unanticipated, benefit: They could learn how to better manage their own expertise and knowledge. This benefit should be especially attractive to those with mature enterprise architectures in place , because such clients are now in a good position to leverage knowledge previously lying dormant. But to gain the benefits, clients must step up to the challenges of managing expertise themselves and collaborating with their outsourcing providers. The starting point is to look carefully at each provider's practices during the provider assessment phase – looking for processes, systems, and practices that you could adopt.

For example, some large U.K. clients reported to us in 2005 that their offshore providers had far superior system development methodologies and project management practices. With provider assistance, these outsourcing clients improved their own capabilities in these areas, which also improved the working performance between the two parties.

Too often, outsourcing is considered one-sided: Handing over assets, people, activities, and knowledge to third-party management. However, it can be more. Clients can learn from providers. They can also contract for collaboration services to release their own knowledge potential, while also releasing the provider's potential, for mutual gain.

Notes

1. This article is based on ongoing research at TCS between 2001 and 2007. During this period, we conducted over 150 interviews with senior executives and staff at several levels in Mumbai, Gurgaon, Bangalore, Amsterdam, Sao Paulo, Campinas (Brazil), Zurich, and Luxemburg. We also held phone interviews with employees in San Francisco. The interviews ranged from 45 to 90 minutes in length. Each was transcribed, and subjected to software coding and analysis. We also collected a range of documents, including presentations, annual reports, and internal management papers.

2. See Willcocks, L. and Lacity, M. (2007) *Global Sourcing of Business and IT Services*, London: Palgrave Macmillan. Willcocks, L. and Cullen, S. (2005) *The Outsourcing Enterprise: How the CEO Should Be Engaged*, London: LogicaCMG.

3. This issue of the need for providers to develop domain expertise of a client's sector (such as banking) and its organization (i.e., its culture, structure, political configuration, and idiosyncratic systems and processes) arose in our previous research. Technical expertise is necessary but not sufficient. And it is not the same as domain expertise. See Feeny, D., Lacity, M., and Willcocks, L. (2005) Taking the Measure of Outsourcing Providers. *Sloan Management Review*, April: 41–48.

4. A discussion of knowledge issues in outsourcing appears in Willcocks and Lacity, op. cit, 2007, chapter 7.

5. Orlikowski, W. (2002) Knowing In Practice: Enacting a Collective Capability in Distributed Organizing. *Organization Science*, 13(3): 249–273.

6. TCS Annual Report 2006 and internal documents.

7. See Rottman, J. and Lacity, M., chapter 9, in Willcocks and Lacity, op. cit., 2007; and Willcocks, L., Cullen, S., and Lacity, M. (2006) *The Outsourcing Enterprise 3: How to Select and Leverage Effective Suppliers*, London: LogicaCMG.

8. The knowing-doing gap was identified in the pioneering work of Polanyi, M. (1983) *The Tacit Dimension*, Gloucester, MA: Peter Smith. The gap refers to how an organization can know *what* to do and the know-how required to act, but still lack the processes to translate knowledge into effective action. We have also observed this gap in our outsourcing research. For example, see Willcocks, L., Hindle, J., Feeny, D., and Lacity, M. (2004) IT and Business Process Outsourcing: The Knowledge Potential. *Information Systems Management Journal*, Summer: 7–15. Another source, with corporate examples is Pfeffer, J. and Sutton, R. (2000) *The Knowing-Doing Gap: How Smart Companies Turn Knowledge into Action*, Boston, MA: Harvard Business Press.

9. Avoiding such damage and increasing outsourcing flexibility are reasons both researchers and practitioners argue for subdividing large-scale IT projects into smaller ones, with short timelines and frequent business outcomes. See, for example, Willcocks, L., Petherbridge, P., and Olson, N. (2003) *Making IT Count: Strategy, Delivery and Infrastructure*, Oxford: Butterworth.

10. The issue is discussed in Lacity, M., Willcocks, L., and Cullen, S. (2008) *Global IT Outsourcing: 21st Century Search For Business Advantage*, Chichester: John Wiley& Sons.

11. For details, Finnegan, D. and Willcocks, L. (2007) *Implementing CRM: From Technology to Knowledge*, Chichester: John Wiley& Sons.

12. For a detailed discussion about component reuse see Kotlarsky, J., Oshri, I., van Hillegerberg, J., and Kumar, K. (2007)Globally Distributed Component-Based Software Development: An Exploratory Study of Knowledge Management and Work Division. *Journal of Information Technology*, 22: 161–173.

13. Op. cit., Finnegan and Willcocks, 2007 and Kotlarsky et al., 2007.

14. See Oshri I. and Newell S. (2007) Component Sharing in Complex Products and Systems: Challenges, Solutions and Practical Implications. *IEEE Transactions on Engineering Management* 52(4): 509–521.

15. Gartner report. The Benefits of the Capability Maturity Model for Application Development, Gartner, London, 2007 (available on

http://www.gartner.com/4_decision_tools/measurement/measure_it_articles/2003_0424/ben_cmm.jsp).

16. Full details are in Kotlarsky, J., Oshri, I., and van Fenema, P. (2008) *Knowledge Processes in Globally Distributed Contexts*, London: Palgrave Macmillan.

17. For 12 research-based predictions for the period 2006–2011, see Willcocks, L., Cullen, S., and Lacity, M. (2006) *The Outsourcing Enterprise 3: Selecting and Leveraging Effective Suppliers*, London: LogicaCMG.

18. See op. cit., Willcocks and Lacity, 2007, and Reynolds, P. and Willcocks, L. (2007) IT Outsourcing and Rebuilding Core IT Capabilities at Commonwealth Bank Australia: Case Research, Paper at the 2007 ICOIS conference, Heidelberg, Germany, May 29–30.

INDEX

ABN AMRO–TCS contract 290–1, 292–303
abstract systems 209
Agerfalk, P. 47
Alavi 242
Amsterdam 299, 306
Anglo-America 58
anxiety 177, 178, 179, 180, 183, 190, 194, 201, 204, 205
application service provision (ASP) 13
architecture 84–5, 89
  IT architecture 89
  relationship architecture 19–20, 30–1
  strategic architecture 19
asymmetrical interactions
  in technologically mediated
    communication 137–8
atmosphere developments 81–3
  innovation 82–3
  sourcing strategy 83
Avison, D.E. 130

Bangalore 79, 134, 139
Bannon, L. 131
Barley, S.R. 130
Basel II 81
Bechky, B.A. 220
Beulen, E. 245
Blau, P. 12
Blount, G. 99
Boland, R.J. 49
Boston 134, 137, 138, 140
boundary spanning 49, 54, 66, 103, 304
  boundary objects 49
  forms, cultural and cognitive 55–6
Brazil 291
Bredenlow, T. 154
Brocklehurst, M. 99, 103
brokering 200–1
Brown, J.S. 241, 243, 253, 262
Brown, S. 145
Budapest 2, 7

capability maturity model (CMM) 102, 111, 113, 114, 131, 232, 302–3
Casson, M. 185
Centers of Excellences (COEs) 296–7, 300
Chase-Dunn, C. 133
Chin, W.W. 13, 14
China 44, 79
  see also mediated business model
classical reengineering methods 53
client knowledge 263
client organizations 77, 78, 79, 80, 82
client-specific capabilities 101–2, 103, 108, 119
  established firm 113–14
  high growth publicly held firm 109–10
  slow-growth joint-venture firm 115
  slow growth small firm 112
client–vendor relationship 20, 22, 48, 53, 58, 73, 76
CMMI 52, 59, 60, 100
codified knowledge 60, 111
cognitive dimension practices 165–72
cognitive distance 56, 59–60
Cohabitation phase 179, 190, 206
  stable collaborative order,
    constructing 195–203
collaboration
  distributed collaboration: and
    culture 129–30; ICTs and global
    processes 130–2; World-systems
    theory 132–4; integrated collabora-
    tion, across distributed site 127;
    knowledge transfer and collabora-
    tion development 260; stable order,
    constructing 195–203
collectivist cultures 58
comfort 179, 180, 181, 186, 204, 205
commodity supply relationship 32
communication 48, 58, 130, 132, 137–8, 166–8, 170, 196, 217, 219, 232, 248, 251, 275–6
  face-to-face communication 250, 279
  and transactive memory system 7